MALLARMÉ AND THE POLITICS OF LITERATURE

Crosscurrents

Exploring the development of European thought through engagements with the arts, humanities, social sciences and sciences

Series Editor
Christopher Watkin, Monash University

Editorial Advisory Board

Andrew Benjamin
Martin Crowley
Simon Critchley
Frederiek Depoortere
Oliver Feltham
Patrick ffrench
Christopher Fynsk
Kevin Hart
Emma Wilson

Titles available in the series:

Difficult Atheism: Post-Theological Thinking in Alain Badiou, Jean-Luc Nancy and Quentin Meillassoux
Christopher Watkin

Politics of the Gift: Exchanges in Poststructuralism
Gerald Moore

Unfinished Worlds: Hermeneutics, Aesthetics and Gadamer
Nicholas Davey

The Figure of This World: Agamben and the Question of Political Ontology
Mathew Abbott

The Becoming of the Body: Contemporary Women's Writing in French
Amaleena Damlé

Philosophy, Animality and the Life Sciences
Wahida Khandker

The Event Universe: The Revisionary Metaphysics of Alfred North Whitehead
Leemon B. McHenry

Sublime Art: Towards an Aesthetics of the Future
Stephen Zepke

Mallarmé and the Politics of Literature: Sartre, Kristeva, Badiou, Rancière
Robert Boncardo

Forthcoming Titles:

Visual Art and Projects of the Self
by Katrina Mitcheson

Visit the Crosscurrents website at edinburghuniversitypress.com/series/cross

MALLARMÉ AND THE POLITICS OF LITERATURE

Sartre, Kristeva, Badiou, Rancière

Robert Boncardo

EDINBURGH
University Press

Edinburgh University Press is one of the leading university presses in the UK. We publish academic books and journals in our selected subject areas across the humanities and social sciences, combining cutting-edge scholarship with high editorial and production values to produce academic works of lasting importance. For more information visit our website: edinburghuniversitypress.com

© Robert Boncardo, 2018

Edinburgh University Press Ltd
The Tun – Holyrood Road
12(2f) Jackson's Entry
Edinburgh EH8 8PJ

Typeset in 10.5/13 Sabon by
Servis Filmsetting Ltd, Stockport, Cheshire

A CIP record for this book is available from the British Library

ISBN 978 1 4744 2952 8 (hardback)
ISBN 978 1 4744 2954 2 (webready PDF)
ISBN 978 1 4744 2955 9 (epub)

The right of Robert Boncardo to be identified as the author of this work has been asserted in accordance with the Copyright, Designs and Patents Act 1988, and the Copyright and Related Rights Regulations 2003 (SI No. 2498).

Contents

Acknowledgements	vi
Abbreviations	vii
Series Editor's Preface	ix
Introduction: Comrade Mallarmé	1
1 Jean-Paul Sartre's Mallarmé: Hero of an Ontological Drama, Agent of the Counter-revolution	22
2 Julia Kristeva's Mallarmé: From Fetishism to the Theatre-Book	79
3 Alain Badiou's Mallarmé: From the Structural Dialectic to the Poetry of the Event	122
4 Jean-Claude Milner's Mallarmé: Nothing Has Taken Place	175
5 Jacques Rancière's Mallarmé: Deferring Equality	191
Conclusion: From One Siren to Another	227
Bibliography	245
Index	251

Acknowledgements

I wish above all to thank three intellectual influences, without whom it would have been impossible to carry out this project: Elizabeth Rechniewski, Françoise Grauby and Claude Perez, my advisors at Sydney University and Aix-Marseille University. I would also like to thank my closest comrades, Christian R. Gelder, Claudia Hill and Bryan Cooke, who read the manuscript and offered advice on how to improve it. I am solely responsible for the faults that remain.

This book is dedicated to my family: Guy, Debbie, Philip and Felicity Boncardo.

Abbreviations

Alain Badiou
BE   *Being and Event*
C   *Conditions*
HI   *Handbook of Inaesthetics*
TOTS *Theory of the Subject*

Jean-François Hamel
CM   *Camarade Mallarmé*

Julia Kristeva
RLP   *Revolution in Poetic Language*

Stéphane Mallarmé
OC   *Œuvres complètes I*
OC II *Œuvres complètes II*
CP   *Collected Poems: A Bilingual Edition*
D   *Divagations*
PV   *The Poems in Verse*

Quentin Meillassoux
NS   *The Number and the Siren*

Jean-Claude Milner
C   *Constats*
MP   'Mallarmé Perchance'
MT   *Mallarmé au tombeau*

Jacques Rancière
MS   *Mute Speech*
PL   *The Politics of Literature*
PS   *Mallarmé: The Politics of the Siren*

Jean-Paul Sartre
MPN *Mallarmé, or The Poet of Nothingness*
FI *The Family Idiot: Gustave Flaubert, 1821–1857. Volume 5*

Series Editor's Preface

Two or more currents flowing into or through each other create a turbulent crosscurrent, more powerful than its contributory flows and irreducible to them. Time and again, modern European thought creates and exploits crosscurrents in thinking, remaking itself as it flows through, across and against discourses as diverse as mathematics and film, sociology and biology, theology, literature and politics. The work of Gilles Deleuze, Jacques Derrida, Slavoj Žižek, Alain Badiou, Bernard Stiegler and Jean-Luc Nancy, among others, participates in this fundamental remaking. In each case disciplines and discursive formations are engaged, not with the aim of performing a pre-determined mode of analysis yielding a 'philosophy of x', but through encounters in which thought itself can be transformed. Furthermore, these fundamental transformations do not merely seek to account for singular events in different sites of discursive or artistic production but rather to engage human existence and society as such, and as a whole. The cross-disciplinarity of this thought is therefore neither a fashion nor a prosthesis; it is simply part of what 'thought' means in this tradition.

Crosscurrents begins from the twin convictions that this re-making is integral to the legacy and potency of European thought, and that the future of thought in this tradition must defend and develop this legacy in the teeth of an academy that separates and controls the currents that flow within and through it. With this in view, the series provides an exceptional site for bold, original and opinion-changing monographs that actively engage European thought in this fundamentally cross-disciplinary manner, riding existing crosscurrents and creating new ones. Each book in the series explores the different ways in which European thought develops through its engagement with disciplines across the arts, humanities, social sciences and sciences, recognising that the community of scholars working with this thought is itself spread across diverse faculties. The object of the series is therefore nothing less than to examine and carry forward the unique legacy of

European thought as an inherently and irreducibly cross-disciplinary enterprise.

Christopher Watkin
Cambridge
February 2011

Introduction:
Comrade Mallarmé

Throughout his posthumous reception, in particular in the post-war period, the late nineteenth-century poet Stéphane Mallarmé has been a privileged object of reflection for French intellectuals. Intriguingly, his writings have been drawn on not only to lend support to positions in philosophy or poetics: they have also been seen as politically significant. In stark contrast to the image that circulates of him as an aloof aristocrat unconcerned by history, Mallarmé has frequently been the writer of choice for twentieth-century French thinkers concerned with the politics of literature. From the work of Jean-Paul Sartre to that of Julia Kristeva, Alain Badiou, Jean-Claude Milner and Jacques Rancière, among many others, Mallarmé has been at the centre of political thought in French intellectual life. In fact, he has become 'comrade Mallarmé',[1] the glorious ancestor of all those who would seek to argue for the progressive or revolutionary virtues of literature.

The aim of this book is to investigate this history of political appropriations of Mallarmé's writings. Our focus will be on the work of Jean-Paul Sartre, *Tel Quel*'s theoretician-in-chief Julia Kristeva, Alain Badiou and Jacques Rancière. The book also contains a short chapter on Jean-Claude Milner, and closes with a brief consideration of Quentin Meillassoux's recent intervention into Mallarmé studies. Throughout the book, our key concern will be to determine how Mallarmé has been constituted as an object of political reflection; what conceptual resources have enabled his writings to be construed as politically significant; and in what conjunctures – both intellectual and political – his work has been mobilised by French intellectuals.[2]

Whether these intellectuals proclaimed Mallarmé to be a privileged agent in the revolutionary transformation of society; feted his writing's uncompromising complexity as the sign of an heroic attempt to resist, albeit in relative isolation and by the sole means of his literary art, a politically contemptible period; or condemned his difficult poetry and prose as symptomatic of a fatal withdrawal into obscurity, French thinkers have consistently linked Mallarmé's writings to politics. Crucially, however, these links have been far from univocal. While Mallarmé's alleged aristocratism has made him the perfect instantiation of the 'legend of the irresponsible poet',[3] to use Sartre's famous formulation, his 'commitment' has also been praised – and by none other than Sartre himself – for being as 'all-embracing as possible – social as much as poetic'.[4] And while thinkers like Kristeva have admitted that Mallarmé's radical linguistic practice was confined in his time – and perhaps also in ours – to 'elitist refuges', they have also argued that this was 'an entirely conjunctural compromise' (RLP 439) and that Mallarmé's writings could one day still become what they always, already were: 'a sort of anarchist attack that would strike at the most tenacious dogma, that of a codified language, the last guarantee of sociality' (RLP 434). In short, Mallarmé has been a distinctly ambivalent figure politically: at once a contemptible counter-revolutionary (MPN 37; MT 63); a conservative who, despite the corrosive negativity of his poetry, 'participated in the maintenance of vacillating structures' (RLP 455); but also a rigorous egalitarian whose poetry was 'destined to everyone' (HI 31).

In the five chapters of this book, we will investigate five different cases in which Mallarmé has been the object of explicitly political concerns. Beginning with Jean-Paul Sartre's reading of the poet proposed in the immediate aftermath of the Second World War, we will explore the entirety of the existentialist's writings in order to determine how Sartre conceived of Mallarmé's politics. In our second chapter, we will turn to the works of Sartre's most notorious successors: the collaborators of the journal *Tel Quel*. We will be particularly concerned with Julia Kristeva's *Revolution in Poetic Language* (1974), a work that channels the prophetic promise of May '68 and attends closely to the political significance of Mallarmé's writings. Our third chapter will be devoted to Alain Badiou's career-long dialogue with Mallarmé. Beginning with *Theory of the Subject* (1982), a work that only just postdates the Telquellians' most significant interventions on the matter of Mallarmé's politics, we will go on to explore Badiou's post-*Being and Event* (1988) reading of Mallarmé and show how the poet helps him negotiate the post-'89 conjuncture. Our fourth chapter on Jean-Claude Milner will engage with the same political context, but this time from the perspective of Milner's radically counter-revolutionary Mallarmé, a figure Milner first presents in his 1999 book *Mallarmé au tombeau*. In our fifth and final chapter, we will turn to the work of Jacques Rancière, whose dense monograph *Mallarmé: The Politics of the Siren* (1996) offers a revisionist reading of Mallarmé's poetico-political project at the same time as it critically engages with the entire interpretative tradition we will have studied in this book. In our conclusion, finally, we will briefly consider Quentin Meillassoux's efforts to reopen the question of Mallarmé's political significance for today.

Unfortunately but inevitably, this book will not cover the complete set of political readings that have been proposed of Mallarmé. Such an unmanageably large set could conceivably include the interpretations of Maurice Blanchot, Roland Barthes, Jean-Pierre Faye, other collaborators of *Tel Quel* such as Philippe Sollers and Jean-Joseph Goux, and even the work of Philippe Lacoue-Labarthe.[5] Furthermore, the specifically political focus of this work means that we will have to exclude the more philosophical readings of Mallarmé, such as those by Jean Hyppolite,[6] Michel Foucault,[7] Jacques Derrida,[8] Gilles Deleuze[9] and Jean-François Lyotard,[10] not to mention the more recent contributions of André Stanguennec[11] and Pierre Campion.[12] Finally, while we will take into account works of contemporary Mallarmé scholarship, in addition to well-established contributions from the past, this book is very much focused on the poet in so far as he is read by Sartre, Kristeva, Badiou, Milner, Rancière and Meillassoux. In other words, our principal concern will always be with how Mallarmé has been made to function within their singular conceptual schemes, as well as in terms of the socio-political and intellectual conjunctures these thinkers have confronted.

*

In his initial engagement with Mallarmé in the post-war period, Jean-Paul Sartre positioned Mallarmé at the negative pole of possible forms of literary engagement. As a member of the postromantic movement, inaugurated by Gustave Flaubert and Leconte de Lisle in the aftermath of the bloody events of June 1848, Mallarmé's writings constituted part of what Sartre considered a disastrous detour in the history of French letters. Certainly, for Sartre, this detour had since been corrected by his own doctrine of 'committed literature', but it was an historical error nonetheless and a warning to any future writer concerned with their political responsibility. Famously, Sartre claimed that he held 'Flaubert and Goncourt responsible for the repression that followed the Commune, since they did not write a line to stop it'.[13] But he could well have included Mallarmé in his sweeping condemnation of the late nineteenth-century literary field – a field he argued was ontologically continuous and ethically complicit with 'a social order based on exploitation' (FI 380). In works such as *What is Literature?*, *Mallarmé, or the Poet of Nothingness* and the third volume of *The Family Idiot*, Sartre read the poet as a radical nihilist whose ideology gave expression to 'the terror of the propertied class, which [was] becoming aware of its inevitable decline' (MPN 84). The figure of Mallarmé thus enabled Sartre to mark out the negative contours of his own literary and political vision.

However, as every commentator on Sartre's work on Mallarmé has noticed, in *The Poet of Nothingness* the philosopher also claims that Mallarmé's singular achievement was inventing a paradoxical form of poetic 'commitment'. Indeed, in that work Sartre explicitly refers to Mallarmé as 'the hero of an ontological drama' (MPN 122) and praises his lucidity in the face of 'the impossibility of Man' (MPN 144) – a lucidity that presages Sartre's own in *Being and Nothingness*. How are we to account for Sartre's oscillation between treating Mallarmé as a counter-revolutionary and as a 'hero'? Can Sartre truly conceive of a 'committed' poetry? Our first chapter will enter the debate and will attempt to clarify the political significance of Mallarmé's writings for the Marxist existentialist.

As members of the intellectual generation that succeeded Sartre's dominance, the writers and theoreticians of the journal *Tel Quel* initially turned towards an affirmation of the autonomy of literature – an autonomy that was defined in opposition to the political imperatives Sartre was perceived, in a quasi-Zhdanovian fashion, as having submitted literature to. In such a context, with their exemplary self-reflexivity and inventiveness, Mallarmé's poetry and prose became the perfect instantiation of a literary theory and practice capable of affirming its autonomy not only from politics but from the world as such, which it no longer had the servile duty to represent. Formal innovation, as well as theoretical reflection, could be pursued without reference to the directives or demands of politics. However, with an increasingly politicised student body as their main readership and an alliance with the PCF beginning in 1967, *Tel Quel* were forced to find resources within their essentially formalist theory of literature in order to demonstrate the continuity of their area of expertise with the task of social revolution. Mallarmé's writing, construed as a radical praxis that dissolved the standard semantic and syntactical unities of language and re-organised them according to more expansive, more flexible structures, would thus come to stage, at a microcosmic level, the radical transformation of the 'social order at its most fundamental level', that of 'the logic of language' (RLP 78), as well as to figure the ideal social arrangement. This vision was given its most sophisticated expression in the works by

Julia Kristeva, notably *Revolution in Poetic Language*, an examination of which will constitute the centrepiece of our second chapter. While Sartre had taken Mallarmé's famous provocation 'I know of no other bomb than a book' to signify that to 'the real and consequently particularized destructions of anarchism', Mallarmé had 'set the harsh, universal and intentionally ineffective abolition of the world by language and of language by itself' (FI 163), Kristeva argued that the poet's linguistic praxis truly was a sort of 'anarchist attack' that could bring forth 'the revolution of poetic language'. But how, precisely, did Kristeva argue for the revolutionary credentials of Mallarmé's work? And why, if such a transformative power was present in the poet's writings, had it not yet been fully realised?

With Alain Badiou's work we find an engagement with Mallarmé that is as indifferent to the *linguisterie* of the Telquellians as it is to Sartre's problematic of 'committed literature'. However, as we will see, Badiou's Mallarmé also oscillates between being a glorious ancestor – a political and intellectual companion from whom vital resources can be drawn – and a suspicious conservative, a 'hermetic recluse' (TOTS 65) who believed, in contradistinction to the militant philosopher, that there was 'no temporal advent of the new' (TOTS 108). While *Tel Quel* persistently maintained a prophetic posture, anticipating the moment that the 'revolution of poetic language' would come about, Badiou's staunch commitment to the revolutionary promise of May '68 was made in full recognition of its fragility (TOTS 327). What role could Mallarmé play in helping the philosopher navigate the long aftermath of the May events? In *Theory of the Subject*, Badiou turns to Mallarmé as the radical thinker of the 'structural dialectic', a form of thought that marks out the limits beyond which a committed revolutionary must pass if they are to properly think revolutionary change. While Badiou also finds in Mallarmé an image of the political endurance he needs to wait out, without compromising on his convictions, a moment of political reaction, he will only be able to treat the poet's 'structural dialectic' as a 'precious legacy' (TOTS 108) that falls short of the 'historical dialectic' required by the Maoist revolutionary. Thus, as we shall see, the figure of Mallarmé that emerges from *Theory of the Subject* resembles a curious amalgam of the petty bourgeois nihilist condemned by Sartre and the intellectual radical praised, with certain precautions, by *Tel Quel*.

Badiou's engagement with Mallarmé does not end with *Theory of the Subject*. Rather, it continues, indeed intensifies, following the publication of *Being and Event*. In this latter book, instead of arguing that Mallarmé set an arbitrary limit to thought and practice, Badiou treats him as the unprecedented poet-thinker of the 'event' – a thinker to which he, as a philosopher, must henceforth remain faithful. Despite this shift, Badiou's own political project remains marginalised. How does Badiou mobilise the resources of Mallarmé's writings after the shift in his philosophy that occurs in *Being and Event*? What political significance can Mallarmé have during a period that saw the apparent defeat of Marxism and the downfall of the Soviet Union? Our third chapter will explore this question through a close reading of the essay 'A French Philosopher Responds to a Polish Poet', along with other texts from the latter half of Badiou's philosophical trajectory.

It would be hard to imagine a reading of Mallarmé more opposed to Badiou's than Jean-Claude Milner's. In our fourth chapter, we will turn to the Lacanian linguist's 1999 book *Mallarmé au tombeau*, which on first glance seems geared towards undermining the image of Mallarmé as a 'comrade' to progressive causes. In his short but devastating book, Milner steadily zooms out of a close reading of Mallarmé's sonnet 'The virginal, enduring, beautiful today' to take in the entirety of the last two centuries of revolutionary politics. For Milner, Mallarmé was not only a counter-revolutionary but also a nihilist who refused to even recognise the existence of revolutions and the hopes and dreams people invested in them. As Milner argues, for Mallarmé the truth of the modern era was not the steady march of progress but the installation of a commodity society, which reduced all things to a 'quotidian nothingness' (D 218), including attempts at collective emancipation. The aim of our fourth chapter will be to present Milner's challenge to the interpretative tradition that has produced the figure of 'comrade Mallarmé'. How does Milner argue for the hidden complicity between Mallarmé's nihilism and his progressive readers' 'political vision of the world' – a complicity that makes readers like Badiou 'strict Mallarméans' (MT 88), albeit in an entirely unexpected sense? Is Milner's interpretation grounded in a serious reading of Mallarmé's *œuvre*, or does it distort his poetry and prose in the service of polemical ends?

The reading of Mallarmé proposed by Jacques Rancière initially appears to resist the general tendency of the poet's post-war political appropriations. Returning as he does after the pathbreaking work of Bertrand Marchal to a recognisably philological approach that seeks to reconstruct the way Mallarmé conceived of his own project, we will see that Rancière – to whom our fifth chapter is devoted – is not concerned to enlist the poet in a punctual intellectual or political struggle. After Sartre's strategic positioning within the post-war literary field, which led him to posit Mallarmé as a surpassed moment in the trajectory of French letters leading towards 'committed literature';

after the Telquellian's extraction from the poet's writings of a 'textual practice' that was thought to be the necessary poetic prolegomena to any further revolution; after Badiou's identification of Mallarmé's famed intransigence with the commitment and patience required of the Maoist revolutionary during a period of calm after May '68; and after Milner's polemic against the twentieth century's 'strict Mallarméans', Rancière's work cannot but appear as an attempt to read the poet strictly on his own terms. The 'politics' in the title of Rancière's monograph *Mallarmé: The Politics of the Siren* is not a revolutionary politics or a tool-kit for today's progressives. Rather, it refers, quite simply, to the way Mallarmé conceived of the central political problematic of his time and the role his poetry was to play within it. As we will see, Rancière reinterprets all of the major motifs of Mallarmé's posthumous reception – from his isolation from the public sphere to his writings' extreme difficulty – in terms of the immanent principles of this 'politics'.

But Rancière's intervention is not only an exercise in exemplary scholarship. By restoring Mallarmé's work to its proper horizon of significance, Rancière is also able to identify the constitutive ambivalence of this 'politics' – an ambivalence that is strikingly congruent with the diverse and contradictory estimations of the poet's political significance explored throughout this book. In our fifth chapter, we will follow Rancière as he shows how, despite recognising that it was the poet's duty to prepare 'the celebrations of the future' (PS 33), Mallarmé was led to eternalise 'the poet's solitude' (PS 33) and to infinitely defer the transcendence of his posture of aristocratic elitism. But the question then becomes what Rancière's own position vis-à-vis Mallarmé's 'politics' is. Despite consistently confusing his own voice with that of the poet's, it is not clear whether Rancière endorses or condemns Mallarmé's chosen mode of political engagement. What is the relation between the poet's 'politics of the siren' and Rancière's own? What stance does Rancière ultimately take towards the ambivalent political significance of the poet's writings? Our final chapter will close with a close consideration of these questions.

Each chapter of this book can be read individually as a relatively self-enclosed study of one thinker's engagement with Mallarmé. Yet the reader will undoubtedly see threads common to all five chapters progressively emerge. Indeed, these threads will converge in our conclusion, where, on the basis of a brief discussion of Quentin Meillassoux's book *The Number and Siren*, we will consider the more general implications for the politics of literature that Mallarmé's post-war reception poses. What does it mean for our ideas of literature and politics that Mallarmé has been both a hero and a villain, a comrade and a class enemy? Are our conceptions of these two categories consistent, or are they a tangle of assumptions, fantasies and anxieties about literature's political significance? The book will end by broaching these pressing questions.

*

Contemporary Mallarmé scholarship continues to flourish. Ever since the late 1980s, when Bertrand Marchal published his two monumental works *Lecture de Mallarmé* (1985)[14] and *La Religion de Mallarmé* (1988),[15] the area of Mallarmé studies has enjoyed a period of intense productivity, in both the Anglophone and Francophone worlds. Coming after a period during which the poet had been annexed by proponents of 'high theory', Marchal's philological approach opened up vast regions of Mallarmé's *œuvre* to renewed exploration, in particular the *Divagations*. Today, Pascal Durand's[16] and Patrick Thériault's[17] sociological and psychoanalytic approaches exist alongside passionate investigations into Mallarmé's 'occasional' verse,[18] while in the Anglophone world the works of Roger Pearson,[19] Rosemary Lloyd[20] and Damian Catani,[21] among others,[22] have deepened our knowledge of the immanent concerns and principles of Mallarmé's project. Today, the interested reader has a far greater array of interpretative options open to them than readers of half a century ago – not to mention a new and masterfully edited two-volume *Pléiade* edition of Mallarmé's complete works.

It would be impossible to do justice to this novel scholarship in the space of this introduction. More seriously, however, to do so would potentially jeopardise our project from the outset. For in fact, the rise of today's philological approaches to Mallarmé has occurred in direct opposition to the speculative and philosophical readings treated in this book. A recent call for contributions to a collective work on Mallarmé's reception, launched in late 2016 by the eminent French Mallarméan Thierry Roger, remarks that philosophical readings of the poet make up 'a volatile but very productive zone' of scholarship – one that nevertheless 'poses questions of hermeneutical legitimacy from a philological point of view'.[23] How can we return to the readings of philosophers like Sartre or theorists like Kristeva when they seem to have been superseded by careful contemporary scholarship? What is the use of exploring their political appropriations of Mallarmé when a consensus seems to exist regarding their very limited value? There are a number of ways to respond to these questions. First and foremost, there is no absolute distinction between speculative readings of Mallarmé and readings that adopt a more philological frame. As we will see in some detail, all of the thinkers treated in this book offer serious and synthetic readings of Mallarmé's œuvre. In each case, they present ample evidence to support their claims. In fact, they frequently go further and pose questions that are often neglected in mainstream Mallarmé scholarship – questions that turn around the ultimate foundation of Mallarmé's thought and its relation to other domains of human experience: politics, theology, science, and so on. Secondly, it is not clear that these theoretically inclined readings have been thoroughly understood and digested by today's Mallarméans. Is it so obvious that Marchal's claims regarding Mallarmé's 'religion' trump Milner's conviction that Mallarmé abandoned this post-secular project (MT 78)? Are Marchal's arguments to be preferred over Badiou's claims that the poet's religious designs are the most derivative part of his œuvre?[24] If a line of division has to be drawn between two kinds of Mallarmé scholarship, then we hope that the present work will help draw this line with the greatest possible accuracy.

In the remainder of this introduction, instead of engaging with the main lines of contemporary Mallarmé scholarship, we will discuss four recent works, all from the French-language scene, which have a similar focus to our own: Jean-François Hamel's *Camarade Mallarmé: Une politique de la lecture*, Thierry Roger's *Archive du Coup de dés: Etude critique d'Un coup de dés jamais n'abolira le hasard de Stéphane Mallarmé (1897–2007)*, Vincent Kaufmann's *La faute à Mallarmé: L'aventure de la théorie littéraire*, and finally Laurent Jenny's *Je suis la révolution: Histoire d'une métaphore (1830–1975)*. These works will help us situate ourselves within the contemporary debate around Mallarmé's politics.

Roger's *Archive du Coup de dés* studies the various readings of Mallarmé's *Un coup de dés* produced in France during the twentieth century. By means of an archaeological approach inspired by Foucault, Roger seeks to 'exhume the invisible substructures'[25] that undergird the multiplicity of discourses that have taken Mallarmé's masterwork as their object.[26] In addition to revealing the unconscious systematicity of the archive of statements made about *Un coup de dés*, Roger also aims – this time from a philological perspective – to 'show how readings [of *Un coup de dés*] have over- or under-valorised certain aspects of the letter of the text, by way of truncated citations or the displacement of textual unities'. Roger even goes so far as to 'invalidate certain interpretations' in the name of 'a certain idea of Mallarmé'.[27] His critique of *Tel Quel*'s reading of the poet, for instance, is particularly severe: Roger eviscerates the journal's 'violent de-historicisation' of *Un coup de dés* and Kristeva's generalised 'filtering' of Mallarmé's work, which he argues was achieved by 'augmenting certain traits . . . and by reducing, even occulting, others that were not compatible with the dominant frame of reading'.[28] Roger's *Archive du Coup de dés* is thus at once a retrospective and critical work, which rigorously assesses the relative value of the readings made of Mallarmé's testamentary text.

In stark contrast to Roger's archivistic, archaeological and oftentimes explicitly critical approach, Jean-François Hamel frames his recent work *Camarade Mallarmé* as an affirmation of what he calls a 'politics of writing' – a 'politics' that has decisively influenced twentieth-century readings of Mallarmé and whose 'strategy has consisted', he argues, 'in wrenching [Mallarmé's] works away from their time so as to illuminate contemporary debates and so transform literature into a discourse of resistance to power' (CM 62). As Roger writes in his review of *Camarade Mallarmé*, in contradistinction to his own approach Hamel 'does not seek to demystify these political readings'.[29] Wondering whether they are thus 'truly put at a distance', Roger argues that the author of *Camarade Mallarmé*, like the literary theorist and philosopher Yves Citton, whose recent work on hermeneutics inspires Hamel's own approach, inevitably 'passes from a pragmatism of literary reading to a militant conception of literary reading'.[30] This passage is encapsulated in the conclusion to *Camarade Mallarmé*, where Hamel calls for 'a use of the counter-times of literature in order to act against the stases of the present' (CM 203) – a use that would take inspiration from Mallarmé's writings themselves, as well as from the many and varied political uses to which they have been put in the twentieth century. Thus, while Hamel's work surveys with an encyclopaedic enthusiasm the 'chains of memory' that have 'fashioned the interpretative tradition surrounding the name of Mallarmé' (CM 62), he supplements this historical account with a confident proposition for future political actualisations of Mallarmé.

Vincent Kaufmann's 2011 work, *La faute à Mallarmé: L'aventure de la théorie littéraire,* takes a different approach altogether. Framing itself as an intervention into contemporary discussions in France about the teaching and production of literature, Kaufmann's book seeks to argue against the idea that the French literary theory of the 1960s and '70s, whose figurehead was Mallarmé himself, is responsible for the 'decline of literature'; for literature being 'cut off from the world of experience'; for its nefarious effects in 'high schools';[31] and for having 'prepared the terrain for the nihilism that characterises the contemporary literary field'.[32] In order to resist this false diagnosis, Kaufmann chooses to present a sympathetic survey of 'the adventure of literary theory'. This survey occupies the majority of his book and deals with the themes of literary autonomy, the death of the author, literature's revolutionary or subversive pretensions, as well as a selection of the major works of the key actors in this 'adventure'. What emerges from Kaufmann's essay is thus a passionate portrait of a moment of intellectual effervescence, a moment in which literature in general and Mallarmé's work in particular were seized with intellectual tools that had 'an aura of scientificity'[33] and were invested with extraordinary political powers. Far from being 'the name for the radical autonomisation of a literature become solipsistic',[34] as Tzvetan Todorov or William Marx would have it, Mallarmé and the French literary theory that so often took him as its privileged object stand for a vigorous defence of the powers of literature to effect change. In a manner somewhat similar to Hamel, Kaufmann thus affirms the 'pleasure of appropriation, of the use of texts, or of their actualisation',[35] and remarks that despite 'the innumerable reproaches bearing upon the lack of culture or ignorance directed against the commentators situated in the theoretical movement' it is finally 'these commentators that are read and who themselves read'.[36] Kaufmann does finally concede, however, that 'the adventure of literary theory' and the political readings of Mallarmé it produced constitute 'a chapter that is no doubt closed in the history of literary criticism'.[37] Moreover, he intersperses his book with critiques of the literary theories that were proposed during this 'adventure', in particular of their utopianism. For instance, when writing of Kristeva's *Revolution in Poetic Language*, Kaufmann argues that its claim for the revolutionary power of literature 'was only ever a horizon or a sort of revolutionary index destined to give credibility to a theoretical construction'.[38] Thus, *La faute à Mallarmé* constitutes a sort of synthesis of the retrospectively critical approach that Roger adopts and the affirmative attitude of Hamel's *Camarade Mallarmé*. The difference with the latter work lies in the fact that Hamel's prophetic posture, which he assumes at the close of his book when he invites his readers to 'augment the power of texts, and, with an antagonistic aim, inscribe a dissidence within them' (CM 203), contrasts with Kaufmann's definite sense of the closure of 'the adventure of literary theory', however passionate his survey of its achievements might be.

The last of the four contemporary works relevant to the present book, Laurent Jenny's *Je suis la révolution*, explores the various metaphorical transfers that have occurred between the literary enterprise and political revolution. Like Kaufmann, Jenny relegates this hermeneutical act to the past. Pleading for a future 'reconciliation with our language',[39] Jenny's project details the ways in which an anti-classicist aesthetic, which either accorded the component parts of a literary work an anarchic autonomy from the work as an organic whole, or conceived of it as an absolute rupture with the common run of the world, came to be a mirror for the political fortunes of democratic and revolutionary modernity.[40] By way of a sensitive investigation of the various modalities of this metaphorical relation, Jenny shows how it was able to 'arouse the adhesion and interest'[41] of some of the main actors in the literary and political dramas of the modern age, from Hugo to Maurras, Blanchot to Paulhan, Barthes to Sollers. Nevertheless, Jenny convincingly demonstrates that these readers 'incessantly alluded to different aspects of the revolutionary event in order to pinpoint changing forms of literature'.[42] The confident stance of a Sollers, for example, who affirmed that 'writing [was] the continuation of revolution by other means',[43] is thereby revealed in all of its conjunctural contingency and theoretical fragility. While Hamel still looks forward to a future 'art of political interpretation' (CM 203), Jenny's 'archaeology',[44] just like Roger's, has an undeniably critical dimension that suggests that this literary adventure is over. As he writes in his conclusion, the 'time of the revolutionary metaphor has passed'.[45] It would seem that the time of 'the figure of comrade Mallarmé' (CM 14) is therefore over as well.

What we have here, then, is a series of contemporary works that differ wildly in their methodologies and axiologies. While dealing with relatively distinct objects, Roger and Jenny both practise an archaeological approach with a view to both comprehending and surpassing certain interpretative *dérives* involving Mallarmé. Kaufmann, by contrast, is situated somewhere between the latter critics' critical approach and Hamel's prophetic confidence. While he seeks to defend 'the theoretical movement' of the 1960s and '70s against those who would treat it as 'the scapegoat'[46] for today's literary decadence, Kaufmann does not go so far as to call for its re-actualisation. As a result, *La faute à Mallarmé* is at once a welcome corrective to contemporary reactionary diagnoses regarding the status of literature and a nostalgic review of a period of intellectual effervescence. Finally, despite recognising that 'it would be easy to point out the historical misinterpretations' manifest in the various political readings of Mallarmé he explores, Hamel revels in their capacity to 'valorise literature as a discourse of resistance to power' (CM 62) and proposes them as models for a future 'politics of reading' (CM 203).

The contemporary significance of political interpretations of Mallarmé is therefore not the object of a consensus. Rather, there appears to be a distinct oscillation between, on the one hand, a sense that political appropriations of the poet are interpretative extravagances, while on the other hand critics like Hamel treat these readings as an inspiration for a revitalised 'politics of literature' (CM 203).

What place does our work have amongst these contemporary efforts to understand how Mallarmé has been read? Given that our own corpus and set of guiding questions coincides almost entirely with those of Jean-François Hamel's *Camarade Mallarmé*, it behoves us to discuss his work in more detail, thereby situating our own perspective with greater precision.

*

As we mentioned above, Hamel's book sets out to give an historical account of the phenomenon of 'comrade Mallarmé', a paradoxical figure of literary engagement constructed by politically minded readers, for the most part on the broad French left, during the latter half of the twentieth century. Registering the various problematics confronted in Hamel's work, Roger writes that *Camarade Mallarmé* 'bears less on Mallarmé than on what we ourselves have called "Mallarmisme" ... and just as much on the avatars of "Mallarmisme" as on the becoming of Marxism and the revolutionary paradigm within French intellectual life in the twentieth century'. Roger continues, underscoring the fact that Hamel's book is thus 'a sort of history of French intellectual lefts, situated between history and philosophy, and approached through the projective test of Mallarmé'.[47] Despite this plurality of points of interest, it is crucial to point out that *Camarade Mallarmé* should be understood, in least in part, as a viable move within contemporary Mallarmé scholarship. Why is this the case?

To answer this question, we must first of all remark that the principal focus of *Camarade Mallarmé* is hermeneutics as such, or 'the act of reading' in itself, the examination of which Roger tells us has 'had the wind in its sails' ever since contemporary literary studies in France displaced 'the active centre of literature from the author to the reader'.[48] What this focus tells us is that, however fruitful Hamel's discussion of 'the act of reading' might be, the implicit assumption of his work is that the readings of Mallarmé in question are not in themselves wholly viable propositions for reading the poet today, at the very least from a philological perspective. Their contemporary interest lies less in expanding our knowledge of the poet's *œuvre* than in exploring a more general thesis, which Hamel puts as follows:

> the hermeneutical engagement of 'militants of restricted action' demonstrates ... that it is through the gestures of reading and interpretation, which are always gestures of memory, that the political significance of texts is

produced and reproduced, beyond the first intentions of the writer and his ideological commitments. (CM 17)

In other words, since it would arguably be implausible to revive many of the readings he deals with as fruitful proposals for contemporary Mallarmé research, the demonstrative force of Hamel's book lies in his arguments, presented consistently and compellingly throughout, regarding the nature of 'cultural memory' (CM 10) and the practices of various 'interpretative communities' (CM 199). Indeed, Hamel approvingly cites the following passage from Pascal Durand's recent attempt at a sociological reading of Mallarmé's trajectory, which aims in part to rectify many of the interpretative *dérives* of the past century: as Durand writes, Mallarmé's reception 'teaches us less, perhaps, about his *œuvre* than about the theoretical uses to which it has successively been put'.[49] However, despite the fact that Hamel recognises the questionable nature of these readings from a philological perspective, his thesis regarding 'cultural memory' is conspicuously doubled, as we have already noted, by a confident claim regarding the potential for political 'dissidence' (CM 203) possessed by certain interpretative practices:

> New critical theories, which prolong the interest of Western Marxism for art and literature and which have imposed themselves at the turn of the twentieth and twenty-first century, could in turn – if this hermeneutical practice appears fruitful to them – appropriate for themselves the poems and prose works of Mallarmé. (CM 189)

Curiously, then, while Hamel registers and even seems to subscribe to a certain consensus within contemporary Mallarmé studies regarding the validity of the political readings of the poet's *œuvre*, he also explicitly reproduces one of the principal tropes that characterised them: namely, as Kaufmann would have it, that of conceiving literature as possessing 'a singular symbolic efficacy'[50] capable of 'transforming social reality'.[51] Thus, while Hamel suggests at the beginning of *Camarade Mallarmé* that the only way one can read these interpretations is to 'suspend one's incredulity' (CM 10), he closes his book by declaring his fervent belief that such hermeneutical practices can function as 'discourses of resistance to power' (CM 62). There is thus a palpable tension in *Camarade Mallarmé* between a position of critical, indeed oftentimes ironic, distance from these past literary-theoretical extravagances, and a position involving the enthusiastic affirmation of the emancipatory powers of literature.

But if we are required to 'suspend our incredulity' towards the readings of Mallarmé proposed in the twentieth century, why should we invest any more faith in the 'politics of reading' that Hamel champions?

How can we avoid having to choose between an attitude of enlightened incredulity, which would relegate these political readings of 'comrade Mallarmé' to the past, and an incongruously enthusiastic attempt to replay a moment of this history?

In our view, the key to resolving this deadlock is first of all to reconstruct as precisely as possible, and in terms of their own individual integrity, the specific conceptual schemes that Sartre, Kristeva, Badiou, Milner, Rancière and Meillassoux bring to bear on Mallarmé's writings, as well as the political and intellectual conjunctures these thinkers confront with these schemes. For the fact is that these conceptual schemes, by force of their own internal consistency and capacity to respond to the conjunctures our thinkers confront, *compel belief* and adherence, not incredulity. If Hamel claims it is not possible to believe, today, in the seriousness of these twentieth-century readings of Mallarmé, then we must go further in the direction of faithfully reconstituting the situations in which such a dynamic of belief did operate. It is crucial to give an exact account of each thinkers' intervention – an account that restores them to their proper horizon of significance. While it is true that Hamel himself also attempts to situate the various constructions of the figure of 'comrade Mallarmé' in their intellectual and political context, we can briefly remark upon two significant divergences between our own account and the one provided in *Camarade Mallarmé*. Firstly, while Hamel claims that each of these political appropriations of Mallarmé pursues 'a deliberate art of anachronism' (CM 62), it is not at all clear that this is an accurate description of what Sartre, Kristeva, Badiou, Milner, Rancière and Meillassoux set out to do. In fact, it seems to better describe his own proposed 'politics of literature'. As Roger makes clear, 'Rancière and Lacoue-Labarthe would no doubt be surprised by such a judgement of their practice', since their respective writings 'converge with the reading produced by Bertrand Marchal in 1988 under the title *Religion de Mallarmé*, a reading it is difficult not to describe as philological'.[52] But it is also clear that Sartre, in his painstakingly totalising account of nineteenth-century literature, did not seek to 'wrench Mallarmé's *œuvre* away from its time' (CM 62) but rather to exhaustively analyse 'the Objective spirit' (FI 41) that nourished his writings. No doubt Sartre, like the Telquellians after him, also deployed his understanding of nineteenth-century literature to intervene in intellectual and political conjunctures contemporary to him, such as when he made Mallarmé's 'pure literature' the negative double of his own 'committed literature'. But as with theorists like Julia Kristeva this was always done on the basis of a purportedly accurate account of Mallarmé's significance: the aim of *The Family Idiot* is a total account of nineteenth-century France, just as *Revolution in Poetic Language* seeks to describing as precisely as possible the entirely 'new phenomenon' (RPL 15) that the poet's *œuvre* represented for the Telquellians. Likewise, Badiou's reading of Mallarmé involves the very precise claim that 'Mallarmé's poems and prose pieces [were] enquiries whose grouping-together defines this indiscernible as the truth of French poetry after Hugo' (BE 404). Finally, as we mentioned above, Rancière's approach is guided by a concern for philological accuracy. To claim, then, that these interpretative practices are examples of 'a deliberate art of anachronism' is to obscure the immanent teleology of the works of the thinkers treated in this book.

Secondly, while Hamel claims that these political appropriations of Mallarmé all seek to constitute 'literature as a discourse of resistance to power' (CM 62) in a manner identical to his own proposed project, this only holds for *some* of the political appropriations of the poet's writings. Indeed, the irony of Hamel's prophetic affirmation regarding his 'politics of reading' is that Mallarmé has often stood for the *failure* of literature to actualise its subversive power or to fulfil its political responsibilities. Rather than being a heroic figure who resisted 'power' or who intervened decisively in the 'social order at its most fundamental level', Mallarmé has also been deemed a counter-revolutionary and a conservative. Thierry Roger seems to pick up on this point when he writes that 'the readings of Mallarmé produced by Blanchot, Mondor, Valéry and the Sartre of *What is Literature?* have nothing specifically "left-wing" about them and therefore have little to no relation with the idea of comrade Mallarmé'.[53] Indeed, as Sartre would have it, Mallarmé is no 'comrade', but rather the perfect example of 'the legend of the irresponsible poet'. Against Hamel, we might say that the case of Mallarmé actually provides a lesson in the possible failure of his own proposed 'politics of reading'.

In our intervention, then, by restoring the political appropriations of Mallarmé made by Sartre, Kristeva, Badiou, Milner, Rancière and Meillassoux to their proper horizon of significance, we will seek to give full expression to the conflicting assessments that have been made of Mallarmé's writings, some of which already contest the pertinence of Hamel's proposal. It is only on the basis of such a reconstruction that their contemporary significance can then be determined.

*

The above points of criticism should nevertheless not obscure the fact that Hamel's work is a significant and in parts unprecedented contribution to our understanding of Mallarmé's reception. Indeed, it should be recognised, for instance, that *Camarade Mallarmé* presents many of the key contextual determinants of the pre-war reception of the poet. Hamel's reconstruction of the chain of interpretative practices leading from the very first editions of *La Nouvelle Revue Française* to the works of Gide, Valéry and Claudel, the communists of *L'Humanité*, the Surrealists, and finally to the pathbreaking work of Henri Mondor, will from this point on be indispensable to any reconstruction of the context in which Sartre and his successors write on Mallarmé – the moment from which our own work departs. In his first chapter, entitled 'The Invention of a Politics of Reading', Hamel identifies at least three distinct uses of Mallarmé in the pre-war period. By briefly reviewing these, we will be able to launch into our first chapter on Sartre with the proper context of the philosopher's intervention in mind.

Firstly, as Hamel points out, Mallarmé had come to be a model of the writer who, with an almost inhuman patience, valiantly refused to compromise with the status quo. Unsurprisingly, the actual content of this status quo is unstable. For Valéry, it was the political disorder of the 1930s in particular, as well as the violence, vulgarity and spiritual emptiness of modern life in general, which rendered the intellectual powerless. Highlighting the specifically ethical character of Valéry's reading, Hamel concludes that 'the disclosure of the ethical implications of a deliberately separated poetry, that is, of an autonomous literature subtracted from the laws of the market as well as from universal reportage, is Valéry's major contribution to the political interpretation of Mallarmé' (CM 52–3). As this passage also makes clear, Valéry was able to transform Mallarmé's famed isolation into the property that made him politically – or ethically – significant, instead of being a handicap or a sign of his irresponsibility. For Michel Leiris, by contrast, the status quo against which Mallarmé's stance could provide a model of resistance was the moral degradation of France during the Occupation (CM 21–7). Against the corruption of language that Leiris claimed had occurred after the capitulation to the Nazis, Mallarmé's 'defence of a pure art, radically distinct from universal reportage, signalled, according to Leiris, a literary resistance to the ideological instrumentalisation of language' (CM 27). The apparently anti-democratic aspects of Mallarmé's writings were thus transformed by Valéry and Leiris into signs of his ethical heroism.

Secondly, however, and in contradistinction to this first interpretative tendency, Mallarmé had also become an example of a general tendency witnessed in modern literature towards a corrosive – or, in Paulhan's terms, *terroristic* – approach to literary creation. Hamel describes this terroristic literature as a 'pure literature, stripped of commonplaces and attacking the language of contemporaries and the existence of a public space open to democratic deliberation' (CM 86–87). Intriguingly, in so far as this terroristic tendency was associated with the idea that modern literature had subtracted itself from communal life, both the right *and* the left critiqued the withdrawal of the writer from public affairs, their investment in a 'pure literature' and finally in an artistic individuality that came at the expense of the construction of a national – or democratic – culture. A work like Julien Benda's *La France Byzantine, ou, le triomphe de la littérature pure* (1945),[54] for example, prefigures Sartre's defence of democracy, associating as it does literary purists, from Mallarmé to the Surrealists, with an aristocratism that, as Jean Paulhan had already argued in *Les Fleurs de Tarbes* in 1941, manifested a 'disgust in the face of clichés [and] ended in hatred for current society and common sentiments' (CM 91), leading ultimately to 'the divorce of the writer from the public' (CM 81). Mallarmé thus stood for the corrosive negativity of modern literature – its terroristic assault on the foundations of a shared culture, however the latter was construed.

Thirdly, Mallarmé's writings were treated as a symptom via which the state of French culture could be diagnosed more generally. This diagnosis was made by the right before and during the Occupation and sought to explain the weakness of French culture compared to that of the Germans – a weakness that was seen as the result of the writer having either become 'separated from national life' or from propagating the 'disorders of individualism' (CM 22). But it was also made after the Liberation by the left, who aimed to identify the origins of collaborationist tendencies and to purge them from French letters.

At the moment, then, of Sartre's decisive intervention in the postwar intellectual field, Mallarmé was already a figure who condensed a number of decisive political and ethical questions. Was the poet's alleged distance from the public sphere a mark of his principled commitment to an art that represented, as Valéry would have it, 'the spiritual destination of man, that is, his capacity to raise himself above animality by the recognition of the absolute' (CM 52)? Or was Mallarmé – that 'being of refusal' (CM 80) – guilty of failing to cultivate a viable common culture characterised by 'democratic deliberation'? Did the negativity of his poetry manifest a disdain for ordinary people's prosaism, or a liberation of fundamental human capacities? Questions such as these will animate not only Sartre's engagement with Mallarmé, but those who come after him as well.

NOTES

1. J.-P. Faye, 'Le camarade Mallarmé', *L'Humanité*, 19 September 1969.
2. For interpretations of the political significance of Mallarmé's work that were contemporary to him, see B. Marchal (ed.), *Mallarmé (Mémoire de la critique)* (Paris: Presses Universitaires de Paris-Sorbonne, 1998).
3. J.-P. Sartre, 'Introducing *Les Temps Modernes*', in R. Aronson and A. Van Den Hoven (eds), *We Have Only This Life To Live: The Selected Essays of Jean-Paul Sartre, 1939–1975* (New York: New York Review of Books, 2013), 137 (translation modified).
4. J.-P. Sartre, 'The Purposes of Writing', in *Between Existentialism and Marxism*, trans. John Matthews (London: Verso, 2008), 13.
5. These readings have nevertheless been the object of Jean-François Hamel's recent work, which we will soon discuss in detail. J.-F. Hamel, *Camarade Mallarmé: Une politique de la lecture* (Paris: Editions de Minuit, 2014).
6. J. Hippolyte, 'Le *Coup de dés* et le message', in *Figures de la pensée philosophique* (Paris: Presses Universitaires de France, 1971), 877–84.
7. M. Foucault, *The Order of Things: An Archaeology of the Human Sciences* (New York: Vintage Books, 1994).
8. J. Derrida, 'The Double Session', in *Dissemination*, trans. B. Johnson (Chicago: University of Chicago Press, 1981), 173–286.
9. G. Deleuze, *Nietzsche and Philosophy*, trans. H. Tomlinson (New York: Columbia University Press, 1983), and G. Deleuze, *The Fold: Leibniz and the Baroque*, trans. T. Conley (London and New York: Continuum, 1993).
10. J.-F. Lyotard, *Discourse, Figure*, trans. A. Hudek and M. Lydon (Minneapolis: University of Minnesota Press, 2011).
11. A. Stanguennec, *Mallarmé et l'éthique de la poésie* (Paris: Vrin, 1992).
12. P. Campion, *Mallarmé, poésie et philosophie* (Paris: Presses Universitaires de France, 1994).
13. 'Introducing *Les Temps Modernes*', 137.
14. M. Marchal, *Lecture de Mallarmé: Poésies, Igitur, le Coup de dés* (Paris: José Corti, 1985).
15. M. Marchal, *La Religion de Mallarmé: poésie, mythologie et religion* (Paris: José Corti, 1988).
16. P. Durand, *Mallarmé: Du sens des formes au sens des formalités* (Paris: Seuil, 2008).
17. P. Thériault, *Le (Dé)montage de la fiction: La révélation moderne de Mallarmé* (Paris: Honoré Champion, 2010).
18. B. Bohac, *Jouir partout ainsi qu'il sied: Mallarmé et l'esthétique du quotidien* (Paris: Classiques Garnier, 2012).
19. R. Pearson, *Unfolding Mallarmé: The Development of a Poetic Art* (Oxford: Oxford University Press 1997); R. Pearson, *Mallarmé and Circumstance: The Translation of Silence* (Oxford: Oxford University Press, 2004).

20. R. Lloyd, *Mallarmé: The Poet and His Circle* (Ithaca: Cornell University Press, 1999).
21. D. Catani, *The Poet in Society: Art, Consumerism and Politics in Mallarmé* (Oxford: Peter Lang, 2003).
22. See the very recent book by R. H. Bloch, *One Toss of the Dice: The Incredible Story of How a Poem Made us Modern* (New York: Liverlight Publishing Corporation, 2017).
23. See http://www.fabula.org.actualites/contre-mallarme-contre-attaque-con trepoint-contretemps_76726.php (accessed February 2017).
24. A. Badiou, 'Mallarmé Said It All', in R. Boncardo and C. R. Gelder, *Mallarmé: Rancière, Milner, Badiou* (London: Rowman & Littlefield, 2017), 92.
25. T. Roger, *L'Archive du Coup de dés* (Paris: Éditions Classiques Garnier, 2010), 15.
26. See, for Roger's discussion of Foucault's archaeological approach and his application of it, *L'Archive du Coup de dés*, 15–19.
27. *L'Archive du Coup de dés*, 22.
28. *L'Archive du Coup de dés*, 482.
29. T. Roger, '"Camarade Mallarmé": mallarmisme, anachronisme, présentisme', *Acta fabula*, Vol. 15, No. 6, 'Réinvestissement, rumeur & récriture', Juin–juillet 2014.
30. '"Camarade Mallarmé": mallarmisme, anachronisme, présentisme'.
31. V. Kaufmann, *La faute à Mallarmé: L'aventure de la théorie littéraire* (Paris: Seuil, 2011), 7.
32. *La faute à Mallarmé*, 8.
33. *La faute à Mallarmé*, 27
34. T. Roger, 'La faute au mallarmisme', *Acta fabula*, Vol. 13, No. 9, 'L'aventure Poétique', Novembre–Décembre 2012.
35. *La faute à Mallarmé*, 194.
36. *La faute à Mallarmé*, 195.
37. *La faute à Mallarmé*, 15.
38. *La faute à Mallarmé*, 191.
39. L. Jenny, *Je suis la révolution: Histoire d'une métaphore (1830–1975)* (Paris: Editions Belin, 2006).
40. *Je suis la révolution*, 212.
41. *Je suis la révolution*, 211.
42. *Je suis la révolution*, 211.
43. Cited in *Je suis la révolution*, 181.
44. *Je suis la révolution*, 6.
45. *Je suis la révolution*, 211.
46. *La faute à Mallarmé*, 10.
47. As Roger writes in his review of *La faute à Mallarmé*, 'Mallarmisme is a reductionism that consists in reducing the poet to the *Sonnet en -yx* and to a few decontextualised formulas', 'La faute au mallarmisme'.
48. 'La faute au mallarmisme'.

49. Cited CM 14.
50. *La faute à Mallarmé*, 31, n. 1.
51. '"Camarade Mallarmé": mallarmisme, anachronisme, présentisme'.
52. '"Camarade Mallarmé": mallarmisme, anachronisme, présentisme'.
53. '"Camarade Mallarmé": mallarmisme, anachronisme, présentisme'.
54. J. Benda, *La France Byzantine, ou le triomphe de la littérature pure: Mallarmé, Gide, Proust, Valéry, Alain, Giraudoux, Suarès, les Surréalistes. Essais d'une psychologie originelle du littérateur* (Paris: Gallimard, 1945).

1 Jean-Paul Sartre's Mallarmé: Hero of an Ontological Drama, Agent of the Counter-revolution

In a 1959 interview, after admitting that he had drawn on his writings extensively in *Saint Genet* and in his work on Flaubert – work which would soon become the monumental *The Family Idiot*, published in 1971–72 – Jean-Paul Sartre confessed that he had 'only just begun' to read Mallarmé.[1] Yet as we will see in this first chapter, despite being, on his own admission, both provisional and incomplete, Sartre's reading of Mallarmé was remarkably consistent. Developed at greatest length in his 'existential biography' *Mallarmé, or the Poet of Nothingness*,[2] a half-finished manuscript published in a 1979 edition of *Obliques* but composed much earlier in the years 1948–52, Sartre's interpretation of Mallarmé can be found throughout such majors works as *What is Literature?*,[3] 'Black Orpheus',[4] and the third and final volume of *The Family Idiot*.[5] For Sartre, the poet was the 'hero of an ontological drama' (MPN 122), an ingenious artistic precursor to the philosopher's own tragic vision of human existence, as developed in *Being and Nothingness*. Yet he was also a member of a late nineteenth-century French literary generation that Sartre, partisan of 'committed literature', constantly excoriated. The aim of this chapter is to explore this foundational tension.

In the scholarship on Sartre's *Mallarmé* to date, commentators seem to have taken their cue from the philosopher's own remarks. As Sartre states in the same 1959 interview: 'I mention [Mallarmé] only to indicate that "pure" literature is a dream. If literature is not everything', he continues, 'it is worth nothing': 'This is what I mean by "commitment".'[6] It wilts if it is reduced to innocence, or to songs. If a sentence does not reverberate at every level of man and society, then it makes no sense. What is the literature of an epoch but the epoch appropriated by its literature?'[7] Commentators from Rhiannon Goldthorpe to Carey Wolfe, Benoît Denis to Jean-François Hamel,[8] have all read *The Poet of*

Nothingness as a significant chapter in Sartre's development of his concept of 'committed literature'. Echoing this critical consensus, Hamel argues that in *Mallarmé* Sartre 'envisages the possibility of a committed negativity of poetry: that is, of a terroristic politics of literature that ruptures with his own doctrine of commitment' (CM 95). As this passage suggests, the stakes of Hamel's argument are high: in *What is Literature?* Sartre had prohibited poets from ever entering the pantheon of 'committed' writers; yet less than five years later, he had allowed Mallarmé back in – or so it seems. How could Sartre have shifted so quickly from treating the poet's 'icy silence'[9] as the culmination of a politically irresponsible tendency in French letters, to affirming that the poet was 'conscious of [his] commitment'?[10] What was the political significance of Mallarmé's writings for Sartre?

In the first section of this chapter we will briefly present Sartre's views on modern French poetry in order to introduce the problematic of Mallarmé as a paradoxically 'committed poet'. Then, in the second and longest section, we will present a detailed exegesis and commentary of Sartre's *The Poet of Nothingness*, turning at the end to *The Family Idiot* in order to evaluate the scope of Sartre's claims about the poet. Finally, we will conclude with a discussion of occasional remarks made by Sartre on Mallarmé's 'religion' – remarks that foreshadow the concerns of later commentators.

*

Why does Mallarmé's status as a 'committed poet' have the value of a paradox? For Sartre, modern French poetry presents two characteristics that make it radically unsuitable for political engagement.[11] Firstly, it instantiates a corrosive linguistic practice that breaks apart everyday language and approximates what Sartre, following Jean Paulhan, calls *terror in letters*.[12] Secondly, it manifests an inhuman indifference to the world of common action, preferring instead the autonomous world of words used as *things* rather than as *signs*. Mallarmé is discretely present in a formula Sartre obsessively invokes in his early literary essays to describe the first of these characteristics – a formula that is less a direct citation of the poet and more a mobile assemblage of fragments from Léon-Paul Fargue, Georges Bataille and Mallarmé's own 'Crisis of Verse'. Thus, in a passage from his 1945 essay 'The Nationalisation of Literature' in which Sartre confidently affirms the reinstated dignity and democratic virtues of *rhetoric* over its destructive opposite, *terror* – a pair of terms adopted from Paulhan – we find one iteration and variation of this formula:

> Today, things have changed: the dignity and power of both literature and rhetoric have been re-established. It is no longer a question of lighting fires in the scrub of language, of joining together 'words that burn' so as to attain the absolute by the combustion of the dictionary, but of communicating with other Men by modestly using the means at hand.[13]

As this passage makes clear, Sartre is speaking at a moment of rupture in which a dividing line needs to be drawn between past literary practices and those that are better adapted to present exigencies.[14] Critics such as Anne Boschetti have shown how, in the post-war context, Sartre set out to assert his intellectual hegemony by breaking with past literary forms judged to be unsuitable for progressive politics after the Second World War. But alongside this necessary moment of critique, Sartre also had to defend the intrinsic pertinence of literary practice – of his *own* literary practice – against the suspicions of the politically ascendant Marxists of the PCF, who privileged different modes of action.[15] Sartre made modern French poetry, including Mallarmé's, serve both ends: on the one hand, he pre-emptively exorcised the possible points of failure of 'committed literature' by exteriorising them in past forms of poetry; and on the other hand, he ruthlessly critiqued, from a quasi-Marxist perspective, the late nineteenth-century literary field to which Mallarmé belonged – a critique we will explore soon. This bolstered his Marxist credentials and, as Boschetti puts it, helped to 'rid [his own] literature of suspicion'[16] – the 'suspicion' of being complicit with a politically deleterious literary ideology. Thus, when it came to positively articulating the characteristics of 'committed literature', in particular its privileging of communicative clarity and its attempt to address a wide cross-section of contemporary readers,[17] Sartre consistently contrasted it with the negativity of modern French poetry. In 'Black Orpheus', an essay published three years after the inaugural issue of *Les Temps Modernes* and devoted to the phenomenon of 'negritude', Sartre reprises parts of the formula quoted above:

> It strikes me that from Mallarmé to the Surrealists, the profound aim of French poetry has been this self-destruction of language. The poem is a camera obscura in which each word bangs insanely into the next. Colliding in the air, they set each other on fire and fall down in flames . . . And since French lacks terms and concepts for defining negritude, since negritude is silence, to evoke it, they will use 'allusive, ever-indirect words, reducing themselves to an equal silence'. Short-circuits of language: behind the words falling down in flames, we glimpse a large, black, mute idol.[18]

Here, Sartre uses the same selective citation from 'Crisis of Verse' as he had in 'The Nationalisation of Literature' – namely 'words . . . light each other up through reciprocal reflections like a virtual swooping of fire across precious stones' (D 208)[19] – and connects it with another well-known phrase from Mallarmé's 'Magic': 'To evoke, with intentional vagueness, the mute object, using allusive words, never direct, in an endeavour very close to creating' (D 264 – translation modified). In this game of literary mix-and-match, Sartre draws on a famous Mallarméan description of language's autonomous production of meaning ('words ... light each other up through reciprocal reflections'); links the poet's evocation of fire and heat ('light', 'a virtual swooping of fire') to Léon-Paul Fargue's maxim, 'poetry is made up of words that burn';[20] and finally claims that the outcome of this poetic process is 'silence' ('reducing everything to an equivalent of silence'). This is the 'icy silence' mentioned in *What is Literature?* – a 'silence' that lies beyond the clamour of common language and which Mallarmé's work exemplarily produces. Against this self-cancellation of language, 'committed literature' advances the democratic virtues of communication and clarity.

In addition to dissolving language as a means of intersubjective comprehension, Sartre argues that modern French poets had also undermined language's essentially practical function. In his 1944 essay 'Man and Things' Sartre speaks of the poet Francis Ponge's work as being 'built out of word-things',[21] a description he immediately qualifies in the following terms: 'Of things: that is to say, of the inhuman.'[22] As a typical poet Ponge does with words what he also does with things: namely, he 'divest[s] them of their *practical* significations'.[23] In other words, he treats them in abstraction from any human 'project'[24] that would take them, as Heidegger would put it, as a 'Zeug', a tool. At the end of this process, the poet's words are returned to a state indifferent to human ends. Thus, in terms of the 'undifferentiated choice' that lies at 'the origin of every artistic calling',[25] poets manifest a suspicious indifference to the practical exigencies people normally respond to with language, and prefer instead the anti-world they can construct with the sensible properties of words. In *The Poet of Nothingness*, Sartre claims that Mallarmé himself made a choice in favour of poetic language since he realised that he 'could, at a single stroke, use words both to annihilate the world and to create it by words' (MPN 113). In *The Family Idiot*, Sartre makes explicit what adopting this attitude implies: 'To choose the sumptuousness of names is to prefer the universe of the Word to that of things and to prefer satisfaction through words – or false satisfaction – to the real pleasure of the things of the world.'[26] Compared to the prose writer, for whom words are nothing but 'useful conventions [and] tools'[27] to be put into the service of unveiling the extra-literary world to the reader, the poet is a politically suspect quietist.

From this short exploration of the key characteristics of Sartre's early account of modern French poetry, we can both appreciate this account's idiosyncrasy as well as glimpse the logic that lies behind it. Firstly, the suggestion that poets purposefully subtract language from its originarily pragmatic existence – the corollary of which is their incapacity to act linguistically within a common world – tells us that Sartre's ideal is, unsurprisingly, a literature that would produce determinate effects similar to those of political action more narrowly defined.[28] Secondly, the exclusion of poetry from 'committed literature' on the grounds that, like a painting or a melody, it proposes no 'definable signification'[29] – poetry's purpose, recall, is to produce 'silence', not any intelligible sound – demonstrates that Sartre's ideal is, again unsurprisingly, a literature of communicative clarity and precision. More than this, his ideal involves both writer and reader participating in a homogeneous present in which ideas can be perfectly transmitted between the diverse strata of a society.[30] By contrast, the poet will stand for the writer wilfully subtracted from the social world, their voice resonating within the confines of 'an audience of specialists'.[31] Furthermore, their refusal to be actively engaged with the pressing practical concerns of their times reeks of cowardice: in an exemplary passage from *Baudelaire*, Sartre writes that 'poetic creation, which [Baudelaire] preferred to every form of action ... attracted him in the first place because it allowed him to exercise his freedom without any danger'.[32] This damning sentence could be extended to all poets, including Mallarmé. In exact opposition to this poetic attitude, we can place Sartre's famous affirmation from 'Introducing *Les Temps Modernes*': 'We don't want to miss out on anything of our time ... we have only this life to live, amid this war, and perhaps this revolution.'[33]

This, then, is the intellectual and historical context in which Sartre's 1959 statement that Mallarmé was 'conscious of [his] commitment' becomes a paradox. In the remainder of this chapter, we turn to the work that scholars have read as a radical revision of Sartre's concept of 'committed literature': *Mallarmé, or the Poet of Nothingness*.

*

As Carey Wolfe writes, *Mallarmé, or the Poet of Nothingness* seems to represent 'Sartre's attempt to extend and fundamentally revise the concept of commitment':

> What began in 1947 in that text as a more or less courteous reprimand of contemporary poetry becomes five years later in *Saint Genet* a full-blown anatomy of a generic pathology. But in the same year, *Mallarmé*, in a startling reversal, develops a new and unabashedly ontological concept of

poetic commitment not really present in Sartre's work either before or since.³⁴

What is curious about this critical consensus is that Sartre only once uses a cognate of the French term *engagement* in the entire manuscript of *Mallarmé*. Stranger still, this occurs in the context of his description of the corrosive negativity of the poet's writing – a characteristic that would have counted against Mallarmé in *What is Literature?* Sartre writes: '[Mallarmé] was a Poet to the core, wholly *committed* to the critical self-destruction of Poetry' (MPN 145 – our emphasis). Moreover, as we will soon see when we explore the context of its composition, Sartre never frames *The Poet of Nothingness* as a work designed to reflect on the concept of 'commitment'. And even if a revised conception of literary action is one of its unexpected products, Wolfe's argument implies that 'commitment' remains a consistent concept when stretched between its *political* and *ontological* meanings.

In what follows, we will examine in their order the two main sections of *The Poet of Nothingness*: first, a polemical study of the post-1848 French literary field, in which Sartre extends insights from *What is Literature?* and lays the foundations for his account of 'postromanticism'³⁵ in the third volume of *The Family Idiot*; and second, a biographical account of Mallarmé's childhood and early adulthood, which places the young poet in the context of Parnassianism and a nascent Symbolism. In the first section, Sartre radicalises his assessment of his literary predecessors, bringing a more explicitly Marxist perspective to bear upon their lives and works and adding an unexpected dose of sarcasm and scorn to his critique. In the second section, he pursues the project of 'existential psychoanalysis' announced in *Being and Nothingness* but in fact presaged in his *War Diaries*. In studying Sartre's *Mallarmé* our main concern will be with the following tension that traverses it: while Mallarmé emerges from the first section as an 'agen[t] of the ... counter-revolution' (MPN 37) in the aftermath of the June Days of 1848, in the second Sartre presents him as 'the hero of an ontological drama' – the guise in which he supposedly qualifies as a 'committed poet'. How are we to evaluate the relation between these two distinct descriptions? Does Mallarmé's ontological commitment save him from political condemnation?

*

There were many reasons for Sartre to attempt a biography of Mallarmé in the years 1948–52. For the most part, these reasons had to do with the way contemporary publications on Mallarmé and related topics resonated with Sartre's long-standing concerns. As Hamel has shown, despite the way being prepared by Valéry's discipleship throughout the 1920s and '30s, both inside and outside of the pages of *La Nouvelle Revue Française*, the period of the Occupation and the Liberation represented the true moment of Mallarmé's canonisation in French letters (CM 53–63). In 1941 and 1942, Henri Mondor published the two parts of his ground-breaking *Vie de Mallarmé*,[36] a biographical and literary study of unprecedented scope. Almost immediately, the literary critic Maurice Blanchot favourably reviewed Mondor's book in the *Journal des débats*. Blanchot's piece, his first of many 'Chroniques de la vie intellectuelle', marked the beginning of a series of essays on Mallarmé that he would publish in the following years. Two of these, 'Literature and the Right To Death' from *The Work of Fire*, and 'Mallarmé's Experience', first published in the journal *Critique* in 1952 and later in *The Space of Literature*, are cited as authoritative works in *The Poet of Nothingness*.[37] The attention paid to Mallarmé at this time by another prominent and philosophically inclined critic no doubt encouraged Sartre to produce his own reading of the poet. Returning to Mondor, two years after his *Vie de Mallarmé* appeared, in 1944, the famous surgeon published *Mallarmé plus intime*,[38] a follow-up work to *Vie de Mallarmé* in which he made available even more previously unseen letters and documents. A year later, Mondor collaborated with Georges Jean-Aubry to curate the first Pléiade edition of Mallarmé's *Œuvres complètes*. And finally, in 1951, Mondor's book *Eugène Lefébure: Sa vie, ses lettres à Mallarmé* was published.[39] In this last work, through a close reading of the future Egyptologist's epistolary exchange with Mallarmé, Mondor shed light on a hitherto unrecognised line of influence on the young poet, all the while offering an intimate account of his famous spiritual crisis of the years 1866–67.

This wealth of new biographical information undoubtedly made Sartre's project of an 'existential biography' of Mallarmé both desirable and possible. Envisaged, perhaps, as a sequel to his then recently published *Baudelaire*, Sartre's manuscript on Mallarmé took up the thread of his reflections on the relation between the individual and their historical moment, which he had begun to note down in his *War Diaries*. Briefly returning to this work will help us properly situate *Mallarmé* in Sartre's intellectual trajectory.

In *Notebook 14* of his *War Diaries*, Sartre recounts how he and Simone de Beauvoir had been both intrigued and provoked by Aron's work *Introduction à la philosophie de l'histoire, Essai sur les limites de l'objectivité historique*, published in 1938. In particular, their attention had been drawn to the problematic treated therein of 'the various layers of signification' on the basis of which one can give an 'explanation of the historical event'.[40] In the *War Diaries*, Sartre sets out to explore this problem by posing the following question: to what extent was Kaiser William II a *cause* of the First World War?[41] This focus on the role of an exceptional individual in an historical situation presages his attempt in *Mallarmé* to demonstrate how the 'Idea' of late nineteenth-century poetry could be 'transcended' by a singular subject and their irreducible margin of freedom. In the case of William II, Sartre seeks out 'an inner relation of comprehension between … English policy and [the] withered arm' of the Kaiser.[42] In other words, he argues that William's very *being* as Kaiser – his 'being-to-reign',[43] the meaning of which was decisively inflected by the congenital atrophy of his left arm – had a relation of reciprocal determination with the politics of the Prussian State towards England. The way that Sartre attempts to demonstrate this is instructive. Focusing on William's intra-familial relations, Sartre insists on the way his 'disability' was lived as being that of a future Kaiser – and *not* as the 'disability' of 'a simple citizen'.[44] That William's 'disability' was treated with contempt within his family, in particular by his English mother, the daughter of Queen Victoria, determined that it was 'towards England that he ha[d] his inferiority complex'.[45] Thus, for William, his 'disability' was inextricably bound up with his vision of England such that 'conquering England' became equivalent to 'suppressing his disability'.[46] The way that a political situation is mediated by the family unit thus becomes the key explanatory move Sartre makes in order to totalise and hierarchise the 'various layers of signification' constituting the Kaiser's life. In *The Poet of Nothingness* Sartre will also turn to Mallarmé's familial situation as the key determinant in the poet's ability to interiorise and surpass a collective problematic. The intellectual inspiration and orientation for his *Mallarmé* biography is thus present well before the publication of *Being and Nothingness*.

With the flurry of publishing activity on Mallarmé during and after the war years, Sartre had ample material at his disposal to pursue the questions he could only jot down in his *War Diaries*. Yet the reader expecting to find in *The Poet of Nothingness* a sober historical account of post-1848 France alongside reflections on Mallarmé's life will be sorely disappointed: Sartre's manuscript, in particular its first section 'The Atheist Heritage', reads more as the continuation of his polemic against his literary predecessors. In fact, Sartre seems principally concerned in this section to accumulate evidence against the post-1848 generation of French poets, demonstrating with an almost perverse analytical glee how their bleak vision of the world betrayed an allegiance to the ruling capitalist class. To understand why the tone of 'The

Atheist Heritage' is so ferocious, it is crucial to point out that it was written during the period of Sartre's feverish work on the first of three articles that would make up his notorious essay *The Communists and Peace*. At this moment, Sartre became, by his own admission, 'a fellow traveller'[47] of the French Communist Party. Disgusted by the Henri Martin Affair and by the sins of French imperialism both at home and abroad, Sartre 'swore a hatred of the bourgeoisie that will end only when I do', as he later wrote in 'Merleau-Ponty'.[48] Sartre's Marxism was thus at its most doctrinaire at the time of composing his manuscript on Mallarmé. Indeed, the violently polemical tone of 'The Atheist Heritage' irresistibly suggests that some of Sartre's 'hatred' animated his uncompromising condemnation of those who, from Flaubert to de Lisle, had made themselves the 'agents of the counter-revolution' (MPN 37) in the aftermath of 1848. But to fully appreciate how Sartre could so easily displace his class hatred onto a century-old incarnation of the French bourgeoisie, it is essential to mention the mediation of Henri Guillemin's book, *Le Coup du 2 décembre*.[49] A classmate of Sartre's at the Rue d'Ulm, in his 1951 book Guillemin assembled an extraordinary array of documents – newspapers, journals both public and private, letters and speeches – made by the main actors of the events that occurred between the failed revolution of 1848 and Napoleon III's rise to power. For Sartre, the book proved that the leading bourgeois of the time had acted consciously and with a sickening cynicism, helping to install a veritable dictatorship after crushing the people's democratic aspirations in the early months of 1848. As Sartre stated in a 1976 interview, the documents made available in *Le Coup du 2 décembre* – documents which he draws on liberally in 'The Atheist Heritage' – revealed the profound cruelty of the bourgeoisie, which he had again seen at work in contemporary events. Thus, if *The Communists and Peace* could be considered a radicalisation of Sartre's already-stated allegiances to socialism, then Guillemin's book helps bring his polemic against the late nineteenth-century French literary field, begun in *What is Literature?*, to boiling point. This is why *Mallarmé, the Poet of Nothingness* could never have been the sober historical study presaged by the *War Diaries*.

Yet Sartre's book on Mallarmé is not only an exercise in political assassination. Indeed, had he sought simply to verify the superstructural account of art found in Marx, whose *German Ideology* he twice references (MPN 65, 83), then he would have contradicted the most profound motivation of his work. In fact, Sartre's fundamental aim in *Mallarmé* is the same as in his contemporaneous book *Saint Genet*, where he writes that he seeks to 'indicate the limit of psychoanalytical interpretation and Marxist explanation and to demonstrate that freedom alone can account for a person in his totality'.[50] Sartre puts this same point in the following passage from *The Poet of Nothingness*: 'if we have chosen the case of the "Obscure Sphinx" of Tournon, it is because it seemed to provide us with the privileged opportunity to confront, in a concrete case, the psychoanalytic and Marxist methods of interpretation' (MPN 87). While the reference to freedom found in *Saint Genet* is strikingly absent from this second passage, we can be sure that it remains at the centre of Sartre's concerns, in particular since his purpose in *The Poet of Nothingness* is to show how Mallarmé transcended the constraints of 'the poetic complex' (MPN 64 – translation modified) of his time. For indeed, this is a 'complex' that the philosopher *cum* Marxist polemicist eviscerates in the first half of the book. Thus, when Sartre announces at the close of 'The Atheist Heritage' that an individual will emerge with 'an all-embracing lucid consciousness' that will be able to 'hold all [of the] nuances' of French postromantic poetry 'together' – an individual who will consequently 'elude Marxist interpretations and escape social conditioning' (MPN 64) – it suddenly seems as if all of the polemical fire and analytical power of this first section of *The Poet of Nothingness* existed only to make the final victory of Mallarmé's freedom all the more spectacular. We will explore this explosive tension in the final part of this chapter. First, however, we must take the full measure of Sartre's Marxist *reduction* of post-1848 French poetry, restaging step-by-step his arguments for the ethical complicity and ontological continuity between the victorious French bourgeoisie's ideology and the fundaments of postromanticism.

*

Sartre begins the narrative of 'The Atheist Heritage' at a critical juncture within French history: the June Days of 1848. Importantly, on his reading the bloody events of this month represented less a moment of radical structural change in nineteenth-century France and more an apocalyptic revelation of the most profound truth of this society. He puts this point forcefully in *Critique of Dialectical Reason*, another work intimately concerned with the history of class struggle in France: with the massacres of workers in the streets of Paris, 'the struggle of the classes was stripped bare; having been hidden for so long, the fact that it was a *struggle to the death* was revealed in all its brutality'.[51] This passage perfectly matches the sense of the opening lines to 'The Atheist Heritage': 'In 1848 the fall of the monarchy blows the bourgeoisie's cover' (MPN 19). In other words, the events of 1848 showed that the bourgeoisie – even if it had been hidden beneath the mystifying mask of a monarchy, and even if it would soon seem to submit, in 1851, to another form of authoritarianism – was ultimately the class whose interests were served by the reigning social order. Moreover, with the June Days it had demonstrated that it was willing to defend its interests *qua* the ruling class through murderous violence. Unless one adopted a posture of bad faith, after 1848 no one could think of France as a unified community, a people marching in lockstep towards a glorious future, as Victor Hugo's Romantic poetry had famously – and falsely – presented it. The fracture at the heart of France had been revealed.

Commentators have recognised the importance Sartre accords 1848 in *The Poet of Nothingness*. Yet few have been able to explain with precision the nature of the link he establishes between the political events of 1848 and their repercussions in the realm of poetry. Why, for instance, does Sartre continue the opening sentence of 'The Atheist Heritage' with the claim that, in the wake of 1848, 'Poetry loses its two traditional themes: Man and God' (MPN 19)? Is it a matter of a direct causal connection between the political, poetical and metaphysical levels? Or is there simply a suggestive temporal contiguity between changes occurring in each of these realms separately? The mystery is deepened when, on the following page, Sartre explains that the de-Christianisation of France was a long, drawn-out process, whose key stages were marked less by political events and more by the shift between generations (MPN 20). But if this is the case, then unlike the revelation of class struggle, the death of God could hardly have been 'staggering news' (MPN 19) for the French people of 1848; it could not have taken the form of a newswire received all of a sudden by a country of unsuspecting Catholics, even if this is how Sartre describes it on the first page of 'The Atheist Heritage'. If postromantic French poetry could no longer take God and Man as stable points of reference, then it could not have been because of the violence of 1848 alone. How, then, does Sartre understand the relation between 1848, atheism and postromanticism?

The first step in Sartre's argument turns around the nature of the atheism shared by the post-1848 intelligentsia, Mallarmé included. For the bourgeois revolutionaries of 1789 and 1793, a scientific form of atheism inspired by the physical and natural sciences of the time had helped them 'dissolve', as Sartre puts it, 'the monarchy's great syntheses' (MPN 19). Within the infinite Universe of mathematised modern science, society could no longer be situated in a unified cosmological hierarchy with God at the highest level and the monarch just below Him in the role of His worldly representative. The sciences were therefore an effective means for eroding the monarchy's claim to social prestige. Moreover, the sciences' *de facto* link to the rise of a new ruling class meant that their object, Nature, was implicitly associated with predicates such as benevolence and progress – a reflection of the sciences' ideological submission to the bourgeoisie's strategy. Yet as Sartre explains, the members of this first generation were 'too much involved in the struggle' (MPN 20) to pose the fundamental question of whether the sciences could in turn ground the bourgeoisie's claim to being the rightful ruling class. This would be left to later generations. Sartre narrates: 'the children, gritting their teeth, took stock of the consequences' (MPN 20) of their predecessors' strategy. For beyond their pragmatic use in a situated struggle, the sciences progressively revealed a universe in which no class – indeed no human being – could lay claim to any form of superiority whatsoever. As for the sciences' object, Nature, it was now 'older and hardened' and 'no longer even offered those comforting vestiges of finality that once had justified the high hopes of the revolutionaries' (MPN 19). In short, in order to defeat its first enemy, the monarchy, the bourgeoisie had used a weapon that would inevitably work against them. Sartre summarises this movement as follows:

> Analytical reason – that most potent of bourgeois weapons – after demolishing the monarchy's grand syntheses, quietly and unwittingly did away with the ultimate crowning synthesis: Self-caused Being, a whole that produces and governs its parts. The universe had come apart. Nature had become nothing more than an infinite dance of dust particles. Under the unctuous chemicals of life, man began to suspect his true mineral nature. If the universe is now nothing more than a jumble of atoms, where is the basis for a moral order? (MPN 19–20 – translation modified)

This is the fundamental question for the generation of bourgeois that come to power at the time of the failed 1848 revolution. Here, Sartre reprises a dialectical move made famous by Marx, for whom the bourgeoisie necessarily holds within itself the seeds of its own destruction. This time, however, the contradiction is between the bourgeoisie's atheistic ideology, which dissolves all natural hierarchy, and its obvious need to justify its reign. As Sartre audaciously puts it: 'God drags down with him the very gravediggers who had dug his tomb' (MPN 20).

We are beginning to see the nature of the relation between 1848, atheism and poetry. With the events of the June Days, the bourgeoisie is revealed to be the ruling class in France, with the stability of its reign bolstered only by violence. Yet it had no reliable means besides force to justify its position: atheism by definition failed it in this task. Thus, while the atheism of the revolutionaries of 1789 was affirmative and victorious, for the bourgeois who felt the fragility of their position after 1848 atheism was a philosophy that induced despair. The consequences of this inversion are profound. As Sartre explains, a new precomprehension of Being *as such* – or of 'Nature' (MPN 37), to use the terminology of the time – had emerged, one that involved a radical shift in the ideological significance of the categories of Being and Nothingness. Comparing the new ruling class to the old, Sartre writes that 'the nobleman, secure in his faith and proud of his birth, is eminently satisfied with nature and unabashedly exhibits his own' (MPN 56). But if Nature is now what 'makes men equal' (MPN 56), then the bourgeoisie cannot affirm itself through the category of Being: only the various species of Nothingness are appropriate: 'unable to found its privileges in Being', Sartre writes, the bourgeoisie 'claims to distinguish itself from the people by means of self-inflicted privations and taboos, that is, through Negations' (MPN 56). Sartre will name *distinction* the ensemble of social practices that derive from this fundamental decision in favour of Nothingness.

*

We will return to *distinction* at length, since it constitutes the principle point of contact between bourgeois ideology and French postromanticism. First, however, we must turn our attention to the poets of the post-1848 period themselves. While the bourgeoisie may well have suffered from the death of God, especially since the event dynamited the rational basis for their domination, Sartre explains that the poets were in a singularly fragile position:

> the poets of 1850 felt to the very marrow of their bones the cleavage produced by the extraordinarily swift advance of irreligion in European history. They are witnesses of this irreparable breach as well as its first victims. As children, they had been raised on the poems of Lamartine, Hugo, and Vigny and conceived their own futures on the model of those glorious careers. (MPN 22)

Hitherto poetry had always had a theological horizon; indeed, its most profound source could only be God himself: 'the poet was only the trumpet; God supplied the breath' (MPN 24). Furthermore, the poet's words, even if he spoke only of his most intimate affects, immediately resonated with a community: 'the Word functioned as an intermediary between poet and reader' (MPN 62). The act of reading was therefore the equivalent of a kind of mass, which gathered a community together. But with God dead, all existing means for understanding the practice of poetry, along with all of the justifications for its existence, were now dead letters. Poetry became an impossible vocation: its new recruits had wagered on the theological fundaments of the Universe remaining in place, yet these had been irreversibly removed.

Jean-Paul Sartre's Mallarmé

But did not many of the Romantics have an at least ambivalent relation to God? What of their pantheism, their paganism, or their agnosticism? Sartre recognises the syncretic nature of much Romanticism. Nevertheless, in his view poets like Lamartine, Hugo and Vigny had failed to pose the question of the ultimate coherence of their world vision: the contradictions within their work had not yet matured to the point of exploding. But this is not the case for the poets of the post-1848 period:

> the austere sons of these heedless and prodigal fathers could not help looking reality in the face. For them, neither atheism nor the poet's Calling was one of those notions you think up, but whose real implications only appear later through experience. They were but hand-me-downs from a previous generation, thoughts already thought by other people and viewed with a certain detachment. It was impossible to cover them over. (MPN 23 – translation modified)

Everything therefore happens as if the shift between generations forced certain logical contradictions into the light. To live with intellectual inconsistencies in a state of practical immediacy was the prerogative of the Romantics. Simply because they had to inherit their predecessor's syncretic ideology, the postromantics, by contrast, had to come to terms with its internal contradictions.

Interestingly, this same intergenerational dialectic is operative in the determination of the specific nature of the postromantics' atheism. If the first generation of bourgeois atheists had negated their fathers' Catholicism, then it would seem *prima facie* that, when it came time to stage their own revolt, the next generation of bourgeois would simply return to religion. Indeed, such a return would have been a welcome ideological move in the wake of 1848 since the bourgeoisie desperately required a source of transcendental legitimacy. And yet, as Sartre explains: 'From 1850 on, faith is a negation of the negation':

> Nothing can save us from inhabiting a world forsaken by God; if someone still wishes to believe in Him, it will be despite His absence (the cynic would say it is *because* of it); and if one obstinately insists on predicting the ultimate triumph of Religion, it is only after acknowledging its devastating defeat. (MPN 22 – translation modified)

In other words, while both the movement of generations and the ideological demands of the time pointed to a return to religion, the undeniable advance of atheism meant that such a return could *only* take the form of a kind of theology of the negative. The poets of the post-1848 period therefore raised God's absence to the status of a paradoxical proof of his existence, turning the gnawing lack they felt into a heartfelt demand for His presence. Then, in a second move, they transformed this demand into the mark of God's presence in Man: our desire for Him is a sign that He is already at work within us. Yet this is small consolation: God's absence is undeniable and inevitably leads to despair; and if despair is the sole affective tribute to His existence, then the postromantics are doomed to a life of misery. Referring to Verlaine's 1866 collection *Poèmes saturniens*, Sartre writes that the postromantics were therefore 'Saturnine poets, born under an unlucky star' (MPN 27). Sartre claims that, in a point of striking similarity with the bourgeoisie's ideology of *distinction*, the postromantics had 'at last found [their] favourite theme: non-being' (MPN 25). They rejected the world *in its entirety* in the name of an absolutely absent ideal, whose sole mark of existence was precisely its inexistence.

This rejection extends, of course, to other human beings as well. Armed with their absent yet exigent Ideal in the form of a vanished God, the postromantics inevitably turned their resentment towards their compatriots, whom they could only contemplate with contempt: 'The wrath of the poets was awesome. The most violent immediately proclaimed their hatred of Man, that impostor whose grievous fault consisted in not being the son of God' (MPN 21). While the Romantics had addressed, with an almost childlike generosity, 'the sovereign people' (MPN 60), in the post-1848 period the possibility of such a universal address had been destroyed – first by the revelation of the profound line of division running through France, and second by the fact that the sciences had dissolved Man's privileged status within the Universe, thereby determining that no living reader could ever reflect back the poets' work in the spiritual light they desired. But if poetry sought to raise itself up above this vulgar humanity, its transcendence could not be taken for granted. The death of God placed the postromantics in the midst of an apparently insurmountable metaphysical dilemma: if the Universe of modern science showed them that 'all men, without exception, [were] merely vain figures of matter' (MPN 37 – translation modified), why would poetry be any different? Is it possible to *create* now that God – that is, the Creator – is dead, and all action is reduced to the rearrangement of existing materials? And if Being is now understood as 'dispersion, inertia, and exteriority', how can the poet's creative syntheses resist being 'reduce[d] to a purely random dispersal' (MPN 34)?

Under the tutelage of Leconte de Lisle – and, more distantly, of Edgar Allan Poe, whose essay 'Philosophy of Composition' was translated by Baudelaire in 1846 – the postromantics took a first step towards addressing these problems by refusing all forms of *inspiration*, which they feared risked giving voice to 'the discordant noises of Nature'

(MPN 25). As Sartre explains, this suspicion was only one consequence of their choice in favour of 'non-being', since the *inspiration* of the Romantics offered a powerful vision of the productivity of Being. In refusing to be a conduit for an impersonal force, the postromantics turned to the controlled artifice of technique: poetry could no longer be an involuntary act; instead, it required the ever-active mediation of the poet's will. Since this change occurred at exactly the same time the poets lost the universal addressee of the Romantics, the postromantics' turn to technique seemed to coincide with a simultaneous shift from unguarded generosity to cynical manipulation. As Sartre explains, the postromantics' impassivity and pursuit of technical perfection thus implied an attitude of contempt:

> As a direct consequence of the disappearance of the Divine Word, Poetry becomes a technique. I cannot help seeing in this preoccupation with producing effects a sign of hostility toward the public. In the days when the poet sang, his enthusiasm had swept his audience along: they shared communion. Deprived of their God, these poets wish to act on their readers by conveying emotions they do not feel; coldly and impassively, they manipulate their readers, contemptuous of the magic spell whose mechanism they understand only too well. (MPN 25)

Yet both aspects of this new orientation in poetry remain half measures: they merely postpone a confrontation with the dilemma of the death of God. On the one hand, the turn to technique fails to resolve the problem of creation: 'They claim that they are merely *sculpting*', Sartre writes, invoking Verlaine's 'Epilogue'. 'But what sort of work of art does this produce? Is putting a human stamp on matter enough to warrant the name creation? Shouldn't matter and form be created simultaneously, in a single flash of inspiration?' (MPN 26 – Sartre's emphasis). On the other hand, even if their audience is now seen as made up of a manipulable material, the asymmetry between author and addressee is so great that no circuit of reciprocity can ever be established. Only God could be an appropriate addressee for the postromantics. As Sartre goes on to explain, one way to resolve this last problem is for poets to write *exclusively* for other poets – that is, for poets who recognise and reflect back to one another the same ethos. However, as Sartre reminds us, all of this remains a case of necessity transformed into virtue: for the postromantics, *there simply was no more public*. In a sarcastic – even scatological – passage, Sartre mocks this new generation of poets, including Mallarmé, whose early work 'Art for All' he paraphrases here:

> Constricted to the point of constipation, the newcomers jealously conceal their poems from indifferent crowds. To ward off prying fingers, they put

golden clasps on their books: the public is requested not to touch. One writes principally for oneself, then for one's fellow poets, and finally for a few collectors of rare objects. (MPN 35)

As Mallarmé writes in 'Art for All', 'man can be a democrat; the artist must double himself and remain an aristocrat' (OC II 362). For Sartre, this reveals the most profound truth of these various transformations in poetry: through all of the postromantics' despair, misanthropy and impassivity, the 'real aim of all this is to restore an aristocracy' (MPN 35). If they could no longer count on God's support, nor on the patronage of a public who had treated their predecessors as spiritual guides, then they would write *against* the Universe from which God had flown and *against* the people who now ignored them. In this way, they maintained their superiority – their election.

Yet the very fact that they wished to 'restore an *aristocracy*' poses a problem for Sartre's Marxist reading. How can the postromantics' ethos be considered consistent with bourgeois ideology if it involves, as it appears to, an attempt at recreating a noble class that is historically *opposed* to the bourgeoisie, as it is to the workers? Sartre might well resist, both political and ethically, their misanthropic quietism; yet it seems difficult to do so on the grounds that it is a variant of bourgeois ideology. In the next section, we will see how Sartre nevertheless demonstrates the postromantics' fundamental complicity with France's ruling class.

*

The first step in Sartre's argument is to recall that the sciences implied not only an *ontological* egalitarianism, unveiling as they did a single level of Being on which all entities were situated – an egalitarianism registered, on Sartre's reading, in Mallarmé's 'Music and Letters', which speaks of 'the obviousness of being in its sameness' (D 188 – translation modified); the sciences also implied an *epistemological* egalitarianism as well: 'By holding that Truth can be conveyed', Sartre explains, the sciences 'destroy the objective basis of all hierarchy (MPN 35). These principles sit uneasily together, since the vision of Man as a mere 'jumble of atoms' (MPN 20) suggests nothing concerning a common intelligence. Yet Sartre convincingly shows that the postromantics held – or rather feared – both principles, since they at once *condemned* Man for having 'souillé', in Leconte de Lisle's words, 'ce miserable monde / D'un sang si corrompu, d'un soufflé si malsain, / Que la mort germe seule en cette boue immonde', and *resisted* the attempts of the masses to gain access to their writings, as Mallarmé openly does in 'Art for All'.[52] Indeed, the existence of a common intelligence was the real risk for the postromantics, just as it was for the ruling bourgeoisie: 'Everyone agrees, bourgeois and poet alike, that the inroads of public education are deplorable' (MPN 35). For there can be no natural hierarchy if all have the same capacity to learn, and therefore to lead. To defend itself against this danger, Sartre explains that the bourgeoisie turned to a solution that already served well as a response to their fear of Nature – *distinction*:

> the workers ... must be reminded on every possible occasion that there are innate differences among men. The bourgeoisie speaks neither of blood nor of breeding but alludes casually to tact, to good taste, to the *esprit de finesse*, and to all such other qualities which cannot be acquired. When a 'superior' class sees its superiority challenged, it defends itself by a resort to the esoteric, all the while keeping open the option of bloodier and more effective measures. (MPN 36)

This is the first major point of intersection between bourgeois ideology and the ethos of postromanticism. Just as the postromantics created esoteric works which functioned to divide humanity, excluding those who failed to perceive the minute aesthetic differentials they mobilised, so too did the bourgeoisie arbitrarily make the possession of certain indefinable qualities a prerequisite for belonging to the *true* humanity. To the degree that they participated in this rear-guard action, Sartre concludes that the postromantic poets made themselves 'the agents of the "Précieuse" counter-revolution' (MPN 37).

Yet the bourgeoisie's and the poets' common recourse to *distinction* seems immediately to divide in two. For as Sartre recalls, a certain strain of Romantic – and now postromantic – anti-capitalism was a defining feature of nineteenth-century artistic life. As he writes in *The Family Idiot*, 'All of the bourgeois intellectuals of the nineteenth century were in agreement on one point: to be bourgeois was to be philistine.'[53] Indeed, while the new generation of poets condemned the vulgarity of the masses, their polemical fire was just as intense when it was directed against the bourgeoisie, whose cold, calculating instrumentalism ran counter to their sense of the intrinsic value of Art.

This double and contradictory meaning of *distinction* poses a challenge to Sartre. How can he claim that the ethos of Parnassianism and Symbolism were continuous with bourgeois ideology if they explicitly opposed its fundamental feature, the pursuit of profit? Does poetry not offer a form of resistance to the infinite extension of a market logic? Sartre's answer is without ambiguity: 'Never do they resemble the bourgeoisie more closely than when they attempt to set themselves apart from it' (MPN 56).

To understand this claim, we can begin by briefly passing over an inessential, though striking, component of Sartre's argument. While diatribes against the bourgeoisie can be found throughout the postromantics' writings, Sartre claims that these poets demonstrably misunderstood both the nature of class and its contemporary modes of existence: 'On close inspection, however, the bourgeoisie they pillory doesn't really exist' (MPN 53). The image of the bourgeoisie attacked by the poets was a fantasy, cobbled together from their contempt for the crude anxiety of shopkeepers, who were only one step above workers, and from their boredom in the face of the Administration's banalities. The postromantics therefore effectively did the work of the bourgeoisie, obscuring the true lines of division in society and allowing the ruling class to pursue its interests without scrutiny. Yet this is not the most essential sign of their objective solidarity. To see this, we need to return one final time to the theological problematic the postromantics struggled with.

With the death of God, poetry lost its sole source of transcendental legitimation. The scope of this loss cannot be underestimated: where once it was continuous with a Universe and a human community grounded in God, poetry now seemed senseless – a reflection of the ultimately void nature of the world in which it currently found itself. As we know, the poets responded to this unprecedented situation through a theology of the negative, which allowed them to transform their profound dissatisfaction into a fragile proof of their spiritual existence (MPN 29). All of the marks of Man's failure, all signs of his deficiency, were proofs that he required God. The same goes for poetry: if it no longer functioned after 1848, then this was only to be expected in a world whose decrepitude was by definition resistant to poetry's purity.

Crucially, however, this blanket condemnation of the Universe and of Man was not the only possible conclusion the postromantics could have drawn from the death of God. Sartre is very clear that other intellectual – and political – options were available at the time:

> it was not absolutely necessary that their loss of faith should have driven them back to eighteenth-century analytic materialism. Neo-Kantianism, Agnosticism, Neo-Hegelianism, Relativism, Pragmatism, Dialectical Materialism: all these philosophies would soon arise or had already arisen from the Death of God. (MPN 47)

The question then becomes: why did the postromantics embrace a scientistic vision of cosmic decline with such fervour? For Sartre, the answer is clear: it was because 'they tied their fate to that of the possessing class' (MPN 47 – translation modified) – a class which, as the philosopher's Marxism dictates, is in decline, or at the very least threatened in its very existence. Yet isn't the ideology of the nineteenth-century French bourgeoisie also infused with optimism? This is indeed what Sartre argues in *Baudelaire* (1947):

> After the seventeenth century which rediscovered the past and the eighteenth century which made an inventory of the present, the nineteenth century believed that it had discovered a fresh dimension of time and the world. For the sociologists, the humanists and the manufacturers who discovered the power of capital, for the proletariat which was becoming conscious of itself, for Marx and for Flora Tristan, for Michelet, for Proudhon and for George Sand, the future existed and gave the present its meaning.[54]

To understand why the postromantics' pessimism is nevertheless still a sign of their deep allegiance to the bourgeoisie, we need to understand a key moment in Sartre's argument: poets like de Lisle, Verlaine, Coppée, Heredia and Mallarmé were members of the *petty bourgeoisie*, not the bourgeoisie. For Sartre, the petty bourgeoisie occupies a unique position in capitalism, which makes it fertile ground for historical pessimism. As he explains, given their stake in Capital, the petty bourgeoisie 'never stop seeking admission into what are called the "higher circles"' (MPN 38): they identify with their economic superiors and imagine their social trajectory to rightfully be one of upward mobility. However, when they are not being 'ruined by big industry and big business' (MPN 40 – translation modified), their precarious position means they are the first members of the capitalist class to suffer from economic crises. Thus, the petty bourgeoisie's class position inevitably leads to the cultivation amongst its members of an attitude of generalised resentment, doubled by a deep misunderstanding of their situation:

> The *petit bourgeois* diabolicizes History, that scourge which periodically ruins him. He diabolicizes Nature and Life itself because they smack of the rabble. He contrives to bask in the light that radiates from the ruling classes and, since he foolishly insists on maintaining an order that victimizes him, has no recourse other than raising himself above the crowd in an attitude of affected and sulking negativism. (MPN 40)

In other words, while the upper layers of the bourgeoisie understandably promulgated an ideology of progress, the petty bourgeoisie betrayed its allegiance to this class by adopting the exact opposite ideology. If it had cast its lot in with the workers it might have been receptive to the promise of a different economic order beyond the current one, whose cyclical crises were the principal cause of its misery. As Sartre confidently claims, with God now dead a 'member of the working class would claim his place in the sun; he would even try to conquer it by force' (MPN 39). But with capitalism as its unsurpassable ideological horizon, the petty bourgeoisie doomed itself to an eternal pessimism.

Thus, when the postromantics interpreted the sciences as announcing the decrepitude of the Universe, without exploring any of the more positive intellectual possibilities opened up by the death of God, they signalled their belonging to the petty bourgeoisie. In a cruel twist, Sartre even suggests that the poets' resentment as typical members of this class came first, and their turn to poetry second: 'the ruin of poetry became emblematic of their own personal failures, endowing these with an unsuspected death' (MPN 41). Furthermore, Sartre implies that the metaphysical dilemmas the poets faced, despite appearing as autonomous metaphysical problems, were also derived from a fundamentally petty bourgeois ideology. Thus, as we know, their condemnation of Being in its entirety meant that, for them, Being was fundamentally 'dispersion, inertia, and exteriority'. And yet they also claimed – or rather desperately wagered – that their very *refusal* of Being through poetry, even if it remained illusory, ensured their transcendence. This left them oscillating endlessly between truth, as they understood it, and the contestation of truth by value – an oscillation perfectly captured in an early letter of Mallarmé's to Henri Cazalis, which Sartre paraphrases in the following extraordinary passage:

> Perhaps not enough stress has been laid on the reciprocal negation whereby the Ideal seeks to negate Matter and Matter seeks to negate the Ideal: I personally see this as one of the most striking characteristics of the epoch . . . The poet feels comfortable in the midst of this hall of mirrors. He repudiates the Dream in the Name of Truth and Being. This is his lofty despair, his secret suffering, at once corrosive and ennobling. He then re-establishes this Dream by bracketing matter in the name of Ideal Being and Ideal Value. (MPN 49)

What the postromantics presented as an insurmountable metaphysical problem, however, was nevertheless built on the assumption that the Universe was meaningless; that it all came down to Nothing. Yet this axiom is a product of a hasty and demonstrably *interested* interpretation of modern science – an interpretation that expressed the petty bourgeoisie's entrenched historical pessimism. And given that the petty bourgeoisie ultimately takes the side of big Capital, the postromantics' tragic metaphysics can be traced back to the fundaments of the bourgeoisie's class interests.

One final point needs to be made before we conclude this section on Sartre's Marxist reading of French postromanticism. We have seen how the poets' pessimism betrayed their allegiance to the ruling class, even if their practice of *distinction* was directed against it. Yet in fact we have not yet explained why Sartre believes their practice of *distinction* itself remained within the ambit of bourgeois ideology. How can Sartre claim that the postromantics should be considered bourgeois if he also argues that they attempted to constitute 'a phantom Nobility' (MPN 37) *against* the bourgeoisie?

The first point to recall is the poets' adoption of what Sartre calls the 'faith which courts failure' (MPN 30): their theology of the negative transformed their suffering and dissatisfaction into signs of election, allowing them to preserve a margin of transcendence over the corruption of the world, even if this margin collapsed when they took the full measure of their condemnation of Being. As individuals, they refused to identify with any of their worldly predicates, choosing instead to associate their true existence with the pure power to take a reflexive distance from their circumstances. Sartre mocks their empty gesture of bad faith, and criticises the role it plays in ensuring – rather than undermining – their social conformity: 'This dual identity is beneficial to the established moral order. While "the Prince of the Clouds" works hard at cultivating "his own pure vision", his *alter ego*, the compartmentalized and conformist civil servant, attends to his duties' (MPN 58). Yet it is not because the postromantics' *distinction* made them conform socially that they were objectively complicit with bourgeois ideology. It is not even because their individualism reflected the bourgeoisie's favoured philosophy of social atomism, as Sartre also seems to suggest (MPN 50–3). Rather, it is for a far more profound reason. As we know, the poets instituted their 'phantom aristocracy' (MPN 55) by negating the world in its entirety, including their empirical selves, and by finding in their perpetual dissatisfaction a mark of election and transcendence. Yet the true nobility – the nobility of before the French Revolution and the de-Christianisation of France – had grounded their legitimacy in Being, not in any category of Nothingness. Nature was on their side. And yet, as we mentioned above, the post-1848 bourgeoisie had to turn to the various subcategories of Nothingness to achieve the same goal. *Thus, when the postromantics set out to institute a new nobility through a practice of negativity, they betrayed their participation in bourgeois ideology.* A nobility based on the practice of *distinction* is no nobility at all, only a subset of the bourgeoisie. From beginning to end, postromantic French poetry was thus a bourgeois phenomenon.

*

Despairing, manipulative, misanthropic and misguided: the postromantic ethos was a reactionary response to the death of God; an elitist retreat in the face of France's newly discovered lines of division; and a variation on the bourgeoisie's practice of *distinction*, which disguised itself as an aristocratic anti-capitalism. Everything opposes it to Sartre's committed literature: while the latter aims to address 'the sum total of men living in a given society',⁵⁵ the postromantics write for a narrow elite made up only of their peers. And while Sartre's committed literature seeks to 'disclose the world and to offer it as a task to the generosity of the reader',⁵⁶ the theology of the negative of Parnassianism and Symbolism condemns all human action in advance, sapping it of its situated meaning. Worse still, it obscures the real lines of division in the world.

Yet we also know that 'The Atheist Heritage' is ultimately only a prologue to Sartre's true project in his book on Mallarmé. His aim is not principally to show how postromanticism was an expression of the economic and political infrastructure of mid-nineteenth-century France, even if he achieves this; it is to explore how one singular poet – Mallarmé – was able to transcend it.

This is the project announced in the extraordinary final paragraph of 'The Atheist Heritage'. As Sartre begins by explaining, the postromantic ethos was shot through with fantasies and contradictions, the most significant of which was the fact that, while it explicitly rejected all empirical addressees, it made a secret appeal to God: 'They don't say it; they don't even think it; and yet their dissatisfaction with everything, their conviction that human failure somehow magically implies a victory of man – all this points to an infinite and unnamed presence' (MPN 62). This fatal pragmatic contradiction should be enough to undermine the intellectual integrity of the postromantics' writings. Yet as Sartre claims, '[n]ot one of them is capable of holding together, in a single overarching tension, the various and contradictory aspects of their situation' (MPN 63). Like their predecessors the Romantics, they lacked the philosophical endurance required to take the axioms of their ethos to their ultimate conclusion. Moreover, as we know, postromanticism involved an exhausting oscillation between a crushing despair and an intoxicating sense of divine election. For Sartre, this meant that many postromantics simply 'give up midway' (MPN 63). Others took an alternative route, seeking out the stability of institutional recognition: 'Flaubert received a decoration, Baudelaire was a candidate for the Académie Française, Leconte de Lisle and Heredia were academicians' (MPN 59). If the postromantics adopted the contradictory metaphysical assumptions of their ethos, it was not because they understood – let alone cared deeply about – their implications. Instead, 'each poet borrows them. No one thinks them through; they are accepted because *Other People* are supposed to think them' (MPN 64 – Sartre's emphasis). Such a logic of imitation is what Sartre will later come to call *seriality*: that is, the poets do not adopt the axioms of postromanticism out of personal conviction; they do so only because an indefinite series of Others are supposed to have adopted them, and the imagined weight of their number makes it impossible for them *not* to adopt these axioms, for fear of artistic irrelevance.

But the dissemination of the postromantic ethos via seriality comes at a price: its axioms remain '[a]nonymous . . ., taken up, rejected, then taken up again haphazardly by a bevy of distinguished and pedestrian minds' (MPN 64). If, then, they are to be thought together, with their combined consequences taken to their logical end and thus, hopefully, transcended, someone will have to receive them *not* according to the logic of seriality but in a fundamentally different mode: 'Yes, if someone could appear for whom the idea of poetry could become a mortal and self-inflicted illness, if an all-embracing lucid consciousness could, in one single act, hold all its nuances together, it would then elude Marxist interpretations and escape social conditioning' (MPN 64). In the following section, we will follow Sartre as he tracks Mallarmé's individual trajectory in order to determine how, for the poet, the postromantic ethos could not merely be an impersonal ensemble of ideas and affects, but a cultural creation that it was existentially essential for him to work through. Then, in a final section, we will consider whether Mallarmé's transcendence of his peers' poetry corresponded to a transcendence of their specifically *political* limitations, or whether it remained continuous and complicit with 'a social order based on exploitation'.

*

In the second section of his book, titled 'The Chosen One' by the editors of the 1979 edition of *Obliques* devoted to Sartre – a choice inspired by a phrase from Mallarmé's late prose piece 'The Court',[57] whose significance we will see shortly – Sartre sets out to explore Mallarmé's childhood and early adult life. His aim is firstly to find clues as to how the poet was able to fully assume the antinomy at the heart of post-1848 French poetry, and secondly to show how Mallarmé's individual trajectory determined the nature of the poetry that would result from his 'sublation' (FI 349, n. 51 – translation modified) of his contemporaries' pessimistic Parnassianism. In order to distinguish Mallarmé from the other poets of his generation, Sartre begins by presenting the then-provincial schoolteacher through the eyes of his Paris-based peers. Quoting from Catulle Mendès, Leconte de Lisle, François Coppée and Théodore de Banville, Sartre picks up on a common thread in their testimonials: despite belonging to 'the species of poet-bureaucrat' (MPN 68), and despite his fervent adherence to a Parnassian aesthetic, these poets find Mallarmé's poetry unintelligible, his personal suffering pointless in its extremism, and his intransigent disdain for the wider public positively harmful for their aesthetic cause (MPN 68–9). Mallarmé seems to know the codes of Parnassianism, and his personal circumstances match those of his peers: like them he 'suffers conveniently from the prevalent Mid-Century Malaise' (MPN 69). Yet something in his poetry and person seems to misfire: an almost-imperceptible margin of difference separates him from the Parnassians. As Sartre describes it, this difference consists in the lack of reflexive distance Mallarmé places between himself and the fundaments of the Parnassian aesthetic. Far from pleading in his favour, in the eyes of leading poets like de Lisle, Mallarmé's 'unyielding intransigence' (MPN 68) with regards to the rules of the 'poetic complex' that Sartre had studied in 'The Atheist Heritage' makes him a 'suspicious character' (MPN 69). By being absolutely faithful to the Parnassian ethos, Mallarmé unwittingly exposes its implicit premises:

> these gentlemen of the *Parnasse Contemporain* devote themselves to scorning everything, but not without treating themselves with a certain indulgence, if only to help them survive. The road is long and has just begun, so they indulge themselves. But this young madman doesn't dream of sparing himself. He will drop from exhaustion a few yards from the starting line. (MPN 69)

While his peers, as far as Sartre is concerned, are hypocrites – in many cases their despair is nothing more than an alibi for their misanthropy, or a cover for their 'conformism' (MPN 59) – Mallarmé seems gripped at the very core of his being by the metaphysical dilemmas Parnassian poetry throws up. While his peers should 'have recognized in him a perfect image of themselves' (MPN 68), Mallarmé fails to follow the unwritten laws of their ethos, which stipulate that their nihilist aesthetic is a mere rhetorical ploy, not a guide for living. Yet this error – or *excess* – of interpellation is also an opportunity: it means Mallarmé can give 'the poetic Idea . . . his personal stamp' (MPN 64) – he can make it his own 'mortal and self-inflicted illness' (MPN 64) – and thus open up the possibility that its contradictions will finally be confronted and overcome.

After highlighting this paradoxical disconnect between Mallarmé and the poetic corporation he emulates, Sartre reinforces the sense of the poet's existential despair by referring to four worldly objects – his profession, family life, friends and nature – that demonstrably fail to win his affections. While his profession leaves him, in Mallarmé's own words, 'wiped out, a wreck' (MPN 69), Sartre wonders whether his wife might have offered some consolation: 'Does he at least love her?' (MPN 69). In responding to this question, Sartre unexpectedly launches a powerful feminist critique of Mallarmé's marriage. In fact, Sartre's long section on Mallarmé's relationship to Maria Gerhard shows just how deeply the poet was marked by the misogyny implicit in Parnassianism. As Sartre explains, if Mallarmé was first attracted to Maria Gerhard, it was because he saw her through the eyes of both 'Baudelairean poetry' and the exigencies of the 'contemporary bourgeoisie' (MPN 69). With respect to the first frame of reference, Maria Gerhard seemed to match the quiet melancholy of a character like Madame de Cosmelly from Baudelaire's *La Fanfarlo*, while her withdrawal from the world conveniently matched the desire of the bourgeois men of the time for 'domestic tranquillity' (MPN 72). Aesthetics thus bolstered a base misogyny, ornamenting a systematic attempt to silence women with false metaphysical profundities. Commenting on Mallarmé's tendency towards practical inertia, Sartre writes that 'Maria Gerhard favours the attempt of these quietists who, to remove themselves from life and from Being, sought to create a permanent confusion of past and present' (MPN 71). The poet's early prose piece 'Winter Shudder' seems to confirm this. There, Mallarmé speaks of his wife's alleged distaste for 'new things', which she finds 'frightening, with their noisy healthiness'. They impose their potentially fatiguing instrumentality upon her – 'and that's very difficult for those who shun activity' (D 16). Conveniently, her unobtrusive presence allows Mallarmé to '[a]void reciprocity' (MPN 73) and to possess a home-bound incarnation of his fundamental metaphysical conviction: *nihil novi sub sole*.

To prove that Mallarmé's marriage exposed his participation in the Parnassian ethos, Sartre remarks upon his use of the term 'sister' to refer to his wife. Quoting from Verlaine's 'Lassitude' and 'Mon rêve familier', as well as from Corbière's 'Steam Boat', Sartre argues that this appellation betrays Mallarmé and his peers' attempts to infantilise and de-sexualise women, in the sense of stripping them of their autonomous desire. However, Sartre admits that in later years Mallarmé will refer to Maria simply as his '*wife*' (MPN 74 – Sartre's emphasis). Yet this is only a minor metamorphosis, since it marks nothing more than the poet's public adoption of the mores of his time. His break with his friend Eugène Lefébure over the latter's 'illicit companion' demonstrates that, as far as his participation in polite society was concerned, he wanted his wife to be respected – but only because she was *his* wife, and *he* had to be respected: 'in private', Sartre clarifies, Mallarmé 'makes her progressively younger' (MPN 74).

Having shown that Mallarmé could not alleviate his despair through his marriage, Sartre admits that '[c]ertainly he loved his daughter' (MPN 75), Geneviève. Again, however, this will only be because she can accompany him, like a trophy, in public life, such as when she serves punch to the visitors of his famous *Mardis*. As a child, by contrast, Geneviève inspired Mallarmé's resentment: as he writes to Aubanel on 27 November 1864, 'This crying, naughty baby drove Hérodiade away.'[58] Could Mallarmé's friends have drawn him out of his despondency? No, replies Sartre: his long and rich letters to them may well have sustained him during his exile in Avignon and Tournon, but they do not attest to any profound affection (MPN 76). Without friends or deep family attachments, Mallarmé seems an utterly solitary figure, with no affective investment in anything of this world.

'Will nature', Sartre asks, 'help him get outside himself?' (MPN 76). Having extensively documented the Parnassian's anti-naturalism, Sartre must address the unavoidable fact that, in apparent contrast to his peers, one of Mallarmé's key images is the sunset. Moreover, as the poet writes in a passage from 'Bucolic' – a passage cited by Sartre – 'nature ... imparted to my youth a fervor I call passion' (D 268). But as Sartre argues, Mallarmé's vision of nature is not that of a realm of contingency understood as a productive power outstripping our reason. For this loyal disciple of Baudelaire, nature cannot represent 'sweet and absurd abundance' (MPN 76 – translation modified). Instead, finding a clue in the very same passage from 'Bucolic' in which Mallarmé expresses his 'passion' for nature, Sartre points out that for the poet the sunset was 'a tangible Idea', one that actually kept him at a safe distance from nature's contingency. Indeed, for Mallarmé it was primarily a reliable spectacle:

> he, along with most of the poets of his age, sought generality and repetition. From his window he could observe the yearly and daily renewal of celestial ceremonies. But since it was he who ordained them, he ran no risk of being startled by their course or of learning from them anything whatsoever. (MPN 76)

While it undoubtedly connotes cyclicity, Mallarmé's nature, Sartre clarifies, is fundamentally an image of decadence, with the figures of sunset and autumn both standing for the slow descent of humanity towards nothingness. Furthermore, Sartre refuses Mallarmé's claim to be able to 'account for his tastes', as the poet does in the following passage from 'Autumn Lament' (1864):

> Ever since Maria left me to go to another star ... I've been attracted to anything that could be summed up in the word 'fall'. Thus, my favourite time of year is those last, lazy days of summer which immediately precede autumn ... Similarly, the literature my spirit turns to for pleasure is the dying poetry of Rome's last moments ... (D 13)

According to Sartre, who quotes here from Baudelaire's 'Brumes et pluies', as well as from Verlaine's 'Un soir d'octobre' and 'Crépuscule du soir mystique', Mallarmé's taste for the word 'fall' cannot be derived from the singular tragedy of his sister's death: 'this dead young woman is also merely a symbol' (MPN 78), Sartre explains, since her passing had already been filtered through the lens of the poet's class-based ideology: 'What the poet reads in Nature is the decadence of poetry, the imminent death of Man, the final empyrosis: in a word, the fears of the bourgeois intelligentsia' (MPN 78). The key that unlocks all other symbolic codes, for Sartre, is thus the declining fortunes of the bourgeoisie: as he had demonstrated in 'The Atheist Heritage', if Mallarmé and his peers returned obsessively to figures of decadence, then it was because, as good members of the petty bourgeoisie, 'they tied their fate to that of the possessing class' (MPN 47 – translation modified). Mallarmé's class allegiances, as with the way he sublimates them poetically, are no different to those of his peers.

And yet, a question remains: if he seems to fit so snugly into the mould of French postromantic poetry, 'Why is it ... that his fellow poets don't quite accept him as one of their own? (MPN 78). In response to this question, Sartre has shown how detached Mallarmé was from four typical sources of affective investment, thus ensuring that 'he *lived* according to [the] principles' (MPN 78 – translation modified, Sartre's emphasis) of French postromanticism. But in the next stage of his argument, Sartre will have to demonstrate why, as a function of his individual trajectory, Mallarmé was not only personally receptive to his generation's 'soft, spiteful thought' (MPN 67), but could also 'hold all its nuances together' (MPN 64) and transcend it.

At this point, Sartre confronts the then-recently published work of Charles Mauron, *Introduction à la psychanalyse de Mallarmé* (1950).[59] In this book, the inventor of *la psychocritique* claims that the network of images and ideas that makes up Mallarmé's *œuvre* ultimately leads back to the death of his mother and sister. While Sartre will accept that Mallarmé's affections for his sister derived from their shared connection (or lack of connection) to their dead mother, he is more uncertain than Mauron as to the exact nature of the impact his mother's death had on his poetry. Firstly, Mallarmé's poetry makes only a few allusions to childhood as 'a lost Paradise' (MPN 82): unsurprisingly, Sartre cites the reference to 'the adorable / infancy of rose-woods under natural / blue' (PV 39) from 'Sick of unquiet rest', as well as the 1863 poem 'Apparition' and select lines from *Hérodiade* (MPN 82). Furthermore, just like his references to 'the incestuous eroticism, the taste for failure and for Non-Being', Mallarmé's infrequent invocations of an Edenic childhood participate in the '*objective spirit*' (MPN 83 – Sartre's emphasis) of his time. As such, Sartre argues that they 'express the historical and social conjuncture as much, if not more than, the history of a particular individual' (MPN 82 – translation modified). Sartre concedes to Mauron that, with respect to typical postromantic tropes, Mallarmé 'profoundly impressed his own indelible stamp on them' (PN 83). By contrast, a contemporary like Verlaine, whose *Poèmes saturniens* Sartre incessantly cites throughout *The Poet of Nothingness*,[60] swiftly abandoned these motifs; indeed, as Sartre reminds us, 'Verlaine ... later would radically change his conception of poetry' (MPN 61). This speaks in favour of Mauron's focus on Mallarmé's 'individual sensibility' (MPN 83 – translation modified). Yet the philosopher is still not convinced: taking as an example the motif of the ocean from *Un coup de dés*, Sartre wonders whether Mauron is correct to read it as the expression of an Oedipal drama. As Sartre rightly points out, 'the theme of the Ocean does not undergo any noteworthy development prior to 1873'. Thus, when it appears in early pieces such as 'Sigh', Sartre is correct to remark that 'the function of water seems to be exclusively that of a mirror' (MPN 85): the 'jet of white water [that] sigh[s] towards the Blue!' (PV 53) from this poem reflects the poet's aporetic desire, as Georges Poulet argues in an essay contemporaneous with Sartre's and which Sartre directly references.[61] This is profoundly different to 'the Abyss / blanched / spread / furious' (CP 128) from *Un coup de dés*, which is not a mirror for the young poet's narcissism but rather a figuration of 'the infinite disorder of matter and the reign of Chance' (MPN 86). Furthermore, given that Mallarmé uses the ocean to represent matter *qua* 'an inhuman power of exteriority' (MPN 86 – translation modified) that dissolves all of the meaningful unities produced by human action – as the poet puts it, the ocean in *Un coup de dés* takes the original and deliberately minimal form of 'some splashing below', whose sole effect is to 'disperse the empty act' (CP 142) – then Mallarmé, Sartre argues, is ultimately giving expression to 'the misery of man without God, the *collective* theme of the epoch' (MPN 86 – Sartre's emphasis). On the one hand, then, Mallarmé's chosen symbols are 'self-consciously refashioned' (MPN 86) by him across the course of his life; and on the other hand they 'very accurately reflect the terror of the propertied class, which is becoming aware of its inevitable decline' (MPN 84). Not only are the dramas he stages consciously manipulated, they express a social and not a personal reality, one that is intimately linked to his class allegiances.

*

Sartre's first strike against Mauron's psychoanalytic approach is thus made in the name of a Marxist reading of the poet's work. Yet as we mentioned above, Sartre's main question is: how was Mallarmé able to confront and transcend the contradictions of the 'poetic complex'? What elements of his individual life made him receptive to – and gave him the resources to resolve – a common poetic and metaphysical problematic? Like Mauron, but also against him, Sartre will now turn to the challenges Mallarmé faced in his childhood and deduce from them the fundamental characteristics of his *'being-in-the-world'* (MPN 88). As he will then show, this *a priori* structure of his affectivity will find unmistakeable expression in his poetry.

The first step in Sartre's argument is to distinguish psychoanalysis from phenomenology – an essential move, since his claim that the death of Mallarmé's mother 'was at the origin of a deep trauma in the life of the young boy' (MPN 82) seems identical to the centrepiece of Mauron's account. According to Sartre, the kind of psychoanalysis pursued in *Introduction à la psychanalyse de Mallarmé* falls into the positivist trap of failing to interrogate its objects of study transcendentally. Thus, while the psychoanalyst may map with perfect accuracy the relations between a child and their parents, they end up positing what are ultimately unintelligible – in the sense of purely fortuitous – causal relations between the different components of a child's existence. In other words, the psychoanalyst 'overlook[s] certain essential structures' (MPN 88). Invoking Heidegger, Sartre explains that these structures include:

> *the way he fits into the very heart* of human reality, *the extent to which he is affected by the world*, his *absolute distance* from concrete reality, etc. These structures, which give everyday experience its meaning, its sense of direction and its range are themselves determinations of a synthetic relation of the individual with being, which is called *being-in-the-world*. (MPN 88 – Sartre's emphasis)

If Sartre interrogates the death of Mallarmé's mother, then it is to find clues as to the nature of his fundamental orientation to the world; his *'attitude towards being'* (MPN 90). As a young child, Sartre explains, Mallarmé's lived relation to Being was essentially mediated by his mother. More precisely, every empirical object he encountered, every engagement with others and with himself, was bathed in the light of his mother's omnipotent gaze, as if all things were all modes of a single, benevolent substance. *Pace* Mauron's positivist strain of psychoanalysis, '[t]heir original connection is not one based on contiguity, or even on knowledge'; rather, it is 'a mute affinity which arises from the fact that, as fruits of the same love, they ... appear to be illuminated by the same clear light' (MPN 92). As evidence of this, Sartre cites, both explicitly and implicitly, numerous pieces of Mallarmé's poetry and prose. Despite the heterogeneity of their themes, Sartre seeks to capture their common and striking evocation of an absent presence, which seems to dissolve itself in the face of the ontic entities making up the poet's world – but also, mysteriously, to ground them. For instance, when Sartre writes that '[t]his tender giant emerges and vanishes into Nature through a thousand roots and branches' (MPN 91), he is paraphrasing and displacing the following verses from 'The Afternoon of a Faun', which recounts the Faun's initial discovery that the two nymphs of the previous evening's hypothetical encounter have vanished:

> My doubt, a mass of old night, ends
> in many a subtle branch which, by remaining the real woods,
> proves, alas! that alone I offered myself
> the idea error of roses as triumph. (PV 91)[62]

Similarly, Sartre invokes 'Funeral Toast' (MPN 98), where the poet expresses his desire that there remain of the dead 'Master', Théophile Gautier, not some supernatural 'shadow', but only 'a solemn agitation in the air / of words':

> ... drunken purple and great shining calyx
> that, rain and diamond, the transparent glance
> fallen upon these never-fading flowers
> isolates in an hour and in the daylight ray! (PV 107)[63]

Sartre also pinpoints the evocation of the gaze of an absent female presence in the prose poem 'The White Waterlily'. There, having 'been beached on a tuft of reads, the mysterious end' of his fluvial adventure to seek out a mysterious 'Madame', the poet imagines that 'the silvering mists that coats the willows became the transparency of her gaze, which knew every leaf' (D 33, 34). In each of these instances, the natural world is a world that is *looked at* by a figure whose absence correlates with the presence of the world's affective essence.

Commentators like Charles D. Minahen have mocked Sartre's use of citations to deduce the poet's originary relationship to Being. As Minahen writes, the above-quoted verses from 'The Afternoon of a Faun' demonstrably 'express a mature male's lusty desire to seduce nymphs', thus making the example 'altogether unsuitable and inappropriate'[64] for understanding a child's relation to his mother. Minahen would no doubt say the same for the passage from 'The White Waterlily', since its context is also that of a failed erotic encounter between adults. But for Sartre, this is beside the point: while there have been – and will continue to be – innumerable poems devoted to lust, what marks Mallarmé's out is the singular and recurring technique by which the objects of his poetic world frequently evoke some evanescent presence. That this is a transposable technique is proved by its use in 'Funeral Toast', which it is hard to consider a romantic declamation. Furthermore, Sartre is not seeking to show how 'a child's ephemeral vision of his lost mother',[65] as Minahen puts it, is transposed thematically, or even unconsciously, into a poem or prose piece. Rather, he is attempting to locate the subjective source of those moments of Mallarmé's writings – their evocation of vanishing objects, their infusion of the world with a sense of a palpable absence – that mark these writings out in their singularity. For Sartre, to explain the poet's originality is not only to describe his innovations with respect to an established canon of writings; it is to follow the explanatory thread back as far as it can go, locating the possible sources of these innovations in the dispositions determined by a subject's *'being-in-the-world'*.

This becomes even clearer when Sartre considers what happens when the poet's mother dies. If her absent presence within the totality of the world had given this world its ontological – and not epistemological – substructure, simultaneously making it a space of safety for the child who could consequently go on to appropriate it, her death affects every empirical encounter Mallarmé will henceforth have. The world is now struck by an irredeemable *lack*: 'The Gaze is extinguished. The great white body slips lifelessly away. A void opens up in the midst of plenitude' (MPN 93). The worldly objects surrounding the child are no longer modes of a munificent mother-substance; rather, '[t]hey acquire truth *in their own right*' (MPN 93 – Sartre's emphasis). Furthermore, their self-sufficient indifference to the young Mallarmé is accompanied by the sense that each constitutes an impenetrable barrier to the dead mother, identically denying her return to presence: 'The emergence of a specific object is the end result of a disappointment, the ashes and cinders which remain after the flames of a dream have died out' (MPN 95). In an almost parodic paraphrase of 'Crisis of Verse', Sartre writes that Mallarmé's mother is 'the absent of every house' (MPN 97 – translation modified). Again, Sartre locates signs of this transformed affective relation to the world in Mallarmé's writings. The famous phrase from 'Music and Letters', 'We know, held captive by an absolute formula that, doubtless, only what is, is' (D 187), for instance, transcribes the uniform nullity of Being *qua* the space from which the mother is lacking. The same goes for the following passage: 'Whatever agony, also the Chimera suffers, pouring out its golden wounds, the obviousness of being's sameness, no untwisted curve has falsified or transgressed the omnipresent Line' (D 188 – translation modified). As the term 'the Chimera' suggests, however, the child is still a subject of desire; he is still drawn to 'a superior attraction', a 'Chimera'. Yet in so far as his desire is oriented towards his dead mother, the object of his desire is 'a void' (D 187). An evanescent movement, found throughout Mallarmé's major works, has its origin here: as Mallarmé writes in 'Music and Letters', when faced with the impossibility of creating anything *new* – that is, with creating anything that is not struck by the basic inadequacy of Being – the poet can only do something that is '[e]qual to' – and not *identical to* – 'creating': that is, they can poetically produce 'the notion of an object, escaping, which is lacking' (D 187 – translation modified). The dead mother is the primordial object whose 'vibratory disappearance' (D 210 – translation modified) will repeatedly occur throughout the poet's *œuvre*. In an extraordinary passage, Sartre paraphrases some of the fleeting apparitions Mallarmé stages in poems like the 'Sonnet en -yx', 'Does all Pride smoke of an evening', 'Arisen from the aspirant rump', and the swan sonnet:

> Reality remains a pale presence on whose surface there hovers an absence. Sometimes it seems as if a form might emerge from this dark shape, that hidden in the shadows, a wing will start flapping, that the downy whiteness of feathers will begin to flutter. (MPN 94)

We are beginning to glimpse the manner in which Sartre will coordinate Mallarmé's individual trajectory with the intellectual climate of France's post-1848 'infantile disorder of atheism' (MPN 30): just as God is lacking from the world, so is Mallarmé's mother lacking; and just as the Parnassians transformed this ontological lack into a normative orientation to the world, the young Mallarmé 'can't help levelling an accusation against Being': from the age of six onwards, '[h]e affirms the infinite superiority of what ought to be over what merely is' (MPN 96).

The next stage of Sartre's argument consists in showing why this primordial wound was never overcome by the young Mallarmé. For as he admits, '[t]here are numerous instances of orphans who were able to impose this "labor of mourning" upon themselves' (MPN 97). In the poet's case, identification with the mother was impossible, and not only because she was dead: as Sartre explains, 'he respect[ed] her too much' (MPN 111). Moreover, she represented not a subjective position he could one day come to occupy, but the very ontological foundation of his desolate world. Yet Mallarmé was similarly barred from identifying with his father. Taking his cue from Mallarmé's 'Autobiography', where the poet writes that his 'paternal and maternal families present, ever since the Revolution, an uninterrupted series of functionaries in the Administration and the Registry' (D 2), Sartre claims that the young poet could not have missed the fact that his '[f]amily life [was] a hall of mirrors' (MPN 98). Repeatedly taking up a profession whose essential social function preserved it from the political volatility of modern France, successive patriarchs of Mallarmé's family had all been functionaries; the ethos within the family, Sartre claims, was that 'man and job are identical' (MPN 99) such that no space of aspiration or resentment could ever legitimately take root. Furthermore, the Administration required of its workers no individual initiative, only a steady hand and good connections. Everything, then, points towards a fundamental familial inertia: there was no indeterminacy for Mallarmé, no open space of innovative action on his horizon; he could only be 'the seventh reincarnation of the same family administrator' (MPN 98). This fundamentally transformed his conception of temporality – another of his subjective dispositions that will make him particularly receptive to Parnassianism:

> Faced with a life relived so often and so listlessly *by others* with whatever family memories he can see buried in the depths of his future, the child perceives things from the vantage point of death. From this perspective everything is forever complete; tomorrow is merely a mirage; you touch it, and it was *yesterday*. (MPN 98 – Sartre's emphasis)

This sense of time as infinite repetition resonates with Mallarmé's already-established orientation to the world: nothing new can ever come about, every action ends with the same sense of nullity: the poet's desire *never* attains the mother, whose absence expresses 'the hollow futility of everything' (MPN 100). Citing *Igitur* as if it were an autobiographical text, Sartre remarks that from an early age Mallarmé consequently suffered from 'a crushing sensation of finitude' (MPN 101 – translation modified).

But it was not only the *ennui* provoked by his father and grandfather's professional inertia that prevented him from identifying with them. Rather, in quickly remarrying and producing four children with his new wife, Anne Mathieu, his father had acted in criminal contradiction with his son's basic subjective orientation: that is, if Mallarmé remained faithful to an inexistent phantom – as Sartre writes, 'he [was] at once [the] terrestrial witness and ... memorial' (MPN 111) to his dead mother – his father had chosen to add to the absurd abundance of Being. In short, no new constellation came into Mallarmé's sky that could help him reorient himself in a more positive direction. He had no resources with which launch himself into a future in which he would no longer be marked by mourning.

*

Sartre's exploration of Mallarmé's formative years ends with the philosopher discerning an abstract dilemma the poet will eventually have to face. On the one hand, Mallarmé's fidelity to his mother means that 'he throws himself toward something ineffable, toward pure singularity' – toward his mother in her irreplaceable role as the lost foundation of his world. On the other hand, her absence means that she now stands for nothing more than 'the impossibility of her existing anywhere in time and space' – the negation of singularity in its necessarily empirical specificity. Unflinching fidelity is thus transformed into a peculiar kind of betrayal: Mallarmé is left with only 'the pure concept of the negative' (MPN 101 – translation modified). As Sartre shows, Mallarmé is faced with an isomorphic problem in his attempts to respond practically to his situation. While the testimony of his grandmother, which Sartre cites, points to Mallarmé being a recalcitrant and self-absorbed child, as does the fact that none of his childhood friends remained alongside him as an adult, Sartre clarifies that the young Mallarmé was not, in fact, rebellious. As far as staging a revolt against his situation was concerned, the child had 'deprived himself of the means to do so', since 'nothing escape[d] his damning verdict' (MPN 107) against the world, including the value of any eventual resistance. Referring to the 1862 version of 'The Jinx', Sartre pinpoints an affective impotence in Mallarmé, just as he had done with respect to the other poets of his generation. He takes the verb *convoiter* from the verse 'Ils convoitent la haine et n'ont que la rancune'[66] to mean *to yearn for*, showing that he thinks Mallarmé cannot even summon a sense of revulsion vigorous enough to lead him to action: 'Lacking hatred, he is overcome by a coldheartedness and a sense of sterility which increase with each passing day' (MPN 102 – translation modified).

How will Mallarmé emerge from this stultifying situation? Sartre's answer is simple: through poetry. As he explains, quoting Hegel via Blanchot, if Mallarmé

> looks for salvation in words rather than in sounds or in colours, it is because he detects a secret ambiguity in them. What is involved in the act of naming? Destruction of creation? 'The first act by which Adam made himself master of the animals was by imposing a name on them, which is to say, by annihilating them in their existence (*qua* existents).' Ideally, language should serve both purposes. In this way one could, at a single stroke, use words both to annihilate the world and to create it by words. (MPN 113)

The creation of a poem *qua* something that negates Being *in its entirety*, including the poet in his facticity, offers Mallarmé a concrete means for remaining faithful to his mother and rendering effective his otherwise diffuse sense of dissatisfaction. Separating himself from his corrupt lineage, Mallarmé will seek to *'create himself anew'* (MPN 113 – Sartre's emphasis) through his poetry. On Sartre's reading, this is the sense of the well-known opening passage from Mallarmé's homage to Villiers de l'Isle-Adam: 'This crazy game of writing, it only exists by virtue of a *doubt* – the drop of ink related to the sublime night – some duty to recreate everything . . . to prove that we are truly here where we ought to be.'[67] It is also the sense of the final tercet from the sonnet 'Lace cancels itself out':

> such that towards some window,
> by means of no womb but its own,
> filial, one might have been born. (PV 187)[68]

Yet Mallarmé's project begins badly. Far from cutting the thread of his past, early poems like 'Apparition', 'The Flowers', 'The Jinx' and 'The Afternoon of a Faun' owe a lot – and unexpectedly so – to his predecessors, in particular to Hugo, Gautier, Baudelaire and Banville. His desire for an absolute beginning returns him to the past. Mallarmé is thus again struck by a form of impotence. As Sartre argues, he finds a provisional passage through this deadlock by composing poems *about* his sterility: these include 'The Azure', 'The Jinx', 'The Clown Punished' and 'Bell Ringer' (MPN 117). Yet this is not a sustainable solution, since 'he cannot spend his whole life repeating, in every imaginable tone of voice, that he has nothing to say' (MPN 117). The stakes are therefore very high when he sets out to compose *Hérodiade*, which, as Sartre remarks, is 'a drama . . . or a tragedy' (MPN 117 – translation modified) and thus possesses a narrative thrust entirely lacking in the other poems' circular dialectics. Nevertheless, its theme is still sterility. Sartre claims that, leaving aside *Hérodiade* during the summer of 1866, Mallarmé composes 'The Afternoon of a Faun' with a surprising facility. As the philosopher explains, the reason for this is that 'the unfinished *Hérodiade* . . . provid[ed] him with a pretext', thus allowing him to 'lowe[r] his standards a notch' (MPN 118). Yet this only postpones a final confrontation with his creative sterility. Sartre believes that it is when Mallarmé returns to *Hérodiade* that his spiritual adventure reaches a point of total crisis. As the poet admits in a letter to Cazalis from July 1866, 'I put my entire self into it without knowing, and this is the cause of my unhappiness.'[69] For Sartre, the sense of this admission is that, in attempting to recreate himself through his poetry, Mallarmé had written a poem whose refusal of any empirical form of inspiration and whose striving for complete artistic purity had rendered it unexpectedly *empty*. In a manner consistent with the formal dilemma sketched out above, Sartre explains that Mallarmé 'put the Absolute in his poem and the Absolute is *nothing*' (MPN 120). Mallarmé's uniform refusal of Being in the name of his vanished mother had prevented his 'Absolute' from having any concrete content – any effective existence. Certainly, Mallarmé wrote so 'that he may rise from his ashes and give birth to himself' (MPN 120). But the nothingness coiled around *Hérodiade*'s heart – around Mallarmé's heart – revealed that his wish for resurrection was nothing more than 'a disguised death wish' (MPN 120 – translation modified). Creation had become synonymous with absolute annihilation. Sartre claims that Mallarmé's deadlock is best expressed in the following passage from a letter to Lefébure:

> Yes, *I know it*, we are only vain forms of matter, but quite sublime to have invented God and our soul. So sublime, my friend, that I want to enjoy this spectacle of matter which knows that it exists and yet flings itself wildly into the Dream which it knows does not exist, celebrating the Soul and all the similar divine impressions which have been building up in us since the earliest times, and proclaiming these glorious lies before the Nothingness which is truth![70]

For Sartre, this dramatic oscillation occurs between two distinct forms of Nothingness, thus guaranteeing Mallarmé's creative impotence. On the one hand lies 'the Truth' (MPN 119), which is Being in its uniform nullity as revealed to Mallarmé following the death of his mother. On the other hand, opposite Being *qua* matter is 'the Dream', which names the poet's desperate and always disappointed quest to re-find his mother, or to create a concrete form that transcends Being. Yet 'the Dream', too, is a form of Nothingness, albeit one that names the impossibility of existing in any determinate space or time whatsoever.

Mallarmé's use of poetry to heal his primordial wound thus led to an impasse: in attempting to recreate himself, he succeeded only in engendering two reciprocally annihilating forms of Nothingness. Importantly, at this stage of his individual adventure, Mallarmé has already reached the point his contemporaries had attained, albeit with varying degrees of awareness as to its aporetic nature. It is as if the poet's personal trajectory had accelerated the logical process by which the axioms of Parnassianism unfolded their consequences. Moreover, since these axioms corresponded to the fundaments of Mallarmé's '*being-in-the-world*', resolving the tension between them became a task of vital necessity for him. The next step Mallarmé takes in order to 'loosen ... the bonds of his destiny' (MPN 114) will therefore be decisive: it will correspond to his transcendence of the poetry – indeed of the very worldview – of his contemporaries.

'The English teacher suddenly finds himself swept up in an extraordinary adventure' (MPN 121), announces Sartre at the opening of the final section of his manuscript: this is the moment that was presaged at the close of 'The Atheist Heritage'. And just as the philosopher had promised, with the contradictions in the poetic Idea about to explode within – or *as* – the very person of Mallarmé, the time is close when 'the errors ... will topple over and reveal the truth of man behind them' (MPN 64 – translation modified). Indeed, in this next stage of his personal phenomenology of the poetic spirit Mallarmé will do nothing less than come to consciousness of the truth of human existence. For indeed, Sartre very seriously considers Mallarmé to have arrived, via the inner dynamics of his poetry, at a truth the philosopher himself will later express in *Being and Nothingness*. Despite their apparent political differences, on this point philosopher and poet are in complete conceptual solidarity.

To explain, Mallarmé has so far made two discoveries: firstly, that it is impossible for him – for Man – *not* to seek out a form of necessity, an essential foundation to Being; in Mallarmé's individual trajectory, this search is propelled forward by the primordial loss of his mother. But secondly, it is equally impossible for him *not* to be the unwitting victim of Being in its fundamental contingency; he will never be able to create something *new* in the form of an 'irreducible synthesis' (MPN 24 – translation modified) – that is, in the form of a creation whose constitutive parts will not, ultimately, disperse. Mallarmé gives a canonical expression of this second point in 'Music and Letters': 'Nature has taken place; it can't be added to' (D 187). Sartre presents Mallarmé's dual discovery as follows:

> Suddenly the sterile poet's torment takes the shape of a universal consciousness torn between an absolute necessity and the radical impossibility of creating ... *What* can they produce if not random combinations, so scattered and external to one another that they resist the act of synthesis which the poet would impose on them? And what can they work with, if not words which chance has stuck together in their minds according to some archaic affinity whose influence lingers on, long after the original meaning has been forgotten? (MPN 122)

In the wake of the death of God, these are questions that *all* human beings must ask themselves. As such, Mallarmé is justified when he 'confuse[s] [his] personal drama with that of humanity as a whole' (MPN 136). Importantly, when the poet claims that he is 'Man himself' (MPN 145 – translation modified), Sartre is quick to clarify that this is not a matter of affirming the existence of 'some Idea of Human Nature'. Rather, his conception of human existence is that of 'a conflict incapable of synthesis' (MPN 123) between contingency and necessity. Every human action is performed in light of an end freely posited by the subject; the moments of this action constitute a synthetic unity, with their reciprocal relations giving each of them an equal necessity *qua* moments that help achieve the end. And yet, this future-oriented action is but a volatile illusion flickering over the surface of matter. For fundamentally, as we know, Being is 'dispersion, inertia, and exteriority': there is no necessity – and no future – except as properties of an action that will inevitably crash against the rock of Being's contingency. Mallarmé articulates this 'drama' once and for all in *Igitur*: 'inaccessible hence insoluble, it cannot be fathomed in a state of illumination, for it is resolved in an instant, just the time of showing its defeat, which unfolds in a flash'. This 'drama' also reveals the meaning of 'Chance' for Mallarmé: as Sartre writes, '[w]e will speak of chance each time the supposed result of a premeditated action discloses itself as the pure and simple production of the intersection of causal chains' (MPN 125). In other words, 'Chance' is the name for the defeat of man's future-oriented project. The necessity of this defeat derives from the irreducible nature of the subject's pro-jective action: like the young Mallarmé who incessantly sought to re-find his mother *qua* the absent presence that had given his world its necessity, the human subject is always oriented towards necessity in the form of a future totality in light of which the present has its meaning. Yet reality is actually composed of an infinite chain of causes flowing from the past: the apparent priority of the future is thus a mere 'lure' (D 187), as Mallarmé puts it in 'Music and Letters'. Crucially, then, 'Chance' is not opposed to determinism: a universe of efficient causality may still lack any *reason for being*. Indeed, if determinism is the true nightmare, then it is precisely because it transmits its (anti-)foundational contingency to every ontic entity in the universe. The sole distinctive mark of human beings in this universe is that they must be *conscious* of this contingency, all the while attempting to overcome it. As Sartre writes, commenting on the same letter to Cazalis in which Mallarmé admits to being nothing more than 'an aptitude the spiritual has to see itself', for the poet – as for the philosopher – 'within matter – that shapeless infinity – there seems to be some obscure appetite to turn back on itself in order to know itself' (MPN 136) – an 'appetite' named consciousness. Furthermore, as in *Being and Nothingness*, existential structures such as possibility only come into existence with consciousness. Without the human subject, 'an infinite and eternal series of causes is all that it ever could be' (MPN 135 – translation modified). This last ontological postulate, which captures the mode of being of the *in-itself* in Sartre's ontology, is powerfully conveyed by Mallarmé's sonnet 'When the shadow threatened with unalterable law', in particular by the following tercet, which ends with an evocation of a human power existing beyond the brute massivity of Being:

> Space, self-identical, if it inflate or deny itself
> rolls out cheap fires in this boredom as witness
> that genius has ignited in a festive star. (PV 159)[71]

Mallarmé's poetry thus stages the human drama *par excellence* – the most fundamental structure of our existence. We set off in search of necessity, yet we have always-already failed to reach it, just like the sea foam from *Un coup de dés*, which is 'fallen back in advance from being unable to dress its flight' (CP 128). We are like the swan from 'The virginal, enduring, beautiful today', who silently dreams of an escape from his ice-bound prison, yet who remembers that all of his previous efforts to do so have failed. Faced with this horror, 'he is paralysed in the cold dream of contempt' (PV 161). Sartre comments: 'the semblance of movement vanishes, leaving only the infinite, undifferentiated surface of ice' (MPN 143).

We will soon return to consider whether Mallarmé's transcendence of his contemporaries, as Sartre has here presented it, also constitutes a transcendence of their *political* limitations. For the time being, we can remark on the fact that Sartre lauds what might be called the *ontological egalitarianism* of Mallarmé's worldview: in contrast to his peers, for whom poetry seems exclusively a means to assert their superiority over other human beings, Mallarmé believes his poetry stages a drama whose tragic dignity is played out in all of our lives. Quoting from Mallarmé's late prose piece 'The Court', Sartre comments on the poet's paradoxical sense of self-importance:

> As for credentials, yours are just as good as mine: 'Anybody can be the Chosen One – You or I.' What magnificent pride! Aggrandizing yourself to the point of becoming the incarnation of Man and not to take any credit for it; wishing to measure up to God, or to anyone else; everyone's equal: superior only to those superior men who, in a panic, preferred voluntary mutilation to the systematic destruction of their circumstantial Self, all the while clinging to their accidental virtues. (MPN 123)

*

Having discovered a compelling philosophical vision of the human subject's fundamentally tragic mode of existence, Mallarmé still needs to find a way to transpose it poetically. *Hérodiade*'s fatal flaw was that it staged an Absolute that was revealed to be a paradoxical figure of Nothingness – a deception isomorphic to Mallarmé's own unwitting transformation of his mother *qua* 'a pure singularity' into 'the pure concept of the negative'. After discovering, in desperation, that his most important poetic creation was metaphysically *empty*, Sartre explains that Mallarmé 'seriously contemplated killing himself' (MPN 121). For if his project to recreate himself betrayed 'a disguised death wish' (MPN 120), why not go all the way and actually commit suicide? On Sartre's reading, *Igitur* recounts the unrelentingly logical process by which, from generation to generation, the poetic Idea slowly revealed its fatal inconsistency: namely, that while poetry demanded a divine guarantee, it now existed in a universe without God. Just as the dialectic of generations meant that the post-1848 poets could not return to Christianity *simpliciter*, Igitur had to confront the irreducibility of 'Chance'. Like him, Mallarmé was caught between 'a purity whose demands were becoming each day more aggressive [and] a Contingency whose presence was each day becoming more obvious' (MPN 125). Can this conflict end in any other way than an absolute immobility akin to death? Sartre answers yes: as Mallarmé has already realised, this conflict is the very motor of human existence; as such, to decide that its exigencies are so contradictory, so despair-inducing, as to warrant suicide – a suicide that Igitur himself finally performs when he 'lays down on the ashes of his ancestors' – is to make a decision about the value of human existence *tout court*. This is the sense of Sartre's seemingly hyperbolic claim that it was up to Mallarmé '[w]hether or not Man disappeared from the earth' (MPN 127): his suicide, in other words, would be a kind of microcosmic genocide.

But if Mallarmé did not kill himself, it was because he discovered in his very refusal to do so an effective means by which to cut himself off from his paternal lineage: his life was no longer the involuntary perseverance in Being of his father's gratuity but a gift which 'Mallarmé now bestows ... on himself because he pardoned himself' (MPN 127). Furthermore, in consciously keeping himself, day after day, from slipping into Nothingness, Mallarmé could produce a poetry whose 'theme' would be 'the lucid desolation of an Art which knows itself to be impossible' (MPN 128); a poetry, in other words, whose assumption of its own inconsistency would match his own heroic decision to keep living – the only truly *free* act a human being can ever perform. But what are the properties of Mallarmé's mature poetry in so far as it transcends the vacuity of *Hérodiade*? If this latter poem failed because 'it oppose[d] a pure form of human thought to the determinations of life and experience', just as the Stoic does in Hegel's *Phenomenology of the Spirit* – a figure of consciousness Sartre considers a perfect model for 'Mallarmé's purity' (MPN 130) – then the poetry which surpasses it must take the form of an *act*; it must be a 'negative labor' (MPN 131) performed on a determinate content. In Hegelian terms, Mallarmé's 'conversion' (MPN 130) must involve the passage from Stoicism to Scepticism.[72]

In an unpublished section of his 1953 preface to Mallarmé's *Poésies*, Sartre describes the technique Mallarmé invented to give his poetry an effective *force* of negativity, as opposed to *Hérodiade*'s empty evocation of the Absolute *qua* Nothingness. As Sartre explains, in his post-conversion work Mallarmé set out to '*treat* any object at all with a certain technique that drains it of its matter and enables it to function as an idea, that is, as the synthetic and transcendent unity of diversity' (MPN 140–1 – translation modified). Of course, in so far as Mallarmé's implicit ontology holds that Being is 'dispersion, inertia, and exteriority', he is not concerned with poetically reproducing the rational structure of the real: in what could be considered his negative theological version of Platonism, for Mallarmé the unity of the multiple is nothing other than what it *lacks*. Sartre gives the second verse from the sonnet 'In victory having fled fair suicide' as an example of this technique: 'a brand of glory, blood in foam, gold, tempest!' (PV 163). As Sartre explains, in this verse 'what [Mallarmé] means to *say* is not "sunset" but the effect on the reader is such that the sunset emerges as the *non-verbal* unity of the multiplicity of colors' (MPN 141 – Sartre's emphasis). While distinct, each of the objects in this nominal phrase are struck by an identical *lack*: they are all *not* the object suggested. Just as Mallarmé's mother was lacking from the world in its entirety – a world whose unity thus lay only its uniform nullity – his poetry makes the objects it names seem radically *insufficient*. Each of them is the deficient, worldly sign of an absent object of desire. Mallarmé's poetry thus plays out, again and again, the same experience of radical deception experienced by the human subject as it 'flings itself wildly into the Dream which it knows does not exist'. Necessity is absent from the world; it is only a lure that makes us crash all the more surely against the rock of contingency.

We have almost reached the end of Sartre's exploration of Mallarmé's individual trajectory and of the poetry it helped him produce. The last turn of the dialectical screw involves the poet's recognition that his technique, however locally successful it might be, is still impotent in the face of contingency: 'If chance appears at the outset, "no throw of the dice shall ever abolish it"' (MPN 143). Nothing, in other words, guarantees the success of his poetry. Yet as Sartre shows, Mallarmé had an ingenious response to this seemingly insurmountable logical difficulty. Firstly, he accepted that his actual poems were failures – something they incontestably were in so far as they set out to 'conquer' chance 'word by word' (D 236), yet inevitably failed to do so. This allows Mallarmé to make his second move. As Sartre recalls, for the last thirty years of his life the poet claimed to be working on a great Book that would be the 'orphic explanation of the Earth' (D 3) – a Book for which his actual poems were only the abandoned drafts. He would die without having completed it. But with his passing, this relation between his failed poems and the Book is rendered eternal: the poems' faults – their failure to abolish chance – consequently take on 'an absolute necessity' (MPN 144) in so far as they were all meant to one day be rectified in the form of the Book. In other words, Sartre considers Mallarmé's death an almost wilful act.[73] More precisely, he sees the propagation of the myth of an incomplete Book as part of a logically grounded strategy to overcome chance – the only strategy possible.

*

The Poet of Nothingness was written just over five years before Jacques Scherer published *Le 'Livre' de Mallarmé*,[74] the first work to contain Mallarmé's scattered notes for an elaborate literary ceremony. When Sartre refers to the poet's Book in *The Poet of Nothingness*, he therefore principally has in mind the Book as it is referred to in the following tantalising terms in Mallarmé's 'Autobiography':

> I have always dreamed and attempted something else, with the patience of an alchemist, ready to sacrifice all vanity and all satisfaction, the way they used to burn their furniture and the beams from their ceilings, to stoke the fires of the Great Work. What would it be? It's hard to say: a book, quite simply, in several volumes, a book that would be a real book, architectural and premeditated, and not a collection of chance inspirations, however wonderful ... I would even go further and say *the* Book, convinced as I am that in the final analysis there's only one, unwittingly attempted by anyone who writes, even Geniuses. (D 3)

The consequences of Sartre's understanding of the Book are profound, as we will see in the final section of this chapter. In *The Poet of Nothingness*, the Book has no concrete existence: it refers only to an imagined work of absolute literary value, but one whose content is nothing more than the hypostatisation of the faults of every existing literary work in so far as the Book will have retrospectively redeemed them. In this guise, the Book's role is to render Mallarmé's poetry *necessary*. On this point, it is worthwhile clarifying the understandable misapprehension of some critics regarding the scope of Sartre's claims about Mallarmé. Thierry Roger has argued that 'the essence of Sartre's reading ... is in fact founded on Mallarmé's Parnassian and post-Baudelairean period, as well as on the crisis he suffered in Tournon during the years 1866–1869, a crisis which led to *Igitur*'.[75] Similarly, speaking of the third volume of Sartre's *The Family Idiot* – a work to which we will soon turn – Pascal Durand praises the philosopher's 'analysis of the Parnassian *ethos*', which, according to him, 'was raised to a degree of critical intelligence for which there is no equivalent'.[76] Yet Durand's own approach to Mallarmé does not follow the philosopher's any further than a few analytical points concerning the poet's early years. Both of these eminent scholars therefore read *The Poet of Nothingness* as a brilliant yet limited book, which subsumes all of Mallarmé's poetry under the rubric of a dialectic discovered in his youth, then later abandoned. Rancière, as will see, holds a similar view.

Yet we know that Sartre ranges across the entirety of Mallarmé's corpus, from poems like 'Sa fosse est creusée' (1859), written when the poet was only seventeen, to late prose pieces like 'The Court' (1895) and his testamentary text *Un coup de dés* (1897). Moreover, Sartre demonstrates a conceptual coherence in Mallarmé's *œuvre*, albeit one that involves a dialectical progression. In the remainder of this chapter, our principal aim will not be to judge whether the poet's writings are best understood on Sartre's terms, although we will gesture towards some of their limitations. It will be to interrogate the coherence of Sartre's reading at a different level – a *political* level.

*

Mallarmé is the 'hero of an ontological drama'. But does this save him from being an 'agent of the counter-revolution'? In our view, *this* is the fundamental question posed by *The Poet of Nothingness* in the context of an investigation into the politics of literature. To confront this question, we will momentarily turn away from *Mallarmé* and consider one of Sartre's last published books: the third volume of *The Family Idiot*, paying particular attention to its ominously titled first section, 'Objective Neurosis'.

Sartre refers frequently to Mallarmé throughout the three volumes of *The Family Idiot*. The book can therefore be used to test whether he significantly altered his views on Mallarmé in the twenty years that followed his abandonment of the manuscript of *The Poet of Nothingness*. Our approach will initially be slightly different: taking up the long section Sartre devotes to Leconte de Lisle (FI 317–400), we will ask whether the characteristics the philosopher identifies in de Lisle's work – characteristics which he condemns politically in the most unequivocal of terms – apply also to Mallarmé.

Helpfully, in the following passage, which is worth quoting in its entirety, Sartre lists four key characteristics of de Lisle's exemplary work:

1. *Misanthropy*, the only adequate response to the common infamy of victims and executioners. By which we mean the only hyperbolic ruse permitting the acceptance of a social order based on exploitation by dissolving classes in the universality of evil, the most evenly shared thing in the world.
2. *Disengagement*, an immediate and practical consequence of human wretchedness – there is no just cause, there are no unhappy wretches. It ratifies as well the resounding failure of every generous action (the Republic finds its grave diggers among the same folk it might have showered with benefits), and more generally of our claimed activity.
3. And equally *the autonomy of literature*, too often betrayed in the name of so-called political or social ideals, simple masks for our passions and interests. Here autonomy reveals itself by the denial of human aims – a denial of needs and of the body, a denial of ambition, a denial of the public, a denial of spontaneity in the name of impassivity and of inspiration in the name of work – to be the fundamental negation of man or, if you will, the passage to the negative absolute.
4. The *nonbeing of the real* – as a consequence of that hyperbolic extrapolation – in short, the denunciation of our passions' cherished illusions, and the *being of the nonreal*, a valorization of the imaginary. We understand this to mean appearance offered as such and revealing, in the static evolution of a beautiful work, insubstantiality as the ontological rule of cosmic totalization (FI 380 – Sartre's emphasis).

Our question is to what degree Mallarmé overcomes the flagrant political faults concentrated in de Lisle's vision of literature. Before answering in detail, it is worthwhile considering the explicit remarks Sartre makes throughout *The Family Idiot* concerning the continuity between Flaubert and de Lisle's literary ideology, on the one hand, and Mallarmé's on the other. In fact, these remarks converge towards an unequivocal conclusion: Mallarmé not only remains within the lineage of French postromanticism, he refines – indeed he perfects, as Sartre at one point suggests (FI 335) – the literary vision of those writers born of the conjoined cataclysms of 1848 and the death of God.

Generally speaking, Sartre claims that Mallarmé transformed what had remained the merely thematic content of de Lisle's work into a precise technical procedure, which he put to work at the level of his poetry's form. As we know, Mallarmé's practice of allusion empties out the substance of every object his poetry explicitly names and forces it to suggest an absent object – ultimately necessity itself – in light of which it appears as radically deficient. In a second move, every single one of Mallarmé's poems repeats the same gesture at a higher level, since they exist only in the shadow of the Book. But at no point in this procedure does Mallarmé give the game away; his poetry lacks the incessant denunciations of the world that we find throughout de Lisle's monotonous work. As Sartre writes, Mallarmé's 'radical despair is magnificently hidden' (FI 353). Yet a silent force of negativity is still constantly at work in his poetic world – in *our* world – and draining it of its self-sufficient meaning. If Mallarmé is different to de Lisle, then this difference lies not at the ideological level, since on Sartre's reading Mallarmé too seeks to strip the world of its immanent meaning, rendering both it and our projects within it equally null. Rather, it is to be found at the *formal* level. In another passage in which he comments on de Lisle's preface to *Poèmes antiques*, Sartre makes this very claim: 'We recognize in passing the techniques of derealization that Gustave [Flaubert] refined as early as 1844, and that Mallarmé *would perfect* under the Third Republic. Leconte de Lisle – who owed nothing to Flaubert – used cruder techniques; yet, they issue from the same intention' (FI 335 – our emphasis).

In short, postromanticism finds 'its theorist and its hero in Mallarmé' (FI 12). In light, then, of Sartre's remarks in *The Family Idiot*, Mallarmé's transcendence of the 'poetic complex' that emerged from the post-1848 conjuncture seems to involve a refinement of its poetic technique and a more subtle expression of its principal themes. But is this aesthetic continuity doubled by a political fidelity to de Lisle's bleak vision? Taking the four components of his ideology one by one, let us consider, firstly, whether de Lisle's *misanthropy* is reprised by Mallarmé. In our view, Sartre recognises the tragic dignity Mallarmé accords to what he considers the fundamental drama of our existence. This was the sense of the passage from 'The Court', which we cited above: 'Anybody can be the Chosen One – You or I'. Thus, unlike de Lisle, Mallarmé does not adopt an aristocratic distance from those who suffer the tension between necessity and contingency: the poet is on the same level as all other people. Moreover, Mallarmé's own reprieve in the face of his possible suicide shows that he considers Man's grandeur to lie in his unflinching lucidity in the face of the aporia of his existence: the genocidal themes of a de Lisle poem like *Aux Modernes* are consequently entirely absent. Certainly, as we noted above, there is a tension between Mallarmé's position as the person who *knows* the tragic essence of human existence and his ontological egalitarianism, a tension which Sartre captures in *The Family Idiot* when he writes that 'Mallarmé – at once more aristocratic and, by his own choice, more plebeian – will judge himself mandated by *being from below*, by what Merleau-Ponty calls "the fabric of being in a rough state," in order to bear witness to a universal aspiration of the world to deliver itself from chance'.[77] But his poetry betrays less a hatred of humanity and more a desire to render it in its truth; a truth which, while tragic, gives humanity a new and unexpected source of dignity.

This point allows us to address the third characteristic of de Lisle's literary vision: namely, the *autonomy of literature*. For Mallarmé, on Sartre's reading, literature is certainly not a partisan of any 'cause'; it does not sacrifice itself on the altar of any political struggle. Yet it is transitive to the very essence of human existence. As such, it seems impossible to ascribe to Mallarmé the same intention to *extract* literature from all human affairs, as de Lisle wanted to. By stark contrast, for Mallarmé, literature's innermost movement is the same as that which animates every subject.

In terms, then, of the first and third characteristics of de Lisle's literature, Mallarmé undeniably shifts their meaning, even rejecting them out of hand. Mallarmé is no more a misanthrope than Pascal; and his conviction concerning the ontological significance of his writing makes it impossible for him to separate literature's movement from the lives of other human beings.

It is when we turn to the second and fourth characteristics, however, that the gulf separating Mallarmé's writings from Sartre's political axiology begins to come into view. For Sartre, the characteristics of *disengagement* and of the *non-being of the real* have a close affinity. After 1848, de Lisle's literary ideology was the perfect conformist discourse, since it 'contest[ed] any rebellion against the established order by striking at its root, dramatizing the vanity of action and systematically derealizing the real, finally making the reader and the poet himself the dreams of a dream' (FI 351). It is hard not to see how Mallarmé *also* stages the ultimate vanity of every human action. All human projects, including political ones undertaken within a singular context of struggle, fall under the implacable law of Mallarmé's dialectic 'without synthesis'. Sartre seems to confirm that this crushing verdict applies to political action when, following a discussion of Flaubert and his classmates' failed insurrection at the Lycée de Rouen in 1832, he writes: 'I cannot evoke their defeat without thinking of the original drama as Mallarmé retraces it: "He throws the dice, the bet is made . . . He who created finds himself again to be matter, blocks, dice." Between July and October the schoolboys have lived, each for his own account, the Mallarméan moment, pebble of eternity, *paradox*.'[78] In other words, in his juvenile political engagement Flaubert experienced 'the transformation of a tempting future synthesis into what is revealed as being the analytic past' (MPN 124 – translation modified). The passage from *The Family Idiot* continues as follows:

> these children believed they were historical agents, they threw the dice, made their bet and – he who created finds himself matter once again – these subjects have once again, through the necessary failure of their enterprise,

become the objects of history, inert barrels buffeted by its waves. They believed that just causes always prevail (you cannot be a revolutionary without optimism: the advent of Man is near, this will be the end of history, virtue, happiness; it will be done by their hands). However, they discover their defeat: history continues *without them*, what they took as the end of history was only their own end; as historical subjects, they have fallen into a pit, whether because their mistakes ruined their enterprise or because the targeted object was beyond reach. In this last case, Man, the supreme purpose of men, chose these scamps in order to manifest in principle his impossibility.[79]

This final line echoes the invocation of 'the tragic impossibility of man' (MPN 144) from *The Poet of Nothingness*. From first to last, then, Sartre reads Mallarmé as a poet who posits the inevitable failure of all human action. The world, in so far as it is the site of our illusions – our pursuit of necessity – is thus insubstantial. Or, more precisely, its truth is radically different to how it appears in the context of human action. Thus, like de Lisle, Mallarmé can indeed be said to affirm the *non-being of the real*. As for his predecessor's ethics of *disengagement*, however, the balance sheet is more uncertain. As Sartre writes in *The Poet of Nothingness*, Mallarmé understands that 'an experience must be undertaken because of and not in spite of the fact that its outcome is known in advance' (MPN 130 – translation modified): that is, even if he recognises that 'no particular experience could ever contradict the principles in whose name it was established' (MPN 130), Mallarmé still chooses to throw the dice. In contrast to de Lisle, who preserves an illusory space of poetic autonomy outside of, and above, human affairs, Mallarmé accepts the irreducibility of an *ontological* engagement in the dialectic of contingency and necessity.

But is this the same as acknowledging the inescapable nature of *political* engagement? To approach this question, it is worthwhile citing a crucial passage from 'The Atheist Heritage' where Sartre appears to speak in his own voice, unequivocally condemning the postromantics' fetishisation of failure:

> For someone totally committed to History, losing is unbearable: it is the triumph of the forces of Evil. If he is told that posterity will appreciate his virtues two hundred years hence, he will hardly be impressed. In fact, it couldn't matter less to him. He knows very well that his grand-nephews will no longer be abreast of what was going on, and that they will appreciate his courage and self-abnegation from a quasi-aesthetic perspective since they won't care about the causes which inspired them. (MPN 61)

There can be little doubt that in the context of this passage Sartre identifies with 'someone totally committed to History'. As we know, throughout 'The Atheist Heritage' Sartre unfavourably contrasts the postromantics' nihilism with the utopian project of the proletariat; that is, with the project of a class which 'claim[s] its place in the sun' and 'even strive[s] to conquer it by force' (MPN 39). Against these egalitarian aspirations, the postromantics had eternalised the reign of the bourgeoisie, treating the period's limits as an absolute horizon and translating its contingent characteristics 'into psychological or metaphysical terms' (MPN 54). Mallarmé, too, participated in this process of ideological sublimation. Thus, whatever the *ontological* dignity of his poetic dialectic,[80] his tragic perspective not only fails to capture the stakes of situated political struggles, it cannot accord them any intrinsic value. Mallarmé's poetry thus stands opposed to Sartre's 'committed' literature. From first to last, Mallarmé is a literary predecessor whose influence must be appreciated yet ultimately exorcised.

The tension in Sartre's reading of Mallarmé between praising the poet as 'the hero of an ontological drama' and ranging him, with varying degrees of explicitness, amongst 'the agents of the "Précieuse" counter-revolution', offers an unexpected lesson in the politics of literature. By promising to show how the poet would transcend the limits of postromanticism – a promise that, on balance, Sartre keeps – the philosopher leads us to expect that he will also demonstrate how Mallarmé escaped from the bleak and misanthropic ideology in which his peers had imprisoned themselves. That Sartre describes Mallarmé's poetic dialectic with such unmediated sympathy in *The Poet of Nothingness* seems to support this expectation. Yet, after careful examination, we have shown how Mallarmé's poetry still falls foul of the political axiology Sartre works with both openly and polemically in 'The Atheist Heritage' and which also orients his judgement in *The Family Idiot*. There is no way to overcome the tension between Sartre's Marxist view of the movement of History and the following claim inspired by Mallarmé's *Igitur*: 'The meaningless spiral of generations: this is the movement of history' (MPN 125). Ingenious as they are, the poet's writings thus remain wedded to the ideology of the post-1848 French bourgeoisie, transforming it into 'an ontological and metaphysical adventure' that obscures its social origins. At root, far from reflecting the entropic essence of the Universe, Sartre claims that Mallarmé's pessimism – like that of Leconte de Lisle before him – betrays the blunt 'refusal to take the side of the proletariat' (FI 381). In a word, his literature is irrevocably complicit with 'a social order based on exploitation' (FI 380). Yet an implicit lesson of Sartre's procedure here is that Mallarmé nevertheless *did* overcome many of the limitations of Parnassianism and Symbolism. His achievements in this domain are incontestable: he took the implications of the death of God to their end and refused facile solutions concerning the possibility of poetic creation. He also broke with the inconsistent elitism of writers like de Lisle, and instead recognised the universality of the existential dialectic he had uncovered. Finally, he transformed the postromantics' theology of the negative into an 'extraordinary negative logic' (MPN 143), which he put to work within the form of his poetry. The point is that all of these veritable achievements were made *within* the parameters of postromanticism's counter-revolutionary politics. Concomitantly, whatever its truth-value as an ontology, Mallarmé's 'ontological drama' remains radically refractory to any egalitarian politics, which necessarily imply attending to the situated intelligibility of specific struggles and affirming the possibility of success – not the equivalence-in-failure of all human action. Poetry, in other words, can evolve according to its own internal criteria; indeed it can even take vast strides forward, as it did with Mallarmé. Yet when it is measured against a certain scale of political values, such as Sartre's militant Marxism, these transformations can come to nought. Mallarmé *is* both 'the hero of an ontological drama' and an 'agent of the counter-revolution'. The very political ambivalence of his poetry has to do with the fact that both of these theses are true.

*

As we announced at the opening of this chapter, in occasional remarks made in an interview given during the latter half of his philosophical trajectory, Sartre seems to offer a very different vision of Mallarmé's writings to the one developed in *The Poet of Nothingness* and reprised in *The Family Idiot*. In the brief remarks we will now explore, the philosopher attributes to Mallarmé a utopian and universalist literary project that cannot be captured within the terms of French postromanticism. By contrast, this project manifests some of the key features of 'committed literature', in particular its ideally universal address.

In an interview with Madeleine Chapsal in 1959, Sartre is confronted with the following apparent paradox: despite arguing for a literature whose prose would be 'an instrument, an extension of one's arm, one's hand'[81] – in a word, an effective *praxis* within the world – Sartre had nevertheless devoted his attention to writers such as 'Flaubert, Genet, Mallarmé – all of whom seemed to regard writing as an end in itself'.[82] Resisting Chapsal's idea that literature can actually be autotelic, Sartre responds first by affirming that 'literature, understood as a pure art deriving all its rules from its own essence, conceals its author's commitment and his fiery opinions on every sort of subject – including social and political questions'.[83] As we have seen him argue in *The Family*

Idiot, the autotelism of literature was in fact an historical by-product of the disenchantment that followed the failed revolution of 1848. But despite this historicist refutation of the notion of literary autonomy, when it comes to addressing the particular case of Mallarmé, Sartre does not aim to expose the social causes that undercut the poet's apparent absolutism. Rather, he articulates what he conceives Mallarmé's positive poetic vision to have been:

> [Mallarmé] rejected his epoch, but he preserved it in the form of a transition, a tunnel. He hoped that one day what he used to call 'the crowd' – by which he meant a mass public assembled in a godless cathedral rather than in a theatre – would see Tragedy played before them. The one and only Tragedy – at once the drama of man, the movement of the world, the tragic return of the seasons – a tragedy whose author (as anonymous as Homer) would be dead, or else be just one of the audience, present at the unfolding of a masterpiece that did not belong to him, or which *all* would stage for him as for all. Mallarmé linked his Orphic and tragic conceptions of Poetry to the communion of a people rather than to individual hermeticism. The latter was no more than a rejection of bourgeois stupidity. To be sure, Mallarmé did not think one could write 'openly' for a mass public. But he felt that for a united people, the obscure would become clear.[84]

Sartre demonstrates here his extraordinary intellectual fluency. In these remarks from a spoken-word interview, he presents a brilliantly compact account of Mallarmé's mature *œuvre*, which he recognises as an attempt at a secular religion. The addressee of this religion – 'the crowd' – is radically indeterminate and suggests a generic humanity beyond the artificial divisions that a 'phantom nobility' (MPN 37) might attempt to institute. By contrast, the poet is a part of this 'crowd', not a member of some 'aristocracy' (MPN 35). Furthermore, rather than Mallarmé's infamous difficulty being a function of his refusal of a fallen public sphere, Sartre argues that it is a sign of the inadequacy of the present situation. Instead of working to distinguish two distinct humanities in the face of an 'unbearable egalitarianism' (MPN 34), his difficult poetry inscribed a utopian desire for what Sartre calls, in an interview from 1964 where he also mentions Mallarmé, 'the time when everyone will read'.[85]

Despite this thorough re-organisation of his vision of Mallarmé's *œuvre*, what is perhaps most striking about Sartre's 1959 remarks is that he does deal with the communitarian element of the poet's work in *The Family Idiot*. In this book, however, he predictably attempts to integrate it within the framework of postromanticism. Writing of the troubling transformations of the idea of literary autonomy amongst this generation of poets, Sartre advances the following account of Mallarmé's secularised religion:

> In the end, demanding that the tragic poet preserve anonymity in his lifetime and until the end of time, Mallarmé embodies the ultimate meaning of the writer's inessentiality when he dreams of a great tragedy that would portray before the assembled people, like the medieval passion plays, the mystery and fatal contradiction of man plunged once again into the rhythms of nature. (FI 91)

Here, the anonymity of the author is not linked to a utopian universalism but to a radical conception of literature's autonomy. Sartre explains: 'Refusing to serve, to be integrated into a class literature, the work becomes its own end; it stands on its own in an inhuman solitude, resting on the related suppression of reader and author' (FI 91). In other words, the rejection of all extra-literary aims means that literature had become disconnected from human action, including those of reading and writing. If both author and public are negated by Mallarmé's *œuvre*, this is not because they participate in a poetic 'communion', but rather because 'the literary absolute' (FI 90) transcends them both. However, as can no doubt be sensed, the interpretative framework of postromanticism – which manifests itself in the above passage in the form of a conception of the work of art as an 'absolute' – is clearly straining against the material Sartre is working with. If Mallarmé 'dreams of a great tragedy' to be played before 'the assembled people', it is difficult to see how the 'suppression' of this 'people' could be the aim of the poet's work. And if the author must 'preserve [his] anonymity', then this is more reasonably understood as a consequence of the essentially collective nature of the power that manifests itself in and through this 'great tragedy', and not as a consequence of its 'inhuman' character.

Sartre offers a far more coherent interpretation of this dimension of Mallarmé's *œuvre* in his interview with Chapsal. While in *The Family Idiot* he operates on the assumption that 'Mallarmé beautifully summed up thirty years of literary history' (FI 177), in this 1959 interview Chapsal implicitly invites Sartre to differentiate the poet from Flaubert. In accepting this invitation, Sartre is able to admit that he is 'in complete sympathy with Mallarmé'.[86] And indeed, that he is sympathetic to the poet is ultimately unsurprising, for the utopian dream of 'the communion of a people' through the mediation of literature is precisely the project he himself had proposed in *What is Literature?* If Sartre did not turn to Mallarmé to articulate this utopian vision in the aftermath of the Second World War, this was no doubt because the poet was too closely associated with a period of French literary history that was the negative double of 'committed literature'. As we have argued, Sartre consistently exteriorised the ever-possible errors of the writer onto Flaubert, de Lisle, Mallarmé and their contemporaries. From his Marxist perspective, which was at its most doctrinaire at precisely the moment he wrote *The Poet of Nothingness*, Mallarmé's obscure poetry and isolation from the public sphere could only too easily be condemned as an example of '[t]he legend of the irresponsible poet'. It is for these reasons, then, that Sartre's recognition of the poet's communitarian utopianism in 1959 is so out of the ordinary. However, as we will see in the following chapters, in the political appropriations of 'comrade Mallarmé' that succeed Sartre's pathbreaking writings, this dimension of the poet's *œuvre* will assume unprecedented importance.

NOTES

1. 'The Purposes of Writing', 13.
2. J.-P. Sartre, *Mallarmé, or The Poet of Nothingness*, trans. E. Sturm (University Park: Pennsylvania State University Press, 1988).
3. J.-P. Sartre, *What is Literature?*, trans. B. Frechtman (London and New York: Routledge, 2010).
4. J.-P. Sartre, 'Black Orpheus', in Aronson and Van Den Hoven (eds), *We Have Only This Life To Live*, 149–86.
5. J.-P. Sartre, *The Family Idiot: Gustave Flaubert, 1821–1857, Volume Five*, trans. C. Cosman (Chicago: University of Chicago Press, 1993).
6. Throughout this chapter, we will consistently use the term 'commitment' to translate the French term 'engagement', irrespective of the choices made by Sartre's different translators.
7. 'The Purposes of Writing', 13–14.
8. R. Goldthorpe, 'Mallarmé: Sartre's Committed Poet', in M. Bowie et al. (eds), *Baudelaire, Mallarmé, Valéry: New Essays in Honour of Lloyd Austin* (Cambridge: Cambridge University Press, 1982); R. Goldthorpe, *Sartre: Literature and Theory* (Cambridge: Cambridge University Press, 1984), 184–97, 222–41; C. Wolfe, 'Rethinking Commitment: Ontology, Genre and Sartre's *Mallarmé*', *Diacritics*, Vol. 21, No. 4 (1991), 69–85; B. Denis, 'Le dernier des poètes. Sartre lecteur de Mallarmé', *Courrier du Centre international d'études poétiques*, No. 225 (2000), 45–61. For more examples of reliable scholarship on Sartre and Mallarmé, see C. Abastado, 'Portrait d'un nihiliste (Sartre, au lecteur de Mallarmé)', *Obliques*, 'Sartre', Nos. 18–19 (1979), 195–7; T. König, 'Pour une phénoménologie du discours poétique moderne', in C. Burgelin (ed.), *Lectures de Sartre* (Lyon: Presses Universitaires de Lyon, 1986), 283–94; C. D. Minahen, 'Poetry's Polite Terrorist: Reading Sartre Reading Mallarmé', in M. Temple (ed.), *Meetings with Mallarmé in Contemporary French culture* (Exeter: University of Exeter Press, 1998), 46–66; M. Scriven, *Sartre's Existential Biographies* (London: Macmillan, 1984), 76–84; P. Verstraeten, 'Sartre et Mallarmé', in *Sartre/Barthes, Revue d'esthétique* (1991), 27–38.

9. *What is Literature?*, 100.
10. 'The Purposes of Writing', 13 (translation modified)
11. Sartre is very clear that his discourse on poetry applies to modern French poetry: 'I repeat that I am talking of contemporary poetry. History presents other forms of poetry', *What is Literature?*, 26, n. 4.
12. J. Paulhan, *The Flowers of Tarbes, or Terror in Letters*, trans. M. Syrotinski (Champagne: University of Illinois Press, 2006).
13. J.-P. Sartre, 'La Nationalisation de la littérature', in *Situations, II* (Paris: Gallimard, 1948), 34 (my translation).
14. For an excellent description of this moment of rupture, see Hamel, CM 64–77.
15. For an account of the ascendency of Marxism in this period and the concomitant suspicion of literature in favour of other forms of collective militancy, see A. Boschetti, *The Intellectual Enterprise: Sartre and* Les Temps Modernes, trans. R. C. McCleary (Evanston: Northwestern University Press, 1988), 104–17.
16. *The Intellectual Enterprise*, 110.
17. For these features of 'committed literature', see Sartre's comments on the necessity of a common backdrop of contextual information and on the writer's attempt to simultaneously speak to the diverse strata of a society in *What is Literature?*, 51–3, 120–1.
18. 'Black Orpheus', 160–1.
19. For other selective iterations of this passage in Sartre's œuvre, see MPN, 158 and J.-P. Sartre, *Saint Genet: Actor and Martyr* (New York: Georges Braziller, 1963), 410.
20. Cited in J.-P. Sartre, 'There and Back', in *Critical Essays*, trans. C. Turner (London, New York and Calcutta: Seagull Books, 2010), 325–6. Sartre also frequently links Fargue's maxim to Bataille's expression 'the holocaust of words'. For Sartre's numerous iterations of Bataille's maxim, which is originally found in *L'Expérience intérieure*, see J.-P. Sartre, 'A New Mystic', in *Critical Essays*, 225, 239. See also 'Black Orpheus', 161, and MPN 139.
21. J.-P. Sartre, 'Man and Things', in *Critical Essays*, 94.
22. 'Man and Things', 396 (our emphasis).
23. 'Man and Things', 401 (Sartre's emphasis).
24. 'Man and Things', 402.
25. *What is Literature?*, 1.
26. J.-P. Sartre, *The Family Idiot: Gustave Flaubert, 1821–1857, Volume One* (Chicago: University of Chicago Press, 1981), 272.
27. *What is Literature?*, 6.
28. See Boschetti's remarks regarding 'the dogma of action' that the PCF enforced in intellectual spheres, *The Intellectual Enterprise*, 109.
29. *What is Literature?*, 3.
30. On the necessity of contemporaneity in *What is Literature?*, see Hamel, CM 192–3.

31. *What is Literature?*, 96.
32. J.-P. Sartre, *Baudelaire*, trans. M. Turnell (New York: New Directions, 1967), 190.
33. 'Introducing *Les Temps Modernes*', 133.
34. 'Rethinking Commitment', 70.
35. This is the term Sartre systematically uses in the third volume of *The Family Idiot* to refer to Flaubert, de Lisle and Mallarmé's literary generation: see the section entitled 'The Literary Situation of the Postromantic Apprentice Author', FI 57–410. We will henceforth use it without quotation marks.
36. H. Mondor, *Vie de Mallarmé* (Paris: Gallimard, 1941).
37. For the reference to 'Literature and the Right to Death', see MPN 113, and for the reference to 'Mallarmé's Experience', see MPN 137.
38. H. Mondor, *Mallarmé plus intime* (Paris: Gallimard, 1944).
39. H. Mondor, *Eugène Lefébure: Sa vie, ses lettres à Mallarmé* (Paris: Gallimard, 1951).
40. J.-P. Sartre, *War Diaries: Notebooks from a Phoney War, 1939–1940*, trans. Q. Hoare (London and New York: Verso, 2011), 294.
41. *War Diaries*, 301.
42. *War Diaries*, 300.
43. *War Diaries*, 304.
44. *War Diaries*, 312.
45. *War Diaries*, 316.
46. *War Diaries*, 309.
47. J.-P. Sartre, *Sartre By Himself*, trans. Richard Seaver (New York: Urizen Books, 1978), 72.
48. J.-P. Sartre, 'Merleau-Ponty', in Aronson and Van Den Hoven (eds), *We Have Only This Life to Live*, 355.
49. H. Guillemin, *Le Coup du 2 décembre* (Paris: Gallimard, 1951).
50. *Saint Genet*, 584.
51. J.-P. Sartre, *Critique of Dialectical Reason, Volume One. Theory of Practical Ensembles* (London: Verso, 2004), 755 (Sartre's emphasis).
52. 'Everything sacred and which wishes to remain sacred is enveloped in mystery. Religions take refuge in mysteries revealed only to those predestined to them; art has its own', OC II 362.
53. *The Family Idiot*, 592.
54. *Baudelaire*, 165.
55. *What is Literature?*, 119.
56. *What is Literature?*, 45.
57. 'Otherwise, I suspect that the mysterious order pushing the gratuitous crowd toward false idols is aiming to obstruct the advance of the Chosen One – whoever he is, whether you or me – the only one in whose name social change or revolution occur . . .', D 283 (translation modified).
58. Cited MPN 75.
59. C. Mauron, *Introduction à la psychanalyse de Mallarmé, suivie de*

Mallarmé et le Tao et Le Livre (Neuchâtel: Editions de la Baconnière, 1968).
60. See MPN 25–6, 27–8, 32, 33, 43, 50, 70, 71, 72.
61. G. Poulet, *Etudes sur le temps humain*, 2 (Paris: Plon, 1952). For Sartre's reference to Poulet see MPN 163.
62. 'Mon doute, amas de nuit ancienne, s'achève / En maint rameau subtil, qui, demeuré les vrais / Bois mêmes, prouve, hélas ! que bien seul je m'offrais / Pour triomphe la faute idéale de roses', OC 23.
63. '... pourpre ivre et grand calice clair, / Que, pluie et diamant, le regard diaphane / Resté là sur ces fleurs dont nulle ne se fane, / Isole parmi l'heure et le rayon du jour !', OC 28.
64. 'Poetry's Polite Terrorist', 52
65. 'Poetry's Polite Terrorist', 52.
66. See the transcription of this first version of the poem in the 1945 edition of Mallarmé's complete works, S. Mallarmé, *Œuvres complètes* (Gallimard, 1945), 1411.
67. OC 481. This translation comes from Michel Deguy's *A Man of Little Faith*, trans. C. Ellison (New York: New York University Press, 2003), 57.
68. 'Telle que vers quelque fenêtre / Selon nul ventre que le sien, / Filial on aurait pu naître', OC 43.
69. Quoted in MPN 120.
70. This translation comes from L. W. Marvick, *Mallarmé and the Sublime* (New York: State University of New York Press, 1986), 160.
71. 'L'espace à soi pareil qu'il s'accroise ou se nie / Roule dans cet ennui des feux vils pour témoins / Que s'est d'un astre en fête allumé le génie', OC 36.
72. Sartre also refers to this dialectical passage in *What is Literature?*, 233 n. 6.
73. 'The Purposes of Writing', 13.
74. J. Scherer, *Le 'Livre' de Mallarmé. Premières recherches sur les documents inédits* (Paris: Gallimard, 1957).
75. *Archive du Coup de dés*, 376.
76. *Mallarmé: Du sens des formes au sens des formalités*, 278.
77. J.-P. Sartre, *The Family Idiot: Gustave Flaubert, 1821–1857, Volume Three* (Chicago: University of Chicago Press, 1989), 475.
78. *The Family Idiot: Gustave Flaubert, 1821–1857, Volume Three*, 235.
79. *The Family Idiot: Gustave Flaubert, 1821–1857, Volume Three*, 235.
80. Arguably, Sartre describes Mallarmé's poetic dialectic with such enthusiasm – and, concomitantly, with such a striking lack of critical distance, which contrasts with his eviscerating overview of postromanticism – because it irresistibly recalls aspects of his ontology in *Being and Nothingness*. For instance, in his account of value, Sartre describes the for-itself's attempts to found itself in similarly tragic terms: 'The being of human reality is suffering because it rises in being as perpetually haunted by a totality which it is without being able to be it, precisely because it could not attain the

in-itself without losing itself as for-itself. Human reality therefore is by nature an unhappy consciousness with no possibility of surpassing its unhappy state', J.-P. Sartre, *Being and Nothingness*, trans. Hazel Barnes (London and New York: Routledge Classics, 2005), 114.
81. 'The Purposes of Writing', 12 (translation modified).
82. 'The Purposes of Writing', 12.
83. 'The Purposes of Writing', 12.
84. 'The Purposes of Writing', 13.
85. J.-P. Sartre, 'A Long, Bitter, Sweet Madness', trans. A. Hartley, *Encounter*, Vol. 22 (June, 1964), 62.
86. 'The Purposes of Writing', 13.

2 Julia Kristeva's Mallarmé: From Fetishism to the Theatre-Book

In this second chapter, we turn to the reading of Mallarmé produced by the chief theoretician of the avant-garde journal *Tel Quel*, Julia Kristeva. As is well known, Kristeva's reading of Mallarmé was produced at a time of great intellectual effervescence in France, which marked the end of Sartre's dominance and the rise of structuralism and poststructuralism. It is during this period that a former collaborator of *Tel Quel*, Jean-Pierre Faye – who in 1968 had gone on to found the journal *Change* – sparked a violent polemic between the two rival journals by penning his article 'Comrade Mallarmé'.[1] In this piece, Faye enlists the poet in the political and theoretical struggle for universal emancipation:

> Mallarmé is not who we think he is. He is with us – with the largest 'us', the 'us' that is working towards the complete liberation of the human powers of invention, and towards the creation of a society with a new language, a language that will weave and articulate this society. For language is not an ornament: it is the armature that links the gestures of work with those of play. And Mallarmé represents nothing less than the moment of the most extreme audacity in the exploration of this linguistic power – of the power that the most recent research in the linguistic sciences calls its 'true creativity'.[2]

For the intellectual period we are about to study, Faye's passage is strikingly representative – so representative, in fact, that it can be surprising to discover it was part of a polemic meant to articulate the differences between two avant-garde journals.[3] By linking linguistic creativity to political emancipation, and then by suggesting that, up to this point, Mallarmé had been misunderstood and that only the 'the most recent research in the linguistic sciences' could restore him to his proper place in the language-centred struggle for a 'new society', Faye reproduces some of the key tropes of the political appropriations of Mallarmé in this period.

Numerous readings of Mallarmé were offered within the ranks of the Telquellians and their collaborators, from essays by Philippe Sollers[4] to lengthy studies by Jacques Derrida,[5] to Kristeva's own engagement with the poet throughout her 1969 work *Sèméiôtiké: Recherches pour une sémanalyse*[6] and her 1971 essay 'Sémanalyse et production de sens, quelques problèmes de sémiotique littéraire à propos d'un texte de Mallarmé: *Un coup de dés*'.[7] Our focus, however, will be exclusively on Kristeva's monumental 1974 work *Revolution in Poetic Language*, whose full French title is *La révolution du langage poétique: L'avant-garde à la fin du XIXème siècle: Lautréamont et Mallarmé*.[8] This work secured Kristeva's fame in both France and the Anglophone academic world. Despite this, only a third of *Revolution in Poetic Language* has ever been translated into English. Most importantly for our purposes, the remaining 400 or so pages include Kristeva's long and detailed reading of key texts by Mallarmé, as well as her monumental study of late nineteenth-century France. Consequently, and despite Kristeva's fame, there exists no sustained analysis of her reading of Mallarmé in either English or French.[9] This chapter will make up for this lack. Slightly rearranging Kristeva's order of presentation in *Revolution in Poetic Language*, we will start by sketching her account of late nineteenth-century France. Then we will follow her as she analyses Mallarmé's texts 'Prose (pour des Esseintes)' and *Un coup de dés*. Finally, we will return to the socio-historical level of Kristeva's analysis and determine how she understands the relation between Mallarmé's writings and their time.

Revolution in Poetic Language could well be considered the most sophisticated expression of the journal *Tel Quel*'s innovative literary theory. It both integrates and, on its own terms, surpasses the work of all other Telquellians, including Kristeva's own early work. Yet it is unmistakeably inscribed in *Tel Quel*'s collective avant-garde project.[10] As Philippe Sollers announced in 1968 in the pages of *Les Lettres Françaises*: 'it is necessary to go back before the effects that can be situated in the 1920s (Surrealism, Formalism, the extension of structural linguistics) in order to correctly situate a more radical reserve inscribed at the end of the last century (Lautréamont, Mallarmé, Marx, Freud).'[11] The Telquellians believed, in other words, that there was a latent power of social transformation contained in certain literary artefacts of the past, notably Mallarmé's. With the correct theoretical tools, this power could be actualised in the present by way of new literary creations that overcame the limitations of the old. Doubtless because it was originally written as her 1973 Doctorat d'État and was thus subject to the stringent requirements of the French university system, Kristeva's

Revolution in Poetic Language constitutes the most exhaustive attempt by any of the Telquellians to make good on their promise of demonstrating literature's virtual political power. For Kristeva, Mallarmé will be an ambivalent figure, just as he was for Sartre. On the one hand, Kristeva will set out to demonstrate the virtual power of political change at work in his writings. On the other hand, however, in order to preserve the promise of the 'revolution in poetic language' – a 'revolution' that demonstrably has not yet come about – Kristeva will have to explain why Mallarmé failed to actualise his writing's transformative potential. Mallarmé will thus be at once the inaugurator of a politically transformative linguistic praxis and a traitor to its true power. Our aim in this chapter will be to track the stages of Kristeva's argument and evaluate her attempt to both comprehend and surpass 'comrade Mallarmé'.

*

We begin with Kristeva's analysis of the nineteenth century in France, an analysis that differs in intriguing ways from Sartre's. Unlike Sartre, who focused on the Second Empire and the rallying of the ruling bourgeoisie to Napoleon III – a rallying reflected in the work of the most significant postromantic poets, Mallarmé included – Kristeva's main concern is with the Third Republic and the way its rolling economic crises and political scandals undermined the French state's pretensions to represent the unity of the French people. Consequently, Kristeva does not read Mallarmé as a nihilist. Instead, her attention is drawn to the way the corrosive negativity of his writings both emerged from, and participated in, the general weakening of symbolic efficacy during the Third Republic. In what follows, we will start at the macrocosmic level, studying the general tendencies of French society in the nineteenth century as Kristeva sees them, before turning to the microcosmic level and identifying the traces of these tendencies in Mallarmé's writings. Then, we will return to the level of large-scale historical phenomena and follow Kristeva as she asks how, if Mallarmé's writings so ingeniously disarticulated the unities of the symbolic order, they have yet to have any measurable 'impact' (RLP 620) on the social whole, as *Tel Quel*'s literary avant-gardism promises they will.

At the opening of the section entitled 'Maintenance and Limitation of Power and Class Consciousness', the second section of the final chapter 'The State and Mystery', Kristeva claims that the series of 'revolutionary leaps' (RLP 375) running from the French Revolution to the events of 1848 had ultimately contributed to the ramification of state power. While universal suffrage had been briefly won in the aftermath of the 1848 revolution, the French people's emancipatory demand for equality, represented in the goal of universal suffrage, had resulted in 'the centralisation of the state apparatus' – a process 'represented and made explicit by the accession to power, following a *coup d'état*, of a mini-dictator' (RLP 375). But even after the fall of this 'mini-dictator' in 1870 and the installation of the Third Republic, Kristeva claims that the state of the Third Republic was primarily geared towards establishing and maintaining a legal and repressive framework for the functioning of the market, not instituting an egalitarian society. As Kristeva puts it, 'by an apparently paradoxical logic, the revolutionary process of the bourgeoisie leading the people led only to an *Aufhebung* of the institutions of the Ancien Régime' (RLP 375). The revolution's 'most sacred wish' – equality as incarnate in universal suffrage – 'was caught from the very beginning' in the gears of state power. From this point on, Kristeva explains, 'the social organism could do nothing but follow the implacable logic of the institution [of the state] by giving itself a Chief, Hierarchies, Apparatuses of oppression, and so on'. Kristeva continues: 'the bourgeois institutions that follow after 1870–1871 with MacMahon and the Third Republic do nothing more than take up the state apparatus and its juridical and ideological ramifications, with the goal of controlling the growth of commodities' (RLP 376).

In short, the bourgeoisie had become a 'structuring' and not a 'revolutionary' class (RLP 376), and its state apparatus was essentially geared towards the growth of the productive forces. Bourgeois society teemed with technocrats at the same time as it was subject to the anarchy of the market. Most significant for Kristeva, however, was the fact that each social ensemble was now at once isolated from every other ensemble and engaged in a lateral competitive struggle with them. In stark contrast with the communitarian dreams of the nineteenth century – promulgated, for instance, by Hugo – the unity of these social ensembles was 'logically impossible' (RLP 379). That said, even if the French state's primary function was to ensure the existence of a shared framework for the functioning of the market – even if, in other words, it essentially facilitated its citizens' interminable struggle against one another – the French state simultaneously claimed to represent the community's civic, if not spiritual, unity. For Kristeva, an explosive contradiction thus came into existence between the centrifugal forces tearing capitalist society apart and the demand for unity the state fraudulently claimed to respond to. In her view, this contradiction resulted in a generalised devalorisation of symbolic power. A form of social unity was necessary – both economically and spiritually – yet no citizen of the Third Republic could take seriously the French state's claim to be 'the emanation of the common will' (RLP 382). They were subject to its brute force, but they could not fail to see its spiritual emptiness.

As we will see, this collective state of fetishistic disavowal will be the chief condition of possibility for Mallarmé's assault on the symbolic law. For Kristeva, the Third Republic marks an unprecedented moment in European modernity during which there occurred a displacement of the French Revolution's disruptive force from the level of class structure to the level of language. As she will argue extensively, Mallarmé's writings, along with those of Lautréamont, her other main object of study in *Revolution in Poetic Language*, were 'repercussion[s] of the negativity that the French Revolution had unleashed at different levels of the social edifice' (RLP 362). But in contrast to the explicit aims of the revolutionaries, Mallarmé and Lautréamont's writings 'channelled' this negativity into language itself and its ideological outgrowths – sites that the Revolution's negativity had 'brushed up against but bypassed, in order to focus its attack solely on socio-political institutions' (RLP 362). Just as the state's coercive force became obvious to the citizens of the Third Republic at the same time as its pretentions to transcendence were undermined, so too, Kristeva argues, did language – 'the final guarantee of sociality' (RLP 434) – come to be seen as a force that was at once effective, indeed all-encompassing, yet lacking any ultimate guarantee. Language's metaphysical pretensions to truth and substantiality were being steadily corroded.

But how did this very broad historical tendency play out in Mallarmé's poetry? By what specifically literary mediations was the French Republic's crisis of symbolic efficacy 'channelled' into his poetry's form and content? Having very briefly given the context of Kristeva's large-scale analysis, we will now examine her complex account of the 'crisis of verse' in late nineteenth-century French poetry – a crisis that mirrored the social crisis of Third Republic France. We will then turn to her reading of Mallarmé's 'Prose' and *Un coup de dés*.

*

Kristeva offers her most extensive account of Mallarmé's writings in the middle chapter of *Revolution in Poetic Language*, titled 'The Semiotic Apparatus of the Text'. Across the first two sub-sections of this chapter, 'Phonic and Semantic Rhythms' and 'Syntax and Composition', Kristeva studies, respectively, Mallarmé's disarticulation of the rule-governed unities of 'communicative language' in such representative texts as 'Prose (pour des Esseintes)', and his transgression of the rules of syntax, as codified by Chomsky's generative grammar, in *Un coup de dés*. These two sub-sections could be considered an extended meditation on Mallarmé's famous prose piece 'Crisis of Verse', which Kristeva refers to on a number of occasions. Indeed, one of the referents of the phrase 'the revolution in poetic language' is nothing less than the 'crisis of verse' that shook French poetry in the late nineteenth century and saw the alexandrine's prominence undermined by the invention of 'free verse'. What specific forms did this 'revolution' take, and what role did Mallarmé play in it?

Kristeva begins 'Phonic and Semantic Rhythms' with some remarks on the singularity of the French language. As she explains, in their attempt to transcend classical versification before, during and in the wake of the 'crisis of verse', French poets had to confront a peculiar feature of their national language: namely, that in French each syllable is pronounced with the same intensity. Consequently, if French poets were to 'escape the musical regularity of syllabism' (RLP 211), as Kristeva puts it, they could not rely upon a mechanism like the 'variable syllabic accent' (RLP 210) present in languages like English, German or Russian. Whereas Russian poets like Mayakovski were able to reprise the alliterative tonic versification of the Russian *dol'niki*, thus drawing on both stressed syllables and alliteration in their attempt to create innovative rhythmic structures, French poets lacked any similar resources. If they were to bring out a rhythm running transversally to the standard divisions of word, syllable and traditional meter, then only one path was left open to them:

> There remained ... the resources of alliteration: in the absence of a tonic *accent*, a certain *timbre* persisted: that is, the constitution of a phonic network of repeated elements that carried the particularities proper to their articulatory base and, by extension, to the drives that subtended them. (RLP 211 – Kristeva's emphasis)

We will soon explore the link between phonemes, their articulatory base, and the drives, as Kristeva understands it. Her argument here is that French poets, by a necessity inscribed in the pronunciation of their language, privileged their language's potential for alliteration in order to develop new rhythmic structures following the 'crisis of verse'. Defining these new rhythmic structures will be Kristeva's chief theoretical task in 'The Semiotic Apparatus of the Text'. But first she makes two points regarding the ideological consequences of the importance accorded to alliteration in French avant-garde poetry. Firstly, even if the use, as in Mayakovski's poetry, of stressed syllables in combination with alliteration tended to give certain phonemes a relative autonomy from the word as a component of 'communicative language', this technique still privileged the word as the fundamental unit of language (RLP 211). The one-many relation of 'communicative language' was thus maintained, along with the social system it ramified. The extensive use of alliteration in French poetry, by contrast, had the potential to take the phoneme's autonomy from the word even further: crossing the 'lexical frontiers' (RLP 212) of the French language, phonemes caught in an alliterative network tended to disarticulate the unity of the language and even to return it to the pre-social body; a body Kristeva understands to be the site of 'unconscious drive processes' (RLP 212). In other words, the new French poetry unwittingly unleashed a force of negativity that was more radical than the negativity present in any other modern poetry, since its use of alliteration breached the limits of the word, seemingly the most stable component of communication.

Kristeva's second point also concerns the word as a unit of language. If, she claims, the word was linked to communication, and if communication, in the context of traditional 'popular songs and epics' (RLP 211) written using alliterative tonic forms of versification, was linked to the identity and integrity of a community, whether national or other, then the alliterative 'phonic network' of French avant-garde poetry was necessarily an anti- or trans-national phenomenon. Kristeva explains:

> What appeared as a shortcoming (the monotony of the French syllabic accent) proved to be a means by which the poetic experience was saved from the lure of identifying with the national language as a system of communication ... This particularity contributed to the French avant-garde directly and explicitly exploring an unconscious, drive-based, trans-linguistic rhythm inscribed in the national language but aiming through it at *another scene*. (RLP 212 – Kristeva's emphasis)

Mallarmé was one such explorer of this new linguistic continent. As we will soon see, his poem 'Prose (pour des Esseintes)' takes the ontological – and, by definition, political – potential of alliteration in French to the extreme.

Let us recapitulate Kristeva's argument so far. In a general climate characterised by the corrosion of symbolic power, innovative French poetry, by following its own specific paths – namely, privileging alliteration – found itself producing a poetry whose rhythms and distinctive features ran counter to the dominant logic of the national language. Or, seen from another perspective, two phenomena occurring concurrently came to mutually reinforce one another: on the one hand, the French state's pretentions to represent the nation's unity were being undermined, while on the other hand French poetry was corroding the unity of the French language. As Mallarmé writes in 'Crisis of Verse', French poets had begun to create 'entirely new' words that were 'foreign to the language' (D 211). The integrity of the symbolic was under assault on two fronts at once: at the level of social power, and at the level of language.

Mallarmé's 'Crisis of Verse' serves Kristeva as a general introduction to the 'radical change' (RLP 212) that occurred in French letters at the end of the nineteenth century. Generally speaking, for Mallarmé, as Kristeva reads him, this crisis involved the 'division of meaning, of the proposition, and of the word' and the consequent 'loss of their identity' (RLP 212). Language was no longer made up of signifiers solidly linked to signifieds: it was dispersed, multiple and split, with no stopping point to this process of division. However, the integrity and intelligibility of the French language was not entirely lost. Rather, as we have already mentioned, for Kristeva the real achievement of poets like Mallarmé was to create a new language out of the ruins of the old, a language whose 'rhythm' was distinct from the national cadence. Thus, the first, negative moment of the 'crisis of verse' was transcended by a positive moment in which the newly divided segments of language were put back together in order to produce 'a rhythm, a music, a melody' (RLP 212) distinct from the 'rhythm' previously imposed upon them by the alexandrine. Kristeva will find an excellent example of such an innovative 'rhythm' in Mallarmé's 'Prose'.

Before reading 'Prose', Kristeva sets out to define this new 'rhythm' and distinguish it from the metrical patterns of old. Beginning with the well-established distinction between grammatical constraints, on the one hand, and 'rhythmical constraints', on the other – 'constraints', she explains, which have typically been 'identified with traditional meter and versification' (RLP 214) – Kristeva argues that this distinction is inadequate for two reasons: firstly, it applies well beyond the sphere of poetry; and secondly, the 'rhythmical constraints' imposed by traditional verse are only a subset of those that are actually operative in language. But what are these other 'rhythmical constraints', and how do they function in language? To explain, while Kristeva accepts the existence of a phonemic code structuring a given language, she refuses to accord this code any absolute autonomy, 'as structural linguistics would do' (RLP 215). Instead, while the phonemic code constitutes one structuring principle for a language, the 'distinctive traits' (RLP 222) it isolates – phonemes themselves – possess properties that, while effective, are elided when we consider only the significant differences that constitute them *as* phonemes. These properties, Kristeva explains, are of the order of phonemes' timbre. For Kristeva, timbre designates 'phonic differences' between phonemes that are 'dependent on the articulatory basis that produces them' (RLP 225). As we will see in her reading of 'Prose', these 'phonic differences' include differences between aggressive or destructive sounds, on the one hand, and sounds that are softer and thus connote unification or incorporation, on the other (RLP 225). They also include differences between sounds that build tension and those that release it (RLP 242–3). For Kristeva, these sonic properties are irreducible in language, even if different discourses actualise them to varying degrees. Finally, these distinct timbres work together to produce a 'semiotic rhythm' that runs transversally to the 'rhythm' produced by meter. On a first approach, then, when understood as a 'property immanent to the functioning of language' (RLP 215) and not only to traditionally structured verse, Kristeva's concept of 'rhythm', which she forges in order to account for Mallarmé's renewal of the French language, names the fluctuating intensities of language – a fluctuation brought about by the distinct articulatory properties of certain sounds.

This, however, is only part of Kristeva's definition of 'rhythm'. As we recall, the full title of this first section of 'The Semiotic Apparatus of the Text' is 'Phonic *and* Semantic Rhythms'. Thus, as Kristeva reminds us, 'each phoneme is the bearer of semes' since each inevitably belongs to 'morphemes or lexemes' (RLP 222). The phonemic code is thus in solidarity with the morphophonemic code, and both form part of a 'normative use of language' (RLP 213). However, with the constitution in Mallarmé's poetry of an alliterative or other sound-based network running transversally to the symbolic, the semes that phonemes belong to are connected to other semes with which they normally have no relation. Kristeva explains:

> each phoneme is the bearer of semes, such that the morpheme or the lexeme to which it belongs finds itself dislocated, and the phoneme that is thus semanticised tends to constitute a *semantic constellation* in which all of the lexemes comprising this phoneme will participate. (RLP 222 – Kristeva's emphasis)

What this produces, Kristeva argues, is '*a highly ambivalent* if not *polymorphous semantics*' (RLP 222 – Kristeva's emphasis). Thus, 'rhythm' not only involves the fluctuating intensities of a sound-drama – a drama that might otherwise go unheard in 'communicational language'; it also expands the possible set of meanings individual morphemes or lexemes are typically accorded. Given that the linguistic units making up the moments of a poem's 'rhythm' are neither fully phonemic nor phonetic nor semantic in any simple sense, Kristeva has to innovate conceptually in order to name them: her chosen term, which she first forged in *Sèméiôtiké*, is 'signifying differential'. Summarising this section on 'rhythm', she writes:

> Signifying differentials are therefore *more than phonemes*. In addition to the distinctive value of phonemes in the system of language, they bring

with them phonetic particularities that have no distinctive value but which, following their articulatory base, suppose different drive investments. On this basis, they articulate a network of differences which, even if it has no immediate semantic value, comes to acquire one through *displacement* and *condensation*. Signifying differentials therefore condense phonetic values and phonological values and in so doing join the *semiotic chora* to language. Thus, signifying differentials open a given pheno-text onto the code of language as infinity: that is, onto the infinite transgrammatical or agrammatical possibilities of morphosyntactical transformations invested by the drives. (RLP 223 – Kristeva's emphasis)

The 'infinity' in question here is not a positive infinity, even if Kristeva's metaphor of how the 'pheno-text' – the explicit content of a text – opens onto 'the code of language as infinity' suggests the revelation of an existing yet hitherto dissimulated reality. Instead, 'infinity' here names the negation of the finite; specifically, of the finite, determinate limits of the phonemic, morphophonemic or semantic codes of a given language. The modern 'text' thus stages a moment where the discrete identities in a language are dissolved, or momentarily fade; a moment Kristeva calls 'a zero time, during which the distinctive linguistic value of the phoneme is suspended [and] the meaning of a given morpheme is eclipsed' (RLP 224). On her reading, Mallarmé repeatedly refers to this critical moment: 'The numerous "whites" or "voids" or "nothings" in Mallarmé indicate this summit which evokes, moreover, a heavy sleep, one without dreams, sounds, or only mutilated sounds' (RLP 224).

We now have to clarify the link between this 'rhythm' constituted by 'signifying differentials', the drives and the body. Firstly, it is essential to point out that Kristeva understands the body as being, from the very beginning of its existence, the site at which the 'so-called primary processes, which displace and condense both energies and their inscription' (RPL 25, 23), operate. Kristeva explains:

> Discrete quantities of energy move through the body of the subject who is not yet constituted as such and, in the course of his development, they are arranged according to the various constraints imposed on this body ... by family and social structures. In this way the drives, which are 'energy' charges as well as 'psychical' marks, articulate what we call a *chora*. (RPL 25, 23)

What is most important for us to note here is that by drawing on Freud's early energetic models Kristeva can closely associate – if not equate – the primary processes with the drives. Moreover, she situates both in the individual's body, and explains that they are destined to be written over by both the secondary processes – Kristeva's 'symbolic' – and by 'natural or socio-historical constraints' (RPL 27), which dictate the drives' functioning, even if these limitations can never entirely eradicate them.

Returning to Kristeva's analysis of late nineteenth-century French poetry, the 'semiotic network' of 'signifying differentials' present in this poetry seems most analogous to the operation of Freud's primary processes, since both imply a power that runs transversally to standard semantic and syntactical rules. The drives, on the other hand, are linked more closely to the properties sounds possess by virtue of their 'articulatory base'. It is crucial to distinguish these two aspects of Kristeva's concept of the 'semiotic', which seems to cover both of these Freudian concepts. Speaking of the child's first attempts at making meaningful sounds, Kristeva writes that 'by taking into the account the dichotomy of drives' – that is, the death and life drives – 'we can easily explain the constitution of phonological oppositions from the very first morphemes pronounced by the child'. Kristeva then offers a lengthy taxonomy of sounds and the drives they are correlated with:

> /m/ labial, nasal, liquid, and /p/ labial, explosive, translate through articulatory means suction and explosion, the Freudian 'da' and 'fort', incorporating orality and destructive anality. We can note the oral drive of the liquids (l'), (r'), (m) and of the close back vowels; the anal drive of open back vowels; the urethral drive of voiceless constrictives (f), (s), (ʃ) and also the tendency towards phallicisation of this drive in the voiced constrictives (v), (z), (ʒ); the aggressive, rejection drive of the voiceless explosives (p), (t), (k) or the voiced explosives (b), (d), (g); and the erectile-phallic drive of the apical (r). (RLP 225)

This taxonomy should again bring into focus the distinction between the primary processes and the drives. While at a very abstract level the primary processes – and, by analogy, the 'semiotic network' of 'signifying differentials' – name the fact of a determinate, finite limit being breached, such as the limits of the individuated elements of a phonemic code, the drives are in no way as anarchic. First of all, there are strictly two of them: the death and life drives. As far as Kristeva is concerned, these drives denote, respectively, a tendency towards destruction and a tendency towards unification, with the former always prevailing over the latter: 'In this way', she writes, 'the term "drive" denotes waves of attack against stases' (RPL 28, 27). Thus, while Kristeva can justify the link between the primary processes and the drives by way of their shared – yet highly abstract – propensity for crossing the limits of finite identities, the drives, in contrast to the kaleidoscope-like productions of the primary processes, are ultimately reducible to a binary opposition: destruction and construction. Following Ivan Fonagy, Kristeva then maps the drives onto the articulatory properties of certain sounds: their binary logic is thus reprised at the level of language's physiological production. Certain sounds, by virtue of the mouth movements they involve, reflect physiologically a positive, constructive logic, while others reflect a destructive logic. A third group – those Fonagy and Kristeva group under the heading of the 'urethral drive' – constitutes a kind of synthesis of construction and destruction, of incorporation and expulsion, since their physiological production seems to involve a steady release of tension (RLP 242).

In summary, the relation of 'rhythm' to the drives and the body can be stated as follows: on the basis of the articulatory properties of certain sounds, a poem can convey a dynamic – a rhythm – involving three combinatorial possibilities arranged in any order: construction, destruction, or their synthesis. It is crucial to underscore this finite number of possibilities: while the phonic-semantic 'rhythm' discussed above offers an indefinite number of possibilities, this second drive-based 'rhythm' exclusively conveys either a conflict between life and death drives, or the momentary attenuation of this conflict. There are therefore *two* kinds of rhythms hidden beneath Kristeva's term 'semiotic rhythm'.

If we have spent so much time clarifying the stakes of Kristeva's complex and syncretic theory, it is not only because it has rarely been scrutinised closely, but also because her reading of Mallarmé is unintelligible without understanding it well. Most significantly, we have underscored the fact that her concept of a 'semiotic rhythm' covers over *two* kinds of rhythm: one linked by analogy to Freud's primary processes, the other to the life and death drives. The overall significance of Kristeva's theoretical invention still stands, however: at a moment of crisis for the symbolic order in France, poets like Mallarmé set about dissolving the constitutive unities of the French language, from phonemes, to words, to metrical structures like the alexandrine. Yet they also reorganised them according to a new 'rhythm': an 'air or song beneath the text' (D 236 – translation modified), as Mallarmé puts it in 'The Mystery in Letters'. We will now see the operation of this rhythm in Kristeva's reading of 'Prose'.

*

Following her binary model of the drive-bases of certain sounds, Kristeva begins by dividing the sounds of the poem's first stanza into two series. The first series includes voiced or voiceless occlusive labials coupled with the liquid /R/: namely, /pR/, /Rb/, /tR/, /Rd/, /vR/, /f'R/, a series to which is added the stand-alone dental occlusives /t/ and /d/, as well as the voiced velar occlusive /g/, coupled as it also is with /R/. We can see the distribution of these sounds below:

Hyperbole ! de ma mémoire
Triomphalement ne sais-tu
Te lever, aujourd'hui grimoire
Dans un livre de fer vêtu :[12]

For Kristeva, this first series articulates an 'aggressive phallic drive' as well as an 'anal' drive, the latter being produced by the /gR/ sound alone. In other words, this series is on the side of 'explosion' or 'destructive anality' (RLP 225) – of the death drive. It contrasts with a second series constituted by the labial /m/, which can be found in the following places:

Hyperbole ! de ma mémoire
Triomphalement ne sais-tu
Te lever, aujourd'hui grimoire
Dans un livre de fer vêtu :

In opposition to the first series, the series made up of the /m/ sound invokes, in Kristeva's words, 'the incorporating oral drive (suction)' (RLP 242) and thus stands for the life drive in its synthetic, constructive function. In the context of this first stanza from 'Prose', however, it will connote more precisely a fusion with the mother (RLP 246). We will see the significance of this soon.

Thus, at the purely sonic level, the first stanza articulates a tension between the two drives. Kristeva also locates this tension at the level of the vowels. She writes:

The series of vowels begins with a glottal stop /i/, then traverses the entire scale of closed back vowels – /i/, /e/ – before moving to the front open vowel /wa/ from 'mémoire' and 'grimoire', and then, after this moment of relaxation, returns once again to the back – /e/, /i/, /y/ – thus sketching a movement of tension (sublimation). (RLP 242)

Having given the broad outline of the stanza's first sound-based drama, Kristeva turns to its semantics. Beginning with 'Hyperbole', she treats this word not as if it were constituted by morphemes, lexemes or phonemes but rather as if it were made up of signifying differentials – linguistic units that irremediably blur the boundaries between the three aforementioned categories. Thus, the second syllable 'per' – which, all by itself, is neither morpheme nor lexeme nor phoneme – is nevertheless homophonous with the word 'père' (father), which irresistibly stands for a figure of symbolic authority. This initial semanticisation of the signifying differential 'per' is reinforced by the way it rhymes with 'fer' ('iron'), from the fourth verse – a word that lends 'père' the qualities of intransigence and solidity – but also by its rhyme with the word 'ère' ('era') from the syntagm 'l'ère d'autorité' ('era of authority'), found in the fourth stanza. The third syllable, 'bol' – again neither morpheme, lexeme nor phoneme – stands, on Kristeva's reading, for the 'seme of symbolic negation' (RLP 243). Her justification for this is that it forms part of a word frequently used by Mallarmé: namely, 'abolir', 'to abolish', and its cognates (RLP 243). Turning to the first word of the second verse, 'Triomphalement', Kristeva proceeds in a similar fashion to her analysis of 'Hyperbole'. Beginning with the signifying differential 'Tr', this dental sound 'accentuates the aggressivity contained already in the /pR/ of the title' (RLP 244) of the poem. At the level of meaning, just as the differential 'bol' was semanticised by virtue of its belonging to certain significant lexemes, 'Tr' is 'overdetermined', Kristeva writes, 'by its occurrences in lexemes and contexts denoting rupture and birth' (RLP 244). The second syllable of 'Triomphalement', namely 'phal', reprises the paternal or phallic signification of the signifying differential 'per' from 'Hyperbole'.

Kristeva offers a similar analysis of other differentials found in this first stanza. Furthermore, on the basis of a study of the two manuscript versions of 'Prose' she shows convincingly that Mallarmé rewrote certain verses in order to make them phonetically homogeneous or resonant with the others (RLP 244). This lends weight to the primacy she accords the phonic level of the poem. Finally, bringing the semiotic and semantic dimensions of the text together, Kristeva presents her provisional conclusions:

> The extremely elliptical syntactical sequence of this first stanza – which, in this sense, is like the others – with the omission of the verb being marked here by the exclamation and the comma, produces a signification that is completed by the apparatus of signifying differentials we have just remarked upon. Let us be clear first of all that the apparatus thus constructed is far from being exhaustive (the applications, theoretically, are infinite). An irruption of the drives, a negativity, destroys the stases and the finitudes represented by the symbolic code of language. Grammar and memory, authoritarian and paternal, are broken such that, after returning from a maternal fusion, there arises a new signifying possibility. Fictional, exaggerated, disproportionate in so far as it does not respect limits, hyperbolic and triumphal – such is the rebirth the subject will undertake in the text. (RLP 245–6)

A number of elements of the above passage call for commentary. Firstly, Kristeva had announced at the beginning of 'The Semiotic Apparatus of the Text' that Mallarmé 'exclusively uses the rhythmical constraints of language – its semiotic articulations which invest its phonemic system – as his fundamental constraints' (RLP 213). On her reading, this claim is borne out by an analysis of this first stanza. While Kristeva obviously recognises that 'Prose' is a quite traditionally structured octosyllabic sonnet of fourteen quatrains with cross-rhymes, she claims that given its syntactical complexities – or at least those on display in the first stanza, the other stanzas being relatively simple – the only way to restore a unified sense to the poem is by way of its 'semiotic apparatus'. Secondly, Kristeva again links the semiotic dimensions of language to the 'infinite'. Here, the term again very clearly means the absence of a limit, not a positive infinity. Thirdly, while she has given a few examples of how the linguistic units in 'Prose' cross the limits of their symbolic identity, they nevertheless do so in an orderly manner: that is, they work towards conveying a unified thematic meaning, which is none other than the drama of an 'irruption of the drives' and a consequent 'renewal' of language and its subject. 'Prose' is a performative text: it does what it says. Kristeva can therefore not only apply her methodology to it; she can see the theoretical foundations of her methodology reflected in its driving theme.

After her close reading of the first stanza, Kristeva comments on each of the following thirteen stanzas individually and in a similar way. Without following all of the details of her reading, we can remark upon a few of its key features. Just as we predicted, the binary drive model Kristeva works with means that there are only three combinatorial possibilities for the poem's sounds: they either connote an aggressive movement of destruction, a tendency towards unity, or some degree of balance between these two contradictory poles. Thus, while Kristeva describes with perfect precision the phonetic patterns in each of the stanzas, this diverse sonic material is always eventually organised in terms of this model. For instance, moving from the first to the second stanza, Kristeva notes how the /b/ and /p/ sounds from the first stanza are less frequent, as well as how the /R/ sound, which is this time surrounded by more vowels or liquid consonants, is consequently 'less aggressive than in the first stanza' (RLP 246). In a similar vein, the high number of /s/ sounds in this second stanza also leads to a diminution of the destructive phonetic force of the first, representing as the /s/ sound does an instance of the 'urethral drive', a release of tension. Kristeva then links these phonetic changes to the explicit content of the stanza: 'the *aggressivity* which dominated the first stanza is *unified* in the form of a *tension*, represented by the appearance of an *actant* – "je", "ma", etc.' (RLP 246 – Kristeva's emphasis). A balance is therefore struck between life and death drives – a balance that characterises the libidinal economy of a subject, who emerges as if from the synthesis of these forces. In the third stanza, its specific sounds move us away from a state of tension or balance and towards the incorporating, unifying pole of the drives: its vowels, for instance, show a tendency towards 'rounding, nasalisation and closure', all of which are 'indices of a euphoric oralisation, the pleasure of suction' (RLP 247). Again, the stanza's phonetic properties find a correlate at the level of meaning: the poet's 'sister' appears, a figure Kristeva identifies as 'a sublimated mother' (RLP 252). There is thus a rudimentary dialectical progression at work at both the symbolic and semiotic levels of the first three stanzas: 'a return to the mother' is occurring following 'the aggressivity and the phallicism of the first two stanzas, which set off the text's signifying process' (RLP 247). In other words, with the breakdown of the symbolic, the subject returns to its pre-Oedipal state – to its fusion with the mother and its traversal by the semiotic – and will consequently draw on this more anarchic dynamic to revitalise the symbolic itself.

In her reading of the remaining stanzas, Kristeva consistently moves back and forth between sound and sense. For instance, with the labial and dental occlusives of the fourth stanza, which echo those of the first, a destructive aggressivity returns at the sonic level, underscoring the seme of 'division' that dominates the stanza. Similarly, the /k/ sound that opens the fifth stanza, along with the glottal stop that begins its second verse, 'Ils savent ...', both 'accentuate rejection, the destructive drive' (RLP 248) and thus stage sonically the drama of dispersion being played out in the stanza's reference to the 'cent iris', the 'hundred irises'. With the sixth stanza, this centrifugal movement is reversed: with the help of the labio-dental fricatives /f/ and /v/, not to mention the palato-alveolar fricatives /ʃ/ and /ʒ/, 'a more harmonious disposition of the drive charge is achieved', Kristeva writes. Simultaneously, we witness 'the appearance of an affirmation ("oui") and of *an* object that can be localised and identified by the gaze . . .: namely, a flower, which takes the place of the dispersed plurality represented by the "sol des cent iris" from the preceding stanza' (RLP 249 – Kristeva's emphasis). The multiple has thus become the one, and a precarious synthesis has been established. Skipping ahead to the final fourteenth stanza, Kristeva notes how the key thematic opposition of the poem – namely, between a psychotic loss of reason and a renewal of reason by way of the subject reimmersing themselves in the semiotic – is marked by the opposition between the words 'sépulcre' and 'glaïeul'. While the first signifies death pure and simple, the second, qualified as it is by the adjectival phrase 'trop grand', certainly refers to something exorbitant and thus beyond reason. And yet, with its phonetic link to 'gloire' – 'glory' – from the eighth stanza, the 'glaïeul' stands, in Kristeva's words, for 'a death that supposes a posthumous glory and symbolic power' (RLP 256). In other words, it represents a resurrection, the subject having victoriously passed through the trial of their linguistic death. Again, this opposition is doubled at the phonetic level: while 'sépulcre' is 'undergirded by an attenuated phallic drive, as well as by rejection', with its voiceless occlusive labial /p/ and the almost choking sound of its final syllable connoting the negativity of death, the final liquid /l/ of 'glaïeul' stands for an 'oral sublimation' (RLP 256). According to Kristeva, the exclamation 'Pulchérie' unifies these two terms both semantically and sonically (RLP 255).

While we have not picked up on all of the details of Kristeva's reading, those we have discussed are exemplary of its general orientation. On the one hand, Mallarmé's poetry explodes the unity of words in a way that shows his participation in the general climate of symbolic crisis during the Third Republic. This negative moment is figured as a return to a pre-symbolic state – to a point in the subject's ontogenesis where the figure of the 'mother' is predominant. The significance of this link between the pre-symbolic, the anarchic rhythms of the 'semiotic', and the mother will become clear when we return to Kristeva's analysis of French society. On the other hand, however, Mallarmé's poetry is also an exercise in renewal: it reorganises the symbolic order of language according to a more supple principle of structuration – one that integrates 'chance into the One' (RLP 288), as Kristeva puts it. As we will see in the final section of this chapter, this synthesis of the symbolic and the semiotic will become a model for both Mallarmé's and Kristeva's ideal form of sociality. First, however, let us turn to Kristeva's reading of Mallarmé's *Un coup de dés*, which takes up the thread of her reflections on the 'crisis of verse' in French poetry.

*

Introducing the theoretical stakes of her reading of *Un coup de dés*, Kristeva makes an important distinction between, on the one hand, the semiotic dimensions of a text – broadly speaking, those that cross the boundaries of the rule-governed units of language, or which articulate a non-linguistic, drive-based dynamic – and on the other its syntactical organisation. In a short section entitled 'Transposition, Displacement, Condensation', Kristeva sheds light on this distinction by highlighting the increased pertinence of the metaphorical or paradigmatic axis of language in the study of the modern 'text'. As we saw with 'Prose', signifying differentials such as 'bol' or 'gl' condense the various meanings their repeated iterations brought with them, along with the articulatory characteristics proper to their phonetic base. This process of 'condensation' – a term Kristeva takes from Freud and which she prefers to 'metaphor', judged to be too 'confusing' due to its origin in 'classical rhetoric' (RLP 233) – is precisely what makes 'Prose' a truly new and radical work. By contrast, despite the elliptical nature of some of its stanzas, the poem's syntax remains relatively traditional. As Kristeva explains, it is not surprising that the novelty of Mallarmé's writings are to be located on the metaphorical – paradigmatic – axis of language and not on its metonymic – syntagmatic – axis:

> the so-called *metonymic* processes of language, operating as they do on the axis of contiguity, favour intra- and trans-phrastic relations (those expressed by connectors, auxiliaries, pronouns and adverbs, relations of presupposition referring to the context), as well as the metalinguistic capacity (the interpretation of one sign by another). (RLP 232 – Kristeva's emphasis)

In other words, while a text like 'Prose' divides up the linguistic continuum in novel ways and invests its signifying differentials with multiple, polymorphous meanings, its metonymic axis maintains a stubborn complicity with logic, and thus with the symbolic law. However, with *Un coup de dés* what we witness is a disintegration of this metonymic axis itself, and thus of the logical and ontological structures that depend upon it.

Kristeva divides the 'syntactical modifications proper to Mallarmé's poetic language' (RLP 269) into two groups, the second of which is divided again into two sub-groups. First, as in 'Prose', Mallarmé subjects his syntactical sequences to multiple operations of inversion, apposition, ellipsis and elision. However, in the case of this first group of syntactical innovations, the subjacent syntactical structure is always able to be reconstituted. In the second group, by contrast, something rather more radical occurs: on the one hand, we witness a plethora of possible interconnections between nominal and verbal syntagms, yet these connections never give rise to a complete syntactical series. Thus, while each individual syntagm or sequence might be grammatical in itself, their 'interconnections' are 'indefinite and plurilateral' (RLP 269), thus making it impossible to constitute finite phrastic sequences. On the other hand, we also confront 'non-recoverable deletions' (RLP 281):[13] that is, sequences that lack certain terms that cannot be re-established. To get a sense of these 'non-recoverable deletions', we can first consider an example of the opposite case, a 'recoverable deletion'. Kristeva gives the example of the suppression of the agent following the transformation of the phrase 'The dice are thrown by X' into 'The dice are thrown', a phrase that is then nominalised to produce the syntagm 'A throw of dice' (RLP 277). While in this case it is easy to 'recover' the deleted linguistic unit, namely the agent X, in the case of a 'non-recoverable deletion' this is impossible: the surrounding linguistic context offers no sure guidance as to what the deleted unit is.

In order to show the presence of 'non-recoverable deletions' in *Un coup de dés*, Kristeva studies the second double-page of the poem, which opens with 'SOIT'. As she explains, the modal category of this verbal form is uncertain. If it were an imperative, then the following word 'que' would make the sequence agrammatical. If, by contrast, 'SOIT' was the first 'soit' in a sentence articulating an either-or structure, namely 'soit ... soit ...', then it would be grammatical; and yet there is no second 'SOIT'. Finally, if 'SOIT' was a subjunctive, then we would be able to find the rest of the sentence that determines the presence of this verbal form; however, it is lacking. In each of these cases, we lack the means by which to determine the meaning of the term. In this sense, the name of the concept 'non-recoverable deletion' is slightly misleading, since no deletion has ever occurred. We are instead witness to a radical lack for which there never existed a prior plenitude.

Kristeva proceeds to give a number of other examples of 'non-recoverable deletions' on this second double-page. The adjective 'étale', for instance, could be a verb linked to 'l'Abîme', but it could also be a substantive in its own right. However, if we treat 'l'Abîme blanchi' as a subject nominal syntagm and 'étale' as a verb, then the object nominal syntagm is lacking. Likewise, the verbal sequence 'plane désespérément' appears to simply lack the preposition 'qui', a preposition that links it to 'inclinaison' to constitute the phrase 'inclinaison qui plane désespérément'. However, given the spatial distance between these nominal and verbal syntagms, the verb 'plane' attains a degree of autonomy from its function as a verb and becomes – possibly – an adjective, or even a noun. Finally, were it connected directly to 'l'Abîme', we could read this opening page as containing two incomplete sequences, 'l'Abîme étale' and 'l'Abîme plane'. Yet for Kristeva the point is that it is strictly impossible to decide what syntactical arrangements are most appropriate. The basal NS-VS structure has been 'weakened' (RLP 275).

As we mentioned above, such 'non-recoverable deletions' are accompanied by 'indefinite' syntactical articulations, which never settle into the form of decidable sequences. For example, the prepositional syntagm 'du fond d'un naufrage' could be attached to the main phrase of the text to make 'Un coup de dés jamais n'abolira le hasard du fond d'un naufrage'. Yet it could also be the beginning of another phrase that would take the word 'étale' from the following page as its verb. As generative grammar shows, natural languages can embed certain syntactical structures within others of the same or different type, without there being any *grammatical* limit to this process: only the constraints of the subject's memory put a stop to this productivity (RLP 280). As Kristeva explains, all that it takes for 'a series B' to be 'embedded in a series A' is for there to be 'some non-empty element at its left and some non-empty element at its right' (RLP 280). This rule is applicable in *Un coup de dés*. Indeed, in one sense it is extended: as the example given above of an 'indefinite' syntactical articulation shows, multiple phrases are possibly at work simultaneously, making it seem as if the linguistic subject of *Un coup de dés* possessed a 'curiously tenacious' (RLP 281) memory. Yet this rule is also broken, as Kristeva explains:

> we can note that the sequences embedded in the main phrase of the text *Un coup de dés* (the phrase-title) are on the one hand incomplete, and on the other hand are *pseudo-embedded*, since it is difficult – or simply impossible – to find any elements to their right or left. (RLP 280 – Kristeva's emphasis)

For this reason, the 'principle of finite embedding does not seem to be pertinent for this signifying practice' (RLP 280). To read *Un coup de dés*, then, is to witness the breakdown of the syntactical structures that govern normative thought and practice: in Kristeva's terms, the phrastic structure of signification is 'infinitized' (RLP 283), its limits, or rules for completion, being repeatedly breached.

After minutely describing the syntactical innovations of the third double-page section of *Un coup de dés*, Kristeva proceeds to a more general description of what she identifies as the text's six main scansions. For her, the key variables differentiating these scansions are the verbal forms taken on each of the text's double-pages. The third double-page, for instance, which we have just examined, is characterised by a large number of indefinite interconnections and non-recoverable deletions. As such, it represents a general 'loosening of syntactical links' (RLP 287). Just as in 'Prose', then, where the sounds of the first two stanzas connoted a movement of destructive aggressivity, the beginning of *Un coup de dés* sets the text's negativity in motion – the first step of its dialectic of renewal. By contrast, a second scansion made up of the following double-page includes far more verbal syntagms. As Kristeva argues, this 'produces an effect of grammaticality and disambiguates the signification': a form of mastery reappears just in time for 'the upsurge of the Master' (RLP 285) in the text. The text's third scansion takes up the next double-page. Here, we witness a return to the nominalisation of verbs that we saw on the third double-page. This time, however, it is doubled at the semantic level by references to 'atemporality' (RLP 285), which reinforce the predominant present tense of the verbs. Next, the fourth scansion, which is constituted by the sixth, seventh and eighth double-pages, also presents a surplus of nominalisations, along with deletions and indefinite syntactical sequences. For Kristeva, the risk of losing the capacity for predication is denoted by the feather which floats about the abyss. Yet the maintenance of certain syntactical rules means that the feather neither 'flees' from the abyss – thus refusing a confrontation with the semiotic's negativity – nor is it dissolved into the 'whirlpool of hilarity and horror' that would be consequent upon the complete destruction of the symbolic. The fifth scansion takes up the ninth and tenth double-pages, and distinguishes itself by the varied nature of the verbal forms it presents: imperfect, conditional and imperfect subjunctives are all in operation. Finally, the sixth scansion, which is constituted solely by the text's last double-page, sees a return to present-tense verbs, which Kristeva interprets as a reinforcement at the level of syntax of the 'message' (RLP 287) of this final scansion: namely that 'thanks to a surplus of negativity, a new apparatus has come into existence – a constellation, the poem'. Kristeva thus concludes: '*Un coup de dés* affirms the possibility of transgressing the thetic (the syntactical) by exceeding it' (RLP 287).

In one sense, then, when read through the lens of Kristeva's theory, both 'Prose' and *Un coup de dés* say and do the same thing. For its part, 'Prose' brings forth 'a new signifying possibility' by way of a 'maternal fusion' (RLP 246) understood as a return to – or a re-actualisation of – semiotic dynamics, in particular those related to sound. Similarly, *Un coup de dés* also produces a 'new signifying possibility', this time one that thoroughly revitalises language's syntactical organisation. For Kristeva, both texts are instantiations of a new linguistic economy: in the place of the linear sentence we find, as in *Un coup de dés*, indefinite and undecidable syntactical constructions, which by virtue of their very incompletion bring into play the metaphorical axis of language – the condensation of semes and drives Kristeva studied most extensively in 'Prose'; in the place of temporal succession we find 'a *multiplicity of instants*' (RLP 289 – Kristeva's emphasis) – disconnected explosions of sense that resist synthesis; and in the place of the subject-predicate structure – or even of truth as a function of judgement – we find 'a plural and uncertain' (RLP 289) reality: a subject who is de-centred and an object that is in flux. The impact of Mallarmé's 'revolution in poetic language' thus resonates across all registers of experience.

In the next section, we return to the macroscopic level of Kristeva's analysis in *Revolution in Poetic Language*. Having seen the repercussions of the crisis of the symbolic in France in the late nineteenth century at the level of Mallarmé's writings, we now need to understand how Kristeva conceives of the political consequences of Mallarmé's textual negativity. This will involve her advancing a three-part argument. Firstly, Kristeva will have to explain why Mallarmé's writings are politically significant: why should we turn to them in order to better think and do politics? Secondly, she will have to present a model of the social world such that a 'revolution in poetic language' becomes both thinkable and possible. Thirdly, she will have to demonstrate why, despite the transformative power of Mallarmé's writings, their political impact has hitherto been negligible.

*

As we know, the state of the Third Republic was the site of an insurmountable contradiction: on the one hand, its chief function was to keep the competitive capitalist market operating, while on the other it had to reflect the spiritual unity of the French people. This contradiction meant that its aspirations to symbolic power were exposed as being fraudulent. For Kristeva, this set in motion a general process of the weakening of the symbolic order, including at the level of language. As we have just seen, Mallarmé's writings offer a powerful example of this process by which the linguistic logic of the social order was coming undone.

However, it must be noted that for Kristeva, the symbolic order is always, in some sense, at risk of disintegrating. The limits to finite linguistic units are always at risk of fading momentarily or of being swept away completely, as we saw happen to the word 'Hyperbole' when it was dissolved into 'signifying differentials' that together articulated an indefinitely plural meaning. For Kristeva, this means that there is a veritable 'infinity' operative in language – an 'infinity' that marks the absolute impossibility of maintaining the integrity of finite linguistic units. As she writes in the opening section to 'The State and Mystery', titled 'The Text Within an Economic and Social Formation', the 'infinity of the process' (RLP 363) operative within language has an impact well beyond the domain of language conceived in a narrow sense. In fact, as Kristeva argues, 'social institutions and ideologies' are themselves 'systems of communication' and are thus 'in solidarity with language' (RLP 364). As she puts this point even more emphatically further on, the 'fabric of language' is 'the ultimate guarantee of subjective and social identity' (RLP 367–8). For this reason, language's propensity for breaching its own limits – its inner 'infinity' – always risks 'dissolving every linguistic and subjective unity', not to mention 'social structurations' including 'the family [and] the State' (RLP 361). Society, for Kristeva, is thus a set of imbricated, homologous structures, all of which are linguistically constituted and thus constantly at risk of being dissolved.

The situation in late nineteenth-century France, therefore, is historically singular, yet it attests to a more general problematic that all human societies have had to confront. Its singularity is a matter of degree, not kind. As Kristeva goes on to argue, all human societies have had to invent ways of dealing with the risk to their unity posed by language. She proposes a concept for those social practices whose function is to localise and control the 'infinity inherent to unity' (RLP 381): she names these practices 'infinite-supports', or 'supports of the infinite' (RLP 380). On her account, these practices include, most emblematically, religious practices but also artistic practices (RLP 380–1). By quarantining language's force of negativity within safe, designated spaces, 'infinite-supports' function to keep society stable. For Kristeva, despite their radical attack on the integrity of the symbolic order, their marginalisation amongst 'privileged social groups' (RLP 383) meant that Mallarmé's texts 'remained infinite-supports' (RLP 381) in the manner of the religions of the past.

This poses a problem for Kristeva. How can Mallarmé's writings constitute a progressive political force if they ultimately function to support power, albeit in the guise of power's exception? At the opening of 'The Text Within an Economic and Social Formation', Kristeva offers an initial, formal answer to this question in a reflection on the logic of 'infinite-supports'. If a qualitative change is to occur in a social system, she argues, it will only be 'when the infinite stops being a *support* that assures the existence of the system and instead contaminates each of its elements' (RLP 381 – Kristeva's emphasis). By a formal analogy, if the corrosive logic of Mallarmé's writings were to 'contaminate' each subject and each social structure – if, in other words, his writings were somehow to become their animating principle – then the fundaments of the social order would be upturned. Of course, this has not yet occurred, and it seems difficult to envisage how it could ever take place. Nevertheless, there is a deep necessity to the way Kristeva conceives of social change here: if her key concepts refer to language, and if they help her map change at the level of language, then the way to secure the pertinence of these concepts beyond language is first to conceive of society on analogy with language. Then, it is simply a matter of conceiving of the extension of a transformative linguistic practice like Mallarmé's to all social ensembles. In short, Mallarmé must be read by all. In the remainder of the final chapter of *Revolution in Poetic Language*, Kristeva will reflect in depth upon the historical limitations to which Mallarmé's writings *qua* a force for political change were subject – and will propose provisional solutions to the problem of how their 'impact' (RLP 620) might finally be extended to the whole of society.

*

One of the first steps Kristeva takes along the way to discerning the political potential of Mallarmé's writings is to provide an account of French politics in the latter half of the nineteenth century. As we will see, her account focuses on the separation of avant-garde artistic circles from progressive parliamentary and trade union forces. Before we examine her account, however, it is necessary to make two points: one theoretical, the other political. Firstly, adding to the analogies she has already drawn between linguistic and social dynamics, Kristeva now conflates the opposition between 'communicative language' and 'poetic language' with the opposition between 'productivism' – which refers to an ideology that submits everything to a means-end rationality – and 'expenditure' – which refers to an act that breaks with this rationality. Mallarmé's writings, in so far as they not only serve no specific end but undermine any logic that would allow us to posit an end, are examples of 'expenditure'. They are therefore just as opposed to 'productivism' as they are to 'communicative language'. This is the first, theoretical point. Turning to politics, in a long discussion of the Marxist revolutionary tradition, Kristeva argues that implicit in the Marxist account of the proletariat as a class whose historical destiny is to dissolve class society is the idea that the proletariat's ideology cannot be an exclusively 'productivist' ideology. Rather, it rather must synthesise 'productivism' and 'expenditure'. Kristeva's reasoning here is as follows: given that the proletariat has no interests to preserve within capitalist society, its interests cannot be defined in terms of an instrumentalist or 'productivist' rationality. Kristeva explains:

> What the Marxist theory of the dialectic envisages by the concept of 'proletarian class consciousness' is not a class consciousness, but the end of class consciousness in so far as class consciousness 'rests exclusively on the evolution of the modern process of production' – an end that is to be brought about by the introduction of negativity into this consciousness, thus changing the production of a totality into the infinity of a process ... The *subject* of what dialectical materialism designates by the term 'class consciousness' is therefore a subject that 'totalises' in a process what remains divided in class societies: *production, expenditure*. Without this second term, represented in bourgeois society by politics and above all by culture, or more precisely by political and cultural contestation and subversion, such a subject is impossible. (RLP 388 – Kristeva's emphasis)

In other words, signifying practices like those of Mallarmé's are essential to the task of transcending capitalism. For Kristeva, however, no hitherto existing political movement has attempted to 'totalise' these two aspects of society. In the French context, Kristeva locates the roots for this historical limitation in the nature of the political forces that emerged during the Third Republic. The main point of her argument here is easy to summarise: the major political forces of Mallarmé's time, both on the left and the right, were 'productivist' (RLP 396) in ideology. Thus, they failed to incorporate the logic of expenditure found in art and literature. To this day, Kristeva suggests, an effective mass politics incorporating the negativity of texts like those of Mallarmé – a politics that would supposedly seek, by way of the 'semiotic apparatuses' present in 'Prose' or *Un coup de dés*, to 'subtract the proletariat from ideological apparatuses and bourgeois values' (RLP 393) – has quite simply not existed. Unlike the progressive, revolutionary mass movements of the twentieth century, it has therefore not been tested. A union of poet and worker remains, in other words, a viable possibility for the future.

As Kristeva argues, under the Third Republic the most powerful forces of the political right and left were invested in the project of conquering state power, with a view to better running the process of production – whether this meant in a more efficient capacity for the capitalists, or in a more egalitarian fashion for all citizens. Focusing on the left, Kristeva recalls that 'the scission between "socialists" and "Marxists" explode[d] at the Saint-Etienne Congress in 1882, and the Jaurès-Millerand tendency, despite [Jules] Guesde, came to orient itself towards a parliamentary politics' (RLP 393). The CGT, for its part, adopted exclusively economic goals and refused any form of social transformation that did not consist in the mere 'perfecting of the bourgeois system of production' (RLP 394). Kristeva does recognise the existence in the late nineteenth century of more radical political currents that will go on to form, at the turn of the century, the Séction Française de l'Internationale Ouvrière. Yet she also admits that these had little to no political efficacy in Mallarmé's time. In short, the political field was saturated by forces fully invested in an ideology of 'productivism' (RLP 396). A politics of expenditure was nowhere to be found.

Were there any significant ideological currents that critiqued this focus on production? In an ironic twist for her resolutely leftist politics, Kristeva locates the first 'radical critique of the society of consumption' (RLP 397) on the right-wing of the political spectrum. Citing authors like George Sand, Hippolyte Taine and Ernest Renan writing in the aftermath of France's defeat in 1870, Kristeva pinpoints their 'hostility with regards to a "bourgeois materialism" that had diminished the nation' (RLP 398) in the lead up to the decisive years 1870–71. And while these authors either simply criticised bourgeois society and its nominally democratic institutions instead of calling for its abolition, or advocated a return to feudalism – positions that are far from Kristeva's preferred politics – their critiques possessed, in her view, a limited and 'retrospective validity' (RLP 398), in particular since they pinpointed the contradictions of consumerism and overproduction. Their marginalisation, however, meant that their opposition to bourgeois society found no effective expression in an organised politics. In short, no viable 'anti-productivist' politics existed in Mallarmé's lifetime.

It is therefore unsurprising, Kristeva concludes, that Mallarmé and his peers went on a 'political diet' (RLP 399). The circles Mallarmé moved in saw the state's power as insubstantial. And yet, given the state's stranglehold on French society and the lack of any viable alternatives to it, they inevitably fell back on an ironic, quietistic position. Mallarmé, for instance, was so detached from the events of his time that he translated every historical happening into an analogy with the act of writing. Kristeva writes:

> Thus, in the midst of the war of 1870–71, and right up to the time of the Commune, Mallarmé seems only to have been preoccupied with his move from Avignon to Paris and with the 'Republican' functionaries capable of helping, such that the only mark of political events in his correspondence is a reference to the death on the frontlines of his friend, Henri Regnault. (RLP 405)

Kristeva then goes on to point out that in his letters Mallarmé equates Regnault's death with the subjective destitution experienced by the writer in their encounter with the 'signifying process'. All historical events, even the most tragic and extreme, were seen through the idiosyncratic prism of Mallarmé's practice as a writer (RLP 406–7): experiences like Regnault's death were of interest to Mallarmé only as an exterior representation of the writer's internal drama of death and possible rebirth – a drama we saw staged in an exemplary form in 'Prose'. In fact, at a more general level, all social phenomena became mere pretexts for Mallarmé's internal experience of the intra-literary dialectic of the semiotic and the symbolic. As Kristeva puts it, Mallarmé's *modus operandi* was to 'move stealthily through historical experiences and use them as so many homes, shelters and houses, with the mask of a comedian who tricks the entire world and laughs at it discretely' (RLP 407). Mallarmé, in other words, was a master ironist. If he had any contact with the political institutions and ideologies of his time, Kristeva concludes, then it was in a wilfully distant form. Moreover, his social engagements were unilaterally subordinated to his intra-literary concerns.

At this stage of Kristeva's argument, Mallarmé's writings seem to be a perfect example of an 'infinite-support'. His writings course with negativity, yet they are such small-scale productions that they cannot hope to disrupt society at large. Instead, they function as this society's safety valve. Moreover, as Kristeva has just intimated, Mallarmé's negativity in fact took the form of irony, meaning that he relied upon the stability of the social order in order to take his aristocratic distance from it.

This is a running theme of Kristeva's reading of Mallarmé's life. As she points out perspicaciously, what distinguished Mallarmé with regards to his most famous contemporaries, Verlaine and Rimbaud, was the relative stability – indeed conservatism – of his familial and working lives. As Kristeva argues, Mallarmé operated within institutions like the family, *fin-de-siècle* salons and literary circles, leaving each of them perfectly intact but in a slightly unsteady state thanks to the subtle irony with which he inhabited them. As evidence for this attitude, Kristeva quotes the following passage from 'Accusation': 'It is important that, in any contest involving the multitudes for interest, amusement, or ease, there will be rare enthusiasts, respectful of the common motive as a way of showing indifference, who instate, through their different tune, a minority' (D 256). Mallarmé respects, indeed requires, the 'common motive', but only as a pretext for demonstrating his 'indifference' towards it. In his work, the symbolic is shot through with holes, stripped of its essentialist pretensions, and rearranged in the form of a 'semiotic apparatus' that brings language's underlying negativity fleetingly to the surface. But all of this took place in the narrow circles of Mallarmé's artistic peers. As Kristeva evocatively writes, the 'negativity' of his writings were thus 'exiled . . . among the elites' (RLP 389).

At this point of Kristeva's argument in *Revolution in Poetic Language*, there appear to be two limitations to Mallarmé's writings conceived as a potential source of political change. On the one hand, they are marginalised and their impact is extraordinarily restricted. On the other hand, they seem to inflect language's negativity in the direction of a discrete irony. From a political perspective, this irony then devolves into a form of quietism, if not nihilism. Disseminating Mallarmé's writings and 'contaminating' each social ensemble with their negativity is thus a necessary but not sufficient condition for bringing about 'the revolution in poetic language'. However radical the form of Mallarmé's writings might be, their content, Kristeva alleges, is often regressive to the point that their potential to corrode the symbolic law is restricted. Kristeva forges the concept of 'fetish' (RLP 362) to refer to those elements of Mallarmé's writings that function to cover over their radicality: 'the fetish thus becomes', Kristeva writes, 'the obvious mark of the pheno-text' – Kristeva's term for a text's content: 'from syntactical garlands to cults of jewellery, to disputes regarding Catholic or secularised divinities' (RLP 362), 'fetishes' like these offer a false representation of the real dynamics animating Mallarmé's writings. And as this passage suggests, chief among these 'fetishes' is religion. As we already know, for Kristeva religion is an exemplary 'infinite-support'.

Thus, for Mallarmé to frame his writings using a religious vocabulary is for him to falsify, if not betray, the corrosive negativity that is actually operative in his writings. In the next section, we will see an excellent example of such a 'fetish', but we will also begin to glimpse Mallarmé's progressive self-emancipation from these 'fetishes'. Such progress will allow Kristeva to preserve the promise of the 'revolution in poetic language'.

*

In the chapter entitled 'Marriage and the Paternal Function', Kristeva returns to the theme of Mallarmé's ironic orientation to the symbolic order. Here, her focus is on Mallarmé's family life, a site at which he made an exemplary display of his ironic attitude to social formations in general. Like Sartre, Kristeva is interested in Mallarmé's marriage as a key relationship in his life, one that reveals his fundamental attitude towards others, the world and even poetry. Yet the focus of her interest is strikingly different. In a long section from 'Marriage and the Paternal Function', Kristeva reads Mallarmé's 1866 poem *Hérodiade* as a work intimately linked to a period of painful transition in Mallarmé's life: his marriage, his wife's pregnancy, and the birth of their first child Geneviève. For Sartre, *Hérodiade* was Mallarmé's first failed attempt at recreating himself, with the poem vanishing into nothingness at the precise point it attained the absolute. Kristeva also reads the poem in terms of the problematic of 'self-engendering' (RLP 450). Yet she ties it quite plausibly to the intimate context of pregnancy and childbirth in the Mallarmés' household in 1864. Kristeva is frank about the significance of this experience for Mallarmé: 'paternity induced the experience of castration' (RLP 444) in the young poet. For reasons we will soon explore at length, pregnancy and matters of reproduction more generally, linked as they are to sexuality and to *jouissance*, are sites of deep social anxiety for Mallarmé personally. Kristeva writes: 'Mallarmé began *Hérodiade* at the moment of Geneviève's birth, as if the narrative of the social and symbolic power of the virgin Queen of Judea, frigid and sterile in her phallic pause, was supposed to stand up to the genital function of the mother' (RLP 444). The so-called 'genital function' names, most banally, the fact of reproduction. But it also refers metonymically to the entire problematic of the child's pre-Oedipal – that is, pre-symbolic – relation to the mother. It thus also implicates the anarchic logic of the semiotic. If Mallarmé experienced 'castration' during Marie Gerhard Mallarmé's pregnancy and the first months of his child's life, then it was because he realised, however obscurely, that the social reproduction of the paternal law had to pass by way of a site seemingly outside of the law, where sex and its experience of a potentially a-social *jouissance*, the mother-child relation, and the drive-based anarchy of the semiotic, all coalesced. Kristeva continues:

> As her name indicates, Hérodiade refers to the murder of infants, and, as Mallarmé explains, she represents the 'young intellectual'. The sexual prohibition of the Queen is sung over the top of and in the place of the power that the repressed mother-genitor has just acquired, and which her 'naughty baby' represents: Geneviève is described as 'driving Hérodiade away'. (RLP 444–5)

While Mallarmé's *Hérodiade* was never meant to replay the Biblical story of Salomé, Kristeva explains that 'elements of the signification proper to the "historical" Hérodiade enter into the semiotic network unfolded by the text' (RLP 445):

> One of these seems to us to be essential to the signification of the text that we wish to bring out at this point: namely, the renunciation of the drives, which implies a renunciation of the mother and the body, in favour of a spirituality figured by the dead or murderous name-of-the-father. (RLP 445)

Salomé's voluptuous sexuality has quite literally been replaced by the asexual, law-governed logic incarnated in her father Herod's name. In contrast, then, to Hérodiade's 'phallic pause', it is the character of the Nurse in the poem who 'represents the suppressed mother, determinant yet dissimulated' (RLP 446). Hérodiade's infamous self-regard figures her repression of *jouissance* and of the drives, both of which, according to Kristeva, are incarnate in the Nurse-mother: 'Yes, it's for me – for me – that I flower, deserted!' (PV 79).[14] From the moment she appears in the poem, Hérodiade pre-emptively avoids contact with the Nurse, exulting instead her own frigidity and sublimated beauty:

> ... Get Back
> The blond torrent of my spotless hair
> when it bathes my solitary body freezes it
> with horror, and each hair, wound up in light
> is immortal. O woman, a kiss would kill me
> if beauty were not death ... (PV 69)[15]

For Kristeva, *Hérodiade* is a work in which wider anxieties in Third Republic France about the stability of the family – and, by derivation, of the paternal law – are reflected in Mallarmé's personal, poetic trajectory. With the weakening of state and symbolic power, the figure of the mother and her metonymical correlates, from sex *qua* expenditure to the drives' negativity, re-emerge and immediately provoke the forces of reaction. Mediated as its composition was by Mallarmé's own confrontation with the resurgent power of the feminine, on Kristeva's reading *Hérodiade* is thus a product of these reactionary forces. Yet in *Hérodiade* Mallarmé also seeks to preserve the pre-eminence of the paternal law by way of a compromise with what exceeds it. As Kristeva explains, poetry is in fact the perfect site for such a compromise: 'Symbolic power, unstable as it is, seeks to perpetuate itself by integrating *jouissance*, and thus by seeking out realisations in which the position and unity of the symbolic are relativised' (RLP 454). Such 'realisations' include poems like *Hérodiade*, with their supple 'semiotic apparatus' permitting an equilibrium between the semiotic and the symbolic. Furthermore, *Hérodiade* offers the male poet a way of sublimating the – for him – 'castrating' experience of reproduction. Displacing the dialectic of the pre-Oedipal and the Oedipal, of *jouissance* and the law, onto language, Mallarmé can in turn safely take the place of the genitor, usurping the mother's role in the process. Whereas Sartre had seen Mallarmé's concern with 'self-engendering' as an ontological problem, for Kristeva it marks the poet's traversal of the problematic of reproduction. Importantly, this traversal is made in a fundamentally *conservative* mode, since Mallarmé always seeks to maintain the upper hand of the paternal law: in Kristeva's words, Mallarmé 'does not recognise the function of the wife-mother in instituting social constraint, but devalorises it in order to defend himself from it; and, having repressed the wife-mother, he displaces *jouissance* onto the symbolic' (RLP 453).

A similar logic is in play, Kristeva believes, in the salons Mallarmé frequented. The key feature of these *fin-de-siècle* salons is the nature of the woman at their centre. As a single woman without obvious familial bonds, the 'mistress' (RLP 453) of the salon represented the fact that these micro-societies were 'institution[s] running transversally to families' (RLP 510) and thus corroding their claim to be the main unit of social life. Moreover, as a woman, her power as the head of these salons was not something that needed to be 'feared' (RLP 510). It could instead be treated with the same ironic distance as the state's power. Most importantly, however, in so far as the salon's 'mistress' lacked children and her sexual life seemed subordinated solely to (men's) pleasure, she represented a dissimulation – a 'fetish' – of the figure of the mother-as-genitor. Just as Mallarmé had only allowed the 'genital' logic metonymically connected to the 'wife-mother' to enter into his poetry in the form of a 'semiotic apparatus' – the explicit semantic content of his text, for its part, overtly refused the genitor's power – he could only accept the power of a woman in so far as it fell short of, or indeed effectively hid, the awesome counter-power of the woman-as-genitor.

To briefly summarise this section, Mallarmé's early work attests to his precocious confrontation with one of the weak points of the symbolic's chain: namely, reproduction. As Kristeva makes clear, with his textual 'fetish' functioning to dissimulate the figure of the 'mother-genitor' (RLP 457), Mallarmé unquestionably 'collaborate[d] in the maintenance of vacillating structures' (RLP 455), chief among them the integrity of the paternal law. At this point, Mallarmé looks less like a revolutionary and more like a reactionary.

To fully appreciate Kristeva's analysis here, however, we need to delve more deeply into her social ontology and historical anthropology. The two chapters 'Marriage and the Paternal Function' and 'Mystery – Double of the Social Code' flesh out her ideas about the nature of human society and its transformation across time. As we can predict from what we have said so far, the focal point of her attention in these two chapters is the problematic of social *reproduction*. We can begin with the idea that the act of procreation can bring pleasure, or even a more intense, egologically disruptive *jouissance*, which risks exceeding the bounds of social utility. Sex, in other words, is a paradigmatic form of expenditure – a human activity that is not always sucked back into the circuit of production. Closely associated with the *jouissance* of sex is, of course, the child. As a pre-social entity, the child is the locus of anxiety about the failure of the paternal law to reproduce itself: their entrance into the symbolic is never certain – a fact reinforced in Kristeva's theory by the link between the pre-Oedipal child and the anarchy of the drives. As such, in the social ontology promulgated in *Revolution in Poetic Language*, there exists a kind of associative chain linking sexuality, *jouissance*, expenditure, procreation, the child and, finally, the non-law, which is itself incarnated in the drives. This series is in turn summed up in a single, socio-historically contingent signifier: *woman*.

Yet this is only half of Kristeva's social ontology. Drawing on Lévi-Strauss's *The Elementary Structures of Kinship*, Kristeva explores how procreation, while caught in the metonymic chain binding the different figures of the non-law, is also, of course, the privileged site of the law's reproduction. Neither the details nor the cross-cultural validity of Lévi-Strauss' mathematical models matter to Kristeva. What is essential for her is instead that kinship always involves the institution of reciprocal relations of law-governed rights and duties, of credits and debts, that bind a community together. The power implied in these relations has traditionally been possessed almost exclusively by *men*. As Kristeva remarks, there is nothing surprising about the structural proximity between the site of the symbolic's institution and procreation: kinship's web of regulated relations between men function *precisely* to control the site of potential anarchy that is sexuality, *jouissance*, and the pre-Oedipal child. In fact, we are privy here to the most fundamental operation of *repression* in society, whereby the paternal law suppresses the figure of the 'mother-genitor'. Kristeva summarises these complex ideas in the following crucial passage:

> In this way, men gain a social – that is, phallic – power, which they unconsciously 'know' depends on a genitality which exceeds this phallic power, and which opens the symbolic onto biology and history – that is, onto death, where this excess is represented by the *jouissance* of the mother. But of this *jouissance*, society retains only filiation – that is, the contribution of genitality to production: namely, reproduction. In the final instance, filiation, which shows itself to be dependent on a phallic power (that of the father or the uncle), is a way of subordinating *procreation* and the *non-productive jouissance-expenditure which accompanies it and which is inseparable from it* to the needs of the relations of production. (RLP 457 – Kristeva's emphasis)

Returning briefly to Mallarmé's *Hérodiade*, we can now see that Mallarmé's heroine, created as she was at the moment Mallarmé came face-to-face with the precarious passage from the non-law to the law, represents an attempt to bolster the symbolic by sublimating the 'feminine' force of the semiotic. Troubled by the obscure power that his wife *qua* 'mother-genitor' had suddenly acquired, Mallarmé's famously frigid Hérodiade, bearing her father's name and refusing the nurse-mother's 'emotiveness' (RLP 447), offered a poetic bulwark against genitality.

As we have already intimated, however, Mallarmé does not remain a reactionary. In fact, Kristeva will show how in his later work he progressively comes to terms with the problem of sex, *jouissance* and the non-law – a problem that is effective at the level of writing itself. Before we see how he did so, let us return one last time to the social role of 'infinite-supports'.

As we can already guess from our discussion of 'infinite-supports', all human societies have not only had a symbolic system whose paradigm is filiation, they have also had to find a socially useful way of representing – and thus of quarantining – the inevitable path social reproduction takes past the potential anarchy of procreation. In the following passage, Kristeva explains how one of the most enduring ways of representing this passage has been by way of the term 'mystery' – a term that should immediately resonate with Mallarmé's *œuvre*:

> as soon as there is filiation, there is the paternal law as a substitute for the crucial importance of the mother-genitor. In other terms, the paternal law

occults genital *jouissance* and assures procreation for the survival of society – on the condition, of course, that the importance of the mother remains unconscious or shrouded in mystery. In a society where procreation is the determining factor in the production of goods, the mystery of *jouissance* is the reverse side of filiation. Socially, it is in mystery that the *jouissance* that is inseparable from procreation finds refuge; there, sexuality is hypostasised – a sexuality that the relations of production cannot allow to be wasted, but which is channelled into controlled childbirth in the name of the development of the productive forces. (RLP 457)

The term 'mystery' here refers most specifically to an ensemble of practices that Kristeva believes have existed in almost every human society hitherto. Structurally speaking, these practices, while radically distinct in nature from symbolic or state power, are nevertheless power's necessary corollary in so far as they provide the requisite quarantine station for the forces of the non-law. Religion and art – including the art of late nineteenth-century French Symbolism, which is inscribed in the series of these trans-temporal and trans-cultural practices – are the two paradigmatic examples of practices of 'mystery'. In the following passage, by way of the analogy she has already established between 'poetic language' and 'expenditure', Kristeva relates these practices to a specific modality of language:

> in societies anterior to bourgeois society, there exist social groups not directly linked to production and who know nothing of filiation, placing themselves as they do outside of the institution of matrimony. These are the servants of mystery, religious officiants, and later officiants of art, who will emerge from the ranks of the former. The language they use lacks the same exchangist aims as communicative language, just as its subjects do not enter into the relations of the exchange of women which undergirds the relations of production. By virtue of their place in the social ensemble, these subjects constitute the exception to the rule, the rupture in the social relation, its unproductive expenditure; interrupting filiation, they become a complementary opposition to the matrimonial institution. They become the structure necessary to the representation of what filiation hides: namely, *jouissance*, of which the mother is the mute bearer, excluded as she is from the representation of the relations of production. (RLP 458–9)

As we know, Kristeva is not only concerned to place Mallarmé's *œuvre* within the context of her sweeping historical anthropology, but also to account for its historical specificity. There are three crucial features of Third Republic France that determine the uniqueness of Mallarmé's own practice of 'mystery': the generalised weakening of the paternal law, or of symbolic power more generally – a point we are already familiar with; the separation of Church and State; and the presence of a surplus population in capitalist society. As Kristeva explains, at moments of rupture in history – her principal example is the 'Pindaric obscurity' that followed 'Homeric clarity and community' (RPL 15, 13) – the momentary dissolution of the law leads to a 'recrudescence' in 'cults of mystery', as well as 'qualitative transformations' (RLP 459) in their operation. The volatile nineteenth century in France is no doubt one such moment of rupture. While Sartre had focused on the climate of despairing atheism in post-1848 France, Kristeva notes the extraordinary increase in interest in spirituality: 'Satanism, the propagation of the Apocalypse of Saint John, the prophecies, the Assumptionist Fathers, the great popular assemblies and the crowds' pilgrimages, not to mention the erection of Sacré Cœur in 1870, all attest to this rush of the masses towards religion' (RLP 555). Yet a 'qualitative transformation' had taken place, making the 'religious' phenomena of late nineteenth-century France historically unprecedented. For Kristeva, a first historical shift in the nature of the 'cults of mystery' occurred with Christianity. By repressing the function of the 'mother-genitor' by way of the figure of the virgin, Christianity, she claims, 'displaced the jouissance ... of the *sexual act* ... and situated it in language and in symbolic relations alone' (RLP 487 – Kristeva's emphasis). Christianity thus paved the way for considering *language* as the most fundamental site at which social relations were instituted and reproduced. In the Third Republic, a second historical shift occurred whereby the close complicity between the paternal law and the practices of 'mystery' was undone, the sphere of state power and religion being split. As Kristeva explains:

> When the bourgeois Republic separates Church and State, it reveals the very structure of the essential division which supports the diverse forms of state power and which is summed up in the split between the relations of reproduction and the relations of production, a structure that the mysteries gather up both in their 'form' as in their 'content'. (RLP 460)

In addition to this severing of the state and 'mystery', which allowed the latter a degree of autonomy from its safety-valve-like function *qua* the guarantor of social reproduction, the growing atheism of France's population meant that the various practices of 'mystery' lost their transcendent referent: they were no longer an intra-worldly passage to the divine. And since artistic practices, which had hitherto been 'genetically and structurally close' (RLP 461) to religion, were now the privileged site of 'mystery', religion's theological content was progressively evacuated, if not actively negated. In short, a millennia-old machine for ensuring social reproduction was beginning to break down, its component parts becoming disconnected and its internal workings – no longer divinely ordered but mundane and humanly intelligible – were being exposed for all to see. The final significant characteristic of Third

Republic France was that it was a society no longer subject to the imperative to reproduce itself in order to avoid a scarcity of labour power. As Kristeva has it, while they may well have been dissimulated by the 'paternal law' that 'represents the social face ... of the genital function', relations of reproduction were nevertheless 'fundamentally important to societies which had a weak development of productive forces and which thus depended on the quantity of human labour' (RLP 457). By contrast, an industrial society with a surplus population might even 'require for its survival a diminution of the growth rate of the population' (RLP 458) so as to avoid disaster. For this reason, there is no longer an objective necessity to so brutally submit relations of reproduction, along with their accompanying phenomena of sex, *jouissance*, the pre-Oedipal stage of the child, and so forth, to the requirements of the relations of production. In a word, in Third Republic France, the world of *jouissance* began to be separated from a means-end rationality and thus won a degree of autonomy. It tended ever more towards being a practice of expenditure.

Given all of these historical transformations, there was hope that Mallarmé's writings would steadily extract themselves from their initially reactionary function. And indeed, we already have evidence that they eventually did: in Kristeva's reading of 'Prose', a poem published almost twenty years after the composition of *Hérodiade*, we saw that Mallarmé lucidly and poetically staged the genesis of the subject. Indeed, in his 1885 poem Mallarmé showed an extraordinary degree of insight into the logic of the subject's genesis. Not only did he affirm the liberating – albeit anarchic – activity of the drives, he also integrated, in a sublimated fashion, the figure of 'mother-genitor' into the process of subject's birth and rebirth: the figure of the poet's 'sister', on Kristeva's reading, marked Mallarmé's recognition of the irreducible role of the 'mother-genitor' in the reproduction and renewal of the symbolic law. In other words, Mallarmé's poetic career was structured by an arc running from an initial conservatism to an ever-greater radicalism, one that occurred concurrently with an ever-deepening degree of insight on his part into the logic of social reproduction. The culminating point of Mallarmé's trajectory was his project of the Theatre-Book. For Kristeva, Mallarmé's Theatre-Book includes two innovations, both of which bring it tantalisingly close to the ideal work of literature for the Telquellian. Firstly, it refuses the logic of the 'fetish' and attempts to openly synthesise the semiotic and the symbolic, the *jouissance* of reproduction and the stability of the law – in short, to bring together in an equal partnership the two sides of the subject's and society's logic. Secondly, it does this in a veritably collective form: that is, in so far as it is a communal ritual and not an isolated act of reading, the Theatre-Book tends towards the dissemination of Mallarmé's writings to each social ensemble, thus overcoming the intrinsically local character of the 'infinite-support'.

Before we conclude with a brief overview of the Theatre-Book, we can bring its singularity as a political invention into focus by doing what Kristeva herself does: namely, compare Mallarmé's invention to the political current he was at times closest to – anarchism.

As Kristeva recognises, Mallarmé had a complex relationship with the anarchist movements of his time, just as these movements frequently found a reflection of their own destructive and liberating practices in Mallarmé's writings. In the section titled 'Anarchism, Political or Other', Kristeva begins by resisting what she sees as the hitherto prevailing explanation for the solidarity, which was widely attested in *fin-de-siècle* France, between anarchism and certain artistic practices. This dominant explanation involves the claim that it was the 'snobbism' (RLP 425) and 'aristocratism' (RLP 423) of the Symbolists that attracted them to the spectacular force of the individual as manifest in anarchist action. In reality, however, Kristeva argues that it was never simply a case of two forms of aristocratic individualism mirroring each other. Rather, something much more profound was at stake. Kristeva's account of Symbolism's infatuation with anarchism should nevertheless be predictable to us by now. Finding a clue in the many references anarchist writers made to a 'revised religiosity' (RLP 427), Kristeva argues that, like Mallarmé's writings, anarchism was also an attempt to explore the a-social logic of *jouissance*. And if both phenomena made reference to religion, then this was because

> at this time, religion remained the only possible and known discourse on the subject, the discovery of the unconscious having not yet transformed the conception of 'man', nor opened up the principle of God, to the operations of unconscious 'logic' – a 'logic' which would displace the 'secret of the race' onto a new and analysable terrain hitherto maintained, if not reduced, by religion. (RLP 427)

As always, the 'fetish' of religion marks a state of theoretical immaturity or dissimulation, which both Mallarmé and his anarchist contemporaries participated in. This common ground nevertheless offered a lot of space for movement. As Kristeva shows, in terms of his own political convictions and acquaintances, Mallarmé oscillated between the liberal right and the anarchist left, two positions which 'demand[ed] ruptures in the chain of bourgeois institutions' (RLP 429). Yet for Mallarmé, such 'ruptures' should never go so far as destroying the common legal and political framework incarnated in the state. Indeed, one of the most striking results of Kristeva's careful reading in this chapter is that Mallarmé's sympathy for anarchism never went so far as to call for the complete destruction of centralised forms of power. To demonstrate this, Kristeva explores the poet's *National Observer* article from 25 February 1893, titled 'Faits-Divers'. This prose piece, which would later be extensively transformed into the critical poem 'Gold' from 1897's *Divagations*, comments on the Panama Canal scandal and the fate of its main protagonist, Ferdinand de Lesseps. On Kristeva's reading, 'Faits-Divers' presents Mallarmé's views on the fragility of social power, in particular that of the state and its judicial organs. Yet his radical perspective on power exists alongside a traditionally humanistic defence of the individual: as Kristeva writes, 'Mallarmé's unease is palpable in this text' (RLP 432) as he seeks to negotiate between his belief in the insubstantiality of the symbolic order and his maintenance of the individual as a locus of value. Thus, on the one hand, the Panama Canal scandal showed the fickle nature of monetary value, which could unexpectedly grow to unthinkable proportions or disappear in an instant. For Mallarmé, this was a sign of the phantasmagoria of social life in general. As he writes in 'Gold', 'if a number increases and backs up toward the improbable, it inscribes more and more zeros: signifying that its total is spiritually equal to nothing, almost' (D 255). This 'nothing' is the same as the 'central nothing' (D 267) Mallarmé speaks of in 'Bucolic': the 'nothing' that lies at the heart of the modern City, a name for its ultimate insubstantiality. The problem here it is not only that de Lesseps was judged by a factitious form of social power actually subject to the anarchy of Capital. Rather, what is most significant is that the state's judicial apparatus could not restore the money lost in his venture. It was thus exposed as a perfectly impotent institution with fraudulent symbolic pretensions.

On the other hand, in 'Faits-Divers' Mallarmé articulates this critique of power alongside a defence of the individual. Following a predictable anarchist or libertarian line, Mallarmé frames the Panama Canal scandal as a confrontation between 'governmental anonymity' – which he also characterises as a 'monster' – and the 'individual'. In this case, the 'individual', Ferdinand de Lesseps, had also been the object of public adoration, incarnating a series of symbolic values – from individual initiative to entrepreneurial heroism – which 'an abstract state justice' (RLP 431) had simply ignored. On Kristeva's reading, Mallarmé thus shares to a degree the elitism of certain anarchists who sought to cultivate exceptional individuals cutting against the grain of the common. This is confirmed in the prose text 'The Court', which for Kristeva expresses the exigency that a 'spiritual aristocracy' capable of 'remedying' (RLP 438) this situation of crushing abstraction be created. Their main tool for doing so will be the creation of literary works: 'The anonymous master of this religion will be the brilliant producer of books; or, more precisely, all of this religion's adepts will be nothing other than anonymous producers of books' (RL 439). Like Sartre, Kristeva reads 'The Court' as articulating a complex dialectic between elitism and egalitarianism. As she puts it, while the members of this 'spiritual parliament' (RLP 438) are currently restricted, its limits are 'susceptible to being enlarged' (RLP 439). Indeed, they are constitutively open to all since the literary products of this 'spiritual aristocracy' treat a topic that concerns every citizen of the modern state: namely, the 'ambiguous status of power and justice' (RLP 433). This is where Mallarmé's differences with anarchism are most stark. For fundamentally, Mallarmé believes that the state is a necessary but not sufficient condition for a flourishing communal life. In fact, the problem with state power is not its existence, but the modality of its existence. As Mallarmé writes in 'Music and Letters': '*Great damage has been caused* to terrestrial togetherness, for centuries, by conflating it with the brutal mirage, the city, its governments, or the civil code. Otherwise than as emblems or, vis-à-vis our estate, what necropolises are to the heavens they make evaporate' (D 194 – Mallarmé's emphasis). In other words, the members of a society should see the symbolic power that presides over them as a worldly, fragile power – a *fiction*, in other words, which lacks all substance. This is the point at which the works of Mallarmé's 'spiritual aristocracy' take on their importance:

> The social relation is necessary and de-linked, constraining and evanescent, such that only a book – which is itself signification and music, law and transgression – can figure it. Moreover, such a book is necessary at this time in order for consciousness to gain access to this otherwise invisible characteristic of the social relation. (RLP 433)

It is not a matter of destroying symbolic power, but of collectively cultivating an ironic attitude towards it, perhaps even of promoting an attitude of play towards it. And the only means to do so is by way of a literature like Mallarmé's.

This returns us, finally, to Mallarmé's Theatre-Book. As Kristeva understands it, Mallarmé's Theatre-Book was supposed to be an at once edifying and emancipatory experience for its participants. It offered the Third Republic's citizens a direct grasp, by way of their own involvement in the Theatre-Book's movements, of the insubstantiality of the symbolic order. As Kristeva explains, the thematic content of the Theatre-Book attests to the immense progress Mallarmé had made in his exploration of the logic of social reproduction. Having come to an understanding of the dual nature of social power – the equal importance of the semiotic and the symbolic, the 'mother-genitor' and the law, expenditure and production, and so on – Mallarmé set about producing a drama that would stage a subject who was the synthesis of these two poles, and not a subject who refused one in the name of the other. Commenting on a key page from the notes to Mallarmé's Theatre-Book, Kristeva reads the different figures in the drama as a metaphorical synthesis of the two sides of the subject and society:

> The 'equation' between Drama and Mystery consists in the junction of a scission: it is the Hero who, through the Hymn, accomplishes this equation-junction – 'the development of the hero / or heroes / wrongly split into two'. The Hero must condense the dissociation between life (the animals, the workers) and the city (the priest, the crowd and its hunger). Intervening in the Theatre, the Hero brings 'the Hymn / (maternal)' and thus returns the 'mystery' to it. It is then that the theatre and the mystery, the world and time, genius and passion, cease to be separated and obtain an identity that can be called Idea, Book, Self or Drama: The Dr. is caused by the Myst. of what follows – Identity / (Idea) Self – / of the Theatre and of the Hero through the Hymn'. If the hero thus evoked corresponds to what the literary tradition says of him; if he is therefore hymnic and thus tied to the mother; and if he is a poet by his language, then he also appears as the intermediary between the work (the unconscious genitor) and the priest (the man of sublimation); he is the subject who condenses these two experiences and transcends them. (RLP 583–4)

For Kristeva, the Theatre-Book is not only a *representation* of such a subject who totalises the semiotic and the symbolic and all of their analogous structures. It is also meant to be an *act* by which the participants effectively experience their internal scission, along with the scission internal to social power – and do all this with a view to developing a critical, emancipatory relation to their subjection to the symbolic. Summarising Mallarmé's trajectory, Kristeva writes that his 'project did not radically change, save in terms of the following difference: namely, that the project came to fruition by steadily abandoning its status as an aesthetics and becoming an *experience*, composite and variable, undergone by a subject' (RLP 583 – our emphasis).

At the close of her long study of Mallarmé, Kristeva has thus located a literary practice that points towards 'the revolution in poetic language'. Yet it remains subject to the limitations of its time and place. As we intimated above, these limitations are dual. On the one hand, despite his epistemological progress – that is, despite his attempts to adequately represent poetically the nature of social power – Mallarmé's writings, Kristeva claims, remained distorted by a spiritualist vocabulary. His highest achievement, the Theatre-Book – a work in which such 'fetishes' were almost completely shaken off – was something he ultimately decided was not ready for public consumption. As Kristeva has it, the Theatre-Book's discourse was 'an impossible discourse, at least for the end of the nineteenth century, as demonstrated by Mallarmé's chasteness in shutting his notes up in his draw and demanding they be burnt' (RLP 608). Nevertheless, Mallarmé's writings were still 'oriented towards an overcoming of the fetishistic solution' (RLP 609). Future writers could thus take up the thread of his work. Indeed, Kristeva inscribes Mallarmé's writings in an historical teleology: 'James Joyce, Ezra Pound, Antonin Artaud and Georges Bataille take up, albeit in different ways, the same uninterrupted trajectory' (RLP 609). She even elects her husband Peter Sollers' early novels as exemplary works that overcome Mallarmé's theoretical blindspots. As she writes, 'modern texts in effect practice this pulverisation of language, not only to construct a new formalism, but in order to signify this dialectic by taking up a political and psychoanalytic position' (RLP 419). And she adds: 'We are thinking here above all of Philippe Sollers' *Lois* and *H*' (RLP 419 n. 105). In other words, while similarly radical at the level of form, works like Sollers' avoid the logic of the 'fetish' by integrating the most up-to-date and progressive political and theoretical content. As such, there is no possibility of the true nature of social power being dissimulated from the reader.

This leads us to the second historical limitation placed on Mallarmé's work, one that seems much more difficult to overcome: namely, that its reach is radically limited. Almost by definition, this means it falls back to the status of being an 'infinite-support'. As Kristeva puts it:

> It would be necessary for this signifying economy, which Mallarmé glimpsed, to implicate every subject of the bourgeois State or its subsets, for its circulating ideologies to be attacked and, with them, its always-virtually oppressive social structures. The signifying practice sought after in Mallarmé's theatre could have such a social impact if, and only if, it met with favourable economic and political conditions. In a bourgeois State that consolidates its structures of economic expansion and its apparatuses of political liberalism, the Mallarméan project remains a wish whose realisation requires, at the very least, many centuries. It remains the case, however, that this new subject demanded by Mallarmé and orchestrated, in different ways, by the avant-garde literature of the twentieth century, is already emerging, both sporadically and rarely; and that its practice is one of the new but decisive factors in the revolution. (RLP 592)

*

At the end of our long exploration of Kristeva's reading of Mallarmé, we have arrived at a highly symptomatic point. As we noted in our introduction, as a member of a literary avant-garde, Kristeva had to preserve the promise of 'the revolution in poetic language'. To do this, she had to explain why, despite the presence of a transformative linguistic force in his writings, Mallarmé's textual practice had not yet had a decisive 'impact' (RLP 620) on the social world. Correlatively, she had to show how the historical limitations his writings were subject to could be overcome. With exemplary rigour, Kristeva achieved both of these objectives. However, the solution she offers is truly striking. On the one hand, the progressive power of Mallarmé's writings were limited, allegedly, by their content, which distorted their form's radicality by interpreting it in light of a religious or some other similarly regressive framework. Thus, to overcome this limitation, Kristeva was led to argue that it was necessary to produce works like those of Philippe Sollers: that is, works that included theoretical content that scientifically reflected the true nature of textuality, at the same time as expounding a properly progressive politics. Formal innovations had to be supplemented by theoretically correct content. Yet it is obviously very hard to see how Sollers' early novels can in any way be considered improvements on Mallarmé's writings. Likewise, it is difficult to believe that simply adding theoretical content to works of innovative literature could ensure their transformative power. In fact, Kristeva seems to be guided here by the idea of a perfect adequation between literature *qua* cause and its effect on the reading subject. By bolstering literature's form with appropriate content, the reader is supposed to respond in a single, set way: rather than be diverted by references to religion, the reading subject truly will be traversed by the liberating force of the semiotic, their subjectivity being transformed in the process.

Even if this perfect causal connection between literature and its readers were achieved, reading practices would have to be extended to 'every subject of the bourgeois State', as Kristeva herself puts it. This was the second historical limitation Kristeva had identified in Mallarmé. However, her own solution necessarily points to a time in which all people will read Sollers' *H* or *Lois*. For all its extraordinary theoretical achievements, *Revolution in Poetic Language* ends with this implausible scenario as its fundamental fantasy.

Given the theoretical fragility and practical impossibility of Kristeva's proposal, it is not surprising that both her and *Tel Quel* changed their politics and their relation to literature swiftly and decisively in the years following the publication of *Revolution in Poetic Language*. In the next chapter, we turn to a philosopher, Alain Badiou, who maintains a political relation to Mallarmé, yet does so by refusing from the outset to conflate poetry with political action.

NOTES

1. 'Le camarade Mallarmé'. For Philippe Sollers' response on behalf of *Tel Quel*, see P. Sollers, '"Camarade" et camarade', *L'Humanité*, 19 September 1969.
2. 'Le camarade Mallarmé'.
3. For an excellent account of this debate, which places it within the competitive context of the French avant-garde publishing circles in the aftermath of May '68, see B. Gobille, 'La guerre de *Change* contre la "dictature structuraliste" de *Tel Quel*. L'avant-garde à l'épreuve de la crise politique de Mai '68', in *Raisons politiques*, No. 18 (2005/2). See also Philippe Forrest's account in *Histoire de* Tel Quel, *1960–1982* (Paris: Seuil, 1995), 347–9.
4. P. Sollers, *Logiques* (Paris: Seuil, 1968); *Sur le matérialisme* (Paris: Seuil, 1974).
5. Derrida, 'The Double Session', in *Dissemination*.
6. J. Kristeva, *Sèméiôtiké: Recherches pour une sémanalyse* (Paris: Seuil, 1969).
7. J. Kristeva, 'Sémanalyse et production de sens, quelques problèmes de sémiotique littéraire à propos d'un texte de Mallarmé: *Un Coup de dés*', in A. J. Greimas (ed.), *Essais de sémiotique poétique* (Paris: Larousse, 1972).
8. From here on, we will refer to this second work by its English title, *Revolution in Poetic Language*. When we use the abbreviation RLP, we are referring to the original French edition, from which the vast majority of our quotations are taken. See J. Kristeva, *La révolution du langage poétique. L'avant-garde à la fin du XIXème siècle: Lautréamont et Mallarmé* (Paris: Seuil, 1974). All translations are our own. By contrast, when we use the abbreviation RPL, we are referring to the English version. See J. Kristeva, *Revolution in Poetic Language*, trans. Margaret Waller (New York: Columbia University Press, 1984).
9. Michael Payne, who provides a helpful though uncritical exegesis of the English translation of *Revolution in Poetic Language*, does not go on to speak of the details of either section B or C of the original French edition. See M. Payne, *Reading Theory: An Introduction to Lacan, Derrida and Kristeva* (New Jersey: Blackwell, 1993), 162–3, 204. In his 1990 introduction to her work, John Lechte makes only a limited number of remarks regarding the last sections of *Revolution in Poetic Language* – all of which are, as the following analysis will show, problematic. See J. Lechte, *Julia Kristeva* (London: Routledge, 1990), 123, 150, 152. Interestingly, in his otherwise very crucial review of the book, Hans Peter Lund characterises the last section, 'The State and Mystery', as being 'by far the most successful' and congratulates Kristeva on her elaboration of the ways Mallarmé's work was a response to the crisis of French society at the time. See H. P. Lund, 'Mallarmé chez Kristeva', *Orbis Litterarum*, Vol. 31 (1976), 229–33.

10. For the best analyses of *Tel Quel*'s overall project, as well as the way their project was inscribed in the intellectual context of the journal's time, see the work of Niilo Kauppi: *Tel Quel: la constitution sociale d'une avant-garde* (The Finnish Society of Science and Letters, 1990); *French Intellectual Nobility: Institutional and Symbolic Transformation in the Post-Sartrian Era* (Albany: State University of New York Press, 1996); and *Radicalism in French Culture: A Sociology of French Theory in the 1960s* (Farnham: Ashgate, 2010). See also the indispensable work of Philippe Forrest, *Histoire de* Tel Quel, *1960–1982*. Also of interest is P. ffrench, *The Time of Theory: A History of* Tel Quel (Oxford: Clarendon Press, 1995), and D. Marx-Scouras, *The Cultural Politics of* Tel Quel (University Park: Pennsylvania State University Press, 1996).
11. *Les Lettres Françaises*, 30 October–5 November 1968. The same argument is made by Sollers in *Sur le matérialisme*, 21: 'What is thus excluded and repressed by Plato, as by the entirety of metaphysics, can thus be seen as having returned into history at the end of the nineteenth century with the radically different propositions of Mallarmé.'
12. 'Hyperbole! from my memory / triumphantly don't you know / how to raise yourself, today grammar / clad in a book in iron', PV 111.
13. Kristeva borrows this term from Samuel R. Levin, who used it in an analysis of Emily Dickinson's poetry, RLP 281, n. 41.
14. 'Oui, c'est pour moi, pour moi, que je fleuris, déserte !', OC 21.
15. '... Reculez. / Le blond torrent de mes cheveux immaculés, / Quand il baigne mon corps solitaire le glace / D'horreur, et mes cheveux que la lumière enlace / Sont immortels. O femme, un baiser me tûrait / Si la beauté n'était la mort', OC 17.

3 Alain Badiou's Mallarmé: From the Structural Dialectic to the Poetry of the Event

In 1964, Sartre gave an infamous interview to *Le Monde*, titled in English 'A Long, Bitter, Sweet Madness'.[1] In a series of remarks on how contemporary writers could confront the absurdity of creating literature in a world where millions remained malnourished, the philosopher unexpectedly linked Mallarmé to the then-young novelist Alain Badiou, whose work *Almagestes* had recently been acclaimed in the pages of *Les Temps Modernes*. For Sartre, there were two possible tasks for the writer in 1964. The first was to place themselves on the side of the greatest number, even if this meant momentarily giving up their vocation to become, for instance, a teacher in a newly liberated Cameroon or Nigeria. Literature's in-built *telos* towards universal freedom, which Sartre had argued for in *What is Literature?*, could thus lead paradoxically to its self-suppression in the service of emancipation. Literature, for Sartre, was politics by other means. These means could nevertheless sometimes prove insufficient.

As for the second task, Sartre first clarifies that it is 'only applicable to our non-revolutionary societies' such as France. Its utopian goal, he says, is to 'prepare for the time when everyone will read' by 'pos[ing] problems in the most intransigent manner'. As a successful contemporary example of this second task, Sartre refers to Badiou's *Almagestes*. Sartre contends that in this, his first novel, Badiou 'puts language on trial with an intention of cleansing, catharsis'.[2] Struck by the tension between Sartre's enthusiasm for abandoning literature in favour of politics and for pursuing the most uncompromising avant-garde experiments, the interviewer, Jacqueline Piatier, asks: 'Is *Almagestes* readable by all?'[3] Sartre's response brings together Mallarmé and Badiou:

> Be careful. I am not recommending 'popular' literature which aims at the lowest. The public, too, has to make an effort in order to understand the writer who, though he renounce complacent obscurity, cannot always

express his new-hidden thoughts lucidly and according to accepted models. Take Mallarmé. I hold him to be the greatest of French poets. His theory of the hermetic is a mistake, but he can only be difficult to read when he has difficult things to say.

To employ Paulhan's terms, for the Sartre of 1964 terroristic writers like Mallarmé and Badiou actively seek the universal, just as partisans of literary 'commitment' do. Yet the ultimate value of their writings lies in being able to express the tension between their ideally universal field of addressees and the particular public that currently consumes their work. As Sartre affirms, the battle to bring about 'the time when everyone will read' is 'a battle that has to be fought'. But in the meantime, '[a]s long as the writer cannot write for the two billion men who are hungry, he will be oppressed by a feeling of malaise'.[4] As he tells Piatier, Sartre senses this 'malaise' in difficult writers like Kafka. And as he made clear in his 1959 interview with Madeleine Chapsal, which we explored in our first chapter, he senses this 'malaise' in Mallarmé as well, particularly since the poet's hope that 'the obscure would become clear' for a future 'united people'[5] was necessarily doubled, in his present, by a feeling of profound dissatisfaction. Finally, Sartre says that he senses the contemporary writer's 'malaise' in Badiou's *Almagestes* too: 'You see, the contemporary writer must write through his intimations of unease, while trying to elucidate them. He could be a kind of Beckett who would not be totally committed to despair. And the form matters little to me, classical or not. That of *War and Peace* or *Almagestes*.'[6]

Over a quarter of a century later, at a time when many of the national liberation struggles of the post-war years had frozen into new forms of neo-colonial fascism and when the USSR and other communist powers were on the verge of collapse – times, in other words, that were decidedly 'non-revolutionary' – Badiou wrote a short essay entitled 'A French Philosopher Responds to a Polish Poet'. In it he affirms, as Sartre did before him, that literature is 'destined to everyone' (HI 31). Also like Sartre, Badiou claims that if literature cannot reach all people and if, concomitantly, a politics of egalitarian universalism is therefore impossible, the writer must 'stage [a] sacrificial comedy' (HI 31) in their work that serves to 'anticipate the Idea' (HI 32) of humanity's emancipation. Badiou states that Mallarmé puts this point 'superbly' (HI 32) in the following passage from 'Restricted Action': 'The writer, with his pains, dragons he has cherished, or with his light-heartedness, must establish himself, in the text, as a spiritual *histrio*' (D 216). Following both Sartre and Mallarmé, for Badiou the writer bears witness through their 'malaise' to literature's universality as it strains against the inequalities of its time.

In this third chapter, we explore Badiou's career-long engagement with Mallarmé. As we can already see, many of the themes in his dialogue with the poet are classically Sartrean in nature, even if they are taken up within a vastly different theoretical universe. In fact, the similarities with Sartre go further, since at one crucial moment in his trajectory Badiou also fixes Mallarmé at the negative pole of intellectual practice. Both comrade and class enemy, Badiou's Mallarmé will thus be an ambivalent figure for Badiou, as he was for Sartre and *Tel Quel*.

*

In his own words, Badiou 'synthesized [his] reading of Mallarmé in a course given at the Collège Universitaire de Reims during the academic year of 1967–68'.[7] At this time, in contrast to the Telquellians, Badiou's main scholarly reference was, as it remains today, the great Australian critic Gardner Davies. Davies' rigorously conceptual – or, in his own terms, Hegelian[8] – approach contrasts starkly with Robert Greer Cohn's wildly inventive reading of texts like *Un coup de dés*, which appealed to Kristeva and her collaborators (RLP 238–9). For Badiou, Davies' work allowed him to navigate between the two competing theoretical approaches to Mallarmé we have studied in the two previous chapters:

> For my part, as I came out of Sartre, I was in some sense able to traverse the two Mallarmés: the Mallarmé who fascinates Sartre and Blanchot through the motifs of Nothingness, Silence and Anxiety, and the Mallarmé who fascinates *Tel Quel* or the *Cahiers pour l'analyse* through the joint motifs of the powerful neutrality of language and the operational void that is the Subject. This possible traversal of the two different Mallarmés was facilitated – in fact more than facilitated – by the work of Gardner Davies. In truth, I owe him for having been the first to approach Mallarmé outside of any mystery with a conviction in his profound rationality – a rationality that could just as well have originated in Sartre (there is a 'vanishing subject' in Mallarmé, whose entire being lies in Nothingness), as in structuralism (this subject is the active void of a linguistic order).[9]

As Badiou goes on to say, his teaching on Mallarmé in Reims met the same fate as the second part of his course on *The Concept of Model* at the ENS: both were interrupted by the 'brutal beginning of the May '68 movement', after which Badiou was 'catapulted ... into Maoist action'[10] under the auspices of the UCFML, a small Maoist group distinct from both the more traditionally Leninist PCMLF and the anarchistic Gauche Prolétarienne. Badiou's political engagements in this period are significant, for in contrast to Sartre and the Telquellians his commitment to collective organisation, strategic calculation and the winning of enduring victories for the cause of emancipatory politics show that he has never conflated the production or reception of poetry with politics *per se*. Badiou states this explicitly: 'I have never fused poetry and politics: for me, they are distinct truth procedures.' As he clarifies, '[t]he positions of *Tel Quel* always seemed confused to me, and above all fragile'.[11] This is a fragility registered, Badiou believes, in the fact that the Telquellians 'reneged on their political engagements from the 1970's'[12] while Badiou maintained both his intellectual and practical commitments to the communist Idea.

By prising apart poetry and politics, Badiou's reading of Mallarmé seems to render our exploration of Mallarmé and the politics of literature inoperative. In neither of the two stages of his philosophical career – the first being marked by *Theory of the Subject* (1982), and the second by *Being and Event* (1988) and subsequent publications – does Badiou say that poetry can *do* politics, or, reciprocally, that politics must pass *by way of* poetry or linguistic invention. Most significantly, his novel doctrine of *inaesthetics*, developed in the wake of *Being and Event* and the account of the four generic procedures found therein, prohibits philosophy from 'judging the poem' or from 'imparting any political lessons based upon it' (HI 27). As an artistic truth procedure, poetry is *absolutely* autonomous and draws all of its relevant criteria for judgement from itself alone.

When we explore Badiou's writings on Mallarmé in detail, however, we sense a palpable gap between principle and practice. In both *Theory of the Subject* and in essays written after *Being and Event*, Badiou consistently reads Mallarmé in light of specifically political concerns. In the first part of this chapter, we will investigate the long chapter devoted to Mallarmé in *Theory of the Subject* titled 'The Subject Under the Signifiers of the Exception'. In the second, we turn to Badiou's post-*Being and Event* work, with a focus on the short piece 'A French Philosopher Responds to a Polish Poet', an occasional essay we will use to scaffold our discussion of Badiou's later engagement with Mallarmé. These two periods correspond to two distinct and mutually exclusive estimations of the poet's political significance. In *Theory of the Subject*, Mallarmé is read, on the one hand, as playing a role analogous to that of the Maoist militant, who also seeks to preserve and activate the true political capacity of the people. On the other hand, his poetry's 'structural dialectic' marks him out as an incorrigible conservative – even if he is, like Lacan, an enlightened one. With *Being and Event*, however, Mallarmé's significance radically changes: Badiou no longer reads his poetic operations as arbitrarily limited to the 'structural dialectic'; instead, he conceives of them as entirely adequate to themselves *qua* thought-poems of the event, the key category of Badiou's later thought, including his political thought. Correlatively, Mallarmé becomes the philosopher's unequivocal 'comrade', as our reading of 'A French Philosopher Responds to a Polish Poet' will confirm. His poetry's radical universalism means that in this later incarnation Mallarmé is in perfect solidarity with the philosopher's commitment to the communist Idea in a period marked by the downfall of the Soviet states and the fatigue of Marxist thought.

A minute but discernible shift in Badiou's reading of Mallarmé accounts for these two distinct judgements about the poet's politics. To see this, let us turn first to *Theory of the Subject*, where Mallarmé makes his most extensive appearance in Badiou's work to date.

*

Theory of the Subject is Badiou's first systematic philosophical treatise. Yet it is also a vital intervention into a political and intellectual conjuncture. As Badiou understands it, this conjuncture involves the fading political fortunes of the French Maoist movement in the long aftermath of May '68; the dilution or abandonment of the Marxist, structuralist and poststructuralist thought of the late-1960s and their replacement by a tepid liberalism; and finally the electoral victory of Mitterrand in 1981 – a victory which represented, for Badiou, the capturing of the revolutionary forces of 'the Red Years' by the mechanisms of the state. To this situation of extreme fragility and fatigue for the communist project, Badiou responds by developing a 'theory of the subject' – a theory, in other words, of the conceptual and organisational resources required to collectively effect entrenched political change. For Badiou, there is no equivocation as to the direction this change must go in: 'The serious affair, the *precise* affair, is communism' (TOTS 8). What role could Mallarmé play in such a project?

Mallarmé is first discussed in *Theory of the Subject* in the seminar session entitled 'Deduction of the Splitting', dated 5 January 1976. Badiou begins this session by reminding his audience of a distinction previously established between two figures of 'the masses' – a distinction that echoes the famous Maoist slogan *The people, and the people alone, are the motive force in the making of world history*. 'Last time', Badiou says, 'I proposed to you that we split the existence of the masses according to whether they present us with the *being* of history or, as a vanishing term endowed with causal power, constituted the *making* of history' (TOTS 65 – Badiou's emphasis). At the strictly conceptual level, the first instance of 'the masses' – those who *are* history – corresponds to what Badiou calls the *splace*: the synchronic stability of the status quo (TOTS 10–11). Translated into recognisably structuralist terms, the *splace* is equivalent to the system that individuates and structures the relations between each of its elements. The degree of difference between elements of the *splace* – or between individual members of 'the masses who *are* history' – corresponds to what Badiou calls 'weak difference, or the difference of position' (TOTS 55), which he opposes to the 'strong difference' that is made manifest by 'the masses who *make* history' in the course of a revolt or a revolution. Paradoxically, then, while the 'splaced' masses seem to enjoy the most entrenched mode of existence they are in fact brought into being by 'the masses who *make* history'. What this means, however, is that the cause of the *splace* is absolutely heterogeneous to the *splace* in its immanent logic: there is no transitivity between 'the masses who *are* history' and 'the masses who *make* history'. As a result of the distinction, those who partake in a revolt become disoriented and find no coordinates in their 'splaced' existence with which to orient themselves. They therefore inevitably require the mediation of the Maoist militant in order to preserve – and ultimately rediscover – their revolutionary essence.[13]

Badiou presents Mallarmé as having played a similar mediatory role in his time. Thus, at the beginning of 'The Deduction of the Splitting', Badiou makes the striking claim that Mallarmé had 'the strong awareness' that it was within 'the masses who *make* history' that there was to be found 'the silent secret of any art worthy of its name' (TOTS 65 – Badiou's emphasis): 'Mallarmé wanted nothing less than to empower the City with a book and a theatre in which the infinite and mute capacity of the masses – which he names the crowd – would finally find what it takes to produce, by withdrawing from it, its complete emblem' (TOTS 66). In accordance with this reading, Badiou focuses on episodes in Mallarmé's writings where the poet stages 'the crowd' at festivals commemorating 'the foundational riot' (TOTS 66): the taking of the Bastille. While the date of the 14 July fireworks means that 'the crowd' are implicitly celebrating their revolutionary capacity, the spectators remain in a state of what Badiou, following Mallarmé, calls 'self-estranged amazement' (TOTS 67). The poet's gaze, which Badiou identifies with here, sees in the Bastille Day fireworks a representation of the collective's power for revolution – a capacity that this collectivity can only obscurely sense from within their 'splaced' existence:

> Mallarmé's key image here is fireworks: commemorating, on July 14, the foundational riot, they project onto the sky a splendour of which the crowd is only the nocturnal ground: '. . . a multitude under the night sky does not constitute the spectacle, but in front of it, suddenly, there rises the multiple and illuminating spray, in mid-air, which in a considerable emblem represents its gold, its annual wealth and the harvest of its grains, and leads the explosions of the gaze to normal heights'. (TOTS 67)

Given the self-estrangement of 'the crowd', the mediation of the artist – or, by analogy, of the party militant – is essential. It is the illuminating power of the poem that reveals the revolutionary capacity of the French people, surrounded as they are by the parliamentary mediocrities of the Third Republic, just as it is the role of the Maoist militant to preserve 'the memory and the lesson' (TOTS xli) – and thus the promise – of events like the French Revolution for a people alienated under capitalism.

This analogy is reinforced in Badiou's reading of the prose text 'Conflict' (TOTS 98–100). In this late work, Mallarmé, having had his bucolic reverie at his rental property in Valvins interrupted by a group of railroad workers, is overcome by ambivalent feelings that waver between a sense of guilt arising from an imagined complicity with the social order that exploits the workers and a sense of solidarity with those he names, however ironically, his 'comrades' (D 42). This confrontation between poet and worker cannot fail to resonate with the experiences of Badiou and his Maoist comrades in the aftermath of May '68: while the poet obviously did not go so far as to become an *établi*, he was forced to reflect on the relation his poetic practice had to the division of labour in a capitalist society. More importantly, the task that Mallarmé and Badiou set themselves in the wake of their encounter *qua* intellectuals with 'the other class' (TOTS 98) attests to the analogy between their positions: both must produce 'the orders' and 'the plan'[14] that will effectively emancipate 'the workers'. Mallarmé, for instance, interprets the drunken debauchery of the workers as a provisional expression of their 'collective grandeur', which will therefore have to be sublated in order to achieve its properly poetic expression. Revisiting this episode with his own concepts in hand, Badiou writes:

> In the alcohol-sleepiness, this 'momentary suicide', [Mallarmé] deciphers first 'the dimension of the sacred in their existence', the provisory substitute of an interruption for the workers in which we should recognize, for lack of its higher form which would be the revolt, a derivative form of this access to the concept that is the annulment. (TOTS 99)

Like the spectators of the Bastille Day fireworks, these workers manifest a 'self-estranged amazement' (TOTS 67), unaware that their drunkenness reveals a desire to rupture definitively with the cycle of work and rest. As Mallarmé writes:

> Some instinct seeks [the dimension of the sacred in their existence] in a large number, soon to be thrown away, of little glasses; the workers are, with the absoluteness of a ritual gesture, less its officiants than its victims, if one takes into consideration the evening stupor of the tasks and if the ritual observance comes more from fate than will. (D 46)

Without the privileged perspective and intervention of the poet or militant philosopher, however, the workers have only their 'instincts' – 'instincts' that, while revealing their desire to break with the *splace* they are subject to, are nevertheless diverted from their proper course and directed towards practices that pose no threat to the established order.

Despite their analogous positions, Badiou also draws on Mallarmé to draw a line of division between adequate and inadequate forms of thought about political action. Indeed, in his response to the rolling crises of the Third Republic Mallarmé expressly opposed violent political praxis as a means of emancipation. As Badiou recognises, he elected to produce a poetic religion that would overcome the alienation of individual citizens and articulate a *modus vivendi* with a society that had neither God nor an absolute sovereign to provide it with a foundation.[15] Badiou takes the following famous passage from 'Music and Letters' as indicative of Mallarmé's views:

> If, in the future, in France, religion comes back, it will be the amplification of the sky-instinct in each of us, rather than a reduction of our instincts to the level of politics. To vote, even for oneself, does not satisfy, as the expansion of a hymn with trumpets sounding the joy of choosing no name; nor can a riot be sufficiently tumultuous to make a character into the steaming, confounding, struggling-again-into-life hero.[16]

Despite the fact that Mallarmé here opposes, in the name of a poetic 'religion', *both* electoralism *and* violent political praxis, Badiou retains from this passage an element he claims 'makes Mallarmé into an intellectual revolutionary': namely, the imperative of having to 'annul self-nomination in the crowd's ... force' (TOTS 67). In other words, Mallarmé articulated the necessity of dissolving the individual ego in the heroic force of the collectivity. Given the collective aspect of the 'religion' Mallarmé proposes, Badiou is right to say that Mallarmé expresses 'a slight conceptual preference' for 'the riot'. For indeed, relative to 'the riot', the reinstatement of a deprived individualism in the act of voting, particularly within the corrupt parliamentary mechanisms of the Third Republic, is 'the perfect denial' (TOTS 67) of the collective heroism that people are capable of. Badiou can thus count on Mallarmé to reinforce his rejection of electoralism in a political context dominated by 'The Union of the Left', which he believed had stifled the flame of May '68.

However, Badiou will not follow Mallarmé in deeming a novel religion, no matter how divested of theological vestiges it might be, as the solution to the mediocre politics 'the crowd' is presently subject to. While Mallarmé had questioned whether 'the riot' was an adequate expression of 'the sky-instinct in each of us' – a task only his poetic religion of the Book could perform – Badiou rebukes him and proclaims that 'the riot . . . is indeed the exact form of the crowd as vanishing term, which is "sufficiently tumultuous" to cause the spectacular restructuring of time itself' (TOTS 67). Mallarmé's project to 'empower the City with a book and a theatre in which the infinite and mute capacity of the masses' (TOTS 66) would finally be represented can thus only be a provisional and finally insufficient substitute for the true revolutionary expression of the crowd's 'collective greatness'.

We can delve deeper into this play of identification and distanciation between Badiou and Mallarmé by considering the philosopher's reflections on the poet's well-known declaration from 'Magic' that 'there are only two ways open to mental research, where our need bifurcates – aesthetics, on the one hand, and political economy, on the other' (D 264). Badiou reads this declaration as pitting art against politics on the basis of their shared property: that of being *fictions*. As Badiou is aware, the reason Mallarmé places 'aesthetics' and 'political economy' side-by-side is that, as the poet puts it in 'Safeguard', 'the social relation at any particular time, condensed or expanded to allow for government, is a fiction [and] belongs in the domain of Letters' (D 290). In other words, the social bond is not a substance that binds together a self-identical community – how could it be for a poet who posits the 'strong difference' of the Revolution as the vanished cause of French society? Rather, it is the precarious product of a *fiction*. For this reason, the artifice of literature becomes, for Mallarmé, the sole model for understanding the functioning of collective life.

However, it is on the question of how to proceed once the insubstantiality of the social bond has been recognised that Badiou and Mallarmé part company. For his part, Mallarmé attempted to articulate a *modus vivendi* with the essential fragility of the social bond, his poetic religion taking the very artifice of this bond as a reflection of the human animal's fundamentally fictional mode of being. Badiou, by contrast, seeks to overthrow the present order and produce the truly new on the basis of the insubstantiality of what is. The distinction between Mallarmé and Badiou on this point is, in fact, the very distinction between the 'structural dialectic' and the 'historical dialectic' that Badiou will go on to detail in the remainder of *Theory of the Subject*. Mallarmé will thus stand as an exemplary representative of the limits of the 'structural dialectic', which locates the symptomatic where society in its apparent plenitude is undone, but which cannot progress beyond this recognition to an affirmative praxis of creative change.

Turning to Mallarmé's poetic inscription of the 'structural dialectic', Badiou quotes a famous passage from Mallarmé's 'Magic':

Mallarmé thus sets out his programme: 'To evoke, with intentional vagueness, the mute object, using allusive words, never direct' ... The object, reduced to silence, does not enter the poem, even though its evocation grounds the poetic consistency. It is the absent cause. But the effect of its lack lies in affecting each written term, forced to be 'allusive', 'never direct', in such a way as to become equal on the Whole to the silence by which the object was only initially affected. (TOTS 72)

For Badiou, what makes a poem by Mallarmé into a synthetic Whole is the fact that all of its elements work together to evoke an absent object. Like the *splace* that delegates the place of each of its elements, this object is the 'absent cause' of the poem. Since each element of a *splace* can be said to be both itself and its capacity for linkage with other elements from the same *splace*, the words of the poem are 'split' (TOTS 72), being at once themselves and the part they play in evoking the absent object. Finally, Mallarmé adds a dialectical twist to this programme: if it is silence that must be evoked – the silence of the absent object – then 'we must also efface the instrument of the effacement': namely, the words themselves. It is this last twist that Badiou names 'the lack of lack', a second-order lack that he will attempt to show occurs systematically in Mallarmé's poetry and which he will name 'annulment' (TOTS 82). Mallarmé thus adds an innovative move to the 'structural dialectic': as Badiou had promised his materialist audience, 'it will never be a waste of our time to follow [this hero] of nonbeing into the arcane secrets of [his] acidic dialectical alchemy'. However, as we will see, it will also be the task of the materialist reader to detect the ruses of this irredeemably idealist poet, whose 'never-abandoned respect for the real' is matched only by his 'disavowal' (TOTS 55) of its force.

*

The first Mallarmé poem Badiou turns to is 'Stilled beneath the oppressive cloud':[17]

> Stilled beneath the oppressive cloud
> that basalt and lava base
> likewise the echoes that have bowed
> before a trumpet lacking grace
>
> O what sepulchral wreck (the foam
> knows, but it simply drivels there)
> ultimate jetsam cast away
> abolishes the mast stripped bare
>
> or else concealed that, furious
> failing some great catastrophe
> all the vain abyss gaping wide

> in the so white and trailing tress
> would have drowned avariciously
> a siren's childlike side.

After offering an apt presentation of the syntactical development of the poem,[18] Badiou turns first to translating its central figures into the concepts of the 'structural dialectic'. Thus, 'the abyss', in which sea and sky are indistinguishable, is interpreted as a 'figural representative' or a '[m]etaphor of the splace' (TOTS 76), no doubt because of the homogeneity that sea and sky, blended into 'the low-ceilinged oppressiveness of the nothing' (TOTS 76), share with the unicity of the *splace*. To this first metaphorical link Badiou adds a second link, this time between the sea-sky 'abyss' and 'the white page' upon which the poet writes. In addition to this 'abyss', the poem presents 'a trace, the foam', which 'holds the principle of a meaning' (TOTS 77). Upon the blank page, the poet has placed a thin thread of ink; and in the crushing homogeneity of the *splace*, the mark of something heterogeneous has appeared. Badiou suggests that we witness Mallarmé staging here the 'strong difference' (TOTS 87) between 'the mark', a distinctive trait, and 'the void', which names the necessary spacing between distinct marks and which is 'the condition *a priori*' (TOTS 68) of distinctivity and thus of the 'weak differences' that inhere between individual marks. As opposed, then, to being a mere structuralist for whom the 'penchant consists in seeking to combine elements that are identical' or in reducing everything to 'weak differences' (TOTS 55), Mallarmé is an enlightened conservative in so far as he posits from the outset 'an absolutely qualitative difference' between a distinctive trace – 'the foam' – and the non-intuitive process of *spacing* – 'the abyss', the void – that is the *a priori* condition of 'weak differences'.[19]

Badiou then claims that the poem is about the *interrogation* of the meaning of this mark, this minimal difference: 'On the Mallarméan sea, split off from nature, reduced to its anonymity, a trace, the foam, holds the principle of a meaning (*"tu le sais, écume"*: "you know this, foam") which it does not give up (*"mais y baves"*: "but slobber on")' (TOTS 77). There are two hypotheses as to the cause – the meaning – of the foam: it is either the trace of a sunken ship or of a siren's dive. The foam itself marks the eventual irruption of 'strong difference' that breaks with the homogeneity of the *splace* – an event of which the foam is the single, fragile trace. Next, Badiou remarks that '[t]hese two hypotheses are in turn organized according to two metonymic chains': the shipwreck and the siren are evoked by reference to their *parts*, rather than to themselves *qua wholes*. Specifically, the 'ship is made up of a distress signal (the horn), then of a mast stripped of its sail; the siren, of its young flank, and then of its trailing hair' (TOTS 78). In terms of the 'structural dialectic' these metonymies correspond to 'the chain effect' (TOTS 55) since they are the individuated elements of a system that totalises them – the system being either the ship or the siren *qua* 'absent causes'. The more poetic logic behind Mallarmé's decision to evoke these objects in such a manner is that, in so far as they are lacking, Mallarmé reinforces their lack by referring only to their most fragile, insubstantial attributes, and not to the ship or siren in their plenitude (TOTS 78).

Having demonstrated this link between semantics and metonymy, Badiou announces that 'we find ourselves back with all [the] categories' of the 'structural dialectic' that are operative in the poem:

> The strong difference (foam/blank), which opens up the problem of the thing; the network of weak differences, organized in metonymies (ship, mast, horn; siren, hair); the transition from one to the other by way of the causality of lack, supported by the vanishing terms: the ship's wreck and the siren's drowning, of which what is – the foam – is the mark out-of-place on the splace's desolation. (TOTS 78–9)

To this compact set of propositions Badiou adds the claim that the two 'vanishing terms', the shipwreck and the siren, are semantically and conceptually consistent with 'the abyss' *qua* void and hence with the 'strong difference' that is in play in an event: the shipwreck, for instance, is of course engulfed by 'the abyss', and the siren is a marine creature who inhabits the void as its element. A conceptual necessity is thus being actively inscribed in the various figures chosen by the poet.

Finally, Badiou turns to the stage of the 'structural dialectic' at which the 'deduction of the splitting' occurs.[20] In the case of 'Stilled beneath the oppressive cloud' this 'splitting' is evinced by 'the foam', which is at once a part of the sea-sky abyss *qua splace*, and is thus 'captured in the network of mundane differences', and a trace of the vanished event. As such, it is the precise poetic equivalent of 'the trace left behind in the social world by the great mass movements' (TOTS 64) that the Maoist 'lookout' (TOTS 68) is meant to preserve as well as deploy in order to orient their political praxis.

Badiou thus concludes that the poem is 'the emblem of the structural dialectic': its internal logic is integrally geared toward staging its operations. However, the poem does appear to break at a decisive moment with this logic: 'Why two vanishing terms (ship and siren)? Why this second cleavage which, cut in two by the enigmatic coup de force of "or", *ou cela que*, arranges two metonymical chains?' (TOTS 80). If the 'structural dialectic' *qua* the logic of 'structural causality' requires only *one* 'absent cause' to function – if, that is, the structuration of a set of distinctive marks is integrally determined by their belonging to a single system *qua* their 'absent cause'; or if the masses who *are* history are the effect of the vanished masses who *make* history – why does Mallarmé nevertheless stage *two*?

In posing this question, Badiou seems to be submitting his reading to the actual logic in play within the poem, thereby treating it as an autonomous artistic artefact that could potentially take him in a direction distinct from that which is required by his pedagogical – not to mention political – procedure. However, this apparent passivity on the part of the philosopher obscures the fact that Badiou will go on, now and in the following seminar session, to postulate a predictable isomorphism between the poem's two consecutive vanishing terms – the shipwreck and the siren – and the two stages in the passage to communism that French Maoism posits. Thus, while Badiou does permit the poem to unfold itself autonomously, allowing it go beyond the mere figuration of the 'absent cause', he quite brutally stamps the intra-poetic progression from shipwreck to siren with the mark of the Maoist doctrine according to which a *second* revolutionary rupture is required in order to break with the inertia of the socialist states.

Drawing this seminar session to a close, Badiou persists with his provocative interweaving of the Mallarméan and Marxist texts, proffering a set of affirmations that follow the Maoist line but which, on this occasion, mark a decisive difference with the poet:

> From that which put an end to the old tyrannies, we must also know how to liberate ourselves. Those who, after that, persist in talking about socialism and its State as a stable entity certainly share with Mallarmé the hypothesis of a halting point. But they have failed to see its annulation. (TOTS 83)

Here, the poet is clearly aligned with those who persist in believing that the contemporary incarnations of socialism, in particular the CPSU and its French outpost, the PCF, carry the revolutionary flame. There can be no progression beyond these institutions – no novel Maoist politics, for instance – since they effectively constitute 'a halting point' for history. As Badiou will demonstrate in the following seminar session, Mallarmé too posits 'a halting point' in his intra-poetic dialectic. However, his very own operation of 'annulment' contradicts the logic of the 'halting point'. A tension is thus engendered in the *form* of his poetry; a tension which, as we will see, is the mark of the conflict between his ideological conservatism and the latent – though disavowed – radicality of his poetic procedures. Badiou will explore this conflict in depth in the following seminar session.

*

When Badiou returns to 'Stilled beneath the oppressive cloud' he begins by clarifying what the operation of 'annulment' consists in. As he states, 'annulment' constitutes a rupture – a 'leap' (TOTS 87) – in the internal economy of the poem: in other words, it breaks the 'metonymical chains' that had been constituted by the initial hypothesis of the sinking ship (the stripped and abolished mast, the ineffectual horn). By proposing a second hypothesis, the operation of 'annulment' institutes a second and mutually exclusive totalisation that is radically heterogeneous to the first:

> Here the annulment of the vanishing, the shift to a second line of totalization, requires that instead of the metonymy of a supplementary effacement ... there comes – 'or else ...' – the qualitative break in which the strong difference, dismissed before, takes its revenge so that the repressed heterogeneity returns. (TOTS 87–8)

In breaking with the first line of totalisation, which had instituted a series of 'weak differences' between the various parts of the shipwreck, there necessarily occurs a brief return of 'strong difference', which Badiou quite strikingly describes as having been 'dismissed' or 'repressed' beneath the homogeneity of the initial 'absent cause'. Badiou claims that the very punctuality of this 'caesura' is part of a conscious strategy on Mallarmé's part: 'Oh, but Mallarmé would much rather not show this subject that the structural will of his dialectic stumbles up against! If only all this could be kept within the homogeneity of the poetic operations!' (TOTS 88). This last passage follows Badiou's statement that 'Mao discerned the current agency of the communist political subject, the stroke of force that separates it from its alleged prior line of existence.' Mao thus pinpoints a political and philosophical necessity in such a 'caesura', whereas Mallarmé, while equally astute intellectually – and hence, from another perspective, equally supportive of Badiou's position – 'would much rather not show' the unavoidable return of 'strong difference'. Mallarmé would instead prefer, as he writes in *Igitur*, that the 'drama [be] resolved in an instant, just the time of showing its defeat, which unfolds in a flash'.[21] For this unrepentant conservative, his reluctant admission of the necessity of 'strong difference' must be as swift – indeed as invisible – as possible. To cover over the 'the emergence of force' (TOTS 89), Mallarmé contains it within a minimal number of terms – 'or else ...' – in order to return as quickly as possible to 'the monotonous and infinite effectivity of the grinding of being under the law of an absence' (TOTS 89).

Badiou now poses an almost violently incongruous question: 'Why does the poem come to a close?' (TOTS 89). He continues: 'it would be logical for it to remain open-ended, since the combined operations of the vanishing and annulment, by which the cause produces its effect and then delivers its concept, by themselves imply no halting point whatsoever' (TOTS 90). As Badiou puts it further on, Mallarmé cannot be called a Hegelian, since his dialectical operations of 'vanishing' and 'annulment' do not have the perfect circularity of Hegel's idealist dialectic. According to Badiou – who is here provocatively ignoring the fact that the poem *is a sonnet* – the only way Mallarmé's poems can come to an end is by recourse to traditional figures such as the siren or the constellation, with which 'Hugo already end[ed] plenty of poems' and which Badiou suggests are 'signifiers' that are 'in some way separable' (TOTS 95) from the internal logic of the poem, governed as it is by 'vanishing terms' and 'annulments'. Indeed, as Badiou claims, it would be perfectly conceivable for the procession of 'vanishing terms' and their 'annulment' to continue indefinitely: 'The ship . . . or else the siren . . . if not Neptune . . . unless a conch. . . .' (TOTS 90). But Mallarmé's conservatism, Badiou suggests, leads him to produce a vision of 'an implacable finitude' (TOTS 92). To achieve this, Mallarmé must 'inject some familiar connotations' into the closing moments of his poems, which thereby offer an artificial impression of circularity: 'Because the floating language we inherit authorizes us to do so, we tolerate that a poem pauses at the rose of dark night or the swan's exile. We have almost arrived safe and sound, having been guided by the star' (TOTS 96). Thus, despite his relative inattentiveness to the semantic values of Mallarmé's key tropes, Badiou draws on them at this strategic moment in order to advance his vision of the poet as a conservative idealist. On Badiou's reading, Mallarmé is misleading us into thinking that the finitude of the 'structural dialectic' is an absolute horizon for thought and practice. It is therefore up to the Maoist philosopher to call the poet's 'bluff' (TOTS 96) and to deduce from Mallarmé's failed effort to contain the radicality of his poetic procedures the necessity of passing beyond the 'structural dialectic' to the 'historical dialectic'. This conclusion will be reinforced in the following section, where we turn to Badiou's reading of the 'Sonnet en -yx'.[22]

*

Her pure nails on high displaying their onyx,
The lampbearer, Anxiety, at midnight sustains
Those vesperal dreams that are burnt by the Phoenix
And which no funeral amphora contains

On the credenzas in the empty room: no ptyx,
Abolished shell whose resonance remains
(For the Master has gone to draw tears from the Styx
With this sole object that Nothingness attains).

But in the vacant north, adjacent to the window panes,
A dying shaft of gold illumines as it wanes
A nix sheathed in sparks that unicorns kick.

Though she in the oblivion that the mirror frames
Lies nude and defunct, there rains
The scintillations of the one-and-six.

In the final stage of his reading of Mallarmé in *Theory of the Subject*, Badiou turns to the arch-Mallarméan poem, the 'Sonnet en -yx'. Badiou will be particularly drawn to the poem's presentation of a deserted salon after nightfall, suffused as it is with the anxiety that follows the passing of daylight. Unlike other examples of the 'solar drama' in Mallarmé's *œuvre*, the 'Sonnet en -yx' stages a singular scenario in which almost all traces of the setting sun have disappeared. This reinforces the anxiety inspired by the thought that the vanished event – here the sun itself – is *forever* lost.[23] In this poem, even the 'vesperal dreams' of the event, which themselves are already situated at one remove from it as a reality, have been 'burnt by the Phoenix', a metaphor for the sunset. As Badiou states, in this poem the 'burden of lack ... is at a maximum' (TOTS 101). Gardner Davies, whose reading of the sonnet is Badiou's principal point of reference here, describes the sonnet as follows:

> If the allusion to the Phoenix suggests that it is here again a question of the solar drama, this sonnet, unlike the preceding ones, does not offer us a direct evocation of the sunset. The sonnet is as if situated at the second stage of the drama, the task of perpetuating the light of the vanished sun being entrusted to the genius of the poet ... In the obscurity, Anxiety maintains the memory of the vanished light and of all that it had inspired in the poet.[24]

For Badiou, the scenario of the 'Sonnet en -yx' resonates powerfully with the fading political fortunes of Maoism in the aftermath of May '68 – a situation from which all traces of the event seem to have vanished. However, in identifying with what Davies takes to be the task of 'the genius of the poet', Badiou and his Maoist comrades can transform this anxiety into an index of their fidelity to the event of May '68: 'For a militant Marxist, there is the anxiety of the night of imperialist societies, the anxiety of the ashy Phoenix of May '68, or of the Cultural Revolution ... It is also a duty to divide what is obscure, to hold fast to the workers' promise even at the heart of its deepest denial' (TOTS 108).

Badiou also believes that, at the properly conceptual level, the 'Sonnet en -yx' stages the two operations of the 'structural dialectic' we are already familiar with: 'vanishing' and 'annulment'. But it also presents a novel operation, 'foreclosure', which is evinced by the absent amphora, Master and ptyx. The specificity of these objects lies in the fact that, despite appearing to be 'vanishing terms' that could function as traces of the absent sun – the amphora, for example, could have held the ashes of the Phoenix, a metaphor for the sun[25] – they can neither play the role of 'vanishing terms' nor be subject to the operation of 'annulment' *because none of them are present in the room*. As Badiou has it, 'The amphora, the master, and the ptyx have all the attributes of the vanishing term, except the vanishing, from which a trace of the lack should be evinced. They lack without a trace. On this account, they are unsubstitutable' (TOTS 105 – translation modified). In locating this novel operation, Badiou again appears committed to allowing the poem to unfold its various modalities of absence autonomously, without undue interference from the philosopher. But it will now be his task to show what significance the operation of 'foreclosure' has for the 'structural dialectic'. The final line of the above passage gives us an indication: in so far as they are 'unsubstitutable' these terms are the point of departure from which all substitution – deduction – proceeds. As Badiou states: 'This is something you will never be able to deduce: this triangle of the subject [the Master], death [the amphora], and language [the ptyx *qua* pure signifier].' The terms that are 'foreclosed' in the sonnet strictly denote these surd-like foundations to rationality from which all thought and action proceeds. However, the pertinence of the operation of 'foreclosure' is not made particularly evident by Badiou, who makes another characteristic leap to a remark by Mao which contradicts the idea according to which there is, in fact, something unconceptualisable (TOTS 105). Arguably, then, the central though implicit role that the absent amphora, Master and ptyx play in Badiou's reading of the 'Sonnet en -yx' is to reinforce the radical fragility of the solar promise that the poem stages. As Gardner Davies has it, 'the absence of the amphora, the absence of the Master himself, seems to remove all elements that would be able to capture the dreams of light, which Anxiety continues to maintain in the obscurity of the empty salon'.[26]

And so, just as the poet's duty was to guard over the solar promise, the sonnet offers in the figure of the 'lamp-bearer' a precise image of the subjective stance the Maoists must take: 'We are lamp-bearers. Just as the poem does with the deserted salon, we inspect the political place in order to discern therein the staking out of antagonism that will relay the promise and organize the future' (TOTS 108). Indeed, after 'the burden of lack' (TOTS 101) with which the quatrains are invested, the poem will, finally, offer a fragile mark of this promise in the tercets:

> If the obscurity of the room seems once again to triumph over the dreams of light, let us not forget that in a torch relay the lamp-bearers always passed the torch on to the next lamp-bearer. Likewise, here, when the elements of light are threatened with extinction, the decor itself furnishes a symbol to replace them.[27]

The first symbol of the vanished sun, which is announced by an instance of what Badiou had called 'signifiers of the exception' (TOTS 87) – in this case, the 'But . . .' that opens the tercets – is the possible glint of dying sunlight at the mirror's edge: 'But in the vacant north, adjacent to the window panes, / A dying shaft of gold illumines as it wanes'. This, then, is the first intra-situational trace of the vanished event the 'Sonnet en -yx' offers the lamp-bearer-poet; a trace which is equivalent to the 'foam' from 'Stilled beneath the oppressive cloud'. And the first 'vanishing term' that could be its 'absent cause' is the nix that – perhaps – has been drowned in the dark pool of the mirror after being pursued by unicorns. Finally, in an apparent symmetry with the logical progression of 'Stilled beneath the oppressive cloud', the nix *qua* 'vanishing term' is followed by the operation of 'annulment', which is here performed by the upsurge within the frame of the mirror of the constellation of the Great Bear, another possible cause of the brief twinkling on the mirror's edge.

Badiou adds a final twist to his reading that returns to the negative image of Mallarmé as an intellectual conservative, purposefully repressing the immanent heterogeneity of 'strong difference' that is both presupposed and disavowed by his 'structural dialectic'. Indeed, Badiou argues that the 'Sonnet en -yx' is a particularly successful example of Mallarmé's strategy of disavowal. While in 'Stilled beneath the oppressive cloud' the re-emergence of the 'repressed heterogeneity' occurred in the break between the quatrains and the tercets and was marked by the signifiers 'or else', Badiou argues that with the 'Sonnet en -yx' we find only 'a subject of diminished force', a 'subject' that is 'almost folded back – finally! – onto the even surface of the metonymical operations' (TOTS 107). This 'subject' is nothing other than the upsurge of the constellation at the poem's close, which marks the promise of the event and thus of the 'strong difference' it had manifested. It is therefore as if the poet, motivated by a perverse will to dissimulate the necessary moment of 'strong difference', had engineered an ingenious way of having this moment go unnoticed.

But what does Mallarmé's strategy consist in? As we know, the narrative arc of the poem coincides with a search for the traces of the vanished event, the setting sun. It ends, finally, with the reflection of the constellation in the mirror, which confirms the promise of the event in the anxious depths of the night. However, the ruse of the poet consists in making us suppose that the discovery of the evental trace is the result of the creative praxis of the lamp-bearer figure with which the utopian poet and Maoist militant both identify. But in fact, the stars are there from the start: 'The solution to the lamp-bearing problem (here, the reflection of the Great Bear) must be there from the start. Only the poet's dead eye spins the subtle threads that link one object to another so that, in a tricked perspective, the illusion of a surprise may come about' (TOTS 108–9). The temporal progression from anxiety to salvation is nothing more than the imaginary trajectory of a subject stumbling upon signs that have already been laid out for them; nothing new happens in Mallarmé's poetry, only the shuffling between an already-fixed set of possibilities. The narrative arc of struggle followed by success is brutally undercut by the fact that the conditions for this success were always-already in place, set up like a trap by a conservative poet committed to demonstrating that there is 'no temporal advent of the new' (TOTS 108).

*

As we mentioned above, at no stage in his career does poetry *do* politics for Badiou. Only collective organisation, whose goal is to verify people's equality by winning enduring victories in the cause of emancipation, counts as politics. Moreover, politics need make no recourse to poetry in order to qualify *as* politics. However, it is evident from Badiou's reading of Mallarmé in *Theory of the Subject* that the poet's work has an irreducible conceptual and normative content that means it can still be scrutinised *in the light of* a specific political orientation, such as Badiou's revolutionary communism. While Badiou never frames his symptomal reading of Mallarmé as an instance of ideology critique, by interrogating the poet's 'structural dialectic' he engages in an exercise of intellectual vigilance, honing his attentiveness to the conceptual moves he must avoid – or in some cases sublate – if he is to be a properly revolutionary thinker. Importantly, Badiou's preferred dialectic, the 'historical dialectic', both presupposes and must constantly wrench itself away from the 'implacable finitude' (TOTS 92) of the 'structural dialectic' – just as, at the social level, the petty bourgeois intellectual committed to communism must perpetually resist the temptation of remaining a 'hermetic recluse' (TOTS 65) like Mallarmé. Indeed, what makes for the drama of *Theory of the Subject* is the very proximity between Mallarmé and Badiou: both recognise the insubstantiality of the social bond; both reject the false idol of parliamentary democracy, which they believe betrays the political essence of the people; and both set out to remedy their respective situations. Yet they draw irreconcilable conclusions from these premises. It is thus because of, and not despite, their points of agreement that Badiou attends so carefully – and sometimes so critically – to Mallarmé in *Theory of the Subject*. The consensus binding them together is precisely what brings into focus the most essential points of disagreement.

In summary, the key political lesson of 'The Subject Under the Signifiers of the Exception' is that the revolutionary upsurge of 'strong difference' need not be a fleeting, ineffective occurrence, as Mallarmé treats it. It need not inspire the poet's equal parts tragic and ludic conception of the insubstantiality of the social bond. Instead, 'strong difference' can be understood to be something that throws up the resources required to truly effect radical change. Where Mallarmé sees nothing more than an infinite oscillation between the 'vote' and the 'riot', Badiou sees a chance to courageously 'keep steady in the direction indicated by the founding disappearance of the mass movement', no matter how 'impoverished [the] present appears to be' (TOTS 64). In contrast to a true emancipatory politics, Mallarmé's 'sky-instinct' religion is an irredeemably conservative construction, since it leaves the reigning order intact, albeit emptied of all substance. Ultimately, then, 'The Subject Under the Signifier of Exception' is a complex exercise in intellectual purification – with Mallarmé in the position of the purified.

*

In a 2017 interview, Badiou critiques his own early critique of Mallarmé:

> [In *Theory of the Subject*] I present Mallarmé as a great master of the structural dialectic, which without any doubt he is: a poem by Mallarmé always deals with what is lacking-in-its-place in a structured place. And he describes the conditions of anxiety, in the night of the disappearance of the sun. At the time, however, I had not yet established the category of the event. My reading of Mallarmé was therefore unilateral. I did not see that beyond structure and lack (which are Lacanian categories) there is, in a number of his poems, the possibility given by Chance, and that there is therefore an opening in the dialectical division of the place on the basis of a radical event. This is what I later brought to light in *Being and Event*.[28]

By amending his overly 'unilateral' reading of Mallarmé, however, Badiou goes beyond providing a more comprehensive vision of the poet's work. In fact, he inverts its meaning. No longer an ingenious exponent of the 'structural dialectic', in Badiou's post-*Being and Event* work Mallarmé is read as having produced an unprecedented concept of the event, and not as seeking to repress the 'strong difference' that the event manifests. Writing in 'Is It Exact That All Thought Emits a Throw of Dice?' – the essay that marks the first appearance of this new, entirely positive, figure of Mallarmé in his philosophy – Badiou states that *Un coup de dés* is in fact 'the greatest theoretical text that exists on the conditions for thinking the event'.[29] What could have happened to Badiou's thought for Mallarmé to appear in such a different guise?

In one sense, this shift is to be expected. *Being and Event* marks a new beginning not only for Badiou's thought but also, if its claims are taken seriously, for all of Western philosophy *as such*. As a work of fundamental ontology that elaborates an unprecedented mathematical discourse on Being *qua* Being, produces a doctrine of the event as that which breaks with knowledge, and constructs an account of the production of truths, *Being and Event* is a far more ambitious and extensive work than *Theory of the Subject*. Most importantly for our purposes, however, are the following two points. Firstly, in *Being and Event* Mallarmé is said to have provided 'the matheme of the event' (BE 178–83, 191–8): that is, to have poetically depicted the precise multiple that an event consists in relative to Badiou's ontology. Secondly, in contrast to *Theory of the Subject* where Mallarmé's poetry is submitted to a fundamentally political scale of values, after *Being and Event* Badiou affirms the absolute autonomy and truth-producing dignity of art.[30] Rather than marking a limit beyond which the Maoist philosopher must pass, Mallarmé's writings, in so far as they poetically articulate the concept of the event, at once occupy a central place in Badiou's post-*Being and Event* philosophical architecture and are recognised as a 'truth procedure' in their own right (BE 404–5). These two changes mean our approach to Mallarmé's political significance in the second stage of Badiou's career will be markedly different to our reading of *Theory of the Subject*. Is it even possible to speak of a politics of literature in the context of Badiou's engagement with Mallarmé after *Being and Event*?

To introduce Badiou's radically new orientation to Mallarmé, we can begin with a close reading of his interpretation of *Un coup de dés*, which he first presents in 'Is It Exact That All Thought Emits a Throw of Dice?' (1986) before composing a shorter, revised version that would become 'Meditation Nineteen' in *Being and Event*. In what follows we will focus on this latter version of his reading.

The first paragraph of the 'textual meditation' (BE 19) devoted to Mallarmé presents a synthetic overview of what Badiou believes the author of *Un coup de dés* to have achieved. It begins with the following programmatic statement: 'A poem by Mallarmé always fixes the place of an aleatory event; an event to be interpreted on the basis of the traces it leaves behind. Poetry is no longer submitted to action, since the meaning (univocal) of the text depends on what is declared to have happened therein' (BE 191). In the first sentence of this summary, we already find the two-part movement of the 'event-drama' (BE 191) that *Un coup de dés* will stage in its conceptual purity. But before we consider the details of this 'conceptual drama' (BE 197), we should first turn our attention to Badiou's account of the historical originality of Mallarmé's poetry. His comments in 'Is It Exact That All Thought Emits a Throw of Dice?' give us some indication of how he conceives of the poet's innovations:

> It is essential to understand that, at the antipodes of the connection between dream and Nature, in which the Romantic vision had its origins, and which Baudelaire had only half disentangled, since he remained nostalgic for it, Mallarmé holds that, in the epoch of the reign of technology, and of the accomplishment of Cartesianism in its effective possession, Nature has ceased to be of value as a referent for poetic metaphor: 'Nature has taken place; it can't be added to, except for cities or railroads or other inventions forming our material.' I will therefore hold that the real of which the Mallarméan text proposes the anticipation is never the unfolded gesture of a spectacle. Mallarmé's doctrine devotes poetry to the event, which is to say to the pure there is of occurrence.[31]

Poetry, then, no longer contemplates nature, nor is it the passive conduit of its creative effervescence. Baudelaire, the perpetual in-betweener, is the last of the Romantics, albeit a bitter one. What Mallarmé's novel poetry does, by complete contrast, is to turn its focus towards awaiting and welcoming the event. As such, it does not fall into the quietistic pessimism Sartre had diagnosed but rather wagers on the advent of an unforeseeable occurrence. For poetry to no longer be 'submitted to action', then, is for it to no longer have to re-present the generically defined series of actions of French neo-classical poetics, nor any natural plenitude. Rather:

> it organises an experience in which, all factuality being subtracted, the pure essence of that-which-takes-place is captured. The Mallarméan question is not: what is being? His question is: what is it 'to take place' [avoir lieu], what is it for something 'to happen' [se produire]? Is there a being of that-which-takes-place in so far as it takes place?[32]

To put it somewhat simplistically, poetry no longer deals with a string of actions, since all of the action – the event – occurs *prior* to the scene presented in the poem. Or to be even more precise, an event never takes the form of a narrative since it cannot be understood within the terms of what currently counts as an intelligible action or series of actions.

But what, precisely, is the event the poem is dedicated to thinking? As we mentioned above, Mallarmé's poetry presents a two-part movement that is the 'event-drama' itself: firstly, there is the 'staging of its appearance-disappearance ("... we do not have an idea of it, solely in the state of a glimmer, for it is immediately resolved ...")'; and secondly there follows 'its interpretation which gives it the status of an "acquisition for ever"' (BE 191). Intriguingly, the quotation Badiou uses to describe the precariousness of the event's taking-place comes from *Igitur*, which he had previously cited in *Theory of the Subject* to underscore the fleeting fragility of 'the emergence of force' (TOTS 89). Significantly, in the present iteration of the *Igitur* passage Badiou leaves out the following italicised lines, which are those he attends to most closely in *Theory of the Subject*: '. . . we do not have an idea of it, solely in the state of a glimmer, for it is immediately resolved, *just the time of showing its defeat, which unfolds in a flash*'. In *Theory of the Subject* the emphasis was placed on 'the defeat' of the re-emergence of 'force'. For Badiou to excise this latter part of the passage is therefore to shift our focus towards Mallarmé as the heroic poet-thinker of 'the doctrine of the event'[33] and away from him being its conceptual and political enemy.

For its part, the Thucydides quotation, 'an acquisition for ever', signifies that the concept of the event in Mallarmé's poetry will have an effectively trans-temporal validity. As Badiou confidently asserts, *Un coup de dés* is nothing less than the production of 'an absolute symbol of the event' (BE 193) that will form part of the architecture of his philosophical system.

Opposed to the 'pure notion' of the event, however, is 'reality in its massivity', a 'reality' that is 'merely imaginary, the result of false relations, and it employs language for commercial tasks alone' (BE 192). This introduces Badiou's own singular interpretation of Mallarmé's canonical distinction between 'the double state of speech – brute and immediate here, there essential' (D 210). For Badiou: 'If poetry is an essential use of language, it is not because it is able to devote the latter to Presence; on the contrary, it is because it trains language to the paradoxical function of maintaining that which – radically singular, pure action – would otherwise fall back into the nullity of place' (BE 192). Poetry, by guiding the conceptual construction that allows us to rationally discourse on the event, is devoted to at once thinking *and* naming the event. It can therefore be called upon when *any* event is at stake – including political events, as we will see in the last section of this chapter.

Badiou opens his reading of *Un coup de dés* proper with the statement that 'the metaphor of all evental-sites being on the edge of the void is edified on the basis of a deserted horizon and a stormy sea' (BE

129). The key to the homology between the 'evental site' and the figure of 'the Abyss', the setting for the action of *Un coup de dés*, lies in the latter's strict *homogeneity*. We will soon see the significance of this. Firstly, let us secure the semantic link between 'the Abyss' and its indivisibility. Gardner Davies, for instance, speaks of 'the homogeneous void of the sky and the sea'.[34] Badiou echoes this description, writing that within 'the Abyss' 'sea and sky [are] indistinguishable' (BE 192). Thus, 'the Abyss' is a powerful figure of the One: there are no meaningful distinctions within it; nothing of what it contains can be differentiated or discerned; it immediately swallows up anything that would try to assert its difference from 'the identical neutrality of the abyss' (CP 140), such as the wing-like sea foam that is 'fallen back in advance from being unable to dress its flight' (CP 128).

But what does this have to do with the 'matheme of the event'? As we noted above, 'the Abyss' provides Badiou with a sensible image of what he calls 'the evental site'. To be precise, an 'evental site' X belongs to, or is counted-as-one by, a situation S. However, no element belonging to the site X also belongs to the situation S. Badiou states: 'I will term *evental site* an entirely abnormal multiple; that is, a multiple such that none of its elements are presented in the situation' (BE 175 – Badiou's emphasis). We might say that while 'the Abyss' *qua* 'evental site' is counted-as-one by the situation S, nothing that lies within 'the Abyss' can be distinguished from the perspective of the situation S. Hence its indivisible massivity. We can now understand the following topological metaphor: 'The term with which Mallarmé always designates a multiple presented in the vicinity of unpresentation is the Abyss' (BE 192). What is 'unpresentable' here are those multiples that belong to the site X but which, for that very reason, do not belong to the situation S, from whose perspective they are void.

Turning now to the third paragraph of 'Meditation Nineteen', Badiou claims that Mallarmé presents a particular 'paradox' associated with the concept of the 'evental site': namely, that 'it can only be recognized on the basis of what it does not present in the situation in which it is presented'. In other words, its singularity lies in the fact that what it presents – the elements that belong to it – are *nothing* from the perspective of the situation S. Mallarmé offers a figuration of this structural particularity 'by composing, on the basis of the site – the deserted Ocean – a *phantom* multiple, which metaphorizes the inexistence of which the site is the presentation' (BE 192 – Badiou's emphasis). This '*phantom* multiple', whose ghostly character derives from the fact that it is not actually presented on the scene the poet stages, is that of 'the image of a ship . . ., sails and hull', which is 'annulled as soon as invoked' (BE 192). As Gardner Davies notes, 'the poet does not explicitly mention the vessel'; nevertheless, given that on the previous double-page of the poem the word *shipwreck* had appeared, 'the cloud – wing of the Abyss – is transformed into a sail, to which the sea will join its gaping depths in order to form the hull of a phantom ship'. Davies therefore concludes: 'Thanks to the analogy, the Abyss succeeds in evoking this ship which no longer exists and has perhaps never existed.'[35] No trace of the ship remains; its reality is therefore eminently questionable: 'the Ocean alone is presented'. As such, the ship's fragile reality, which emerges in a flash only to disappear, can figure 'whatever unpresentability is contained in the site': namely, those 'inexistent multiples' that are void from the perspective of the situation S. The lesson that Badiou draws from this is that '[t]he event will thus not only happen within the site, but on the basis of the provocation of whatever unpresentability is contained in the site' (BE 192).

To better grasp this point, we can turn to the 'matheme of the event' itself. The event *qua* multiple is written as follows:

$$e_X = \{x \in X, e_X\}$$

In this 'matheme', X denotes the 'evental site' (which therefore belongs to S, the situation); x denotes the elements of the site X, which are 'unpresented' from the perspective of the situation S; and finally e_X denotes the signifier of the event itself. Thus, when Badiou speaks of the evocation of the shipwreck, in other words 'of the provocation of whatever unpresentability is contained in the site', he is referring to those multiples denoted by the algebraic term x.

Badiou then draws on the semantic resources of the idea of a shipwreck: 'every event, apart from being localized by its site, initiates the latter's ruin *with regard to the situation*, because it retroactively names its inner void. The "shipwreck" alone gives us the allusive debris from which (in the one of the site) the undecidable multiple of the event is composed' (BE 192–3 – Badiou's emphasis). Thus, the shipwreck, in addition to being nothing more than a ghostly presence, also carries with it the additional semantic – and conceptual – charge of being that which can 'ruin' its site. Since the unpresented multiples are, relative to the situation S for which X is a site, void, their effective presentation would disrupt the count of this situation, which is precisely what individuates the elements of the site. The 'allusive debris' of the shipwreck – the inexistent multiples – thus threaten the consistency of the situation S and promise its disruption.

We should underscore the fact that in the above-quoted passage

Badiou qualifies the multiple of the event as 'undecidable'. This will be absolutely central for what follows. Before we turn, then, to Badiou's reading of the remainder of the poem, we must specify in what precise sense the multiple of the event is 'undecidable'. As the passage suggests, the issue turns on whether or not the multiple of the event belongs to the situation S. To determine this, it is necessary to investigate its elements. Do the elements of the multiple of the event belong to S? We know that the multiples belonging to the 'site' X – that is, those multiples denoted x – do not. The only remaining element on which to base our decision is therefore the signifier of the event itself, e_X. The question then becomes whether or not the event e_X belongs to the situation S. But the fact is that when we turn to examine the elements of the multiple $e_X = \{x \in X, e_X\}$ in order to determine whether any of them belong to S, we have already identified e_X, since it belongs to this multiple. *One must therefore already have identified the event – in other words, have already determined that it belongs to the situation S, which is also to say have already determined that it is distinct from the multiples x – when one sets out to identify whether it belongs to S or not.* Badiou writes: 'The basis of the undecidability is thus evident: it is due to the circularity of the question. In order to verify whether an event is presented in the situation, it is first necessary to verify whether it is presented as an element of itself' (BE 181). He reinforces this point further on by noting that '[t]he set [e_X] can only be recognized inasmuch as it has already been recognized' (BE 189–90). Badiou's English-language translator, Oliver Feltham, puts the point in the following way:

> This reflexive structure [i.e. that the multiple of the event belongs to itself] not only blocks knowledge but also incites it to re-invent its categories. If, in order to know what kind of multiple the event is, one already needs to know what it is, then the identity of the event is suspended from the acquisition of a knowledge that one evidently does not possess. However, when one does come to possess this knowledge, one will have already possessed it due to its reflexive structure: to know what the event is one has to already know what it is composed of. This strange logic of the future anterior is precisely that of the generic procedure and its enquiries into the consequences of the event belonging to a situation.[36]

Feltham makes it clear here that Badiou's construction of the multiple of the event presages his complex elaboration of the procedure of 'forcing' in the latter part of *Being and Event* – a procedure whose significance we will soon address. What is most important to us at the moment, however, is to again underscore the specific significance of the term 'undecidable' that flows from the 'matheme of the event'. For in addition to the topology of the 'evental-site' figured by 'the Abyss' it is the 'undecidab[ility] [of the event] with regard to its belonging to the situation' (BE 192) that constitutes one of the two key moments at which *Un coup de dés* inscribes the 'matheme of the event' and thus conditions Badiou's philosophy.

Turning now to the fourth paragraph, Badiou writes: 'the *name* of the event – whose entire problem, as I have said, lies in thinking its belonging to the event itself – will be placed on the basis of one piece of this debris' (BE 193 – Badiou's emphasis), these 'debris' being the same 'allusive debris' that Badiou had already linked to the 'shipwreck' and – in terms of his set-theoretical ontology – to the 'inexistent multiples' that belong to the site X. In terms of the 'matheme of the event' the '*name* of the event' is precisely e_x itself. That it is drawn from one of the inexistent multiples can be deduced from the fact that it cannot be a term of the situation, S, for otherwise it would unequivocally belong to this situation, which would mean that the event, in its essential undecidability, would be dissolved. In *Un coup de dés*, this conceptual necessity is figured in the fact that 'the *name* of the event' has an internal semantic link to the shipwreck.

But what, precisely, is 'the *name* of the event' in the poem? It is nothing other than 'the captain of the shipwrecked vessel' (BE 193) himself, who clasps in his outstretched hand two dice that he threatens to throw before sinking beneath the waves. In the following paragraph, Badiou explicitly states that the 'event' at stake in *Un coup de dés* is this very 'cast of dice' itself, which he says 'symbolizes the event in general; that is, that which is purely hazardous, and which cannot be inferred from the situation, yet which is nevertheless a fixed multiple, a number, that nothing can modify once it has laid out the sum – "refolded the division" – of its visible faces'. Put simply, a 'cast of dice joins the emblem of chance to that of necessity' (BE 193). Likewise, the event is absolutely contingent: nothing can prescribe its occurrence. However, once it is given a name – once it has been decided that it belongs to the situation S – it is fixed and therefore necessary.

Badiou can thus say that '[t]he event in question in *Un coup de dés* ... is therefore that of the production of an absolute symbol of the event' (BE 193). However, the goal of poetically staging the event in its conceptual purity places the following strict constraints on Mallarmé:

> given that the essence of the event is to be undecidable with regard to its belonging to the situation, an event whose content is the eventness of the event (and this is clearly the cast of dice thrown 'in eternal circumstances') cannot, in turn, have any other *form* than that of indecision. Since the master must produce the absolute event (the one, Mallarmé says, which will abolish chance, being the active, effective, concept of the 'there is'), he must

suspend this production from a hesitation which is itself absolute, and which indicates that the event is that multiple in respect to which we can neither know nor observe whether it belongs to the situation of its site. (BE 193)

Consequently, 'our sole access ... is to a hesitation as eternal as the circumstances' (BE 193). The reason, then, that Mallarmé never stages the rolling of the dice in *Un coup de dés* is because he is determined to present the event in its conceptual essence. Again, this supposes a particular interpretation of the act of rolling the dice: that to roll the dice is to decide that the event belongs to the situation. Conversely, to definitively *not* roll the dice would be to decide that the event does *not* belong – that it inexists in the same indifferent fashion as the other inexistent multiples that belong to the site X. This would come down to 'the cancellation of the event by its total invisibility' (BE 194). However, in avoiding both of these options – that is, in maintaining the hesitation of the Master, a hesitation that Badiou had already described in *Theory of the Subject* as effecting 'the equivalence of negation and affirmation' (TOTS 94) – Mallarmé presents the 'the concept of the event', or rather 'an absolute symbol of the event' (BE 193).

Badiou now interprets the series of figures that are successively staged in the poem – the 'Nuptial veil', the 'feather' and finally 'Hamlet' – as all representing the '*concept* of undecidability' (BE 194 – Badiou's emphasis): the 'veil' hovers between a union with the situation and, since it is 'on the point of submersion', its dispersal; the 'feather' also oscillates between being scattered across ('strewing') the situation, or escaping it ('fleeing'); and finally 'Hamlet' is 'the very subject of theatre who cannot find acceptable reasons to decide whether or not it is appropriate, and when, to kill the murderer of his father' (BE 194). Badiou reads this series as an accumulation, as well as an intensification, of the idea of undecidability, such that the 'impatient terminal scales' of the siren, who suddenly emerges on page eight, end up dispersing the tense and fragile equivalence between rolling and not rolling the dice:

> the undecidable equivalence of the gesture and the place is refined to such a point within this scene of analogies, through its successive transformations, that one supplementary image alone is enough to annihilate the correlative image: the impatient gesture of the Siren's tail, inviting a throw of the dice, can only cause the limit to the infinity of indecision (which is to say, the local visibility of the event) to disappear, and the original site to return. (BE 195)

Running concurrently to this suite of figures, Badiou locates Mallarmé's 'abstract lesson', namely: 'If... it was the Number, it would be Chance.' He translates as follows: 'If the event delivered the fixed finitude of the one-multiple that it is, this would in no way entail one having been able to rationally decide upon its relation to the situation' (BE 195). The contingency of the event, in other words, is absolute.

However, this absolute contingency of the event threatens to make it radically unthinkable. And indeed, Badiou announces that 'the tenth page', with its nihilist inscription 'nothing will have taken place but the place', suggests that 'the power of place is such that at the undecidable point of the outside-place reason hesitates and cedes ground to irrationality' (BE 196). In other words, this evocative locution signifies that there is no rational thought of the event, and therefore no event as Badiou understands it: 'the place is sovereign . . ., "nothing" is the true name of what happens' (BE 196).

And yet, in a move that is strictly consistent with his construal of Mallarmé as the heroic poet-thinker of the pure event, Badiou does not conclude with this nihilist reading of the poem:

> Page eleven, opened up by an 'excepted, perhaps' in which a promise may be read, suddenly inscribes, both beyond any possible calculation – thus, in a structure which is that of the event – and in a synthesis of everything antecedent, the stellar double of the suspended cast of dice: The Great Bear (the constellation 'towards . . . the Septentrion') enumerates its seven stars, and realizes the 'successive collision astrally of a count total in formation'. (BE 196)

The appearance of the constellation, then, is the *second* event of the poem after that of the never-accomplished roll of the dice. It corresponds to the second moment of Mallarmé's intra-poetic dialectic presaged in the first paragraph, namely, that of the emergence of a 'pure notion', here the 'absolute symbol of the event'. As Badiou states, the upsurge of the constellation shares with the event the property of the absolute contingency of its occurrence – it emerges 'beyond any possible calculation'. Moreover, it arises, on Badiou's reading, as 'compensat[ion]' for 'the courage' required to 'maintai[n] the equivalence of gesture and non-gesture' (BE 197). In other words, Badiou reads the upsurge of the constellation as causally linked to the successful staging of the concept of the event in the preceding pages of *Un coup de dés*, just as his master Gardner Davies did.[37] Indeed, the very emphasis placed on the sovereignty of the 'place', which had momentarily led us to conclude that a rational thinking of the event was impossible, marks Mallarmé's refusal to consider the event as anything but absolutely contingent: 'By causing the place to prevail over the idea that an event could be calculated therein, the poem realizes the essence of the event itself' (BE 197). In contrast to the limitations of Mallarmé's 'structural dialectic' as presented in *Theory of the Subject*, Badiou thus fully affirms the unprecedented thinking of event that occurs, in his estimation, in *Un coup de dés*.

*

As we have just seen, the reading of *Un coup de dés* found in 'Meditation Nineteen' of *Being and Event* occurs in a completely different conceptual universe to *Theory of the Subject*. Most importantly, it reverses Badiou's judgement about the normative and metaphysical orientation of Mallarmé's poetry. In *Theory of the Subject*, if Mallarmé was seen as attributing a radical evanescence to the event then this was in the guise of an ideologically motivated gesture whose goal was to arbitrarily limit the space of thought and action to the 'structural dialectic'. By contrast, in 'Mallarmé's Method' – an essay from 1992 written in the wake of *Being and Event* – Badiou argues that if Mallarmé stages two vanishing terms in 'Stilled beneath the oppressive cloud' then this was not to inscribe as discretely as possible the moment where 'the emergence of force' occurs. Rather, it was to 'mark the undecidability of the event' *qua* an essential component of the event's concept: 'That which took place', he writes, 'must fail in its having-taken-place if the poem is the thought of the event *as such*.'[38] What was once a subterfuge that the materialist reader had to expose is now a sign of unprecedented conceptual precision.

But the differences between the two Mallarmés are most palpable in Badiou's reading of *Un coup de dés*. In 'Meditation Nineteen', when Badiou insists upon the poet's uncompromising commitment to inscribing the event in its complete contingency, he simultaneously insists that this does not exclude but rather entails that Mallarmé affirm 'the place [as] sovereign'. For the event *is* nothing from the perspective of the situation in which it occurs. In *Theory of the Subject*, the swift disappearance of the event was read in light of a project that sought to *make* it disappear. In *Being and Event*, by contrast, to insist upon the event's fragility is not to distort its concept. Rather, it is to be as intellectually rigorous about it as possible. In political terms, while the first of Badiou's Mallarmés set out to make political action seem impossible, the second poetically inscribes its exacting conditions of possibility. For Badiou's second Mallarmé, every political procedure begins with an event, and every instance of politics involves both traversing 'the anxiety of hesitation' – an anxiety figured by the feather from *Un Coup de dés*, which 'hovers about the gulf' – and engaging the 'courage of the outside-place', a 'courage' that orients itself by way of the constellation, 'up high perhaps'.

This last remark offers us a final piece of evidence in our examination of the differences between Badiou's two Mallarmés. In his first reading of the 'Sonnet en -yx' Badiou focuses on the sonnet's evocation of anxiety. In the theoretical universe of *Theory of the Subject* the affect of anxiety always risks immobilising the subject or sends it running into the arms of a superego-like figure (TOTS 291–2). This is precisely the case with the 'Sonnet en -yx' as Badiou reads it in his 1982 work. With no traces of the vanished sun-event to sustain it, the subject lacks all means by which to orient itself: its anxiety is thus provoked. At the same time, however, its trajectory is being computed by a perverse law-giving figure who is none other than Mallarmé himself, whose 'dead eye spins the subtle threads' (TOTS 108) that end up entangling the subject in its finitude. In 'Mallarmé's Method', by contrast, the anxiety provoked by the event's undecidability is conceived as a spur to courageous action. As Badiou writes, 'to the vanishing subtraction of the event annulment *adds* the need to decide its name':[39] in other words, the event's radical fragility does not hamper action, but sparks it. Or rather, it shows that in order to create the truly new the subject requires courage to act without the old Law. Badiou's second Mallarmé is thus a poet *both* of anxiety *and* of courage – a poet who summons us to traverse the first while motored along by the second.

Returning to Badiou's 2017 interview on Mallarmé, his assessment of Jean-Claude Milner's reading of the poet, which we explore in the next chapter, can thus be applied to his own in *Theory of the Subject*. Criticising Milner's 'a-dialectical' interpretation of the sonnet 'The virginal, enduring, beautiful today', Badiou states that 'the Mallarméan poem ... exposes itself to the peril of nihilism only to dismiss it'.[40] Badiou was wrong, then, to accuse Mallarmé of being a 'structural sectarian of weak differences' (TOTS 108). If his poetry so powerfully evoked the crushing homogeneity of the *splace*, this was only out of intellectual honesty – an honesty that ultimately gave rise to a clear-sighted ethics of courage.

It is not our aim here to determine the precise reasons for Badiou's about-face. The most likely, in our view, is that Badiou's meta-ontological transliteration of the mathematical forcing procedure in *Being and Event* makes it possible to conceive of a truth as a production that begins with an undecidable event. Indeed, the specific sense of undecidability that Badiou extracts from *Un coup de dés* is unintelligible without the procedure of forcing – an argument we have made elsewhere with Christian Gelder.[41] Put simply, it only makes sense to see Mallarmé's inscription of the event's absolute contingency as a spur to courageous action if action – or, more precisely, if the production of a truth – requires an undecidable event to begin.

Whatever the case may be, with *Being and Event* Mallarmé emerges as a figure in total solidarity with Badiou's philosophical, normative and even political orientation. However, if we are to establish the precise nature of their *political* solidarity we need to confront the challenge posed by the doctrine of *inaesthetics*, which prohibits any essential relation between poetry and politics. To do this, we will turn for the remainder of this chapter to the essay 'A French Philosopher Responds to a Polish Poet'.

*

Published for the first time in *Handbook of Inaesthetics*, 'A French Philosopher Responds . . .' is an apparently minor circumstantial piece[42] in which Badiou responds *qua* philosopher to the 'fraternal lesson' (HI 28) offered to the French – or to Western Europeans more generally – by the Polish poet and Nobel Prize recipient Czeslaw Milosz.[43] It is also a stunningly compact expression of Badiou's post-*Being and Event* views on Mallarmé's poetry and his conception of the place such poetry could have in a political conjuncture dominated by the failure of Marxism and the downfall of the Soviet states.[44] It therefore not only warrants our close attention but can also be used as a sort of scaffolding for our reading of Badiou's engagement with the poet in the second stage of his philosophical trajectory. In it, Badiou counters Milosz's claim that Mallarmé's poetry is politically irresponsible and attempts to demonstrate its exemplary egalitarianism and universalism – two predicates that determine its indissoluble solidarity with Badiou's own politics.

The essay brings together all of the principal themes of Badiou's post-*Being and Event* thinking of poetry. Firstly, it is written under the sign of *inaesthetics*, Badiou's novel doctrine for dealing with the relation between philosophy and art. This is a doctrine which, as an instance of the more general doctrine of *conditions*, affirms the autonomy of art in its capacity to produce singular and self-sufficient truths that philosophy must think *qua* truths and occasionally integrate into its own operations.[45] Secondly, it draws on ideas related to Badiou's thesis of the existence of 'the Age of the Poets' and of its properly philosophical accomplishments.[46] Thirdly, it deals implicitly with the foundational conflict between 'the matheme' and 'the poem' that animates Badiou's later thinking.[47] Finally, it articulates the relation between Mallarmé's poetry and the key concept of the event.

'A French Philosopher Responds . . .' is also invested, via the mediation of the opposition Milosz posits between the historical experiences of Eastern and Western Europe, in an explicitly political problematic: that of the fortunes of Badiou's communist politics in a period characterised by the fatigue of Marxism and the fragility of the Soviet states. Within this complex political conjuncture, Badiou will turn to Mallarmé as a poet explicitly committed to egalitarianism and universalism – a poetic 'comrade' to his own politics.

We will begin with a brief introduction to Badiou's doctrine of *inaesthetics* before dealing with three points of criticism that Milosz makes of Mallarmé's poetry: that it is elitist, subjectivist and neglects the world of collective historical experience. Against each point that Milosz makes, Badiou will argue forcefully for the universal address of Mallarmé's work.

In 'A French Philosopher Responds ...', Badiou explicitly draws attention to the nationality of the two polemical partners. As far as the national parameters of his essay are concerned, we should note from the outset that Milosz spent much of his youth – including the crucial period of his poetic apprenticeship – in Paris.[48] With such a direct link to the French artistic and intellectual tradition it is unsurprising that the author of *The Witness of Poetry* sees the trajectory of poetic modernity as inseparable from the artistic movements of late nineteenth-century France, particularly Symbolism. Speaking of his youthful sense of inferiority to Parisian culture, Milosz writes: 'In provincial East and Central European capitals a myth was born, of Paris, the capital of the world ... In my youth, apprentices in poetry, if they came from the blank spots on the map, had to undergo a short or a longer period of training in Paris.'[49] Now, however, the tables have turned. At the time of writing his Harvard University lecture series, and after having been awarded a Nobel Prize, Milosz is in a position to proffer 'a fraternal lesson' to the culture he had originally so glorified and felt, as a Pole, so inferior to.

Before we look at the details of Milosz's critique, we should immediately note that, curiously, Badiou frames his response as being itself a sort of lesson – specifically, a lesson in the practice of *inaesthetics*. For according to his *inaesthetic* way of treating the art-philosophy knot Badiou argues that philosophy can only function properly by 'abstain[ing] from *judging* the poem', and from avoiding the temptation of offering it any 'political lessons' (HI 27). This, however, is precisely what Badiou claims Milosz has done. As such, the Pole's entire argumentative procedure risks being invalid. The principal reason for this invalidation is that, for the Badiou of *Handbook of Inaesthetics*, art produces *singular* truths that are *immanent* to it. Drawing together these two main categories, Badiou writes: 'Art is rigorously coextensive with the truths that it generates' and adds: 'These truths are given nowhere else than in art' (HI 9). Thus, philosophy, which is limited to constructing an empty formal model of Truth and does not produce any truths of its own, must respect the fact that both the *thinking* and the *production* of these artistic truths occurs without its mediation. Indeed, 'the poem' specifically 'permits us to forgo the claim that the singularity of a thought can be replaced by the thinking of this thought' (HI 27). For Badiou, any intra-philosophical criteria that could be brought to bear on 'the poem' as a 'truth procedure' are *a priori* irrelevant. Indeed, judging 'the poem' by any extra-artistic criteria at all – including the particular scale of political values that Milosz brings to bear on Mallarmé's poetry – is illegitimate. All criteria relevant for judging 'the poem' are immanent to it and it alone. Art is an absolute.

Badiou thus speaks from a philosophical position that must rigorously *refuse* to judge the poem. Even if there is something politically problematic about Mallarmé's poetry, as Milosz argues there is, then this could only arise from the application to it of a scale of values it is strictly indifferent to. To consider Mallarmé's work as a 'truth procedure', as Badiou does, is therefore to subtract it from the pertinence of any and all political problematics.

However, as we will now go on to show, Badiou will play something of a double game in 'A French Philosopher Responds . . .'. For while he will avoid responding to Milosz's socio-historical diagnosis of the faults of modern French poetry by deferring to the autonomy of Mallarmé's poetry *qua* 'truth procedure', Badiou will also explicitly link this poetry to the stakes of his current political circumstances. We will come back to this peculiar torsion in Badiou's post-*Being and Event* thinking about art.

Returning now to Milosz, we can capture what is essential in his critique of modern French poetry by seeing it as structured according to two interlinked axes: a West–East axis, and a past–future axis. For Milosz, French poetry from Baudelaire through Mallarmé is the origin of modern poetry, and produces the main current of poetic thought and practice after Romanticism: Symbolism. However, the Polish poet will return to this French tradition in order to diagnose its weaknesses and show how poetry from the Eastern bloc has transcended – and will continue to transcend – the various handicaps of this heritage.

Firstly, in terms of the weaknesses twentieth-century poetry was bequeathed by French Symbolism in general and by Mallarmé in particular, Milosz writes:

> The poetry of the twentieth century inherited the basic quarrel between bohemian and philistine, something we should not forget. It was not the best preparation for the encounter with a reality that grew more gigantic

and more ominous with every decade, increasingly eluding the grasp of the mind.[50]

In its withdrawal from a sphere of perceived spiritual inferiority, Symbolist poetry adopted a posture of aristocratic disdain for those people deemed incapable of reading it. The opposition broached here by Milosz between 'bohemian' and 'philistine'[51] is no doubt the backdrop to the question of the *address* of poetry that Badiou deals with in the section of his essay entitled 'To Whom is the Poem Addressed?' For as Milosz remarks, one of the 'basic tenets of modern poetics which was codified by the French Symbolists' was 'the belief that true art cannot be understood by ordinary people'.[52] In other words, the very definition of true poetry depended upon the strict delimitation of a narrow circle of legitimate addressees, a claim that contrasts starkly with Badiou's confident affirmation that '[t]he poem is, in an exemplary way, destined to everyone' (HI 31).

Now, as Milosz is at pains to demonstrate, this 'isolation of speech' (D 211) is not a question of the essence of 'the poem' but is rather a distinctly *historical* phenomenon. It is a conception of poetry's relation to 'the Human family' that arose *after* Romanticism and bears witness to what he calls 'a deep schism'[53] within European culture – a schism that would eventually be closed, at least in Poland, but only at an enormous historical price. Commenting on the now out-of-date separation between poet and people as it is allegedly figured in Mallarmé's sonnet 'The Tomb of Edgar Poe', Milosz writes: 'It is precisely that aspect of poetry in isolation as depicted in this sonnet which strikes us as incompatible with what we have learned in the twentieth century. Social structures are not stable, they display great flexibility, and the place of the artist has not been determined once and for all.'[54] For Milosz, Mallarmé raised to the status of a universal what was merely the outcome of a passing conjuncture. Like Sartre, Milosz sees Mallarmé as having 'postulate[d] the constant repetition in an indefinite future of the handful of readers which he has at present'.[55] However mistaken Mallarmé might have been about the relation between poet and people, Milosz is of the view that the inertial force of his perceived conception of 'the place of the artist' has negatively affected the capacity of poets to deal with the events of the twentieth century. Indeed, even those events during which poetry and revolution were seemingly in lockstep bore the marks of these limitations: 'The suicide of [the Russian Revolution's] bard, Mayakovsky, had more than personal significance. Both Mayakovsky's *œuvre* and his death are marked by contradictions characteristic of the Russian intelligentsia of the preceding century, which were brought to cruel light by revolution.'⁵⁶ The Mallarméan heritage has thus been one of ethical and political incapacitation. Against this heritage, Milosz extols the virtues of twentieth-century Polish poetry, taking care to point out the high historical price that was paid for them. According to him, in mid-twentieth-century Poland a specific set of historical events threw together people from different social strata, thus providing the conditions for the production of a form of poetry much more consistent with the union of poet and people that the Romantics had aimed for:

> When an entire community is struck by misfortune, for instance, the Nazi occupation of Poland, the 'schism between the poet and the great human family' disappears and poetry becomes as essential as bread. I foresee the objection that exceptional situations such as war and the Resistance can scarcely be used as a standard. Yet under the Nazi occupation, class barriers in the Polish underground began to be broken down; that was the beginning of a process intensified later on under Communist rule, until finally another society took shape, the one the world saw in the workers' strike of August 1980. In that new society it was not unusual for 150,000 copies of a book of poems to be sold out in a few hours; the division between the worker and the intellectual was waning too.⁵⁷

Thus, in more general terms, Milosz argues that in Polish poetry

> a peculiar fusion of the individual and the historical took place which mean[t] that events burdening a whole community [were] perceived by a poet as touching him in a most personal manner. Then poetry is no longer alienated. As the etymology of the term suggests, poetry is no longer a foreigner in society. If we must choose the poetry of such an unfortunate country as Poland to learn that the great schism in poetry is curable, then that knowledge brings no comfort.⁵⁸

This, then, is the conception of 'a poetry sung by an entire people' that Badiou sees Milosz as offering on the basis of the historical experience of 'the East, armed with its great suffering' (HI 28). But whatever the achievements of twentieth-century Polish poetry, it remains the case that, for Milosz, the name of the 'schism' that has adversely affected poetry since Symbolism is Mallarmé.

Turning now to a critical exegesis of Badiou's response to Milosz, we can begin with his disagreement over the *address* of modern French poetry, in particular that of Mallarmé. While Milosz focuses on the socio-economic position from which Mallarmé spoke and which he figured in the opposition between the 'angel' who 'purif[ied] the meaning of tribal words' and the 'hydra' (PV 169), a figure of 'the crowd' as an ensemble of philistines, Badiou is inclined to ignore such historical sociologising and to remain content with affirming the ever-present *universality* of the poem's address: 'The poem is, in an exemplary way, destined to everyone.' Whether it arises from within the quasi-aristocratic conditions of the French literary field of the late nineteenth century, or emerges at a moment during which 'the crowd does not declare itself' (HI 30) – that is, during a period lacking a revolutionary politics – poetry's universal address remains a virtual property that no empirical schism between poet and people can take from it. Badiou continues: 'The poem is, in an exemplary way, destined to everyone. No more and no less than mathematics. This is precisely because neither the poem nor the matheme takes persons into account, representing instead, at the two extremes of language, the purest universality' (HI 31). Badiou's response to Milosz's historical diagnosis of the disastrous withdrawal of poetry from the public sphere thus consists in proposing a particular conception of Mallarmé's poetic language as inextricably linked to universality. What the above passage seems to mean is the following: if 'the poem' manifests one of the two 'extremes of language' and 'mathematics' the other, and if 'mathematics' necessarily involves the strict and ever-operative *univocity* of its terms and the rules that govern their relations, then it follows that, by contrast, 'the poem' gives voice to the irreducible *equivocity* of language. To be more precise, 'the poem', rather than maintaining the ruled regularity of a mathematical discourse – or indeed of any normative discourse whatsoever – involves the exploitation of language's capacity for the creative production of ever-renewed effects of sense. If this is correct, what could it mean that 'neither the poem nor the matheme takes persons into account'? As far as 'mathematics' is concerned, the univocity of its marks determines that whoever deploys them must do so in an identical way on pain of the entire mathematical machinery breaking down. But in the case of 'the poem', its exploration of equivocity *qua* one of the two 'extremes of language' poses a different problem: what could the relation between radical equivocity and universality be?

Badiou does not directly address this question in 'A French Philosopher Responds...'. However, the claim that the universality of 'the poem' derives from its exploration of the equivocity of language is dealt with at other moments in his post-*Being and Event* work, albeit not in these precise terms. If we admit that 'the poem' gives voice to the equivocity of language, then we can understand this as an activity by which 'the poem', in its creative exploration of the productivity of language – of 'the power of language' (HI 27) – subtracts itself from the stable meanings of established interpretative communities. This negative, corrosive moment of 'the poem' means it runs transversally to any and all particular set of addressees. In Badiou's terms, poetry approximates 'the generic', which for our present purposes we can describe as that which is subtracted from all of the predicates of a particular situation and which is thus properly 'indiscernible'[59] for the situations' regime of knowledge. It can thus be correlated with people in their universality, or with what Badiou calls 'generic humanity'.[60] Poetry is essentially universal.

It is reasonable to assume that this is what Badiou has in mind when he refers to 'the poem' as the exploration of one of the 'two extremes of language'. To confirm this, we can note that in the post-*Being and Event* stage of his philosophical trajectory Badiou frequently presents poetry as a linguistic practice that subverts the referential value of language by naming that which *par excellence* cannot be discerned by the knowledge of a given situation: namely, the event. As he puts it in the following exemplary passage from *Conditions*:

> naming an event, in the sense I give to the latter, that is, that which, being an undecidable supplementation, must be named for a being-faithful, and therefore a truth, to occur – this naming is *always* poetic: to name a supplement, a chance, something incalculable, it is necessary to draw from the void of sense, in the absence of established significations, and to the peril of language. One must therefore poeticize, and the poetic name of the event is that which throws us outside of ourselves, through the flaming rings of prediction.[61]

As such, 'the poem' effects a *negative universality*. Avoiding any determinate set of addressees and any situationally specific set of referential values, 'the poem' can address itself to the 'egalitarian crowd' (HI 31).

Let us recall that this is Badiou's response to Milosz's concerns regarding the elitism and hermeticism of post-Mallarmé poetry. For the Polish poet, the trajectory he hoped poetry would trace would be from having a restricted circle of addressees to a situation in which – like in the works of Anna Swirszczynksa, Miron Bialoszewski and Aleksandr Wat[62] – the poet's writings would echo with the experiences of a determinate people: '[In Polish poetry] events burdening a whole community [were] perceived by a poet as touching him in a most personal manner',[63] allowing him to give voice to the experiences of a collective. In light of this, it is as if Badiou is attempting to outdo Milosz on the very question of universality. While for Milosz it was still a matter of poetry addressing a particular audience – though one far larger than the circle of 'bohemians' – what matters for Badiou is that poetry refers to no particular audience at all in order to address an even purer universal: 'generic humanity'. For him, 'the poem' is the language of nobody, of no established community; it is veritably 'foreign to the language' (D 211).

We can make two preliminary points about Badiou's procedure here:

Firstly, as 'a philosopher' Badiou has explicitly countered Milosz socio-historical diagnosis with a discourse on the 'Idea' (HI 32) of 'the poem' as it is exemplarily manifest in Mallarmé's work. Whatever the historical vagaries of poetry in its relation to the public, these do not impact upon its essence, which is to represent, at one of the two 'extremes of language, the purest universality'.

Secondly, and as a prolegomena to the next stage of our argument, Badiou has saved Mallarmé from the damning verdict of the Polish poet by recourse to the argument that 'the poem', in contrast to 'the matheme', is the exemplary exploration of language's equivocity; of its capacity for infinite flexibility, which allows it to surpass the limits of all particular communities of sense and to produce a negative universality. However, we will presently see that Badiou's response to Milosz's accusations regarding the 'subjective excess' (HI 28) of Mallarmé's poetry will lead him to make the exactly opposite claim. Let us return, then, to *The Witness of Poetry*.

*

So far, we have considered Milosz's argument that modern French poetry wilfully subtracted itself from the concerns of the collectivity; that this was the result of a socio-economic scission; and that historical circumstances produced a clear and untenable tension between the latent aristocratism of French Symbolism and the poetry that was called for in the twentieth century, particularly during and after the Second World War. To this, Badiou responded by insisting upon the very *subtractive* virtues of Mallarmé's poetry, taking them as the index of an even purer universality.

We can divide the remainder of Milosz's claims and Badiou's response into two parts: the first concerning the poet's accusation of the 'subjective excess' apparently manifest in Mallarmé, and the second concerning Milosz's concomitant claim concerning the 'forgetting of the world and of the object' that occurs in Mallarmé's *œuvre*.

Firstly, then, to the claim of 'a subjective excess' in modern French poetry, to which Badiou will oppose – surely rightly – the 'radical anonymity of the subject of the poem' (HI 30). It would appear that Badiou is here responding to the following view put forward by the Polish poet: speaking of Oscar Milosz, his older relative who lived in early twentieth-century Paris, Milosz writes:

> Twentieth-century poetry suffered 'impoverishment and narrowing' because its interests became limited to 'an aesthetic and nearly always individualistic order'. In other words, it withdrew from the domain common to all people into the closed circle of *subjectivism* ... In Europe, since the middle of the

nineteenth century, the poet has been an alien, an asocial individual, at best a member of a subculture.[64]

Further on in *The Witness of Poetry*, Milosz makes the following comments regarding late nineteenth-century poetry:

> Strange things happen in the poetry of the second half of the nineteenth century: instead of stressing the longevity of art, the solitary rebels who opposed the right-thinking citizens elevated art so high as to remove from it any goals whatsoever and began to glorify it as a thing unto itself, *l'art pour l'art*. In the very midst of a universal weakening of values deprived of their metaphysical foundations, there arises the idea of a poem outside that crisis. Such a poem should be perfectly self-sufficient, submitted to its own laws, and organized as a peculiar anti-world. Now the reward is not recognition by posterity but rather the fulfilment of the poet's personality, as if he were leaving forever a cast of his own face: 'Tel qu'en lui-même enfin l'éternité le change', as Mallarmé says in his poem 'The Tomb of Edgar Poe'.[65]

There are a number of implicit points in Milosz's description of this 'subjective excess' that need to be made explicit.

Firstly, and as we can gather from his above-mentioned socio-historical diagnosis of the fortunes of poetry, the 'individualis[m]' and 'subjectivism' of which Milosz speaks here – and note that the two terms are not meaningfully distinct for him – are both a product of the social scission between 'between bohemian and philistine'.[66] For this reason, the 'closed circle of subjectivism' of late-nineteenth- century poetry, which opposed itself to 'the domain common to all people', is a circle *that is closed off from other classes*. In other words, the 'solitary rebels' are individuated *via* their negative relation vis-à-vis other social collectives; their 'subjectivism' is a sort of ideological outgrowth of a social isolation.

Secondly, in condemning the 'closed circle of subjectivism' of late nineteenth-century French poetry, Milosz is operating on the assumption that the only conceivable counterpoint to a Romantic communion with the people is a kind of radical individualism. But it seems that he is insensible to the tension in his own description of the poetry of the 'solitary rebels' between the poem as a 'perfectly self-sufficient' object that is 'submitted to its own laws', and the poem as a reflection of the individual 'personality' of the author. Surely a poetic absolutism cannot be folded back onto a 'subjectivism' without contradiction?

Milosz thus seems to conflate the narrowing of concerns and the concurrent formal innovations of Symbolist poetry, which reflect its genesis within a highly restricted field of addressees separated from 'the domain common to all people', with a 'subjectivism' *qua* an ideology of the self-sufficiency of the ego. *And it is against the latter conception that Badiou will argue*. In this way, while Badiou correctly makes the case for the 'radical anonymity of the subject of the poem' in Mallarmé, he arguably avoids Milosz's implicit problematic concerning the socio-historical process by which the artistic field has been cut off from society at large.

Let us turn now to a detailed consideration of Badiou's response to the accusation of a 'subjective excess' in Mallarmé. The key to his response will be the notion that there are discrete 'operation[s]' (HI 29) present in Mallarmé's poetry that determine its effective functioning – 'operations' that are, according to Badiou's implicit description of them in 'A French Philosopher Responds . . .', *univocal*. Obviously, this is in stark contrast to his above-mentioned insistence on 'the poem' as the exploration of the equivocity of language. We will have to take care, then, to demonstrate in what precise way Badiou, despite never openly affirming that these 'operations' are univocal, nevertheless depends upon them possessing this property.

To begin, let us cite the opening passage of Badiou's response to Milosz: 'Is Mallarmé a hermetic poet? It would be quite futile to deny the existence of an enigmatic surface of the poem. But to what does this enigma invite us, if it is not the voluntary sharing of its operation?' (HI 29). We can read here a brilliantly paradoxical response to Milosz's implicit equation of the apparent 'hermeticism' of Mallarmé's *œuvre* with its 'subjective excess': that is, Badiou transforms the 'enigmatic surface of the poem' into a safeguard against the reader slipping into a soppy subjectivism or into the hermetic enclosure of an exclusive community, such as 'the club of writers and the public of specialists'[67] that both Sartre and Milosz fear has kept poetry to itself since Mallarmé's time. On the contrary, the surface-level difficulty of the poem is precisely what demands the intersubjective confirmation of 'its operation'.

The poem thus has an inherently *collective* subject on its horizon. As such, rather than being a self-protective move that aims to divert the attention of 'the labouring masses',[68] 'the enigma' of Mallarmé's poetry is in actual fact an invitation to the 'voluntary sharing of its operation'. The univocity of its 'operations', as well as the difficulty of immediately discerning them according to a false *doxa*, are properties directly linked to its *universality*.

Before we go any further, we need to secure the sense in which Mallarmé's poetic 'operations' are univocal for Badiou. Already in *Theory of the Subject* Badiou had rebuked those readers of Mallarmé who, while claiming to enjoy his poems' 'polysemy' (TOTS 74), were in fact avoiding the difficult task of elucidating their logic. For Badiou, by contrast, there was 'One' (TOTS 75) meaning operative in poems like 'Stilled beneath the oppressive cloud', as in the 'Sonnet en -yx' or *Un coup de dés*. Badiou repeats this claim three years later in the essay 'Is it Exact . . .'[69] before reprising it again in *Being and Event*: 'the meaning (*univocal*) of the text depends on what is declared to have happened therein' (BE 191 – our emphasis). In our view, the best way to interpret these provocative claims is simply to see the univocity in question as a *conceptual* univocity: for Badiou, Mallarmé's poems truly do inscribe conceptual operations that are iterable and thus ideal – hence their univocity. As he writes in 'Is it Exact . . .', 'the intelligibility of the most minor of [Mallarmé's] poems supposes that we carefully distinguish three regimes of negation: *vanishing*, which has causal value, *annulment*, which has conceptual value, *foreclosure*, which has null value'.[70] Every reader of Mallarmé's poetry is thus summoned to identify and distinguish between the different operations of negation his poetry puts to work. Failing to do so means that Mallarmé's poetry simply does not function, like a machine the reader has been unable to get running. A reader of a Mallarmé poem is therefore in a similar position to a person tackling a mathematical problem: they can only do so successfully if they allow themselves to be traversed by the effective universality of the mathematical procedure; a procedure which, like the poem, employs rigorously univocal marks.

It is in this way that Badiou deflates the force of Milosz's concerns that Mallarmé's cannot be a poetry that is 'sung by an entire people'. He thereby also resolves the problem of the *de facto* separation of poet and public. For Badiou, the universality of 'the poem' persists despite its formidable complexity; despite its production by a withdrawn, quasi-aristocratic poet; and despite any empirical conditions – such as 'the great schism in poetry'[71] – that could hamper the capacity of 'the crowd' to access it. Furthermore, in contrast to Milosz's wayward accusation of 'a subjective excess', the univocity of the poem determines that when 'we delve into its operation' (HI 29) we are radically anonymous, having submitted ourselves to a universally valid and repeatable procedure.

Now, whatever the force of Badiou's arguments here we can again see that Milosz's attentiveness to, and anxieties about, changing socio-historical circumstances have given way to the philosopher's confidently anti-historicist stance that prefers the assertion of the essence of 'the poem' in its address to 'generic humanity' over the tentative grip on historical trends that the author of *The Witness of Poetry* aims for. While Milosz's wish was for poetry to be concretely reconciled with 'the great human family'[72] – as it had been in twentieth-century Polish poetry – for Badiou such a reconciliation has always-already taken place: 'the addressee of the poem [is] always and everywhere by right the Crowd' (HI 32). Badiou is confident that, for Mallarmé, 'the Crowd' names the collective subject who is the addressee of his poetry:

> If people are defined, in an egalitarian stance, by their capacity for thought – this being the only sense that can be ascribed to the strictest equality – then the operations of the poem and the deductions of mathematics offer the paradigm of what is addressed to all. Mallarmé calls this egalitarian 'all' the 'crowd', and his famous and unachieved Book has no other addressee than this crowd. (HI 31)

Rather than being a term that evokes the phenomena of massification and democratic levelling, 'the crowd' of which Mallarmé speaks is a name for 'generic humanity'. It can come as no surprise, then, that while Milosz regrets the latent aristocratism – if not misanthropy – of some late nineteenth-century French poetry, Badiou sees a direct link between Mallarmé's 'poem' and a revolutionary communist politics. This is confirmed, as far as Badiou is concerned, by the iteration of the term 'the crowd' in the prose text 'Restricted Action', which Badiou draws on in the following key passage:

> The Crowd is the condition for the presence of the present. Mallarmé rigorously indicates that his epoch is without a present for reasons that come down to the absence of an egalitarian crowd: 'There is no Present, no, a present does not exist. Unless the Crowd declares itself.' If – as we shall see, as we have yet to see – there is today a difference between East and West regarding the poem's resources, it should certainly not be ascribed to suffering, but to the fact that, from Leipzig to Beijing, the crowd (perhaps) declares itself. This historical declaration (or rather, these declarations) constitute a present and modify (perhaps) the conditions of the poem. In the naming of an event, the operation of the poem can register the latency of the crowd. The poem then becomes possible as a general action. (HI 31)

As the context of Badiou's remarks make clear, the concept of the 'Present' here designates a political event, which, in the terms of *Being and Event*, involves two components that make it possible for Badiou to link it to 'the poem'. Firstly, it concerns 'generic humanity' and thus the exemplary addressee of the poem (HI 34). Secondly, it involves a rupture with established regimes of knowledge that determine what is discernible within a given (political) situation. This means it involves the *nomination* of what is 'indiscernible'. Hence, it involves poetry. As Badiou writes, 'in summoning the retention of what disappears, every naming of an event or of the eventual presence is in its essence poetic' (HI 26). By virtue of these links, Badiou can henceforth treat Mallarmé's poetry as if it were in perfect solidarity with the politics he affirms.

But what is most striking about the above passage is that Badiou seems to place 'the poem' *under condition of politics*. That is, despite affirming, in the final paragraph of the essay that immediately precedes 'A French Philosopher ...', that philosophy should not judge poetry politically, Badiou here clearly makes the possibility of certain forms of poetic activity dependent upon the political circumstances they are contemporaneous with. Specifically, given the possibility that a political event might be occurring in the Eastern bloc countries in the wake of *Solidarność*, Badiou affirms that 'the poem' can there be summoned, as per its 'Idea', to perform 'the nomination of an event' and so accede to the status of 'general action'. What poetry is capable of doing is dependent upon the current situation of emancipatory politics: poetry's rhythms follow those of political action. On the basis of this idea, Badiou can argue – and here he adopts Milosz's own organising opposition between Eastern and Western Europe – that in 'the West during the melancholy eighties' only 'restricted action' (HI 31) can be envisaged, whereas in the East 'general action' is a live possibility. Continuing to place 'the poem' *under condition* of a political conjuncture, Badiou now puts forward the argument we saw Sartre make at the start of this chapter:

> Restricted action demands that the poet create the theatre of his most intimate defections – of his most indifferent places and his shortest joys – so as to anticipate the Idea. Or, as Mallarmé superbly says: 'The writer, with his pains, dragons he has cherished, or with his light-heartedness, must establish himself, in the text, as a spiritual *histrio*.' (HI 32)[73]

Just as Sartre did, Badiou draws a lesson from Mallarmé regarding the role the poet can play in a 'non-revolutionary'[74] situation: that of attesting through their dissatisfaction to the inadequacy of a situation in which people are separated from their true political being.

Against Milosz, then, on Badiou's reading Mallarmé was in perfect communion with 'the great human family',[75] even and perhaps especially in his withdrawal from a fallen public sphere. For he kept alive the desire for humanity's eventual emancipation as members of 'generic humanity' and refused to address them in a 'demagogic' fashion according to 'how they [were] aligned with their circumstances'. His isolation was thus strictly consistent with his uncompromising commitment to universality.

What is the logic behind Badiou's apparent submission here of 'the poem' to the vagaries of politics? Despite the contradiction that this seems to represent for the doctrine of *inaesthetics*, the answer to this question is quite simple: in so far as 'the poem' is internally related to Badiou's doctrine of the event, it can be invoked in any instance at which such an event and its consequent 'truth procedure' is at stake. Mallarmé is thus paradigmatic in his anticipatory poetic openness to 'the generic', which is what the event involves, as well as in terms of the capacity his poetry has to name the event upon its upsurge. Finally, in so far as Mallarmé himself took part in the singular 'truth procedure' that is post-Hugolian poetry, he can be a metonymy for the basic orientation of Badiou's post-*Being and Event* philosophy, including its commitment to a communist politics in the face of the dominance of 'capitaloparliamentarianism' and the failure of Marxism. Whether or not art *must* do what Mallarmé's poetry does politically is a question we will address at the close of this chapter.

*

We can turn now to the final stage of our critical exegesis of 'A French Philosopher Responds...'. So far, we have shown how Badiou has shifted the terrain of discussion from Milosz's socio-historical diagnosis of the varying relations between poet and public since the end of the nineteenth century to a more strictly philosophical problematic that concerns the 'Idea' of 'the poem'. Against the charge that modern French poetry had irresponsibly withdrawn from 'the domain common to all people', Badiou radicalised the very conception of universality that 'the poem' implied and expanded it to the status of 'generic humanity'. Against the charge of subjectivism, he advanced the idea that the univocal 'operations' of Mallarmé's poetry made it impersonal, the product of a pure capacity of 'thought'. We turn now to the final accusation made by Milosz, namely, that post-Mallarméan poetry has manifested 'a forgetting of the world and of the object'.

First of all, it is important to note that Badiou has again re-inscribed Milosz's problematic into distinctly *philosophical* terms, for the very notion of 'a forgetting of the world and of the object' – a notion that Badiou will read and respond to in terms of the philosophical category of *objectivity* – has to do, predictably, with the Polish poet's concern that post-Mallarméan poetry is 'perfectly self-sufficient, submitted to its own laws, and organized as a peculiar anti-world'.[76] Milosz's name for this kind of poetry is 'pure poetry'.[77] When, in his response to this concern, Badiou refers to 'the world' he is therefore re-inscribing Milosz's terms of reference in a distinctly philosophical register. But of course Milosz's problem here is again the relation of the poet to the public, particularly in so far as this is manifest in the apparent refusal of Mallarmé's work to have any links to specific circumstances, indeed to 'the world' as such. Milosz remarks: 'The poets of the past were not "pure". That is, they did not assign poetry a narrow territory, did not leave religion, philosophy, science and politics to ordinary people who supposedly were unable to share in the initiations of the elite.'[78] While such a characterisation of modern poetry seems incongruous in the case of Mallarmé's *œuvre*, filled as it is with spiritual, philosophical, scientific and political reflections, Milosz is again registering, albeit in a somewhat mystified fashion, the socio-historical split between poet and public. In any case, Badiou shifts terrain abruptly, though not without reproducing in a peculiar way some of the tropes tied to the paradigmatic opposition 'between bohemian and philistine',[79] as we will see. Let us return to Badiou's remarks on 'the enigma' of Mallarmé's poetry:

> to what does this enigma invite us, if it is not to the voluntary sharing of its operation? This idea is crucial: The poem is neither a description nor an expression. Nor it is an affected painting of the world's extension. The poem is an operation. The poem teaches us that the world does not present itself as a collection of objects. The world is not what 'objects' to thought. For the operations of the poem, the world is that thing whose presence is more essential than objectivity. (HI 29)

Badiou continues:

> In order to think presence, the poem must arrange an oblique operation of capture. This obliquity alone can depose the façade of objects that generates the shadow play of appearances and opinions. It is because the procedure of the poem is oblique that we are obliged to enter into it, rather than be seized by it. (HI 29)

Let us first address the substantial *philosophical* point that Badiou is making here. As he claims in *Manifesto for Philosophy*, the poetry of 'the Age of the Poets' is characterised by 'a major novelty': namely, 'the *destitution of the category of object*. More precisely: the destitution of the category of object, or of objectivity, as necessary forms of presentation . . . Poetry is then essentially *disobjectifying*.'[80] The refusal of the referential value of language by the poetry of this 'Age' means that the very category of the 'object' *qua* the referent of language is dissolved. This is what allows 'the poem' to name the event, since the event is what breaks with established regimes of knowledge and is therefore by definition 'indiscernible' or 'unpresentable'.[81] For the same reason, 'the poem' gestures towards a species of what Badiou calls 'inconsistent multiplicity', which is the very being of what is.

Thus, when so-called 'pure poetry' gives up on language's duty to re-present the object-world, it is this world itself that disappears: 'the poem' offers us a glimpse of the 'inconsistent multiplicity' that subtends all 'consistent multiples'. This has intra-philosophical implications such that for Badiou – as his language strongly suggests – it draws us closer to the fundamental reality of things. As an exemplary member of 'the Age of the Poets', Mallarmé helps us to 'depose the façade of objects that generates the shadow play of appearances and opinions' (HI 29) and offers us the following lesson: namely, that 'the world' is not a set of objects exhaustively classified by the operations of knowledge, but rather principally what Badiou here calls 'presence', which names the irruption of the event but which can also be taken as being equivalent to 'inconsistent multiplicity', since the event brings the latter to the surface of knowledge. While Milosz had hoped that poetry would turn itself to the most decisive occurrences of the twentieth century, for Badiou its role has been to relieve us of the illusion of *'the category of the object'*. It is not that modern French poetry has no links with the world, but rather that it has changed the very status of what the world is.

In the above-quoted passage, Badiou reinforces this point by recourse to a set of powerful rhetorical moves. Note, to begin, the important role played by the term 'voluntary': if the meaning of 'the poem' is not immediately clear in terms of some spontaneous *doxa* – and is thus an 'enigma' – then we must take a greater degree of responsibility in elaborating its meaning with clarity. Thus, *passivity* – the passive reception of some spontaneously recognisable *doxa*, similar in nature to the 'imitation of the effect of truth' (HI 2) that art, according to Plato, exemplary produced and which is here associated with 'the pressure of the instant' (D 233) characteristic of the commercialism Mallarmé denounces – is opposed to *activity*, which is associated with the following positively connoted qualities that Badiou links to thought as such: 'labor' (HI 18), a refusal of 'every immediate form of thought' (HI 19), and finally the pursuit of 'an *explicit* procedure of thought' (HI 19 – Badiou's emphasis). Thus, while *passivity* is opposed to *activity*, there is an accompanying opposition between *immediacy* and *mediacy*, the latter being the mark of the temporal duration appropriate for a proper reading of 'the poem' – a reading which, in its submission of the reader to an operation that breaks with habit, helps to 'depose the façade of objects that generates the shadow play of appearances and opinions'.[82] Thus, we have a number of structuring oppositions: *passivity* versus *activity*, *immediacy* versus *mediacy*, and, as this last passage suggests, *doxa* versus *truth* – or, to put this in more properly philosophical terms, between the 'consistent multiples' of established regimes of knowledge and that 'inconsistent multiplicity' that, for Badiou, is the very being of a universal truth.

Badiou thus thinks of the Mallarméan poem not only as univocal and therefore as universal, but also as a sort of exercise into which 'the reader must enter ... in order to reach the momentary point of presence' (HI 29), in the process of which they strip off their submission to *doxa*. The opacity of the poem is not an index of an impoverished aristocratism but rather of its being a critical activity that leads us with implacable rigour to a vision of universality. Intriguingly, the *doxa* to which the truth of the 'present' is opposed is evoked by reference to a passage from Mallarmé's 'The Mystery in Letters', a prose text originally written as a polemical rejoinder to Marcel Proust's accusations of, precisely, Mallarmé's 'hermeticism'. Badiou frames his reference to this text in the following way:

> As for the enigma of the poem's surface, it should really serve to seduce our desire to enter into the operations of the poem. If we give up on this desire, if we are repelled by the obscure scintillation of verse, it is because we have let a different and suspect wish triumph over us – the wish, as Mallarmé writes, 'to flaunt things all in the foreground, imperturbably, like street vendors, animated by the pressure of the instant'. (HI 30)

In other words, those who would reduce Mallarmé to 'a hermetic poet' are complicit with the status quo; with a *doxa* that privileges what is most immediately obvious and which therefore partakes in the essentially repetitive, or circular, nature of ideology. This suspect reader is the willing victim of the habits of mind cultivated by advertising, their thought similar to that of the fast-paced and unreflective reactions of the consumer. Their opposite number is the philosopher or poet, for whom surface appearances are only a collectively accessible *trompe l'oeil* that hides a deeper truth: 'presence'. In citing Mallarmé's 'The Mystery in Letters' Badiou is able to draw on that article's polemical articulation of an opposition between, on the one hand, the refined complexity of his poems' operations, and on the other the vulgarity, superficiality and unthinking spontaneity of the reading habits cultivated by the press and commercial activity more generally. As Mallarmé wrote: 'I prefer, faced with aggression, to retort that contemporaries don't know how to read – Anything but a newspaper; which has, of course, the advantage of not interrupting the chorus of preoccupations' (D 236).

If we return now to Milosz's arguments, we can see that Badiou has again dramatically shifted the terrain of discussion. For the philosopher is now operating with a distinction between 'the world' *qua* a 'collection of objects' and 'presence', the first being fundamentally false and the latter the unprecedented revelation of 'the Age of the Poets'. Next to Milosz's arguments this opposition might appear extreme since it would seem to relegate the Polish poet's preferred form of poetry – namely, a poetry that would manifest 'a fusion of the individual and the historical'[83] – to the negative pole of Badiou's binary opposition: that of a spontaneously comprehensible poetry that would partake in 'the shadow play of appearances and opinions'. But for Milosz, his preferred poetry's accessibility would not arise from any ideological 'shadow play' but rather from shared historical experiences, in particular of catastrophes; experiences in which 'poetry becomes as essential as bread'.[84] The immediacy of such a poetry would be less a product of lazy thinking than of the historical experiences of a particular people.

To summarise this final section, we have drifted from – in Milosz's work – (1) an opposition between 'pure poetry', produced for an exclusive elite and essentially concerned with itself, and poetry as intertwined with the world and with the concerns of the greatest number, to – in Badiou's work – (2) an opposition between 'the world' *qua* 'a collection of objects', a conception denounced as ideological and aligned with 'a demagogic poetry' that addresses people relative to 'how they are aligned with their circumstances', and the 'world' *qua* 'presence', which the true poetry of 'the Age of the Poets' reveals to us and which is in solidarity with its addressees *qua* members of 'generic humanity'. What this means is that Badiou has again re-directed the discussion from Milosz's rather traditional understanding of the opposition between Romanticism and its darker successor, postromanticism – intertwined as this opposition is with his accompanying conceptions of the artist as either communitarian prophet or aristocratic recluse – to a distinctly philosophical problematic. But in terms of *this* problematic, Mallarmé, far from being an irresponsible nihilist, becomes an unequivocally positive model of the praxis of a poet – and, by analogy, of the political militant – in a period during which 'the crowd does not declare itself'.

One final question remains. Throughout this chapter we have demonstrated that while Badiou, unlike the Telquellians or Sartre, never conflates poetry with political action, he still reads Mallarmé's poetry through the lens of his own political commitments. In *Theory of the Subject* this involved interrogating Mallarmé as a poet of the 'structural dialectic', a 'dialectic' that Badiou, as a revolutionary, knew he had to surpass in the direction of an 'historical dialectic'. Similarly, in his post-*Being and Event* work Badiou consistently treats Mallarmé's writings as a body of work that supports his own – both conceptually *and* politically. But does this mean he has broken the rules of *inaesthetics*? In our view, Mallarmé is a political figure for Badiou, just as he is a poetic one. Yet Badiou's doctrine of *inaesthetics* remains intact since neither he nor any future practitioner of *inaesthetics* is obliged to judge *all* art through the same lens as Badiou judges Mallarmé's. An artistic truth procedure remains a truth procedure irrespective of whether it is explicitly egalitarian, as Mallarmé's, on Badiou's reading, conveniently is. The political frame Badiou brings to bear on Mallarmé's writings should not be confused with the evaluative framework of *inaesthetics*.

But is Badiou right to read Mallarmé as an egalitarian? In the next chapter we turn to the strongest possible objection to Badiou's version of 'comrade Mallarmé': Jean-Claude Milner's book *Mallarmé au tombeau*.

NOTES

1. For the French original, see J.-P. Sartre, 'Sartre s'explique sur *Les Mots*', in *Les Mots et autres écrits biographiques* (Paris: Editions Gallimard, 2010), 1254–8.
2. 'A Long, Bitter, Sweet Madness', 62.
3. 'A Long, Bitter, Sweet Madness', 62 (translation modified).
4. 'A Long, Bitter, Sweet Madness', 62.
5. 'The Purposes of Writing', 13.
6. 'A Long, Bitter, Sweet Madness, 62.
7. 'Mallarmé Said It All', 84.
8. See, for example, G. Davies, *Vers une explication rationnelle du 'Coup de dés' (nouvelle édition)* (Paris: José Corti, 1992), 158.
9. 'Mallarmé Said It All', 84.
10. 'Mallarmé Said It All', 84.
11. 'Mallarmé Said It All', 86.
12. 'Mallarmé Said It All', 86.
13. See, for a very clear statement of the necessity of a Maoist political party, one of whose tasks is to preserve the memory of the masses' revolutionary achievements, A. Badiou, 'Théorie de la contradiction', in *Les Années Rouges* (Paris: Les Prairies Ordinaires, 2012), 17–18. See also A. Badiou and F. Balmès, 'De L'Idéologie', in *Les Années Rouges*, 167–8, 180.
14. Cited in TOTS xlii. The provenance of this citation is the passage from Julien Gracq's *Lettrines* from which Badiou quotes liberally in the Preface. There, Badiou takes the hapless Communard commander to be a model of 'the French intellectual' who is 'lost and useless'. What 'the unfortunate delegate of the Commune' was guilty of, on Badiou's reading, was being overtaken by events and failing to produce 'the orders' and 'the plan'. If Badiou identifies, albeit negatively, with this figure, then it is in part because he considers his duty to consist in being 'a realist leader'.
15. For a compact statement of this thesis, see Marchal, *La Religion de Mallarmé*, 389–91.
16. Cited in TOTS 67.
17. We have used, with slight modifications, the translation given by Bruno Bosteels in his translation of *Theory of the Subject*.
18. See, for Badiou's parsing of the single-sentence sonnet, TOTS 75–6.
19. See, for Badiou's more properly conceptual discussion of this point, TOTS 68–9.
20. See, for his properly conceptual demonstration of this point, TOTS 70–2.
21. Cited in TOTS 88.
22. Again, for reasons of consistency, we will use the translation provided in Bosteels' translation of *Theory of the Subject*.

23. See, for a classic presentation of the notion of *le drame solaire*, G. Davies, *Mallarmé et le drame solaire: essai d'exégèse raisonnée* (Paris: José Corti, 1959), 7–39.
24. *Mallarmé et le drame solaire*, 108.
25. *Mallarmé et le drame solaire*, 116–18.
26. *Mallarmé et le drame solaire*, 124–5 (translation modified).
27. *Mallarmé et le drame solaire*, 134.
28. 'Mallarmé Said It All', 87.
29. A. Badiou, 'Is It Exact That All Thought Emits a Throw of Dice?, trans. Robert Boncardo and Christian R. Gelder, *S: Journal of the Circle for Lacanian Ideology*, 'Mallarmé Today', Vol. 9 (2016), 22.
30. For discussion, see E. During, 'L'Acte et l'Idée: Badiou et l'art contemporain', in Isabelle Vodoz and Fabien Tarby (eds), *Autour d'Alain Badiou* (Paris: Germina, 2011), 57–79.
31. 'Is It Exact . . .', 18.
32. 'Is It Exact . . .', 18–19.
33. 'Is It Exact . . .', 21.
34. G. Davies, *Mallarmé et la 'couche suffisante d'intelligibilité'* (Paris: José Corti, 1988), 375.
35. *Vers une explication rationnelle du 'Coup de dés'*, 71.
36. O. Feltham, *Alain Badiou: Live Theory* (London: Continuum, 2008), 102–3
37. *Vers une explication rationnelle du 'Coup de dés'*, 158.
38. A. Badiou, 'Mallarmé's Method', *Conditions*, trans. Steven Corcoran (London: Continuum, 2008), 53.
39. 'Mallarmé's Method', 53 (our emphasis).
40. 'Mallarmé Said It All', 93.
41. See R. Boncardo and C. R. Gelder, 'The Priority of Conditions: On the Relation Between Mathematics and Poetry in *Being and Event*', in A. J. Bartlett and J. Clemens (eds), *Badiou and His Interlocutors: Lectures, Interviews and Responses* (London: Bloomsbury, 2018).
42. Badiou himself calls it a 'brief triptych', HI 28.
43. We will proceed throughout on the assumption that the remarks of Milosz's that Badiou is responding to are those given expression in the English-language publication of Milosz's Charles Eliot Norton Lectures, presented at Harvard University in 1981–82 and published as *The Witness of Poetry* in 1983. See C. Milosz, *The Witness of Poetry* (Cambridge, MA: Harvard University Press, 1983). While this is a somewhat precarious assumption, there are three justifications for it. Firstly, while 'A French Philosopher Responds . . .' first appeared in 1998 in *Petit manuel d'inesthétique*, Badiou clearly states that Milosz's 'lesson' was proffered 'when the socialist states were beginning to collapse' (HI 28), thus at some moment *before* 1989. Secondly, there is sufficient evidence throughout Badiou's essay that he is responding to the specific arguments advanced in *The Witness of Poetry*. Thirdly and finally, it is reasonable to assume that

Milosz's position itself is sufficiently stable as to warrant working with an exemplary expression of it, such as *The Witness of Poetry*.
44. This conjuncture is dealt with more directly in a work with an unmistakably Mallarméan title. See A. Badiou, *D'un désastre obscur. Droit, Etat, Politique* (Paris: L'Aube, 2012).
45. All of these terms and their relations will be defined in detail below. For discussion of the doctrine of *conditions*, see Justin Clemens, 'The Conditions', in *Badiou: Key Concepts* (Chesham: Acumen, 2010), 25–37.
46. See A. Badiou, *Manifesto for Philosophy*, trans. Norman Madarasz (New York: State University of New York Press, 1999), 68–78.
47. See HI 19–21. See also BE 123–9, and 'The Philosophical Recourse to the Poem', in *Conditions*, 36–48.
48. See *The Witness of Poetry*, 7–8.
49. *The Witness of Poetry*, 6–7.
50. *The Witness of Poetry*, 19.
51. *The Witness of Poetry*, 27.
52. *The Witness of Poetry*, 27. As will be immediately obvious, there is more than a little overlap between Milosz's account and Sartre's. See in particular MPN 36.
53. *The Witness of Poetry*, 18.
54. *The Witness of Poetry*, 96.
55. *What is Literature?*, 118.
56. *The Witness of Poetry*, 33.
57. *The Witness of Poetry*, 31. Milosz is of course referring here to the workers' strikes that took place in the city of Lublin in Poland and led to the birth of *Solidarność*. Badiou is also referring to these events when he speaks of the possibility of 'general action' in 'the East', as opposed to 'the West during the melancholy eighties', HI, 31.
58. *The Witness of Poetry*, 95.
59. '"Generic" and "indiscernible" are concepts which are almost equivalent ... The term "generic" positively designates that what does not allow itself to be discerned is in reality the general truth of a situation, the truth of its being, as considered as the foundation of all knowledge to come', BE 327.
60. A. Badiou, *Metapolitics*, trans. Jason Barker (London: Verso, 2005), 97.
61. 'The Philosophical Recourse to the Poem', 42 (Badiou's emphasis).
62. Milosz comments on the work of these poets in the essay 'Ruins and Poetry', in *The Witness of Poetry*, 79–97.
63. *The Witness of Poetry*, 94–5.
64. *The Witness of Poetry*, 26–7 (our emphasis).
65. *The Witness of Poetry*, 46.
66. *The Witness of Poetry*, 19.
67. *What is Literature?*, 118.
68. *The Witness of Poetry*, 28.
69. 'Is it Exact ...', 69.

70. 'Is it Exact . . .', 68 (Badiou's emphasis).
71. *The Witness of Poetry*, 95.
72. *The Witness of Poetry*, 31.
73. In the interests of consistency we have replaced Toscano's translation of the passage from 'Restricted Action' with Barbara Johnson's.
74. 'A Long, Bitter, Sweet Madness', 62.
75. *The Witness of Poetry*, 31.
76. *The Witness of Poetry*, 46.
77. *The Witness of Poetry*, 28.
78. *The Witness of Poetry*, 29.
79. *The Witness of Poetry*, 19.
80. *Manifesto for Philosophy*, 72 (Badiou's emphasis).
81. As Badiou puts it in *Being and Event*: '*Knowledge* is the capacity to discern multiples within the situation which possess this or that property; properties that can be indicated by explicit phrases of the language, or sets of phrases. The rule of knowledge is always a criterion of exact nomination. In the last analysis, the constitutive operations of every domain of knowledge are *discernment* (such a presented or thinkable multiple possesses such and such a property) and *classification* (I can group together, and designate by their common property, those multiples that I discern as having a nameable characteristic in common). Discernment concerns the connection between language and presented or presentable realities. It is orientated towards presentation. Classification concerns the connection between the language and the parts of a situation, the multiples of multiples. It is oriented towards representation', BE 328.
82. This opposition to immediacy, to the spontaneous reception of sense or affect, is a veritable mainstay of Badiou's writings on poetry. See, for example, his comments about syntax in Pessoa, in 'A Philosophical Task', HI 42. See also his characterisation of Lucretius' poetry as being 'entirely oriented towards the deposition of the imaginary', 'The Philosophical Recourse to the Poem', 46.
83. *The Witness of Poetry*, 94.
84. *The Witness of Poetry*, 31.

4 Jean-Claude Milner's Mallarmé: Nothing Has Taken Place

Jean-Claude Milner's 1999 book *Mallarmé au tombeau* was no doubt meant to explode like a well-placed bomb in the midst of the poet's political reception, so destructive are its claims for the interpretative tradition we have studied so far in this book. Yet almost a decade after its publication Milner's short monograph remains all but ignored by scholars. When they have attended to Milner's book at all, scholars have dismissed it as a hasty and far-from-disinterested extrapolation of the meaning of a single sonnet, 'The virginal, enduring, beautiful today', to the entirety of Mallarmé's *œuvre*. However, as we hope to show in this short chapter, the significance of Milner's *Mallarmé au tombeau* extends well beyond Mallarmé's famous swan sonnet. In fact, it extends beyond Mallarmé's *œuvre* itself and strikes at the heart of the 'political vision of the world' (C 19–30) that has produced the figure of 'comrade Mallarmé'. For Milner, Mallarmé was a resolutely counter-revolutionary figure who buried the Romantic tradition that had yoked literature to politics. Our task in this chapter will be to explore the details of Milner's reading – and thus allow, like a delayed explosion, the repercussions of *Mallarmé au tombeau* to begin to be felt.[1]

*

We can begin where Milner begins: with Mallarmé's sonnet 'The virginal, enduring, beautiful today', one of the best-known poems in his *œuvre*:

> The virginal, enduring, beautiful today
> will a drunken beat of its wing break us
> this hard, forgotten lake haunted under frost
> by the transparent glacier of unfled flights!
>
> A swan of old remembers it is he
> magnificent but who without hope frees himself

for never having sung a place to live
when the boredom of sterile winter was resplendent.

His whole neck will shake off this white death-throe
inflicted by space on the bird denying it,
but not the horror of soil where the feathers are caught.

Phantom assigned to this place by pure brilliance,
he is paralysed in the cold dream of contempt
put on in useless exile by the Swan. (PV 164)[2]

In his comments on the sonnet's publication history, Milner remarks that its date of composition might well have been any time during the decade 1865–75 – over ten years before its appearance in *La Revue indépendante* in 1885 (MT 11). This is significant, since it suggests that the doctrine expressed in 'The virginal . . .' was well-established in Mallarmé's mind from the earliest years of his poetic career. Further on in *Mallarmé au tombeau*, Milner confirms this thesis, writing that 'Mallarmé had identified [the] primary elements' of the sonnet's doctrine 'in the years 1863–64, and had laid its definitive foundations when he emerged from the crisis of 1866' (MT 68). As Milner clarifies in a 2017 interview, Mallarmé forged his radically atheistic vision of a universe in which 'Nature has taken place' and 'can't be added to' (D 187) much earlier than scholars typically suggest. Most importantly, this vision remained a guiding framework for the entirety of his poetic career, right up to 1897's *Un coup de dés*. While Milner admits that 'Mallarmé swayed over several decades' between his nihilist refusal of any and all action and his concerted attempt to reforge a human community by way of the Book, in Milner's estimation 'the nihilist hypothesis won out in the end'.[3] Irrespective of his work's utopian dimensions, from first to last Milner's Mallarmé was ultimately a nihilist. Indeed, as we will see, circumstances conspired to ensure the continuity of this vision: after events like the crushing of the Paris Commune (MT 69), the death of his son Anatole,[4] the devolution of his *Mardis* into decadent carnivals,[5] and the manifest failure of the Book (MT 78), Mallarmé's youthful opposition to his poetic predecessors gave way to a full-blown cosmology of contempt. *Pace* Benoît Monginot, 'The virginal . . .' is not an outlier in the Mallarméan corpus: it is its heart – its dead heart.

Milner begins by marking a crucial line of division within the sonnet: while the opening quatrain records a speaker's discourse – a speaker revealed in the second quatrain to be a swan – the rest of the poem consists of a third-person narrative commentary on this discourse (MT 15). Importantly, the pronoun 'we' in the first quatrain is neither a royal 'we' nor a syntactic expletive, as it can be in French phrases like

'Mazarine nous a encore déchiré son bavoir' (MT 17), where the 'nous' plays a strictly grammatical – and not semantic – role. Instead, Milner affirms, the 'we' refers to a really existing collective subject. For reasons that will soon become apparent, the swan-speaker belongs to this 'we' at the same time as he occupies a singular position within it. Transposed provisionally into prose, the exclamative – and not interrogative (MT 17) – discourse of the first quatrain states that a singular day, 'The virginal, enduring, beautiful day', will cut into the continuity of history and break the chains currently binding the speaker and their collective to 'this hard, forgotten lake haunted under frost'. The deictic 'this lake' tells us that the swan proclaims their discourse from the site of a frozen lake: he is therefore in the same predicament as the rest of his collective. That said, he is clearly a singular member of this collective in so far as he prophecies its emancipation. As for the 'beautiful day' itself, it is the referent of the pronoun 'its' in the verbal construction 'will a drunken beat of its wing' and is thus construed as the effective agent of the collective's deliverance. The near future tense of this construction in the French ('Va-t-il nous déchirer . . .') suggests that this day of deliverance is close at hand, and that its advent is certain.

With the shift from the first to the second quatrain, we move from first to third person – or from discourse to narrative, to use Benveniste's terms (MT 15). The swan is now explicitly named: he is 'Un cygne d'autrefois'. Manson translates this as 'A swan of old'. For Milner, however, the word 'autrefois' is not used in an adjectival sense. Rather, it refers through homophony to the 'autres fois', the 'other times', that the swan remembers having 'free[d] himself' from the lake. Thus, the word 'autrefois' does not form part of a nominal syntagm, but is the object complement of the verb 'se souvenir', 'to remember'. In the narrative temporality of the poem, the swan's exclamative discourse has thus been interrupted all of a sudden by its own act of remembering: 'A swan . . . remembers'. The content of his memory is as follows: far from the 'beautiful day' delivering the collective from their ice-prison, the swan-speaker remembers that he has only ever been able to deliver himself. He is thus 'without hope'. The 'beautiful day' has given way to a series of days – the 'other times' that the swan recalls. The singularity and splendour of this 'beautiful day' are thus negated and replaced by repetition and indistinction (MT 25). Milner insists that the pronoun 'lui' in 'se souvient que c'est lui' is not in any way a redundancy, but rather reinforces the fact that it is the swan – and the swan *alone* – who has managed to liberate himself. Collective emancipation has thus given way to strictly individual acts of freedom. Retrospectively, this reveals that the first quatrain was not a proclamation made in full voice but a silent discourse, perhaps even a dream discourse, infused with illusory desire. On this point, Milner notes the absence of quotation marks, which are normally present whenever Mallarmé marks a punctual instance of speech (MT 18–19). Thus, while the first quatrain seems to mime a Romantic poet in full flight, echoing as it does Charles Baudelaire's *Le coucher du soleil romantique* – a poem that is already a mimicry of Victor Hugo, the prophetic poet *par excellence* – Mallarmé has muted the Romantic's discourse, transforming it into an interior monologue. As Milner explains, the word 'Magnifique', in the verse 'Magnifique mais qui sans espoir se délivre' should be read, initially, in the sense of munificence (MT 22–3). But in so far as this adjective is immediately followed by a brutal 'mais', 'Magnifique' is instantly negated: the word is 'plunged back into its inanity', as Mallarmé puts it in *Igitur*. For if the swan delivers only himself, then by definition he cannot be 'Magnifique'.

Milner summarises the sonnet's movement as follows:

> the second quatrain says exactly the opposite of the first. The event it recounts – the intrusion of the memory – cuts the continuity of the preceding discourse. The swan, who was speaking in the first person, brutally interrupts himself in his exclamation of blissful hope, because he remembers. He remembers all of the other times when he realised that he could only ever deliver himself, and that every effort of general liberation was made in vain. (MT 26)

The sonnet's movement of negation and retrospective recomposition does not end with the first and second stanzas, however. On Milner's reading, the first tercet marks another transition involving the negation of the main idea of the second quatrain: namely, that if collective emancipation by way of a 'beautiful day' is impossible, then individual initiative is still sufficient to free at least one swan (MT 29). As Milner points out, the first quatrain had mentioned 'des vols qui n'ont pas fui', which Manson translates as 'unfled flights'. In other words, there had been no lack of flights on the part of the swan-speaker. But in so far as these were 'unfled flights' and the swan is still, by all accounts, stuck in the ice, nothing truly novel ever came from them: 'the trap has always been sprung on him again' (MT 30). Crushed by the knowledge that the 'beautiful day' of collective liberation will never come, as well as by the fact that his own attempts at escape have been fruitless, the swan now 'suspends' (MT 31) all movement, save for an almost imperceptible shake of his neck. In Manson's translation, 'His whole neck will shake off this white death-throe / inflicted by space on the bird denying it / but not the horror of soil where the feathers are caught'. The 'white death-throe' here obviously names the snow that falls – and never stops falling – from the frozen sky. Milner clarifies that the future tense in this tercet's first verse does not signify that the act of shaking the neck follows the swan's awakening from his dream. Rather, it is inscribed in the narrative temporality of the swan's memory: first, the swan recalls the repeated failures of his individual flights; then he remembers that, discouraged by this knowledge, he had repeatedly attempted another, far more modest, gesture of liberation: a derisory shake of his neck, which allowed him to lessen the weight of the snow, at least for an instant.

In fact, it is only with the second tercet that another event in the sonnet's narrative timeline occurs. After waking from his dream and remembering the hopelessness and impotence of his situation, the swan makes a 'decision' (MT 33): as the French has it, the swan 's'immobilise' – he immobilises himself. Manson's translation, 'he is paralysed', unfortunately misses the sense that this is an *act* on the swan's part, and not a description of the swan as he always, and still, is. 'The virginal . . .' thus ends with the swan deciding to do nothing: neither to fly, nor to shake its neck. 'We can now understand retroactively the speech from the first quatrain', Milner announces: 'it is because, precisely, the feathers were always, already caught that only a drunken wing beat – one sufficiently drunk to misrecognise the sad reality – could get out of this trap' (MT 34). Deliverance is radically impossible, both for the collective and for the individual. As Sartre had already seen, all that remains for Mallarmé is the infinite, indifferent surface of ice.

On the basis of this close reading, Milner progressively reveals the complex intertextual web within which 'The virginal . . .' is itself caught. The first and most obvious of the sonnet's interlocutors is Baudelaire's poem 'Le Cygne'. But against much of the scholarly tradition, Milner refuses to consider Mallarmé's sonnet a slightly more extreme transcription, proper to a young admirer, of Baudelaire's habitual motifs: the exile of the poet, the discovery of his inability to extract himself from his finitude, and his consequent contempt for his surroundings. Instead, Milner begins by enumerating the specific differences between the scenario of 'Le Cygne' and Mallarmé's sonnet. First, in Baudelaire's poem the swan speaks, while Mallarmé's remains completely silent. Second, when the swan from 'Le Cygne' speaks it calls for salvation. Moreover, the future tense of the famous lines 'Eau, quand donc pleuvras-tu ? Quand tonneras-tu foudre ?' opens the swan's yearning onto an infinite horizon of hope, which it is impossible to completely negate. By contrast, while the first quatrain of Mallarmé's poem announces the imminent and certain advent of the 'beautiful day', the existence of this 'day' is, as we know, immediately denied. Or rather, it was always, already denied, since its existence was only ever affirmed in the swan's dream. Furthermore, in 'The virginal . . .' there is no sky and no horizon: 'Nothing can be hoped to come from space; everything that can come from it is already there, and it is an agony' (MT 45). Infinite finitude has replaced Baudelaire's gnawing desire for the new. Third, while Baudelaire's swan desires water, Mallarmé's is surrounded by it, albeit in its frozen state. In a cruel twist of fate, the swan from 'Le Cygne' has gotten exactly what it wanted, but this object of desire has turned into a nightmare: 'The water has become harsher than the cruellest of droughts' (MT 45). Fourth, the swan from 'Le Cygne' is eaten away at from within by an intense desire. Mallarmé's, on the other hand, is indifferent, immobile. Indeed, the only affect explicitly mentioned in the sonnet, that of contempt, is not the swan's affect but rather belongs to his environment: 'the cold dream of contempt' that is 'put on' by the swan refers to the freezing snow and ice that surrounds it.

To determine the significance of these inversions, Milner first establishes that Baudelaire's poem, just like Mallarmé's, is a response to a predecessor's work. As Milner argues, this predecessor is none other than Victor Hugo. And the site of this intertextual encounter is politics: specifically, Hugo and Baudelaire's distinct politics in the aftermath of the failed revolution of 1848 and the coup d'état of Napoleon III. While Baudelaire had supported the 'properly proletarian insurrection' of June 1848, Hugo, who Milner describes as being 'strictly centrist in politics' (MT 51), was opposed to it. Despite this disagreement, at the moment of Hugo's self-imposed exile in Guernsey and his refusal, in 1859, of an offer of amnesty, Baudelaire dedicated 'Le Cygne' to the great Romantic. For Milner, this gesture signified that Baudelaire believed the two poets were ultimately comrades, whatever their often violent differences over crucial questions of political action, not to mention poetry. Both were opposed to the oppression of the Second Empire, and both mourned the loss of 'the liberty of all' (MT 51). Most significantly for Mallarmé, Hugo and Baudelaire opposed Napoleon III's regime by way of a specific doctrine of politics and poetry. This doctrine saw history as a triumphant march towards 'Progress, Liberty, Humanity' (MT 63) – a march punctuated by revolutionary events and accompanied by an essential hymn: poetry. For these two poets, revolutionary, progressive politics was thus in perfect solidarity with their poetic inventions. This might come as a surprise to readers of Baudelaire, for as Milner himself remarks the author of *Les Fleurs du mal* is precisely the poet who 'announces the defeat' (MT 51) of Hugo's progressivism. Indeed, Baudelaire's infamous melancholy is on display in 'Le Cygne' itself: as Milner reads the poem, the swan is none other than Victor Hugo himself. And while Baudelaire treats this figure with a deep compassion, Milner notes that 'the homage to the swan is not without a certain dose of mockery: "crazy gestures" both "ridiculous and sublime", pleonasms and an incantatory style worthy of a pastiche of *La Légende des Siècles*' (MT 52) are just some of the marks of Baudelaire's distance from Hugo. If Baudelaire identifies with anyone in the poem, it is with Andromache: that is, with a figure who, while homeless like the swan, also mourns at an empty tomb. Her desire is thus one that can never be fulfilled by an intra-worldly object. Similarly, Baudelaire rejects Hugo's promise of a world-to-come of 'Progress, Liberty, Humanity', yet he retains his predecessor's orientation towards an ideal. He simply places this ideal in an 'unknown out-of-the world' (MT 54), an inaccessible site for mundane creatures such as ourselves (MT 57).

To recap, for Milner the relation between the two giants of French poetry is as follows:

> Separated politically over June, the oppression of the Empire joins them together in a common mourning: that of the liberty of all. Of course, Baudelaire's message to Hugo is an inversion of Hugo himself: to the poet who always promised a final victory, Baudelaire announces the defeat; to the poet who held that everyone and everything are always united – through turning tables, through metempsychosis, through love – Baudelaire speaks of 'those who have lost what can never be refound'. (MT 51)

For Milner, as for Mallarmé, Hugo's hope and Baudelaire's melancholy are nevertheless structurally complicit, since both presuppose the possibility of a day of deliverance – a 'beautiful day' that will break the chains of oppression once and for all. If they disagree, their discord still occurs in a homogeneous discursive space. This shows just how radical Mallarmé's break with his predecessors will be. As Milner writes, for Mallarmé: 'There are no marvellous clouds. There is no unknown out-of-the-world. There is only this place, here-below, where the poet can be nothing but the phantom of himself' (MT 54). Returning to 'The virginal ...', if the first quatrain's discourse of hope, as well as the second quatrain's idea of individual emancipation, both represent Hugo's poetico-political doctrine; and if the swan's shake of the neck in the first tercet signifies Baudelaire's melancholic resignation, then the swan's actions in the final tercet stage the outcome of Mallarmé's 'decision' to break with his predecessors. Mallarmé, in other words, 'immobilises himself' like the swan, extinguishing all desire for revolution or for any measure of change whatsoever. Finally, he dies: he becomes a 'phantom'. Mallarmé places himself in the tomb: *au tombeau*.

*

At this point it is essential to recall that, for Milner, 'The virginal ...' expresses Mallarmé's fundamental doctrine of 'political nihilism' (MP

108), a 'doctrine' that remained the most enduring idea in his *œuvre*, despite the utopianism of some of his writings and projects. It therefore has the value of a programmatic piece. Consequently, we can expect to find traces of this doctrine in Mallarmé's key works. The first piece Milner turns to is 'Restricted Action'. In this late prose piece, Mallarmé implicitly accuses Hugo and Baudelaire of having made distinct yet ultimately equivalent errors, which come down to their belief that they were the 'contemporaries of themselves' (MT 59). In other words, both Hugo and Baudelaire believed their poetry could correspond to real political events – to the 'beautiful day' of deliverance. This is true even if Baudelaire mourned the failure of the two to correspond. Both of their bodies of work were thus governed by the following ideal: namely, that poetry, which takes language and thought to the point of their maximal intensity, would match up with political action's own point of maximal intensity: revolution. On Milner's reading, the key passage from 'Restricted Action' is the following: 'there's no such thing as a Present, no – a present doesn't exist . . . Uninformed is he who would proclaim himself his own contemporary, deserting or usurping with equal imprudence, when the past seems to cease and the future to stall, in view of masking the gap' (D 218).

Mallarmé's 'uninformed' predecessors make two errors. The one who 'deserts' the 'present', withdrawing into mourning, is Baudelaire. In doing so, he betrays the hold the idea of poetry's solidarity with revolution has over him. In other words, while for Baudelaire the revolutionary past had 'ceased' with 1848, it still oriented his every thought and action. Hugo, for his part, is the one who had 'usurped' the 'present': as Mallarmé writes in 'Crisis of Verse', Hugo had 'confiscated, from whoever tried to think, or discourse, or narrate, almost the right to speak' (D 202) and had made his own voice into the only one capable of articulating the revolutionary destiny of the French people. Yet the future in which this destiny was supposed to come to fruition was forever 'delayed'. Hugo's messianism and Baudelaire's mourning had thus conspired together to mask the fact that there is no 'present' – no decisive day of deliverance. For Mallarmé, in contrast to his predecessors, the lack of a 'present' effectively meant that the nineteenth century itself, in so far as it was understood as a century whose essential rhythm was dictated by revolutionary events, did not exist.

In a remarkable feat of interpretative revisionism, Milner then sets out to show how Mallarmé's early, enigmatic prose piece 'The Demon of Analogy' expresses the same nihilist doctrine as the swan sonnet. Milner detects in the piece's repeated refrain 'The Penultimate is Dead' an unsettling and sinister iteration of Mallarmé's judgement regarding the inexistence of the revolutionary nineteenth century. On this reading, the 'Penultimate' refers to the day before the final day of revolution, irrespective of whether or not this final day ends in success. The 'Penultimate' day's significance thus lies in its inscription in a triumphant, revolutionary temporality. But for Mallarmé this emancipatory experience of time and politics is over: 'the Penultimate is Dead'. Milner imagines the malicious significance Mallarmé's prose piece might have taken on it were it read after the defeat of the Paris Commune:

> 'It is dead, quite dead, the desperate Penultimate . . .': who in 1874 could not retroactively hear, in these lines from a text from 1864, the cruel stamping of the survivor, dancing on the memory of the Commune, and sending back in the form of an inverted message the refrain that persists in singing that it is not dead? (MT 69)

But the 'Penultimate' is not only the day that precedes the revolutionary day. It is also, as Milner puts it, the day that 'the last day' – the 'beautiful day' – 'has always-already devalued in advance' (MT 68–9). For Mallarmé, given the impossibility of deliverance, the fact is that all days are like this: they are 'always-already completely forgotten' (MT 69). The refrain 'The Penultimate is Dead' can therefore be read as signifying both the end of revolutionary time and the reduction of all days to the level of 'quotidian nothingness' (D 218).

In light of this interpretation, other enigmas from the piece are unlocked. For instance, that the disoriented protagonist ends up in front of a lutemaker's shop becomes intelligible when we recall that the lute is, in Milner's words, the 'emblem of all the century's lyrics – those of Lamartine, Musset, or Hugo' (MT 69). Moreover, the word 'lute' in French is homophonous with the word for struggle, 'lutte'. The great works of the Romantics, which bound poetry and political progress together, have thus become antiquated commodities as per the logic of industrial capitalism. In the following passage, Milner illuminates another obscure moment in the piece:

> Even more cutting are the following lines: 'on the floor, yellow palms and wings gone off in shadow'; at the site of these debris, the wanderer realises that the lutemaker also sells old birds. In the same stroke, the attentive reader sees that the poem's 'palms' refer to the volatile, not to the vegetal. What is this, if not the swan himself and his flock? Stuffed and lying on the floor, very far from any deliverance, recognisable only by their palmed feet ('yellow palms') and by their wings, no longer outstretched but tucked away – O drunken wing beat, O unfled flights – and lost in the shadow of the bric-à-brac. Thus ends Baudelaire's swan. (MT 70)

Mallarmé is the poet who brings all of the nineteenth century's poetic and political projects to their conclusion. Or, more precisely, he is the poet destined to write at the very moment the revolutionary dream crashes against the rock of reality – a rock that was nevertheless always, already there. For Mallarmé, the truth of modernity was not the steady march towards emancipation, but the installation of a commodity society – a society he was intimately familiar with, as his short-lived journal *La Dernière Mode* attests:

> 'when the boredom of sterile winter was resplendent' is the Mallarméan name for the nineteenth century. Winter of the world, generalised glaciation, indistinction of beings under monochromatic frost, material splendour and spiritual sterility: this is what Mallarmé thought of the modern. We know that he made an inventory of it – in mirrors, splendours, sterility and *ennui* – in *La Dernière Mode*. The history of the nineteenth century can be summed up in a swan who has been caught in the cold. (MT 42)

As we can recall from our first chapter, in his reading of *Igitur* Sartre had discerned in Mallarmé a tragic experience of time where the human being's future-oriented action was always retrospectively revealed to be the product of an infinite series of causes flowing from the past. While Sartre is operating at an ontological level and Milner at a political level, their readings of *Igitur* are strikingly similar: both read the piece's protagonist as a subject who is reduced to saying 'I come after' (MT 73) – Igitur is the last of his lineage – and 'therefore', *igitur* – Igitur is the subject who concludes as to the nullity of his ancestor's dreams. Milner explains: 'The swan sonnet and *Igitur* have the same structure' (MT 72) since both end with the voluntary death of their poet-protagonists: the swan 'immobilises himself', and Igitur 'lies down on the ashes of his ancestors'.

*

As we have insisted on a number of occasions, Milner understands his reading of 'The virginal . . .' to be applicable to the entirety of Mallarmé's corpus, with the exception of projects like the Book and the texts that circulate around it. We will return to this division in a moment. Mallarmé's fundamental aim, Milner argues, was to put an end to the relation his predecessors had posited between poetry and revolution. For this reason, the affect of 'contempt' mentioned in the swan sonnet – an affect attributed, as we saw above, to the swan's surroundings – can now be read in its proper context. It refers to the 'contempt' Mallarmé's peers would have felt towards him once they realised his writings undermined their most fundamental belief about the nature of their practice and its political significance. As Milner explains, this marks another point of distinction between Mallarmé and Baudelaire – indeed between Mallarmé and all of the *poètes maudits* of the late nineteenth century:

> In choosing to be a poet, [Mallarmé] chose, as all the others did, to be scorned by those who expect nothing from poetry; by choosing the appearance of sleep and of dream, he chose – and in this he is alone – to *also* be scorned by those who expect everything from poetry. (MT 66 – Milner's emphasis)

In other words, Mallarmé desired an even purer contempt than that offered by the bourgeoisie in their typical scorn for poets and poetry: he desired the contempt of those who love poetry, particularly in its guise as the revolution's herald and hymn.

Obviously, the irony of Milner's extraordinarily audacious thesis is that if Mallarmé's aim was to de-link Action and Dream – or indeed to dissolve *both* Action *and* Dream in order to disclose the world as a site of indifference and dejection – then he utterly failed, both in his lifetime and in his posthumous reception. For as Milner recognises, and as we know from the three previous chapters of this book, Mallarmé's 'hagiographers' (MT 65) have treated him as a veritable poetic 'comrade' of progressive, revolutionary politics. And even in those cases where these same readers have criticised Mallarmé, they have done so only when his poetry has been seen as falling short of the exacting standards demanded of the revolutionary project – a project these readers have assumed Mallarmé was participating in. Yet for Milner these readers have all failed to see that Mallarmé's singularity lay in *destroying* this project.

However, Milner also recognises that there are aspects of Mallarmé's *œuvre* that have invited the utopian readings proffered by the later Sartre, Kristeva, Badiou and others besides. What of the project of the Book, for instance? While Milner mentions the Book in *Mallarmé au tombeau*, he does so only to immediately dismiss it, writing that Mallarmé's Book, just like the nineteenth century itself, 'does not exist' (MT 78). In his 2016 piece 'Mallarmé Perchance', Milner addresses the Book at much greater length, as well as the more general project it instantiates. As he briefly suggested in his 1978 book *For the Love of Language*, at one stage in his career Mallarmé conceived of poetry as the unique means for abolishing the contingent relation between signifier and signified in language.[6] In 'Crisis of Verse', for instance, Mallarmé lamented 'the chance that remains between the terms, despite their repeated reformulations between sound and sense', and enjoined poets to create 'entirely new' (D 211) words whose sensory properties would match those of the objects they referred to. When read alongside *Mallarmé au tombeau*, we can only assume that for Milner this project was formulated after – and to a degree in spite of – the conclusions Mallarmé came to at the end of his 'spiritual crisis'. Whatever the case may be, Milner sees the Book as continuous with Mallarmé's concern to abolish the chance in language. With the Book, however, the chance in question is one that is derivative of, but not identical to, the equivocity produced by the gap between signifier and signified: namely, the chance that inheres in society. Milner picks up on a passage from 'Bucolic' to articulate this idea:

> 'The artist and the man of letters, who goes by the unique name of poet, has no business in a space devoted to the crowd or chance.' The substantives crowd and chance are treated as synonyms, freely interchangeable for one another. When Mallarmé speaks of chance, he speaks of the crowd and vice versa. A crowd of spoken words or a crowd of speaking beings, a chance encounter of sound and sense or a chance encounter of passers-by. (MP 99)

Milner continues, linking this disorienting series of chance encounters to the end pursued in the literary ceremony of the Book:

> On the basis of the notes that Mallarmé left, it appears that, indeed, the Book was conceived as a means of organising a multiplicity. Mallarmé speculates on the number of participants and attempts to subject that number to the necessary constraint of calculation. An abolition of the crowd should result. One is tempted to take up Lenin's phrase – Lenin, who, in 1901, defined the revolutionary newspaper as a 'collective organiser'. Similarly, one might think of the Book as an organiser by means of which a group of speaking beings who are devoted to realising it in spoken form isolates itself in the midst of the crowd. (MP 99)

Milner's reference to Lenin here is significant, since he argues that interpreters like Marchal are wrong to see Mallarmé's Book as a religious ceremony. In fact, it was distinctly political in nature: 'In the end', Milner writes, 'I would dare to suppose that through the repeated action of the Book, the analogue to a revolutionary party would come into being.' The reason for this, he claims, is that 'revolution undertakes to abolish the chance that, in society, slots someone or other into the class of the powerful or the class of the poor' (MP 99). The significance of this admission on Milner's part should not be underestimated: it effectively means that the counter-revolutionary Mallarmé of *Mallarmé au tombeau* is only *one* incarnation of the poet. During at least one period in his career, Milner implies, Mallarmé unquestionably participated in the Romantic project of rebinding a community split asunder by the abstractions of the modern state and market. The Mallarmé of the Book is not the Mallarmé of *Igitur*, 'The Demon of Analogy' and the swan sonnet.

But what of *Un coup de dés*, Mallarmé's final and most important work? We know that for Sartre *Un coup de dés* was consistent with Mallarmé's earliest nihilist convictions, while for Badiou it presented an ethics of courage that avoided the abyss of nihilism, even while skirting perilously close to its edge. How does Milner position *Un coup de dés* with respect to the two main aesthetic and political orientations of Mallarmé's career? Put simply, he argues that after an intermediary period in which Mallarmé reprised the Hugolian gesture of linking poetry and collective emancipation, *Un coup de dés* joins back up with his precocious nihilism. Yet this time Mallarmé's bleak vision of the universe had been bolstered by a series of intellectual and existential experiences. As Milner explains, the death of his son Anatole shook the poet to his core, awakening his sense of the world's ineradicable contingency.[7] Furthermore, Mallarmé's famous gathering at the Rue de Rome, the *Mardis*, had progressively devolved, Milner claims, into a 'veritable carnival'.[8] This had convinced the poet that any collective form, even one that brought together like-minded artists, was destined to degradation. Published in the second-last year of Mallarmé's life, *Un coup de dés* thus raises the 'political nihilism' (MP 108) of the swan sonnet to a higher power. Its doctrine, summarised in the phrase 'nothing will have taken place but the place', can also be expressed in the following form: 'the Book does not exist' (MT 78). In other words, not only does the revolution not exist, no literary religion capable of abolishing the chance inherent in society exists either.

But what of the constellation that emerges – perhaps – in the heavens on the last double-page of *Un coup de dés*? For Badiou, this constellation marked Mallarmé's intellectual victory over chance: his creation of a poetic thought of the pure event. For Milner, by contrast, the constellation stands for poetry in so far as it is situated at an infinite distance from the world of *ennui*. Milner expresses this idea by way of a comparison between poetry and prose:

> The place of poetry is described as a 'constellation cold with forgetfulness and desuetude'. As for prose, it speaks of the quotidian and says nothing that the newspaper does not say. But the newspaper says nothing which exceeds *la dernière Mode* and the quotidian is nothingness ... Poetry must therefore say something else. It is not enough for it to speak in another way, it must speak of something else. It must speak otherwise of other things. But this other thing is by definition that which does not take place. That which *is* all the more so since it does not take place. Coming from Plato via the intermediary of Hegel, the name 'Idea' – and not 'Ideal' – proposes itself. (MT 81 – Milner's emphasis)

For Mallarmé, the 'Ideal' names an intramundane unity of Action and Dream. As Milner convincingly argues, if the figure of the bird is so frequently connoted negatively in Mallarmé's early work, then it is because birds inhabit the zone between the earth and sky, thus figuring the descent of the idea into matter – something Mallarmé not only considered an impossible eventuality, but also the most dangerous of illusions (MT 70). For Mallarmé, poetry must be absolutely disjunct with respect to the world. It must be eternally distant from the world of the 'newspaper'. Like the constellation, in other words, it must be situated in the heavens from where it can gaze down upon a world made up only of insignificant events. After Mallarmé, poetry encapsulates an extreme aristocratic disdain for the mundane. The contempt suffered by the swan has been returned a thousand times over.

*

In the final chapter of *Mallarmé au tombeau*, 'Prose Redeemed', a stunning shift occurs in Milner's argument. In a discussion of the Russian poets of the early twentieth century, Milner claims, unexpectedly, that their commitment to the October Revolution was a commitment they made *as* Mallarméans:

> The Russians are important here. In their language, Revolution and poetry had mutually summoned each other, and, in some sense, had challenged the other to prove itself to be sufficient. But this challenge itself covered over another. Following the example of Blok, who himself had followed Pushkin's example, poetry alone was capable of speaking of Revolution – whether for or against it – because only poetry was capable of speaking of what took place at the point of its maximal intensity. Had Pushkin not established that only verse could be the language of the December Rebellion, in the same way as poetry was the only language that could make itself the language of love? There was therefore no need to renounce Mallarmé. It sufficed to read him in a negative theological mode. He said: 'nothing has taken place', which meant: nothing has taken place, in so far as the Revolution has not taken place, or a new love. (MT 84)

Far from denying that any revolutionary event could ever take place, for the Russians Mallarmé's poetry had simply elevated the conjoined Ideas of poetry and revolution to hitherto unheard-of heights. Mallarmé's extreme idealist dualism was not antithetical to the revolutionaries' mindset: *it was formally identical to it.* Just as Mallarmé had judged the world to be radically deficient compared with his poetry's purity, so too did the revolutionaries evaluate all of the events that occurred in the here-below according to the exigent standards of the revolutionary Idea.

This homology allows us to pinpoint, finally, the perspective from which Milner himself speaks in *Mallarmé au tombeau*. As we have seen, Milner's reading both inverts and undermines the basis of the political interpretations of Mallarmé proposed by Sartre, Kristeva and Badiou. Yet it is essential to point out that, in contrast to these three readers,

Milner does not openly adopt the poet's position that results from his interpretation. In fact, before the beginning of his final chapter 'Prose Redeemed', it is almost impossible to identify Milner's own voice within *Mallarmé au tombeau*. While Badiou, for instance, freely confused his voice with Mallarmé's and used the poet as a mirror for his own political hopes and disappointments, it is not clear *prima facie* whether Milner shares Mallarmé's views regarding the poetry-revolution couplet. Does Milner set out to subvert the tradition of Mallarmé scholarship in order to present his *own* 'comrade Mallarmé', a 'comrade' who would this time support a counter-revolutionary politics?

In fact, Milner's polemical strategy in *Mallarmé au tombeau* consists in showing, first of all, that there exists a secret complicity between Mallarmé the counter-revolutionary nihilist and revolutionaries like Badiou, and then in opposing both of them in the name of an altogether different political vision. For Milner, the danger of the demanding dualism promulgated by Mallarmé and the revolutionaries was that it allowed them to pass over – or, worse, to treat with derision – many of the most significant events that occur in history, in particular those that touch on Man in his finitude. Against these two profoundly solidary figures, Milner articulates his own position as follows:

> That something take the form of the quotidian, of the today, of the newspaper, of history as written by Herodotus or Thucydides, is not a sufficient condition for it to be deemed a nothingness. But in order for that which is in it and which exceeds nothingness to be grasped, one condition must be fulfilled: that prose exceed the language of the today, of the newspaper, of history, of the quotidian. (MT 83)

Milner's position thus comes down to calling for a literature that can speak of all historical events, including those that seem to bear only upon Man in his utter finitude, but in a way that extracts them from the morass of the mundane. For him, this is especially important in light of the twentieth century, which from one perspective can be characterised as the only century to have ever produced death on an industrial scale. But if the twentieth century was 'distinguished from every other' by the sheer scale of its 'barbarous events, wars, revolutions, massacres and camps' (MT 86), then to capture its essence involves refusing the Mallarméan vision that sees all of the events of the here-below as equally insignificant, at least from the perspective of poetry or literature. For Milner, Varlam Chalamov's *The Kolyma Tales* provides a proof-in-practice of the falsity of Mallarmé's axioms. On Milner's reading, by raising these events above the level of 'quotidian nothingness', Chalamov's *Tales* demonstrated once and for all that Mallarmé had arbitrarily restricted literature's horizon of possibility. 'But if Chalamov is right', Milner concludes, 'then Mallarmé was always wrong' (MT 87).

The polemical genius of *Mallarmé au tombeau*, above and beyond its interpretative precision, lies in its demonstration that this third position, which passes between the Scylla of poetic nihilism and the Charybdis of 'universal reportage', is opposed *both* to revolutionaries like Badiou *and* to counter-revolutionaries like Mallarmé. But even more ingeniously, *Mallarmé au tombeau* shows the hidden complicity of these two positions and even suggests that they are knowingly complicit – that Badiou's discipleship of Mallarmé is made not despite the poet's nihilist idealism, but because of it.

NOTES

1. For reasons of space, we will not be able to discuss the other works by Milner that concern Mallarmé. These works include *For the Love of Language*, *Les noms indistincts*, *L'Œuvre claire* and 'The Tell-Tale Constellations'. Arguably, these works have a different – epistemological and linguistic – focus to *Mallarmé au tombeau*, which is concerned with politics. See J.-C. Milner, *For the Love of Language*, trans. Ann Banfield (London: Macmillan, 1990), *Les noms indistincts* (Paris: Seuil, 1983), *L'Œuvre claire: Lacan, la science, la philosophie* (Paris: Seuil, 1995), and 'The Tell-Tale Constellations', trans. C. R. Gelder, *S: Journal for the Lacanian Circle of Ideology Critique*, Vol. 9 (2016), 'Mallarmé Today', 31–8. For a discussion of these works, see Boncardo and Gelder, *Mallarmé: Rancière, Milner, Badiou*, 6–11.
2. 'Le vierge, le vivace et le bel aujourd'hui / V-a-t-il nous déchirer avec un coup d'aile ivre / Ce lac dur oublié que hante sous le givre / Le transparent glacier des vols qui n'ont pas fui ! // Un cygne d'autrefois se souvient que c'est lui / Magnifique mais qui sans espoir se délivre / Pour n'avoir pas chanté la région où vivre / Quand du stérile hiver a resplendi l'ennui // Tout son col secouera cette blanche agonie / Par l'espace infligé à l'oiseau qui le nie, / Mais non l'horreur du sol où le plumage est pris // Fantôme qu'à ce lieu son pur éclat assigne / Il s'immobilise au songe froid de mépris / Que vêt parmi l'exil inutile le Cygne'.
3. J.-C. Milner, 'I Believed I Owed Mallarmé the Truth', in Boncardo and Gelder, *Mallarmé: Rancière, Milner, Badiou*, 68.
4. 'I Believed I Owed Mallarmé the Truth', 79.
5. 'I Believed I Owed Mallarmé the Truth', 68.
6. *For the Love of Language*, 74–5.
7. 'I Believed I Owed Mallarmé the Truth', 79.
8. 'I Believed I Owed Mallarmé the Truth', 68.

5 Jacques Rancière's Mallarmé: Deferring Equality

Jacques Rancière's 1996 book *Mallarmé: The Politics of the Siren*[1] is written against the entire interpretative tradition we have explored in this book, at the same time as it reinscribes its major motifs within the coordinates of Rancière's novel account of artistic modernity, the 'aesthetic regime of art'.[2] Against Sartre, Rancière thoroughly reorganises the relation between modern French literature and democracy – a relation Sartre had powerfully argued was one of profound conflict.[3] In contrast to Sartre's nihilist Mallarmé, Rancière's will be 'a good democrat' (PS 59) whose poetic language did not pit an artistic elite nostalgic for the nobility against the blind herd of the democratic masses, but rather sought to 'consecrate the community'[4] in a secular world. Against Kristeva, Rancière will not set out to enrol Mallarmé in a situated struggle within the intersecting publishing, political and university fields in France at a moment of social upheaval, but will instead seek to understand him strictly on his own terms. Furthermore, he will refuse Kristeva's claim that Mallarmé's 'religion' was a mere fetish, arguing on the contrary that it is the key that unlocks his writings. Against Badiou, Rancière will reject the philosopher's penchant for extracting philosophically significant concepts from the poet's writings – concepts only the philosopher is capable of fully comprehending.[5] He will also reject Badiou's reading of Mallarmé as an exemplary member of 'the Age of the Poets', whose principle achievement was an anti-representative poetics. By stark contrast, Rancière's Mallarmé will have rigorously mimetic pretensions. Finally, against Milner, Rancière will refuse point blank the idea that Mallarmé was a counter-revolutionary, or even that he was in any way concerned by the problematic of the poetry-revolution couplet: 'Certainly', Rancière states, 'Mallarmé never shared any revolutionary aspirations' – but this is precisely 'why he did not need to produce an assessment of them and declare them over'.[6]

In this fifth and final chapter, we offer a comprehensive exegesis of Rancière's engagement with Mallarmé, an engagement centred on his extraordinarily dense monograph *The Politics of the Siren* but which also includes important chapters in *Mute Speech* (1998), *The Politics of Literature* (2007) and *Aisthesis* (2011). Following the argumentative contours of *The Politics of the Siren*, we will begin by exploring Rancière's dialogue with the critical heritage he sees as having obscured the proper meaning of Mallarmé's writings. Then, we will offer an extensive account of Mallarmé's poetic 'Idea' before comparing it to Saint-Simonism and Wagnerism, two nineteenth-century phenomena Rancière believes were also attempts to respond to the post-Revolutionary problematic of constituting an adequate human community. Finally, following a discussion of Rancière's reading of *Un coup de dés*, we will pose the question of the relation between Mallarmé's politics and Rancière's own. How does Mallarmé's 'politics of the siren' compare to Rancière's commitment to radical equality? What can Rancière's Mallarmé tell us about the relationship between literature and politics more generally?

*

In the 'Foreword' to *The Politics of the Siren* Rancière isolates three interpretative tendencies in Mallarmé's posthumous reception, each of which he intends to refute. The first sees the difficulty of Mallarmé's writings as a mark of the poet's anti-democratic elitism. The second, which is of less importance to Rancière, sees this difficulty as a symptom of Mallarmé's sexual problems. The third is represented by the work of Maurice Blanchot, who frames the poet's project as a strictly impossible project by which the writer struggles with and against the impersonality of language. Rancière responds to each of these tendencies in turn. Against Blanchot, he constructs his own vision of what he takes Mallarmé's true task to have been: namely, to create a poetic religion that would be the secular successor to Christianity. Against the second tendency, he opposes Mallarmé's lucid grasp of his socio-historical situation. And finally, against the first tendency, which reads the difficult form of Mallarmé's poetry as a rampart erected in order to protect its content, Rancière underscores the irreducible imbrication of content and form in the poet's writings. We will begin by working through Rancière's arguments against this latter tendency first.

In the opening to the essay 'The Intruder', published in *The Politics of Literature*, Rancière reads Sartre's *The Poet of Nothingness* as an exemplary instance of the anti-democratic reading of Mallarmé's poetry. Referring as he often does to Sartre's image of the poet's *œuvre* as a 'column of silence',[7] Rancière writes:

> You will have recognised in these lines a certain Mallarméan landscape, the one constructed by Sartre, portraying Mallarmé as the man of letters in the days of art for art's sake: a son of the bourgeoisie, whose revolt makes art sacred, setting it against commercial usefulness and turning this new sacredness of art into a means of building a phantom nobility, custodian of the incommunicable. (PL 80)

For Sartre, as Rancière reads him, Mallarmé's 'obscurity' (PS xiii) was a function of his isolation within the narrow circles of a self-ordained elite concerned to assert its intellectual aristocracy. As we saw in our first chapter, Sartre believed that the French postromantics more generally promulgated a poetry of non-being in order to assert, by conflating refusal with merit, their superiority. While Mallarmé ultimately transcended this elitism, his poetry's nihilism remained indelibly marked by it. According to Rancière, however, Sartre's reading both distorts the immanent productive principles of Mallarmé's poetry and misunderstands its relation to 'the crowd' (PS 5). Yet as our first chapter also showed, it was not for nothing that readers like Sartre saw Mallarmé as an elitist poet, at least at some points in his literary career. An early prose piece like 'Art For All', for instance, is incontestably the work of an elitist – albeit a precocious, unproven, twenty-year-old elitist. As Mallarmé writes there, the 'poet must ... remain an aristocrat' and actively avert the gaze of 'the crowd' from his work: 'Everything which is sacred and wants to remain sacred envelops itself in mystery' (OC II 360) and transforms itself into a secret accessible only to the chosen few. When Rancière speaks in his 'Foreword' of an interpretative tendency that reads Mallarmé's poetry as if it were animated by a 'hermetic intention to say and hide simultaneously the secrets of some gnosis or Cabbala' (PS xiv), he is doubtless referring to a hermeneutical procedure that would take a piece like 'Art For All' as its guide. In fact, as his reference to 'long and mysterious conversations with the poet of the night' (PS xiv) in the same passage makes clear, in these opening pages Rancière is implicitly exhuming a long-forgotten work of Mallarmé scholarship: Charles Chassé's *Les Clefs de Mallarmé*, a work which takes the hermetic reading of Mallarmé to an almost caricatural extreme. In his 1954 book, Chassé argued that after an initial period of productivity prior to 1876 Mallarmé attempted to dissimulate his growing sterility by obscuring banal ideas beneath the pomp of disused words found in *Littré*.[8] Chassé's work is obviously an extreme example of the hermetic reading of Mallarmé, yet the logic of its argument, Rancière suggests, is at work – albeit in a far more sophisticated form

– not only in Sartre's *The Poet of Nothingness* but also in the work of one of Rancière's key polemical partners, Pierre Bourdieu. For what Chassé's argument shares with the work of Sartre and Bourdieu is the assumption that the *form* of Mallarmé's writings – the traditional locus of its 'difficulty' – is exclusively determined by a strategy of distinction, which seeks to split off a circle of initiates from the mass of the profane, just as 'Art For All' had enjoined poets to do.

A cautionary remark is in order here: it should not be supposed that Rancière, in countering the idea that 'the truth' of Mallarmé's writings 'is hidden somewhere beneath the surface apprehended by the eye and the mind' (PS xiv), is arguing, absurdly, that the sense of Mallarmé's poetry and prose is immediately accessible. Indeed, his various descriptions of the formal properties of Mallarmé's writing highlight the necessary work the reader must undertake in order to follow its sinuous syntax and plumb the semantic depths of its words (PS 16). The relevant opposition here is not between Mallarmé the obscurantist mystic constructing Cabbalistic enigmas and Mallarmé the transmitter of transparent sense. Rather, it is between the two following ideas of poetry: on the one hand, the idea of poetry as a set of linguistic operations that obscure or protect an otherwise communicable content; and on the other hand, the idea of poetry as a linguistic phenomenon that *indistinguishes* form and content, making their separation impossible. According to this second idea, poetry's formal difficulties cannot be conceived as a rampart erected around a certain content *since they are inseparable from the content itself.*

For Rancière, as we will see in great detail throughout this chapter, Mallarmé subscribes to this second idea of poetry, and for essential reasons: namely, if his poetry is supposed to be a 'ritual of consecration of the human abode' (PS 16), and if a ritual is something that supposes the unity of a 'spiritual message' and the form it takes, then his poetry's form *cannot* be separated from its content. More importantly still, if it could be, then Mallarmé's poetry would not be able claim to be *the* 'ritual' that attests to humanity's essence: other artistic or spiritual practices possessing their own formal properties would be able to assert their capacity to 'consecrate the community'. As Rancière evocatively puts it, 'the poem is only of worth if its light as well as its night comes only from itself' (PS xiv).

Turning to the second interpretative tendency, Rancière similarly rejects the idea that Mallarmé's poetry is the product of 'the intimate secret of a sexed body' (PS xiv). According to this view, Mallarmé's poems are either the surface-effect of an underlying sexual problematic from which he more-or-less consciously suffered, or the masturbatory matter of a sexual obsessive. For Rancière, such a hermeneutical procedure is always possible since it is never 'wanting in material' (PS xiv): one can always enjoy germinating links between the author's sexual life and his work. However, this not only divests the poet of agency; it trivialises what is really at stake in his poetry, even if he did delight in equivocation: Mallarmé, as Rancière writes, 'also liked to be facetious and certainly took delight in the ambiguity of those poems in which the reader, as he pleases, can read either a metaphysical allegory or the story of an extra-conjugal escapade' (PS xiv). Yet this is a conscious design on the poet's part, not the displaced effect of some sombre sexual impulse. Rancière's opposition to this interpretative procedure is a species of his critique of the scientist who abrogates to themselves the capacity to explain what determines an agent's action, even if the agent themselves is unaware of the effectivity of this determining power. In contrast to this approach, Rancière will insist on according Mallarmé a high degree of lucidity regarding the actual problems that his poetry grappled with – problems that were not sexual but socio-political (PS xvi).

Leaving this more minor interpretative tendency aside, Rancière turns, finally, to Maurice Blanchot's reading of Mallarmé. It should be noted that for Rancière the author of *Faux Pas* is linked to a larger constellation of thinkers, including Sartre, who recognised the distinctly metaphysical destiny of modern literature, as well as its paradoxical impossibility.[9] As such, the discussion of Blanchot in the 'Foreword' to *The Politics of the Siren* should be read as a metonymy for Rancière's response to a whole series of readers who have seen Mallarmé as the exemplary modern writer, grappling with literature's singular aporia.

According to Rancière, Blanchot's engagement with the 'obscure sphinx of Tournon' (MPN 92) is far more compelling than any quasi-Marxist critique of Mallarmé's apparent aristocratism or pseudo-psychoanalytic reading of his sexual problems. For what Blanchot identified in Mallarmé, in particular in *Igitur*, was an exemplary experience of the way language subverted the active will and dissolved the individuality of the writer. For Mallarmé, the act of writing involved an experience of radical passivity akin to suicide. In fact, writing was even more radical, since committing suicide could still be considered an act of the will: 'In the night of writing, the intention of the work reaches the point at which it is experienced as identical to its contrary, the pure passivity of language. Did Mallarmé not record, in his tale of *Igitur*, the equivalence of the two experiences of writing and of suicide?' (PS xv). For all intents and purposes, Rancière's answer to this question is 'yes'. However, he takes his distance from Blanchot on the question of how important *Igitur* is to the rest of Mallarmé's *œuvre*. For Blanchot, the aim of the poet's writings from *Igitur* onward was to 'take account of the parallel experience of an activity of language which is only possible from the very point where it encounters pure passivity'. This made Mallarmé into a 'privileged witness' (PS xv) to our being-in-language. But if this is true, then the discrete products of Mallarmé's *œuvre* would be submitted to a singular and highly prohibitive scale of values: their 'authenticity' (PS xv) would be determined exclusively by their varying ability to bear 'witness' to the 'impotence' of the subject faced with language. As Rancière points out, this can only cast suspicion on the 'deceptiveness of [a] writing that is unfaithful to its nocturnal source' (PS xv). In fact, it is to set the writer a veritably *impossible* task. Furthermore, it is to misunderstand the guiding thread of Mallarmé's later works. On Blanchot's reading, the impossibility at the heart of Mallarmé's literary enterprise remained present even in the 'shattered project of the Book' (PS xv), which he worked on decades later. Rancière believes that just like Sartre Blanchot mistakenly traced 'a straight line' from some of Mallarmé's earliest writings such as *Igitur* to his 'posthumously published booklet of obscure poems' – 'poems' that could only be interpreted as the 'debris' (PS xiii) of his failed encounter with the absolute. A single impoverished and aporetic dialectic was at stake from beginning to end.

For Rancière, however, what 'Art For All' was to politics, *Igitur* is to metaphysics: both represent Mallarmé's youthful vision only, not his mature and most significant poetic perspective. On Rancière's account, both pieces have exerted an undue influence over Mallarmé studies, obscuring the true and constructive task that the older and less sterile Mallarmé set himself: that of producing 'a new Eucharist' (PS 16), not bearing witness to our subjection to language. Importantly, for Rancière, Mallarmé's religious task was one that he took up after having transcended the poetic ideology of his early twenties. Thus, to properly read Mallarmé, we too must go beyond the parameters of his early works: 'It is time to stop reading Mallarmé through the testimonies of his dreams and failures of the course of twenty-five years, or through the shattered project of the Book. The time has come to free him from that from which he strove to free himself' (PS xv). This returns us to the question of 'Mallarmé's specific difficulty' (PS xiii) with which we began. While so far we have been concerned with the 'difficulty' of Mallarmé's writing in so far as it has been understood as either a strategy of distinction or a product of his 'confrontation with the night of the absolute', we should note that in the final pages of his 'Foreword' Rancière subtly and strategically displaces the sense of this term. For the remainder of *The Politics of the Siren* Mallarmé's 'difficulty' will refer, in fact, to the problems the poet confronted and the contradictory exigencies he attempted to respond to. As Rancière states in a 2017 interview, 'the difficulty is Mallarmé's before it is that of the reader'.[10] To come to terms with the challenges Mallarmé faced and the poetic 'mission' (PS 36) in light of which they were disclosed *as* challenges, let us turn to the first stage of Rancière's argument.

*

In the first chapter of *The Politics of the Siren*, Rancière dives straight into Mallarmé's poetry, offering a brilliant exegesis of the sonnet 'Hushed to the crushing cloud':[11]

> Hushed to the crushing cloud
> Basalt and lava its form
> Even to echoes subdued
> By an ineffectual horn
>
> What shipwreck sepulchral has bowed
> (you know this, foam, but slobber on)
> The mast supreme in a crowd
> Of flotsam and jetsam though torn
>
> or will that which in fury defaulted
> From some perdition exalted
> The vain abyss outspread
>
> Have stingily drowned in the swirl
> Of a white hair's trailing thread
> The flank of a young siren girl. (CP 83)[12]

Rancière will read this sonnet alongside 'Toast', another octosyllabic sonnet whose position within the *Poésies*, along with the storm-and-shipwreck scenario it stages, suggest that it is the former poem's uncertain echo:

> Nothing, this foam, virgin verse
> Only to designate the cup:
> Thus, far off, drowns a siren troop
> Many, upended, are immersed.
>
> We navigate, O my diverse
> Friends, myself already on the poop,
> You the sumptuous prow to cut
> Through winter wave and lightning burst;
>
> A lovely drunkenness enlists
> Me to raise, though the vessel lists
> This toast on high and without fear

Solitude, rocky shoal, bright star
To whatsoever may be worth
Our sheet's white care in setting forth.[13]

In analysing these two sonnets, Rancière not only highlights the shift in aesthetics from the 'representative regime' to the 'aesthetic regime' that Mallarmé participates in and that he self-reflexively stages in his poetry – a shift whose meaning we will explore in more detail in the next section of this chapter. Nor is his reading limited to showing how Mallarmé responded to a new and perhaps unprecedented socio-historical setting for poetry. Rather, by studying the singular dynamics of these two sonnets, Rancière will find within them a precise yet paradoxical figure of Mallarmé's poetics and politics: a drowned siren. To understand the significance of the subtitle of *Mallarmé: The Politics of the Siren*, we first need to understand that the siren in question is the one who is paradoxically drowned in the sea-sky abyss of 'Hushed to the crushing cloud'. What could this mean? Let us briefly present Rancière's interpretation of 'Hushed to the crushing cloud' and 'Toast' to find out.

Rancière argues that a number of alternatives are articulated by the clause and relative clause making up the single, sinuous sentence of 'Hushed to the crushing cloud'. As he writes: 'To read the poem is not to reconstitute history but the virtuality of history, the choice between the hypotheses it offers us' (PS 2 – translation modified). In constructing the complex syntax of his poem, Mallarmé did not oppose elitist obscurantism to democratic clarity; instead, he countered an ideologically suspicious univocity with a kaleidoscope of interpretative possibilities. But what are these possibilities? The first is to be found in the opposition between the 'grand drama' of the hypothetical shipwreck and the 'light pantomime' (PS 2 – translation modified) of the siren's dive. In contrast to Badiou, Rancière does not read this as an undecidable opposition as per Badiou's account of the event (PL 187). On Rancière's reading, the sonnet presents the definite and decidable passage between two 'regimes' for the production or poetry: the first is the Romanticism of Hugo and Vigny, which would have presented, in a narrative form consistent with the axioms of the 'representative regime' of art, 'the great dramas of confrontation between intrepid man and raging nature'; the second, by contrast, is an entirely novel poetic universe, one that exists beyond even Baudelaire and his 'flowers of anti-nature' (PS 4), a universe in which we witness the fragile appearance of 'fictional beings' (PS 6) who momentarily emerge from 'any multiplicity whatsoever' (PS 49), such as the foam from 'Hushed to the crushing cloud' or the 'line of azure, thin and faint' that 'could be a lake, perhaps'

(PV 39) from 'Sick of unquiet rest'. Not only, then, is the dialectic of generations played out in the poem; the Aristotelian idea of 'fiction' is radically transformed from 'a representation of actions'[14] regulated by generic conventions to the brief flickering of self-difference undergone by an ostensibly banal object, here a thin thread of sea-foam.

The second kaleidoscope of possibilities concerns the relation between the two hypothetical events – the shipwreck, the siren's dive – and their surrounding milieu, 'the vain abyss of the waves' (PS 3 – translation modified):

> First hypothesis: the grand drama went unnoticed; it remained silent ('tu'), its call – its trumpet – lacked the virtue to disturb the indifference of this site in which it occurred: site of dark clouds like basalt and enslaved echoes, an environment naturally improper to the visibility and the hearing of the drama. Second hypothesis: the great spectacular drama (the high perdition) is, on the contrary, that which the surrounding world (vain chasm of billows) awaited but was denied. (PS 2–3)

At the price of an awkward equivocation over the semantic value of the 'sepulchral shipwreck', which shifts from being a catastrophe to being an object of desire, Rancière personifies the 'abyss', the backdrop to the hypothetical event. On the one hand, this 'abyss', whose 'enslaved echoes' perfectly figure the repetitive and restrictive nature of what Mallarmé called 'universal *reporting*' (D 201 – Mallarmé's emphasis), is responsible not only for sinking the ship; it is also indifferent to its plight and to whatever glory might have been salvaged from its wreck. On the other hand, the 'abyss' is that which, for lack of some 'perdition exalted', has attempted to stage a substitute drama and has drowned in a somewhat derisory fashion a siren-girl (the French adjective 'furibond' denotes an almost comic state of anger or agitation). Its anger thus betrays a desire for a 'grand drama' that would transcend the mediocrity it is currently accustomed to.

This second set of alternatives is clarified by the intertextual link between 'Hushed to the crushing cloud' and 'Toast'. Specifically, the ship in question in the first sonnet is the one the poet of 'Toast' had raised his glass to: 'A lovely drunkenness enlists / Me to raise, though the vessel lists, / This toast on high and without fear'. This ship metaphorises the poetic project undertaken by 'the *Revue indépendante*' and its collection of 'symbolist and decadent poets' (PS 5). Its fortune, as well as its relation to the public of its time, can therefore be seen as being staged in the alternatives articulated by 'Hushed to the crushing cloud': either the ship of the avant-garde ran aground and was lost in a social context unresponsive to the song of these *poètes maudits*, or its poetry was precisely what the public – 'the vain abyss' – had desired but which it had been refused in favour of the mediocrities proffered by 'the current social system' (D 118), as Mallarmé argues it had in 'Scribbled at the Theatre'.

There are two pivotal points to be drawn from the above sketch of Rancière's reading: the first has to do with the two poems' aesthetic, and the second with their politics. Let us turn to their politics first.

On Rancière's reading, 'Hushed to the crushing cloud' stages the exemplary ambivalence of the relation between 'the frail siren of the new poem' and the public for which it was ideally destined. On the one hand, this public is said to possess 'a latent grandeur' that is betrayed by the inadequate forms of art and culture it currently consumes and that arise from a fundamentally inadequate 'social system'.[15] In other words, in a manner consistent with Bertrand Marchal's pathbreaking *La Religion de Mallarmé*, Rancière takes Mallarmé to conceive of 'the crowd' as a collective with a latent spiritual striving, an inner religiosity that corresponds to the essence of humanity.[16] The poet is at once aware of this essence and seeks to create an art form that would, finally, be adequate to it. The desire of 'the crowd' for 'the greatness of high perditions' (PS 6) is a sign of its own latent grandeur. The 'new poem' and its poet are thus on the side of the veritable essence of 'the crowd', and they combat its alienation.

On the other hand, however, this very same 'crowd' is what threatens, as the sonnet itself says, to drown the poem destined to consecrate its grandeur. As Rancière writes, citing equivalent phrases from 'Music and Letters' and 'The Court': 'The fury for greatness of the "jealous hurricane" or of the "famished riot" can only work to bury the frail siren of the new poem inside its voracious stomach' (PS 6). This last metaphor is not insignificant: 'the crowd', in its incarnation as a 'jealous hurricane' or a 'famished riot', is nothing less than a 'monster' with a groaning hunger that will indiscriminately digest the poem. The question then becomes: how are we to think the relation between this 'monster' and its 'latent grandeur' – a 'grandeur' for which the poet claims to speak?

Here Rancière is employing a cluster of terms that Mallarmé frequently uses, particularly in his late prose pieces; terms which capture some of his exemplary anxieties about the relationship between poet and public. That 'the crowd' is represented as a vast collective appetite seems to resonate with other late-nineteenth century images of the 'masses' as rampant consumers or chronically undernourished workers driven by the most base of motivations. That the 'new poem' is 'devour[ed]' means that 'the crowd' can assimilate it only as a sort of foodstuff, not as the spiritual supplement Mallarmé intends it to be. On a superficial reading, Mallarmé's social imaginary thus seems consistent with that of many late nineteenth-century European artists. As John Carey has shown, 'an unprecedentedly large reading public created by late nineteenth-century education reforms'[17] found itself figured as a sombre and threatening mass by new and established writers, who instead of writing *for* it waged a bitter ideological campaign *against* it. *Pace* Rancière, for whom Mallarmé was 'a good democrat' (PS 59), the poet's figure of the 'monster' seems consistent with the constellation of images produced by intellectuals panicked by 'the threat of the masses'.[18] The essayist of 'Art For All' seems very similar to the poet of 'Hushed to the crushing cloud'.

However, the paradox is that this 'monster' is *also* Mallarmé's ideal addressee. The Mallarméan poem, Rancière argues, is destined for 'a crowd still to come' (PS 5). Crucially, this 'crowd' exists on a strict continuum with its fallen contemporary form. That said, given that 'the crowd' presently finds fulfilment in art forms that fail to give proper expression to its spiritual essence, if Mallarmé is 'too well received by the open maw of the monster' (PS 59) then he and his poetry will be seen as *reflecting* the crowd's current desire; as existing on the same level as it. For this reason, the poem-siren dives beneath the waves, 'transform[ing] itself into silence' (PS 7). To think 'the politics of the siren', then, is to think the continuity between 'the crowd' *qua* 'monster' – a figure who seems invested with all of the clichés a late nineteenth-century elitist could conjure up – and 'the crowd still to come' who will inhabit the society that 'succeeds the simple monetary reign of gold used for the exchanging of commodities' (PS 6). *Pace* Sartre and Milosz, Mallarmé's aristocratism is not buttressed by any belief in the essential and eternal distinction between 'bohemian and philistine',[19] but rather by a wager on a future in which each person will be able to share in the 'wealth' that the new poem currently 'reserve[s] for all' (PS 6).

It is in this context that the paradox of the drowned siren takes on its proper meaning. As Rancière notes, 'sirens, in contrast to boats, do not drown in water. On the contrary, they dive down in its depths to escape danger' (PS 6). Thus, while the 'abyss' in its fury may well have thought that 'stingily [it had] drowned in the swirl / Of a white hair's trailing thread / The flank of a young siren girl', this is only a simulacrum produced by the crafty poem-siren. Since 'the crowd', its ultimate addressee, is not yet ready for it, 'the new poem' vanishes from the public stage in order to cultivate 'the latent grandeur' that only 'a crowd still to come' will be able to recognise as its own.

This, then, is 'the politics of the siren', at once elitist and egalitarian. But what of the *aesthetic* at work in 'Hushed to the crushing cloud' and 'Toast'? And how is this aesthetic related to the poet's ambivalent politics? Helpfully, 'Hushed to the crushing cloud' is not only a paradigmatic expression of Mallarmé's politics; it can also be read as an exemplary *mise en scène* of his most fundamental poetic operation.

To approach this operation in its specificity, we can draw on the following beautiful passage from the first chapter of *The Politics of the Siren*, 'The Foam of the Poem', which is worth citing at length:

> the very opposition between the games of the siren and the sepulchral shipwreck tells us that [Mallarmé] was of another era, and his art another cosmology, than [the Romantics] ... He said as much in an illustrious text: 'Nature has taken place, it can't be added to.' And to the – far too few – subscribers of *La Dernière Mode*, he gave the proof: the 'modern image of nature's insufficiency' for us is attested by the very way in which vacationers cross it, 'full steam ahead', to go, at the end of the line, and simply sit down in front of the ocean 'and look at what there is beyond our abode, that is to say, the infinite and nothing'. (PS 3)[20]

In evolving beyond the 'representative regime of art', Mallarmé replaces art's narratives with the brief flickering between 'the infinite and nothing'. As we can see, this is a syntagm employed by Mallarmé himself in *La Dernière Mode*. Yet its meaning is far from clear. However, 'Hushed to the crushing cloud' offers a perfect example of what it stands for in the way it treats the foam: as a unitary, distinctive mark, the multiplication of the foam's meaning – is it a sign of shipwreck or a siren's dive? – is paradigmatic of the way 'the new poem' treats 'any multiplicity whatsoever' (PS 49). Rather than leaving the foam in the repose of its self-identity, the poem demonstrates 'the vanishing difference of every thing to itself' (PS 17); or, as Rancière puts it in the essay 'L'Inadmissible', it shows 'the difference of each One to itself'.[21] As a result, the foam can no longer be counted as a One, but instead becomes irreducibly multiple.

Behind this operation is a more general axiom of the 'aesthetic regime', an axiom with a decisive link to the conditions of democratic modernity: namely, 'the equality of all represented subjects' (MS 50). This nominal 'equality' replaces the generic principle from the 'representative regime' (MS 44–6, 50–1), which we will detail in the next section. Mallarmé's poetic act is indeed concerned with 'the vanishing difference of *every* thing to itself', and not only with the circumscribed set of subjects deemed worthy of artistic treatment by the 'representative regime' (MS 44–6). As such, even if this 'equality' should not be identified without remainder with what Rancière calls 'the molar equality of democratic subjects' since it concerns 'the molecular equality of micro-events' (PL 25), it still has some form of solidarity with the ideal of political equality in the post-French Revolutionary context. Mallarmé's 'anonymization of the beautiful'[22] is the unmistakable mark of the democratic age in the work of this seemingly most aristocratic of poets.

However, the new poem's infinitisation of any distinctive mark or object is constantly threatened with failing – with falling back into nothingness or 'the nothing'. Just like the fictional siren that briefly – if at all – appears above the sea's surface, 'the vanishing difference of every thing to itself' is precisely that: *vanishing*. To inscribe this problem within the logic of the 'aesthetic regime of art', if the poetic act that seeks to idealise 'any multiplicity whatsoever' is essentially precarious, then this follows from a contradiction between two axioms of the 'aesthetic regime': namely, the 'expressive principle of necessity' – the literary work's striving to produce the sensible incarnation of an idea – and the 'anti-representative principle of indifference' (MS 87)[23] – the literary work's refusal of any necessary relation between content and form. To put this in Mallarméan terms, while his poetry purports to produce an 'Idea', in the 'aesthetic regime of art' there is no longer any norm governing the relation between form and content. Thus, despite the ideal unity of form and content we mentioned in our first section on Mallarmé's critical reception, strictly speaking there can be no guarantee that his poetry's form succeeds in idealising its content. The same 'historical mode of visibility of the works of the art of writing' (MS 36) that allows Mallarmé to treat with the alchemy of his verse 'any multiplicity whatsoever' is the same that renders his literary pretensions precarious.

Thus, when Mallarmé inscribes in his 'new poem' the transition from a sublime encounter between intrepid Man and nature to the play of a vanishing siren, he is not only presenting the inter-generational novelty of his aesthetics. He is self-consciously highlighting the precarious status of his aesthetic operations: the poetic idealisation of 'any multiplicity whatsoever' is necessarily a hazardous procedure; there is indeed only a 'thin line of junction and disjunction between the infinite and nothing' (PS 4). We will see the consequences of this in what follows.

*

In the second chapter of *The Politics of the Siren*, 'The Poetics of Mystery', Rancière deepens his exploration of the aesthetic act performed by Mallarmé's poetry. This lays the ground for his comparative analysis of the poet's work and two of its competitors in the race to become 'the last plenary human religion' (D 239), Saint Simonism and Wagnerian opera, an analysis he pursues in his third chapter, 'The Hymn of Spiritual Hearts'. In 'The Poetics of Mystery', however, Rancière's main aim is to elucidate the status of the 'Idea' that Mallarmé's poem seeks to produce in its punctual singularity. Contrasting this 'Idea' with the Platonic *eidos* as well as with the axioms of the 'representative regime of art', Rancière shows how it is tied to a conception of the human being as a 'chimerical animal' (PS 30) and to a community that would finally be appropriate to this 'being of fiction' (PS 6 – translation modified).

In her important article 'Poetic Form and the Crisis of Community', Alison James has argued that in *The Politics of the Siren*, while 'emphasizing the triple crisis of verse, ideas and social forms, Rancière gives surprisingly little weight to the first of these three terms'. Consequently, she claims, 'the fate of metrical forms matters to Rancière primarily as a sign of the death of those archetypes and forms (the Platonic *eidos*) that formerly grounded representation',[24] and not as a sign of the radical transformation in versification that occurred with the explosion of free verse in the last two decades of the nineteenth century. James' diagnosis is confirmed by a close reading of 'The Poetics of Mystery': Rancière is indeed relatively indifferent to the metrical forms of Mallarmé's poetry. Instead, he prefers to operate at a far higher level of abstraction by comparing Mallarmé's 'Idea' to the Platonic *eidos*. Yet this is not for reasons of inattention or professional expertise. Rather, as Rancière himself explains:

> 'Poetry' has always signified much more than the art of writing verse. For Mallarmé, to refuse the solution of free verse is not to refuse a certain form of 'poetic specificity' that would tie poetic form to the question of an equal or unequal number of feet ... For Mallarmé, poetry's specificity is to be an act of language that belongs to a symbolic economy destined to consecrate the community by doubling the material economy of the exchange of goods.[25]

Thus, while Rancière offers no sustained reflection, for instance, on Mallarmé's use of the sonnet form or on his singular prose style, the philosopher's claim is that the analysis of *The Politics of the Siren* captures the most distinctive and essential features of the poet's work. For Rancière, Mallarmé's 'new poem' is not a new invention in versification: it is 'a new Eucharist, a purely human transformation of the human abode' (PS 16) that responds to the death of God, the exhaustion of Catholicism and the manifold inadequacies of the state and the market.[26] Moreover, even if he downgrades the importance of meter and rhyme in interpretation, Rancière insists that some very clear parameters must be respected if Mallarmé's key poetic operations are to succeed. Indeed, at one point this exigency leads Rancière to write that 'this letter' – that is, the poem in its ideal status as 'the Platonic living *logos*', successfully performing its religious function – 'is dead if it is missing the exact ritual by which the reader is instituted strictly as the new theatre where the poem replays its choreography' (PS 22). In other words, Mallarmé's poetry requires a measure of precision from the reader if it is to assume the mantle of the secular successor to the religions of the past: the '*exact* ritual' must be performed.

To determine why this need for precision is so important, we first need to better understand the essentially precarious nature of the Mallarméan 'Idea'. To do so, we will begin by contrasting it with the Platonic *eidos* and with the axioms of the 'representative regime of art', whose logic, Rancière argues, is consistent with the French neo-classicists' interpretation of Plato's theory of Forms.

Beginning with these axioms, Rancière makes it clear that the 'new poem' does not 'recount stories' (PS 44) according to the models of the 'representative regime': as we already know, it does not share the Aristotelean definition of fiction, namely, 'a representation of actions'. But nor does it adhere to the 'generic principle', which regulates the relations between what an artwork represents – its content – and the proper mode of its representation – its form. Similarly, it does not respect the rules of the 'principle of propriety', which, like the 'generic principle', governs the relations between characters; the genre in which they can be represented; their actions and affects; the customs they incarnate; and the particular community capable of appreciating their virtues and faults.[27] And finally, it does not content itself with 'the enunciation of philosophical messages' (PS 44): as we already know, the Mallarméan poem cannot be a vehicle whose form is indifferent to the passage of some philosophical content that could ideally be extracted and communicated by other means. The 'new poem' does not carry a message, hidden or not. Rather, it is the 'act of . . . production' (PS 16) of an ideality – a production that cannot occur by any other means.

But what is the status of this ideality, this 'Idea'? To bring its singular status into view, we can first consider the fact that the 'models' of the 'representative regime of art' are all *ideal* in so far as they are incarnated identically in each different artistic form. This form is therefore inessential relative to the essentiality of the 'model' (MS 44). Furthermore, they are *fixed*, since a particular material form – 'lion', 'eagle', 'serpent' – is predictably related to an abstract idea – 'glory', 'majesty', 'ruse' (PS 12). By contrast, Mallarmé's 'Idea' evacuates the normativity and fixity of the idealities of the 'representative regime' – idealities which, as Rancière reminds us, have 'a venerable model', namely:

the idea or form, the Platonic *eidos*, that which provided every human reality – justice of the city or carpenter's bed, beauty or a louse – with the divine model that it tried imperfectly to imitate. Above these Ideas stands, according to Plato, the Idea of the Good, the light that illuminates the intelligible world in the way that the sun lights up the sensible world. This is what has disappeared. (PS 10–11)

In other words, the generically determined 'models' of the 'representative regime' of art shared the omni-temporal stability of the Platonic *eidos*. With the advent of the 'aesthetic regime' and its dissolution of both the 'generic principle' and the 'principle of decorum', we enter a period in which the model of the Platonic *eidos* becomes inoperable. There can no longer be any correspondence between a particular artistic form and the idea it is supposed to be instantiating.

However, despite the fact that Mallarmé is an atheist who firmly believes that there is no 'divine denominator of our apotheosis', no 'supreme mould for any object that exists' (D 167 – translation modified); and despite the fact that the downfall of the Platonic *eidos* is exacerbated in the domain of poetry by 'the anecdotic crisis of the venerable Alexandrine' (PS 11), Mallarmé is still committed to something like a theory of Forms. Thus, after the disappearance of the Platonic Sun, Mallarmé searches after traces of its 'dust' (PS 11), which are scattered here and there in a world from which the gods have definitively taken their leave. Importantly, among the objects that populate this world and that could 'offer their anonymous magnificence to the seal of the poetic act' (MS 133 – translation modified), Mallarmé privileges those that belong to the domain of everyday life, such as 'hair of foam, clown sequins, golden fringe of light on a stage curtain', or a 'woman's hair as flight of flame'. Despite their banality, these objects, which Rancière selects from the texts 'Hushed to the crushing cloud', 'An Interrupted Spectacle' and 'The Fairground Declaration', partake equally in a world glinting with the traces of the vanished Platonic Sun.

Here we find Mallarmé's version of what Rancière considers a key Romantic notion, but one inherent to the 'aesthetic regime' of art more broadly: namely, that 'any configuration of sensible properties can be assimilated to an arrangement of signs' (MS 60). To be very precise, for Mallarmé it is less that there exists a potential poeticity sleeping in all things, and more that his 'dialectic of verse' has the singular power to produce, almost *ex nihilo*, the poetic transfiguration of 'any multiplicity whatsoever'. For Mallarmé, following the egalitarian ontology of the 'aesthetic regime of art', every thing can be 'differently configured and set to the rhythm of the mystery of the Idea' (PS 11 – translation modified) such that an ideality can spring forth.

Yet if the figures that best exemplify Mallarmé's poetry, such as the siren or the dying glint of sunlight, are all fugitive figures, appearing only to disappear, then this is because his 'Idea' lacks the permanence of the Platonic *eidos*. If, for example, one wished to link a 'mediocrity' (PS 20) like a line of foam to the idea of a shipwreck or a siren's dive, then one could expect only a 'momentary alliance' (PS 13) between this form and its content. Moreover, in contrast to Plato's *eidos*, Mallarmé's idealities are strictly *false*. But this is in a very precise sense. As Rancière has it, Mallarmé 'raise[s]' the objects of his poetry 'to the power of artifice': that is, he at once accepts their brute existence – 'Nature has taken place; it can't be added to' (D 187) – and affirms the human capacity to imagine and create 'that which has no reason to be'; a capacity that transforms 'contingency into an unheard-of power of affirmation' (PS 10). The human being plays. Like Mallarmé's 'new poem' its most characteristic works are those that manifest the 'power of artifice'. As such, for the poet, the 'human animal is a chimerical animal' (PS 30). Rancière puts this point most clearly in *Mute Speech*:

> Nothingness can transform itself into a glorious simulacrum and literature can be the practice of this simulacrum that 'project[s], to a great, forbidden, thunderous height, our conscious lack of what, up there, gleams' ... The foam upon the surf or the reflection of the setting sun, the drape of tresses, the fluttering of a fan or the neck of fleeting glassware can offer their anonymous magnificence to the seal of the poetic act. It suffices to 'compare aspects and count their number' and to arouse 'the ambiguity of a few beautiful figures, at the intersections'. (MS 133)

Yet this literary 'practice' is not as simple as this passage makes it sound. For what *also* follows from the intrinsic fragility of Mallarmé's vanishing idealities is that somebody is required to perceive and, indeed, to record them. This is the task and gift of the poet:

> Not by chance did Mallarmé talk of his 'indubitable wing', the inner fold of the vanished heaven of ideas, that which makes it possible to grasp its golden dust in 'many scattered veins of ore'. 'Dream' designates not the cloud in which the sentimental soul loses himself, but the capacity to 'compare aspects and count their number as it touches our negligence'; it is the gap remarked by the attentive spectator in 'what is', discerning in it the disappearing appearing of that which can or can not be. (PS 13)

As a powerful and paradigmatic example of this process, Rancière turns to the prose text 'An Interrupted Spectacle', in which a bear being exhibited to an audience of workers suddenly assumes the posture of a human being, simultaneously suggesting the constellation Ursa Major. The animal is idealised; at the very same moment 'the crowd is convoked to the spectacle of its greatness' (PS 14). This *collective* moment correlative to the act of idealisation is central. For while the banality of the spectacle of the dancing bear reflected back to the audience their own banality, it nevertheless happens that when the same spectacle is poetically transubstantiated – that is, when a glimpse of a second, higher theatre is given through the transformation of the bear into Ursa Major – 'the crowd' suddenly sees a sensible image of their 'latent grandeur'. The poet's act of idealisation is thus inextricably bound up with a particular conception of a people. This is what strikes Rancière in Mallarmé as an exemplary artist of the 'aesthetic regime': with the downfall of the 'principle of fiction', which had circumscribed an autonomous spatio-temporal domain for art, 'the sphere of literature and of social relations [became] coextensive' (MS 69). As a result Mallarmé inevitably associates the virtual poeticity in things that his gaze and writings actualise with a certain collective power, present in all. While Mallarmé pours scorn on 'the natural way of seeing' common to the clown and the director, who in his pathetic fear throws the bear a morsel of flesh in order to render it docile, thereby returning the spectacle and its spectators to the status of mediocrities, Mallarmé does not condemn 'the crowd' without reprieve. And while he proclaims that the poet's 'way of seeing [is] superior to theirs, and . . . maybe even the genuine one', for him it is not – it cannot be – a capacity that marks a distinction between two *essentially* different humanities.

As we can deduce from the above, the precision necessary for the proper production of the 'Idea' thus pertains to the *ephemeral* – one could even say *circumstantial* – nature of the 'new poem'; the fact that it has 'the instantaneousness of a vanishing tracing' (PS 22 – translation modified); that it is above all 'momentary' (PS 12), particularly since its principal effect is to bring about the becoming-ideal of 'any mediocrity whatsoever' (PS 20 – translation modified), which inevitably sinks back into its banality. As an almost surgically precise operation, the poem's proper functioning will of necessity enter into conflict with what Rancière takes to be a key feature of literary production in the 'aesthetic regime' of art: namely, that it occurs after the breakdown of both the 'generic principle' and the 'principle of propriety', two principles which had regulated the relation between content and form and the immanent characteristics of a literary work and its intended audience. If Mallarmé, like Flaubert, inhabits the time of 'triumphant democracy', in which they witnessed 'the scattering of novels to the four winds' (PS 59) and in which no author can suppose their audience to be the repository of the code proper to deciphering their work, then the poem's 'new Eucharist' is at risk of being perverted, if not entirely lost.[28] There is no guarantee that Mallarmé's poetic 'Idea' will be produced.

Thus, while Rancière scrupulously resists Sartre's and Milosz's tendency to read the difficult form of Mallarmé's poetry as the product of a perverse elitism, he cannot avoid the necessity that its 'exact ritual' be followed by those who know how to operate it. In the same way that he gives us a glimpse of Mallarmé's debt to a certain constellation of anti-democratic ideas in the figure of 'the monster', Rancière allows us to see the concrete – and restricted – forms the consumption of the 'new poem' had to take. For example, when explaining the peculiar ontology of Mallarmé's poetic 'Idea', Rancière refers to the banquet of *La Revue indépendante*, which grouped together *fin-de-siècle* avant-garde poets. Indeed, only the maintenance of a restricted field of addressees capable of verifying the specific relation between form and content could overcome the essential contingency of this relation in the 'aesthetic regime'. Furthermore, only such a tightly controlled regime of reading could avoid the ever-present problem, which democratic modernity exacerbates, of 'orphaned speech':[29] that is, the fact that 'the written word ... drifts all over the place' and is 'incapable of distinguishing whom it should or should not address' (MS 93–4). No text can control the interpretative practices of the infinitely open set of its potential readers.

The poet's act of 'consecration' thus occurs within – we could even say *because of* – the anticipated audience present when Mallarmé first declaimed 'Toast'. It is this audience with their cultivated dispositions towards Symbolist poetry who 'assure[s] the equivalence between the fictional siren and the cup of elevation' (PS 16); it is they who are able to make the metaphorical links Mallarmé's poem establishes, thus enabling its 'Idea' to spring forth. However, these restrictions are not only enabling conditions. Rather, they are also reaction-formations against the fact that there is no longer any necessary relation between content and form, and that the 'new poem' is radically open to the failure of its own project.

This, then is the form taken in Mallarmé's work by the contradiction at the heart of the 'aesthetic regime', a contradiction between the two modes of writing it promulgates: namely, between writing as 'the hieroglyph that bears its idea upon its body', and writing as 'the orphaned speech without a body to guide it and speak for it' – in other words, between necessity and contingency. While Mallarmé's opposition to Christianity is in part based on its regressive reference to 'the "barbaric feast" of the body and blood of the Saviour, designated by the Eucharistic Sacrament' (PS 30), there is an irreducible moment of incarnation operative in his poetry. However evanescent it is, the 'Idea' Mallarmé's poetry produces must become incarnate at the moment of the poem's reading.

But how can Mallarmé hope for this to occur in a context he perceives as 'naturally improper to the visibility and the hearing of the drama' (PS 3) of the poem? As we know from our discussion of Rancière's first chapter, the paradox of 'the politics of the siren' is that the very same community Mallarmé invests with a latent grandeur and whose spiritual capacity it is his duty to both reveal and cultivate is also figured as a 'famished ogre' (PS 24) that threatens to devour his poetry. We can now see that this threat is nothing other than an exterior figuration of the fragility of Mallarmé's 'Idea'. Thus, while 'the crowd' represents the present yet defective incarnation of the glorious community it will one day become, it cannot partake of the poem in Mallarmé's lifetime. It is not present at the poets' banquet, but rather indulging in fallen forms of its spiritual essence.

*

For Rancière, Mallarmé participated in one of the key projects of nineteenth-century European thought and practice: the construction of 'a new religion and a new mythology' (PS 28) that would supplement the insufficient forms of collective existence provided by the Republican state. As Bertrand Marchal puts it:

> It is indeed a public cult – a cult of the State – that Mallarmé, in any case, envisages; a cult under the auspices of the poet. One can, by invoking the title of *Divagations*, refuse to take seriously such an ambition and to see in it only a substitute for national festivals, a sort of 14th of July converted into a day of poetic recreation. But Mallarmé nevertheless still raises a fundamental problem of the time, namely, that of the legitimacy of the State, or of its link to the sacred, as if the purely juridical formula of consent and of the delegation of power by universal suffrage remained insufficient; as if there were no true authority except through a properly religious sanction. ... The problem was certainly not raised during the time of the monarchy, when political and religious authority were united in the person of the king. But since the abolition of the monarchy and the exhaustion of Catholicism, the republican State becomes the sole depository of collective fervour, and for this very reason must give its citizens the elevation of the now-vanished festivals.[30]

Whether it be reactionaries who deplored 'the century of unbelief and dereliction' (PS 28) or progressives for whom the promise of the French Revolution had so far been restricted to the abstract sphere of the law, both 'come together in a common thought . . .: that the bonds of the new community must be built out of the ruins of the old order' (PS 28). Following the German Idealists, Feuerbach and Marx sought in different ways to constitute 'a religion that renders the bread and wine of everyday alienated existence of human powers into divine attributes'

(PS 28),[31] whether this divinity be the Christian God or the impersonal forces of Capital. Similarly, the Saint-Simonians promised a new human community built on the basis of productive labour and technological progress.[32] Arguing forcefully for the continuity of Mallarmé's project with this central tendency in nineteenth-century European society, Rancière writes: 'It is impossible to understand the Mallarméan poem and aesthetics outside of this secular game. But we should also determine its precise part in it: that is, the motives and forms of its "dice throw", of its wager on the "religious" future of the community' (PS 29). This is Rancière's task in the last two chapters of *The Politics of the Siren*. As such, we will discover the precise coordinates of the poet's idiosyncratic religion, which, as Rancière shows, Mallarmé defined negatively in relation to Christianity, the Saint-Simonian notion that Man's essence lies in his labour, and the Wagnerian mythology of national origins.

Working with Mallarmé's *Les Dieux antiques*, the poet's French-language translation of the book by George W. Cox, Rancière draws 'two ... essential propositions' (PS 29) from this apparently marginal moment in Mallarmé's œuvre. The first is that the very notion of a divinity was first born from the *language* that recounted the natural phenomena witnessed by ancient peoples. Language necessarily brought with it theological and metaphysical baggage, which was irresistibly transformed into a religious vision of the world. The second is that the original object of religion was the 'very movement of appearing and disappearing of light' (PS 30): in other words, *the solar drama*, which plays out the fundamental opposition between being and nothingness.[33] From these two propositions Mallarmé draws two conclusions: firstly, that to finally overcome religion, it is not a matter of returning to Man his full powers as Feuerbach had argued, but rather of returning 'to *language* its powers' (PS 30 – translation modified, our emphasis). In other words, what was required was the cultivation of an adequate theory and practice of Man's linguistic capacities. The second conclusion Mallarmé comes to is that the central role of language is to be that which 'glorifies' (PS 30).[34] As Marchal points out, this conception of religion is inspired by the properly scientific pretensions of Müller and Cox's nineteenth-century anthropology. He writes: 'The entire Mallarméan enterprise is indeed an enterprise in recuperating – in the name of art and for the profit of humanity – a common good or secret confiscated since time immemorial by mythology, religion or music.'[35] Furthermore, it gives Mallarmé's conception of the spiritual capacities of mankind a universality that undercuts any claim to national or other identitarian particularities.[36]

To this language-based attempt to overcome religious alienation Mallarmé adds his conception of the grandeur of Christianity, in particular of Catholicism, which he believes had taken a decisive step towards revealing 'the specific nature of the human animal' (PS 30). In the Catholic liturgy, Mallarmé was distinctly impressed by its celebration of that which was *absent*. It thereby exemplifies the human capacity to glorify that which *is not*, like the precarious idealities that the gaze of the 'dreamer' had seen glinting on the surface of everyday objects in 'An Interrupted Spectacle'. Mallarmé thus marks a decisive distinction from other contemporaneous efforts to overcome religion and the post-Revolutionary context of a perceived deterioration of the communitarian bond: rather than the *reversal* that 'Feuerbachian anthropology' (PS 30) had proposed, Mallarmé argues for what might be called a *sublation* of Christianity. Specifically, the poet will empty out all of the *content* from the Christian religion but retain its *form*, that is, the gesture of idealisation and the celebration of artifice. Indeed, as Bertrand Marchal makes clear, Mallarmé is opposed to any attempt to be done with religion once and for all: for him the true utopians were those who thought religion was a pure illusion capable of being overcome.[37]

The stakes of Mallarmé's move within this shared problematic are made evident by two prose texts, 'Conflict' and 'Confrontation', in which the poet engages, albeit implicitly, with the ideas of Saint-Simonism. In fact, on Rancière's reading 'Conflict' and 'Confrontation' constitute nothing less than 'a precise retort' to any religion based on the idea of Man as a labourer. Moreover, they are uncompromising apologies for Mallarmé's refusal to canvass the idea of transforming 'men of the book into manual workers' (PS 32), as if the most appropriate means for overcoming the alienation born of the division of labour and social conflict was for the guilt-ridden poet to down his pen and pick up a shovel. Rather – and this cannot but appeal to Rancière, who has consistently opposed the idea that workers' emancipation involves the affirmation of an identity proper to the world of work – Mallarmé ruthlessly derides the banality of labour, which he caricatures by painting an image of a worker endlessly transporting dirt from one side of a worksite to another: 'a worthless task whose only price is the universal equivalent, the everyday gold that is exchanged for bread' (PS 32).

In 'Conflict', it is crucial to note that Mallarmé does not conceive of the group of railroad workers who disrupt his poetic work as irredeemably sunk in some sort of subhumanity. But neither does he set about composing a 'hymn to work' (PS 32). Rather, he sees that these workers manifest, in their 'Sunday libations' (PS 32), a desire for something other than the cycle of works and days; a desire that no doubt finds inadequate expression in their drunkenness, but which nevertheless bears witness to their latent essence as 'chimerical animals'. Indeed, this assumption about their essence prompts Mallarmé to reimagine his poetic duty: 'the task of the poet-Hamlet thus becomes clear: it is to fix the "points of clarity" which give to the slumped honour of the herd the chimerical glory it seeks instinctively' (PS 32). Rancière then adds a remark that is almost an exact paraphrase of Badiou's *Theory of the Subject*: 'This programme contains no populism' (PS 32). And indeed, 'Conflict' cannot be accused of glorifying labour. Instead, what it does is to veritably exacerbate the distinction between poet and worker.

In addition to distinguishing his religion from the sacralisation of labour, Mallarmé is perhaps even more concerned to resist the form taken by a particular artistic practice in its own response to the problematic of the construction of 'a new community': namely, music, in particular in its Wagnerian incarnation. The first point to make regarding music is that it assumes an unprecedented status within the 'aesthetic regime': it is the form of art that takes the anti-representative tendency of this 'regime' to an extreme. As Rancière has it, music is 'a purified language' (PS 35) that is no longer weighed down by narrative or characters, and which, for this very reason, operates at the furthest possible distance from the mediocre conventions and 'coarse anecdotes' of modern theatre, which reduces art to 'the simple nothingness of banality looking at itself in the mirror' (PS 36).[38] Music is that art form that is closest to the immateriality and interiority of the Idea. Furthermore, it lacks all of the fleshy substance Mallarmé had found so tasteless and out-dated in the Catholic liturgy. Mallarmé is also impressed by the way the performance of a symphony orchestra can bring together a community of individual subjects without imposing any precise *idea* on these subjects in which they would all indifferently participate. But at the same time, it still allows for that act of idealisation that is the proof of humanity's 'chimerical grandeur':

> the people of the musical temple no longer look at themselves in the mirror of banality. But neither do they incorporate any formerly divine greatness. The conductor of the orchestra, like the priest, better than the priest, pushes back the common glory that he exhibits. The chimerical animal only ever appropriates its greatness through an empty space. (PS 37)

This 'distance' is, as Rancière insists, 'a political distance', since music's emptying-out of all representational content prevents any community from forming on the basis of a substantial identity. But this purity also carries a danger: like Hegel, Mallarmé recognises that the flipside of music's anti-representationalism was its tendency to either coincide with the most banal interiority or be appropriated by those willing to anchor its force to a mythology of origins. As Rancière writes, music 'is unable to control its effects, is unable to be reduced to its own principle'. He continues: 'Music is the art of interiority par excellence'; but 'this beautiful interiority is an empty one' (PS 38).[39]

And this void of sense has been exploited, in Mallarmé's view, by Wagner. What the creator of the *Gesamtkuntswerk* had done was to effect a formidable – though for the French poet, perverse – synthesis between the anti-representationalism of music and a nationalist mythology, chaining the awesome though indeterminate power of the former to the latter's identitarian limits. In terms of Rancière's division of the 'regimes' of art, Wagner's music is at once the most avant-garde expression of the 'aesthetic regime' and a regression to the 'representative regime' with its 'its fable[s] and its substantial characters' (PS 39). For Mallarmé, this is nothing less than a 'fraud' (PS 39 – translation modified) that speaks less to Wagner's inventiveness than to his fear of the novel power of an art stripped of all determinate representation. In order to respond to the shared nineteenth-century problematic of the constitution of 'a new community', the composer has chosen the most regressive option: that of 'the celebration of a community of origins' (PS 40).

Against this, Mallarmé refused any symmetrical recourse to an affirmation of *French* national identity. Indeed, he notably resisted calls to have *Lohengrin* banned in Paris.[40] Instead, he radicalised the anti-representative and anti-essentialist logic at play in his art. In political terms, this translates into a rejection of any substantial conception of a community's identity. The generic universalism of Mallarmé's 'religion', grounded as it is in the nominally scientific research of Müller and Cox, is confirmed by Marchal:

> We can now understand to what degree Mallarmé distances himself from the essentially nationalist formula of Wagnerian art. To the concept of the Nation, the poet opposes the notion of the City, to which he gives less a national than a universal content. The Mallarméan crowd has nothing to do with the Wagnerian Volk, even if in both cases an experience of the sacred requires collective fervour. The crowd is not the depository of a national soul that has to be awakened by returning its mythological memory to it; it is rather, by its very diversity, like a sample of humanity, for whom it is less a matter of bathing again in the primitive stream of myth than in the source of nature; less a matter of aiming at the origin of the nation than the origin of man.[41]

The sort of 'social arrangement' Mallarmé imagines to be most appropriate, in this nineteenth century that had 'dissolved the myths of origin and sovereignty' (PS 40), is one that is continuous with the logic of the vanishing idealities his poetry produces. In other words, it must refuse 'all incarnation' (PS 40) and find the means to preserve the empty place of power that the French Revolution had revealed – a place that was isomorphic to the 'nothing' that governs both the productivity and the precariousness of his 'new poem'.[42] Most importantly, however, the art of the democratic age cannot risk the volatility of music's antirepresentative tendency. It must have recourse to what Mallarmé names 'the intellectual word at its height' (D 210). Poetry, as that which can synthesise music and letters and therefore carry out 'the transposition into the Book of the symphony' D 210), reasserts its rights: it alone is appropriate for the 'celebrations of the future' (PS 41). To return to the terms of the previous chapter, it must institute the 'exact ritual' for the consecration of the human community.

As we can see, Mallarmé is engaged with an irreducibly aesthetic and political problematic, which he shares with other contemporaneous social movements, thinkers and artists. His 'small poetic siren' (PS 41), however fragile it might appear when faced with the symphonic deluge of *Tristan und Isolde* or the productive power of Saint-Simonism, is a response to the same key problematic of post-Revolutionary European society. Moreover, it might be suggested that it is a response that finds favour with Rancière himself, who could be suspected neither of being sympathetic to a religion of labour nor of having a taste for the affirmation of national origins. However, as the final chapter of *The Politics of the Siren*, 'The Duty of the Book', will demonstrate, Mallarmé's poetic project encounters a set of decisive difficulties and ends on a note of profound ambivalence. It is only at this point in Rancière's book that we discover what 'Mallarmé's specific difficulty' (PS xiii) consists in.

*

We will begin this final section by detailing the way in which Rancière reinscribes Mallarmé's project in a problematic treated before him by the German Romantics; a problematic whose limits were first circumscribed by Hegel. As we will see, these limits apply to Mallarmé's work as well. Then, we will turn to the way the poet attempted to distinguish his poetry from music and ballet: that is, from two forms of art that could only be simulacra of the 'Idea'. Finally, we turn to a reading of *Un coup de dés*.

As he will go on to do in more detail in *Mute Speech*, Rancière takes the German Romantics – in particular Hegel – to have already laid out the basic parameters for any discussion of poetry's pretensions to thought (MS 86–92). Rancière begins with the 'progressive universal poetry' of Friedrich Schlegel, which he reads as an exemplary expression of the promised powers of poetry for thought – a promise that Hegel will see as an intellectually illegitimate extravagance, for reasons Rancière will show are relevant to Mallarmé's own project. Schlegel's conception of 'poetry-thought' brought together two components: firstly, the 'theory of wit', which named the infinite productivity of language and its capacity to produce strikingly novel meanings that could help the mind break with 'hackneyed words and significations'; and secondly, his 'theory of the symbol' (PS 45). In Schlegel's thought – as Rancière presents it – the 'symbol' is that which inscribed this productive power into a natural history of poeticity, a history of which 'the poetic games of *Witz*' were the crowning and most contemporary achievement. In addition to being continuous with the 'power of ... life', these 'games' were what allowed the human mind to 'deny finite determination and fossilized meaning' (PS 45) and accede to ever-higher forms of reflection

In response to this seductive extravagance, Hegel contrasted the poem's alleged power to 'the clear division of two modes of existence of thought' (PS 46). The first mode is that in which thought finds itself 'outside of itself', effectively existing in materials heterogeneous to it such as paint, stone, prosody or sensuous imagery. The second mode is 'thought in its proper element', which is to say thought that requires no external prop but which is rather perfectly transparent to itself, operating with 'a language of signs that are indifferent to what they signify' (PS 46 – translation modified). This distinction imposes a decisive limitation on the powers of thought one can attribute to poetry, for as in other arts such as painting and sculpture thought manifests itself in poetry in an irreducibly material object – in this case, in language's rhythm and imagery. Certainly, poetry works with 'language', which is the most ideal material for thought; but for Hegel, language itself, particularly in 'the figurativeness of [its] images and the temporal thickness of its materiality' (PS 46), is not self-transparent; it too resists the ideal passage of sense. It is therefore not – *pace* Schlegel – 'the active of power of thought which knows itself'. Rather, it is exemplarily lacking in self-consciousness. As such, poetry cannot fully control what it is thinking or effecting; it is inherently resistant to carrying out a programme, particularly one with philosophical pretensions. And it is even less suited to fulfilling the exorbitant ambitions of Mallarmé's 'new poem' that claims to take up the role of religion, which precisely requires the perfect coincidence of form and content in the production of the 'Idea'.

Hegel, then, emerges as the thinker who first formulated the inherent limitations of a project such as Mallarmé's. But it is crucial to emphasise that Mallarmé does, in fact, conceive of the possibility of his project's failure. However, he does not attribute this possibility to the poem, but rather exteriorises it in two other art forms: music and ballet.

In confronting these two rival arts, Mallarmé finds himself within what Rancière calls 'the circle of mimesis' (PS 48), which here denotes the following complex notion: firstly, the poet must distinguish his own practice *qua* the ostensibly authentic re-production of the 'Idea' from its less successful re-productions, music and ballet. Secondly, these different art forms imitate the 'Idea' but with a greater or lesser degree of success. The difficulty that the 'circle of mimesis' names, however, is the fact that Mallarmé cannot demonstrate the authenticity of his own acts of idealisation – and therefore his capacity to be the privileged practitioner of a poetry that glorifies the community – except by way of asymptotic comparisons with allegedly deficient imitations of the 'Idea'. Mallarmé's poetry will therefore always rely upon a deficient exteriority in order to affirm its authenticity. However, as we will see, this exteriority is an external reflection of properties possessed by poetry itself: an authentic inscription of the 'Idea' is constitutively impossible.

But this is an anticipation of Rancière's argument. For now, let us turn to the specific reasons that music and ballet are, relative to the poem, false imitations of the 'Idea'.

Now, we know that music is, disastrously, 'conveniently exempt from explaining itself' (PS 48). Its a-signifying nature figures the threat of dissemination and thus the ever-present possibility of the breakdown of semantic stability. Ballet, by contrast, is an art that involves sight and the movement of bodies. The principle behind Mallarmé's preference for ballet over music, then, is that like the printed word it has the figural plenitude of a *spatial* art. It therefore seems to avoid the impoverished interiority of music, which is an irreducibly *temporal* art.[43] Furthermore, what makes ballet so evocative and representative for Mallarmé is the way the dancer's movements are – or can be – related to some signification, however multiple and fleeting: 'Never, by its lone act, will a step be able to represent or to suggest any object, story or feeling. But, clearly, an art's pure capacity for fiction stands in inverse ratio to that offered by the ordinary games of recognition' (PS 51). Put differently, ballet does not equate a single movement with a single idea, or institute some constraining set of links between form and content, as an artwork from the 'representative regime' would. Rather, it breaks down standard mechanisms of 'recognition' in favour of a more mobile play of suggestion. As such, what the ballerina 'draws' with her steps is less any single signification linking a bodily movement with an idea, and more the ever-present *potential* of such a signification: 'the pure trajectory between a virtual aspect and a mind able to "divine" it' (PS 51). What she 'mimics' – represents – is the vanishing act by which the idealisation of 'any mediocrity whatsoever' is achieved.

However, the fault of the ballerina lies in the fact that she is a 'rather unconscious revealer' of the vanishing idealities she is otherwise effectively producing: 'Only the gaze of the poet "habituated to dreaming" is able to recognize in it the choreography of the spirit' (PS 52 – translation modified). The gestures of the ballerina must be 'interpreted', and a 'poet-spectator [must] lay "the flower of [his] poetic instinct" at the ballerina's feet' (MS 141). What the poem will require, by contrast, is full self-consciousness.

At this point, after having followed Mallarmé's investigations into the virtues of other art forms, Rancière shows his hand and points out the limits of Mallarmé's procedure: 'Always the "book of verse" appears as the true theatre of the mind, the theatre which imitates only the Idea and of which every other art is a simple imitation' (PS 52 – translation modified). In other words, Mallarmé affirms that it is only poetry that adequately imitates the 'Idea' and that the other arts are therefore straining to be like poetry. Music aims to present pure idealities stripped of denotation and narrative, yet leaves itself open to 'the emptiness of this wordless language, concealed by the clamour of bare sounds' (PS 52). Ballet presents in figural form the movement of idealisation but lacks the self-consciousness required to recognise and to fulfil its potential. However, Mallarmé cannot think of the poem except in its own mimetic relation to these other forms of art: it mimes what they inadequately mime.

Thus, *pace* Derrida's famous reading of the poet, Mallarmé 'maintained a mimetic status for the poem: the poem imitates no model, but traces perceptibly the movement of the Idea, the idea as the movement of its own breaking forth' (PS 52).[44] In terms of mimesis, then, what every discrete poem does is to mime the *act* of idealisation itself. However, as we have demonstrated, this act is constitutively precarious – a precariousness that Mallarmé self-consciously inscribes in the disappearing act of the siren. As such, any supposed act of idealisation can be contested or fail. Indeed, at the limit, with neither the Platonic *eidos* nor the rules of the 'representative regime' to legitimate it, *there is no act of idealisation*. What the poem purports to authentically imitate – and what music and ballet imitate in a deficient manner – *does not exist*.

And yet, given its properly religious problematic, the poem must claim to be re-presenting just such a movement of idealisation. For this reason, it cannot avoid attempting to 'prove itself (PS 57). But such a 'proof' cannot come about by the endless circle of comparison and confrontation with the forgeries of the 'Idea' – with those deficient doubles that are music and ballet. Rather, the 'proof' must come from the poem's own singular materiality.

Rancière now turns to Plato in order to understand the singularity of Mallarmé's practice in the face of the impossibility of authenticating his poetic production of the 'Idea'. Given the irreducibility of the problem of 'mute speech', no immediate presentation of sense is guaranteed; there is an essential precariousness to any linguistic presentation. This is why Rancière claims that 'the writing of the Idea is two things at once: it is both text and interpretation' (MS 140). This constitutive scission means that some other mechanism is always in play in order to guarantee the presentation of the intended and determinate sense. While this mechanism is itself submitted to the same rule of 'mute speech', its presence is nevertheless called upon as a way of trying to control its effects. Rancière gives two examples of such a mechanism: 'ever since Plato another type of writing has always had to stand in for it; one that is both less than written, similar to the breath of the spirit; and that is more than written, either averred in the body of one who fulfils speech, or etched in the very texture of things' (PS 53). In other words, the authenticity of a linguistic presentation can be verified either by saying that it is the materialisation of a self-present spirit or mind – 'the breath of the spirit' – or by the position of the person speaking. Recourse is made to someone who is deemed capable, given a certain distribution of power and authority, to make the statement and for it to be true. In the case of the 'representative regime', this role was played by 'people of taste' (PS 57) who were the repositories of the rules for artistic creation. But as Rancière points out, Mallarmé can turn to neither of these two mechanisms. There is no God, no Platonic *eidos*, and therefore no immaterial 'spirit' who could animate the words of his poems, thereby authenticating them. Furthermore, in the 'aesthetic regime of art', '[n]o writing can designate the rule or the public that testifies for it' (PS 57). And while it may seem that it is the 'man habituated to dream' who can see the vanishing presence of the 'Idea' in 'a popular theatre' or a ballet performance, this privilege must in principle be extended to *all* if the poem is to authenticate humanity's grandeur. No hierarchical conception of the community can come to the aid of the Mallarméan 'Idea'.

Thus, only one path seems to remain open: 'It is necessary then that these two figures of another type of writing' – that is, the writing itself and the supplement that comes to bolster its essential precariousness – 'merge in the sole materiality of the book' (PS 53). In its unprecedented deployment of materials specific to literature – 'the white of the open page, of unequal lines of characters borrowed from diverse fonts' –

Mallarmé's testamentary text *Un coup de dés* is therefore guided by the goal of making matter and form coincide without remainder. Rather than being a superfluous empirical accident attendant upon the ideal passage of sense, the materiality of the book paradoxically becomes the sole means for ensuring the production of the 'Idea'. What the poem says, it must re-present materially.

In his reading of *Un coup de dés* Rancière begins by again recalling the fact that, for Mallarmé, the 'Idea' cannot be a *message* but only an *act*. Thus, if the poet seems to repeat in *Un coup de dés* a gesture performed before him by Vigny, namely that of casting a bottle into the sea – a bottle 'intended for posterity [and] charged with the task that is identical to all of posterity: hosting the heritage of the ideal that was misrecognized in its time' (PS 54) – then Mallarmé's gesture involves a number of novel and distinctive features. Most importantly, in contrast to Vigny, Mallarmé's conception of the Idea is not that of a communicable message, essentially extractable from its poetic form. Rather, his 'Idea' *takes place* in the immanent movement of the poem itself. In terms of Mallarmé's socio-political problematic, this means that *Un coup de dés* cannot simply express a desire for the advent of 'the celebrations of the future'. *It must be these very celebrations themselves*. This is the reason why Mallarmé chooses to perform a 'decisive gesture' in *Un coup de dés* – a 'gesture' by which 'the spirit must, on the place which denies it, institute its place' (PS 55). However, as all readers of the poem know, the 'decisive gesture' at stake in the poem – the throw of dice itself – is never actually carried out. Given the volatile conditions of reception in Third Republic France, 'it is necessary to include in the game the hesitation to play it, to plot in the "cast" of the poem its "victory" over its own chance, the risky game it plays with the chasm' (PS 55). *Un coup de dés* is thus at once an unfolding of the schema of the 'Idea' proper to 'the celebrations of the future', *as well as its withdrawal*. Paradoxically, then, like the siren in 'Hushed to the crushing cloud', the poem must 'hide itself from the present abyss of vain hunger' (PS 55) in order to do its duty.

Admittedly, however, these are the conditions that *all* of Mallarmé's poems are submitted to. What grounds the singularity of *Un coup de dés*, on Rancière's account, is that this text 'must be the *initial* sacrament by which every effectuation, and the siren in particular, are consecrated' (PS 55 – our emphasis). In other words, it is the verification-in-act of the poem's authenticity, which subsequent poetic acts will imitate. As we already know from our discussion of Mallarmé's affirmation of the autonomy of literature, in particular in its recourse to spatiality over the volatile temporal interiority of music, the poem will attempt this self-authentication by 'presenting the figure that resembles materially what it says and what the poem does in general' (PS 57). Mallarmé is thus led not only to narrate the scenario that pits the shipwreck and the Master against the Ocean and which closes with the glorious upsurge of the Constellation; he will also figure this very scene on the page. Noting that this is a 'paradox' for his 'anti-mimetic mimetics of the Idea' – in the sense that, contrary to the entire history of metaphysics, in *Un coup de dés* it is material form alone that guarantees to the upsurge of ideality – Rancière writes that '[o]nly typographical *mimesis* can attest that it really is the primary game of the spirit that inscribes itself here' (PS 55). But this material mimesis is more than a paradox. In fact, there is something singularly bathetic about Mallarmé's recourse to typography. Writing of the poem's attempt to authenticate itself *qua* the inscription of the 'Idea', Rancière states that in *Un coup de dés* Mallarmé is 'only able to [authenticate his Idea] at the price of simply miming, on the double page, the listing of the ship or the constellation's tracing' (PS 56). In order to assert its authenticity in relation to other deficient instantiations of the 'Idea', such as music and ballet, literature had been led back to its own singular resources, in particular to its material, graphic disposition. But what this now means is that the 'new poem', whose ideal had once been the anti-representative character of music, is forced to end with the bathos of a graphic imitation of ship and constellation.

For Rancière, *Un coup de dés* represents Mallarmé's most concerted attempt to respond to the productive contradictions of the 'aesthetic regime of art'. It is a response that, in so far as it took for its ideal the synthesis of the contradictory axioms of modern literature – those of 'the necessity of language' and language's 'indifference to what it says' (MS 172) – was necessarily led to a point of impossibility, if not of failure. *The Politics of the Siren* closes with this unsurpassable 'difficulty'.

*

But what of the specifically political dimension of *Un coup de dés*? Most readers of *The Politics of the Siren* have seen in the book a portrait of a poet in essential solidarity with the cause of emancipation.[45] According to this reading, Mallarmé is a poet whose aristocratic distance from 'the crowd' was a measure only of his 'political prudence' (CM 179). But Rancière's later essay 'The Intruder: Mallarmé's Politics' casts the division between the 'gold' of the poem and the 'mediocrity' of the contemporary manifestations of the community in a different light – one that is implicit but arguably muted in *The Politics of the Siren*. In fact, what Rancière shows in 'The Intruder' is that the division between the 'gold' of the poem and its deficient simulacra *is a division that is doomed to be eternal*. In order to see why this is the case, let us turn finally to 'The Intruder' and to the confrontation Rancière stages there between the workers from his first and arguably foundational work, *Proletarian Nights*, and Mallarmé himself.

Within the implicit axiology of *Proletarian Nights*, Mallarmé could well be construed as an ambivalent figure. On the one hand, as a school teacher he had to 'work hard for his daily bread before devoting his nights to the gold and thought of the poem' (PL 92), in a manner not dissimilar from the workers studied by Rancière. As such, he too struggled against a social order that sought to exhaustively control the tasks, time and capacities of individuals. Furthermore, one moment of Mallarmé's implicit 'nomology' (PL 91) is distinctly egalitarian: contrary to Plato's archipolitics, for the author of *Un coup de dés* 'it is not the lawmaker of the race of gold' (PL 93 – translation modified), himself ordained by the divinity, who alone is capable of performing the poetic task of cultivating 'the glory of a community' (PL 90). Rather, Mallarmé believes that neither the social division of labour, nor any of the predicates attributed to subjects in democratic modernity, can provide infallible guidance as to who has the capacity to perform the poet's task.

On the other hand, however, Mallarmé is a distinctly *negative* figure, since he institutes a certain 'distribution' of roles and capacities that 'had been contested', Rancière tells us, 'all through the century that Mallarmé brought to a close, by the militants fighting for workers' liberation' (PL 91). This inevitably places the poet on the side of those who contest the practice of Rancière's erstwhile heroes: namely, of those workers who resisted the constraining predicates of a so-called workers' culture and set out to create, think and write against their social position.[46] Instead of using their nights to simply rest before another day of work, the workers from *Proletarian Nights* attempted to appropriate for themselves 'the gold of thought and of the community', which in the Platonic schema had been reserved for the exclusive enjoyment of 'the men of leisure and of the night' (PL 91 – translation modified). Intriguingly, these nights are almost perfectly analogous to the night and sleeping workers witnessed by Mallarmé at the close of 'Conflict'. Rather than representing the simple compliance with the proper function of rest, which is to replenish the worker for the following day's labour, in 'Conflict' the sleep of the drunken workers is presented as a mark of their desire for something more; it represents a certain excess relative to 'the economic order of reproduction' (PL 87). Rancière writes: 'In this, the workers *mimic* the work of the poet, they do the work of divination "in the name of some superiority", more precisely in the name of the superiority of the animal, creator of prestiges and chimera' (PL 87 – Rancière's emphasis). What is most important in this passage is the notion that the workers *'mimic'* the task of the poet: they are its simulacrum, one that is equivalent in form and function to the swarm of artistic simulacra against which the 'new poem' had struggled in order to assert its authenticity. The workers' drunken sleep is thus also a flawed means of celebrating their latent grandeur, the spiritual essence of the community.

But why, according to Rancière, is Mallarmé led to 'portray the figure of the old-style worker who can't help but sleep at the end of the day' (PL 92)? What kind of necessity governs this scene? The answer to these questions does not lie in any class-based elitism on the part of the poet, but rather in the very status of literature in the 'aesthetic regime of art'. As we have seen throughout this chapter, the 'Idea' that Mallarmé's poetry purported to produce was an essentially precarious phenomenon. As such, the only means the poet had for affirming the validity of his practice was to exteriorise its immanent faults onto other equivalent practices. Thus, the denigration of the workers in 'Conflict' stems directly from the poet's attempt to assert the authenticity of his own practice. In a sense, Mallarmé could well have been one of the heroes of 'worker's liberation', yet the imperatives of literature in the 'aesthetic regime' corrupted him. While the workers from *Proletarian Nights* broke with 'the ways of being, doing and saying proper to the men of reproduction' (PL 92), Mallarmé could not permit them to be anything more than workers who 'sleep at the end of the day' and dream of a poet who will lay out their path to emancipation.

Again, it is *literature* and its internal exigencies that produce *this* form of 'solidarity' with the workers. Mallarmé provides 'the crowd' with the true meaning – and the true object – of the 'devouring hunger' (PL 94) it has for a better world. Presently, 'the crowd' is seduced only by subterfuges. The multiplication of simulacra of the new 'Idea' is what generates the necessity of defensively adopting the posture of a poet who alone has access to this 'Idea' and who must, as a consequence, maintain 'the gap that half a century of workers' struggles fought to close' (PL 96). Despite, then, the utopian horizon of Mallarmé's *œuvre*, Rancière suggests that literature must keep this horizon at an infinite distance, dooming the poet to being an eternal conservative: 'The inflexibility of places is more than ever called for', he writes, 'when the Idea is merely a simulacrum and yet has to be distinguishable from its simulacra' (PL 94).

Literature, then, is both in abstract solidarity with equality and actively opposed to its effective manifestation. Mallarmé cannot be 'comrade Mallarmé' in these conditions. Rather, the productive contradictions of the 'aesthetic regime of art' mean that he is, once again, as he has been at almost all moments of his reception, a figure of profound ambivalence.[47]

NOTES

1. For existing scholarship on *The Politics of the Siren* see: E. Beaulieu, 'Une sirène de *polis*', *Spirale: arts, lettres, sciences humaines*, No. 220 (2008), 23–4; P. Campion, 'Mallarmé à la lumière de la raison poétique', *Critique*, Vol. 53, Nos. 601–2 (1997), 467–80; P. Greaney, '*Mallarmé: La politique de la sirène* by Jacques Rancière', *MLN*, Vol. 113, No. 5, Comparative Literature Issue (1998), 1190–2; B. O'Keefe, 'Mallarmé: the politics of the siren', *The Comparatist*, Vol. 37 (2013), 309–16. See also the excellent discussion by Oliver Davis in *Jacques Rancière* (Cambridge: Polity, 2010), 119–25.
2. We will detail the main axioms of the 'aesthetic regime of art' and its predecessor, 'the representative regime of art', in the third section of this chapter. For an excellent account of the differences between these two 'regimes', see MS.
3. J. Rancière, 'The Politics of Literature', *SubStance*, Vol. 33, No. 1 (2004), 11–12. See also MS 42.
4. J. Rancière, 'A Singular Invention of Language and Thought', in Boncardo and Gelder, *Mallarmé: Rancière, Milner, Badiou*, 45.
5. 'A Singular Invention of Language and Thought', 53.
6. 'A Singular Invention of Language and Thought', 55.
7. For other iterations of this image in Rancière's references to Sartre, see PS 33 and MS 41, 94, 125.
8. C. Chassé, *Les Clés de Mallarmé* (Aubier: Editions Montaigne, 1954).
9. See in particular MS 32–5.
10. 'A Singular Invention of Language and Thought', 44.
11. As we did with Badiou's reading of 'A la nue accablante tu' in *Theory of the Subject*, we will use the English-language version of this poem adopted by Rancière's translator, Steven Corcoran. We will do the same for 'Salut'.
12. 'A la nue accablante tu / Basse de basalte et de laves / A même les échos esclaves / Par une trompe sans vertu // Quel sépulcrale naufrage (tu / Le sais, écume, mais y baves) / Suprême une entre les épaves / Aboli le mât dévêtu // Ou cela que furibond faute / De quelque perdition haute / Tout l'abîme vain éployé // Dans le si blanc cheveu qui traîne / Avarement aura noyé / Le flanc enfant d'une sirène'.
13. 'Rien, cette écume, vierge vers / A ne désigner que la coupe / Telle loin se noie une troupe / De sirènes mainte à l'envers. // Nous naviguons, ô mes divers / Amis, moi déjà sur la poupe / Vous l'avant fastueux qui coupe /

Le flot de foudres et d'hivers ; // Une ivresse belle m'engage / Sans craindre même son tangage / De porter debout ce salut // Solitude, récif, étoile / A n'importe ce qui valut / Le blanc souci de notre toile'.
14. 'The essence of the poem' in the representative regime of art 'is not found in the use of more or less harmonious metrical regularity but in the fact that it is an imitation, a representation of actions. . . . In other words, the poem cannot be defined as a mode of language', MS 44.
15. Rancière offers us a brief list of these inadequate art forms and their respective audiences: 'refined individuals in attendance at the spectacle of the "twilight of the gods" as played in the Wagnerian temple; the bourgeois, at Ponsard's ancient-style tragedies; and the plebs attending the commonness of the melodrama', PS 6.
16. *La Religion de Mallarmé*, 297.
17. J. Carey, *The Intellectuals and the Masses: Pride and Prejudice among the Literary Intelligentsia, 1880–1939* (London: Faber and Faber, 1992).
18. *The Intellectuals and the Masses*, 4.
19. *The Witness of Poetry*, 19.
20. Arguably, Rancière makes the link between the 'foam' of 'A la nue accablante tu' and the passage from *La Dernière Mode* thanks to the work of Gardner Davies, who writes: 'This line of foam also recalls the evocation, in a passage from *La Dernière Mode*, of a horizon which just separates sea and sky', *Mallarmé et la 'couche suffisante d'intelligibilité'*, 377.
21. J. Rancière, 'L'Inadmissible', in *Aux bords du politique* (Paris: La Fabrique-Editions, 1998), 201.
22. J. Rancière, *Et tant pis pour les gens fatigués. Entretiens* (Amsterdam: Editions Amsterdam, 2009), 347
23. See also MS 172.
24. A. James, 'Poetic Form and the Crisis of Community', in J. Acquisto (ed.), *Thinking Poetry: Philosophical Approaches to Nineteenth-Century Poetry* (Basingstoke: Palgrave Macmillan, 2013), 169.
25. 'A Singular Invention of Language and Thought', 45.
26. See also Marchal, *La Religion de Mallarmé*, 305–6.
27. '. . . four criteria of decorum [overlap]: first of all, conformity to the nature of human passions in general; next, conformity to the character or manners of a particular people or historical figure, as we know them through the best authors; third, agreement with the decency and taste that are appropriate to our own manners; and finally, conformity of actions and speech with the logic of actions and characters proper to a particular genre', MS 46.
28. 'No writing can designate the rule or the public that testifies for it', PS 57.
29. 'Democracy is the regime of writing, the regime in which the perversion of the letter is the law of the community', MS 95.
30. *La Religion de Mallarmé*, 305–6.
31. See also *La Religion de Mallarmé*, 18–21.

32. *La Religion de Mallarmé*, 13–16.
33. See also Davies, *Mallarmé et le drame solaire*, 8–9, 33.
34. See also Marchal's comments about the 'linguistic unconscious' Mallarmé aims to exhume, *La Religion de Mallarmé*, 552.
35. *La Religion de Mallarmé*, 297.
36. See also *La Religion de Mallarmé*, 185.
37. See also *La Religion de Mallarmé*, 314, 318.
38. See also MS 135.
39. See also MS 138.
40. *La Religion de Mallarmé*, 201–3.
41. *La Religion de Mallarmé*, 189.
42. Bertrand Marchal points out the conceptual solidarity between the intra-poetic *nothing* and its social correlate in Mallarmé's *œuvre*, *La Religion de Mallarmé*, 390–1.
43. 'Music drowns art in a temporal pseudo-interiority. Literature reconquers itself by identifying the art proper to the idea with an art of space', MS 139.
44. For the relation of Derrida to Rancière on the question of *mimesis*, see L. Dubreuil, 'Pensées fantômes', *Labyrinthe*, Vol. 17 (2004), 83–6.
45. See Campion, 'Mallarmé à la lumière de la raison poétique'; CM 171–81; and A. Compagnon, 'La place des Fêtes: Mallarmé et la IIIe République des Lettres', in B. Marchal and J.-L. Steinmetz (eds), *Mallarmé ou l'obscurité lumineuse* (Paris: Hermann, 1998), 74–5.
46. J. Rancière, *Proletarian Nights: The Worker's Dream in Nineteenth-Century France* (London: Verso, 2012).
47. For this reason, we cannot follow Hamel when he writes that the 'distance maintained between the worker and the poet signals less a bourgeois conformism than political prudence, one conscious of the limitations of the time as to the integration of workers into the social order', CM 179.

Conclusion:
From One Siren to Another

As our last chapter demonstrated, Jacques Rancière's interpretation of Mallarmé's 'politics of the siren' seems to bring the history of political readings of the poet to a close. This is true in two senses. First, in his systematic re-inscription of the major motifs of these readings, from the infinite deferral of the Book to the poet's aristocratic isolation, Rancière offers a totalising interpretation of Mallarmé – indeed of the entire history of modern literature in which he played a part – and thus seems to close off, at least in principle, all further interpretative possibilities. Second, by showing why Mallarmé's egalitarian politics necessarily had to remain a horizon, an unreachable utopia that could, at best, inspire hope for emancipation and, at worst, justify a provisional aristocratism, Rancière undercuts any pretensions literature might have to successfully take part in a concrete progressive politics. Rather than affirming the contemporary relevance of such a literary politics, Rancière is best read as restoring the conditions of intelligibility for the fact that modern literature had such exorbitant political ambitions in the first place – ambitions that, as the case of Mallarmé exemplarily reveals, it could never, in fact, fulfil. Against Hamel, who claims that Rancière 'maintains, in circumstances hardly propitious for a revolution, the solidarity of literature with the demand of an emancipation founded on a principle of egalitarianism' (CM 181), we would suggest that he both does this and does the opposite: that is, Rancière certainly shows the form of 'solidarity' that a literature like Mallarmé's has with an egalitarian politics; yet he also demonstrates why this 'solidarity' is inextricable from a specifically literary elitism, which disables the poet's political capacities. And while Rancière claims, in the opening of his masterwork *Mute Speech*, that his inquiries aim to resist the widespread notion that 'the complicity of French revolutionaries and German dreamers overturn[ed] everything reasonable and usher[ed] in two centuries of theoretical and political madness' (MS 36), his project is not an unequivocal apology for the kind of poetico-political programme to be found in Mallarmé's writings.

In light of this, it is imperative that we make some brief remarks on the recent work of the philosopher Quentin Meillassoux. For what Meillassoux purports to do in his ambitious book *The Number and the Siren* is to refute Rancière and to demonstrate the stunning yet paradoxical success of Mallarmé's poetico-political project. Via an unprecedented reading of *Un coup de dés*, which he frames as a moment in a poetic attempt to 'build the bonds of the new community' (NS 60 – translation modified) – an attempt Meillassoux construes as being continuous with the comparable efforts of Lamartine, Vigny, Hugo, the German Idealists and Marx, among others – Meillassoux makes the extraordinary claim that Mallarmé was the only utopian of the modern age *to have actually succeeded in his aims*. As he writes in his conclusion, *Un coup de dés* represents 'the strangely successful defence of an epoch we had buried under our disenchantments' (NS 222): in other words, it is a potent reproach to our contemporary cynicism and a reminder of the utopian dreams of the past – dreams which have, in one case at least, come true. To see how *Un coup de dés* could be invested with such extraordinary power, let us turn to a close investigation of Meillassoux's arguments.

To properly frame the implicit debate between Rancière and Meillassoux, we can begin by recalling that Rancière read *Un coup de dés* as the most ambitious expression of Mallarmé's project. But it was also, and necessarily so, his most glorious failure. As he argued, *Un coup de dés* had to authenticate Mallarmé's 'anti-mimetic mimetism of the Idea' (PS 56). However, it could only do so by regressing, in its material mimicry of a shipwreck and the upsurge of a constellation, to the banally mimetic logic of the 'representative regime'. Furthermore, the Master's hesitation to roll the dice was, Rancière argued, a figural staging of the precariousness of Mallarmé's 'Idea': that is, of the risk that it be misrecognised as, precisely, an 'Idea' by the poem's readers. As Rancière writes, Mallarmé had to inscribe in his poem 'the risky game it plays with the chasm' (PS 55) since he registered the inherent threat of failure his poetico-political project implied. And as we also know, the undecidable gesture of the dice-throw was indissociable, for Rancière, from 'the subtraction of the poet' (PS 55) from the public sphere: that is, from his apparently provisional yet actually eternal aristocratism. As such, *Un coup de dés* is a failure; a failure whose principle is, as we underscored above, the contradiction inscribed in the axioms of the 'aesthetic regime' between the essentialist logic implied by the poetic production of the 'Idea' and the anarchic circulation of 'the orphaned letter' (MS 95). Mallarmé's novel poem thus could never properly constitute 'a new Eucharist' (PS 16).

By stark contrast, Meillassoux argues that *Un coup de dés* is nothing less than a secular Eucharist, which ingeniously succeeds in sublating this key element of the Catholic Mass in an atheological age. To see this, we can begin by noting that Meillassoux positions his own intervention in terms of a lineage running from Marchal's *La Religion de Mallarmé* through to Rancière's own intervention. Taking up a point already reinforced by both these readers, Meillassoux writes that the poet was convinced that the duty of art was to 'make up for the default of the old religion by offering a cult capable of satisfying the modern spirit' (NS 107).[1] Meillassoux thus follows his predecessors in interpreting Mallarmé's project as the attempted construction of 'the religion of the future' (PS 56). Indeed, he also recognises that the poet asserted his distance from Wagnerian opera and affirmed, despite his own atheism, the superiority of the Catholic Mass as a properly modern ceremony: as Meillassoux puts it, 'to *represent* to a people its own mystery: such is for Mallarmé the Greek heritage upon which art, including Wagnerian art, continues to nourish itself' (NS 108 – Meillassoux's emphasis). According to the poet, however, modern art had to break with representation and recuperate a specific element of Catholicism, namely, its 'ritual superior in power to those of paganism'; a 'ritual' that involved '*the real convocation of a real drama*' (NS 109 – Meillassoux's emphasis). This 'ritual' is, of course, the Eucharist itself, which does not represent, 'as would a theatre piece' (NS 109), the drama of the Passion but rather 'claims to produce [its] true, effective Presence, to the point where the host is absorbed by the faithful' (NS 109). The task of *Un coup de dés* is thus to sublate the Eucharist and make it a rigorously atheological 'ritual' for a modern people who required 'a collective communion around an effective and present Event' (NS 109 – translation modified).

To specify precisely what this 'ritual' consists in, and having already distinguished it from the 'representative regime' Wagner had regressed to, Meillassoux underscores the fact that the Eucharist is not an instance of 'Parousia' (NS 101), which would involve 'the absolute manifestation of Christ in his glory at the end of Times'. Rather, it institutes 'a paradoxical mode of presence in absence'. In the Eucharist, '[t]he divine is there, among the elect, in the host itself – but is not yet returned': 'It gives itself according to a sufficiently withdrawn mode of reality to leave room for both remembrance (of the Passion) and expectation (of Salvation). It is a presence that is not in the present, but in the past and the future' (NS 101). It is precisely this 'mode of presence' of the Eucharist – and even more importantly its 'real convocation of a real drama' (NS 109), that of a sacrificial Passion – that Mallarmé will attempt to reproduce in *Un coup de dés*. And as far as Meillassoux is concerned, he succeeds.

Meillassoux's demonstration of Mallarmé's atheistic sublation of the Eucharist involves unveiling a precise numerical code in *Un coup de dés*, which is nothing less than the sum of its words minus its title and its famous final maxim, 'All Thought Emits a Throw of Dice'. The number of words in the poem – 707 – becomes the code that constitutes the *denotatum* of the well-known line, 'the unique Number that cannot be another'. On the basis of further evidence sourced from *Un coup de dés* itself, as well as from other moments in Mallarmé's writings, Meillassoux firstly accords the code a symbolic function: the two 7's represents rhyme itself, the foundation of all poetry, whose condition of possibility is that the two rhyming words be separated by the 0 or by a 'Nothingness' (NS 51), the meaninglessness of reality that is momentarily illumined by the spark of rhyme. In terms of the scenography of *Un coup de dés*, this 0 stands for 'the night upon whose ground the Septentrion appears' (NS 55) – the ever-present backdrop of insignificance that a rigorous atheism must presuppose. The 707 thus symbolises the maintenance of rhyme – of an organising principle for poetry – in the face of the 'crisis of verse' and Mallarmé's own atheism.

Crucially, however, Meillassoux insists that it is not sufficient to satisfy oneself with the purely symbolic function of the code: as we know from Rancière, Mallarmé does not traffic in representation. For this reason, the code cannot be reduced to a banally numerical representation of the problematic of poetry after the 'crisis of verse'. And so, in contradistinction to Vigny, Mallarmé does not simply speak of casting his 'bottle in the sea' in the hope of ensuring a posterity. Rather, 'he *actually threw such a bottle*, through the writing and the publication of his Poem – a vessel containing his last wishes in the form of "solitary" and constellatory "calculations"' (NS 113 – Meillassoux's emphasis). The very nature of Mallarmé's work thus prevents us from resting content with a code that would simply be a metaphor.

But further to this, Meillassoux points out that the poem itself provides us with very precise indications regarding the status of the code. Firstly, in so far as the code is the *denotatum* of the famous phrase, 'the unique Number that cannot be another', it must have a strict 'unicity' (NS 101), a property that it could not possess were it simply symbolic. In that case, other numbers could conceivably take its place. Secondly, this 'unicity' is crucially linked to another of the number's properties, which Meillassoux deduces from an ingeniously literal reading of another famous phrase from *Un coup de dés*, namely: 'if it were the Number, it would be Chance'. What this phrase says, according to Meillassoux, is simply that the code – or 'the Number' – is to be identified with 'Chance' itself. As he puts it, 'the Number' is *'chance itself, and* not *one of its effects'* (NS 38 – Meillassoux's emphasis). What 'the Master', who is about to sink beneath the waves, infers 'from this conflagration of the unanimous horizon' – that is, from 'the conflagration of the waves' (NS 20) – is the preparation, in and by *Un coup de dés* itself, of 'the unique Number of Chance as such' (NS 20). We will see further on how Meillassoux justifies this identification of the 707 with 'Chance'.

Thirdly and most importantly, Meillassoux argues that Mallarmé stages in the more immediately representative moments of *Un coup de dés* the possible destiny of his work were its future readers to reduce the code to a purely symbolic function. As Meillassoux has it, if the code were reduced to the status of 'a mere riddle – a charade joined to an enumeration', then it would 'risk ... mak[ing] the poet a universal laughing stock for having given himself over to such games' (NS 103). In *Un coup de dés* we see Mallarmé describe these 'worries' (NS 103) in the hesitations of 'the Master'. As Meillassoux argues, the 'insistent description of these anxieties ... enjoins us to elucidate the profound reasons' (NS 103) Mallarmé has for encoding his poem. In other words, it is not only that Mallarmé was anxious as to whether the code would be discovered. Rather, his anxiety was doubled by the fact that, once discovered, he would have to rely on his readers to properly grasp the full significance of this code, which in itself is meaningless. Against Rancière, then, who had unilaterally interpreted the hesitation of 'the Master' as signifying Mallarmé's lucid grasp of the dangers of the reception of his poetic 'Idea', Meillassoux sees this hesitation as having to do, certainly, with the reception of *Un coup de dés*, but also — and more precisely – with the discovery of the code's significance. His anxiety stems from a fear that the fulfilment of his ambition would never be recognised, but would instead be mistaken for – and mocked as – a mere numerological game, 'something devoid of literary value' (NS 10).

In light of all this, Meillassoux argues that our task as readers of *Un coup de dés* is to determine what the code could mean for Mallarmé: that is, how it allowed the poet to 'arrive at ... a universal truth' (NS 99). The answer to this question is, put simply, to produce a secular Eucharist. Thus, in an atheological mimicry of the Passion of Christ, Mallarmé will stage a *real* sacrificial drama – and not merely a *representation* of one – that is nothing other than the drama of his poem and its irreducible link to his own posthumous destiny. The 'sacrifice' by which *Un coup de dés* acquires 'the depth of a Passion' (NS 116–17) is that of the 'the meaning of the work' (NS 123) itself: in other words, the 'sacrifice' that would be consequent upon no one ever discovering the code. This selflessness, as Meillassoux has it, allows the poet to 'rival the absolute devotion of the old Christ' (NS 123).

Furthermore, in order to ensure that his sacrificial drama was properly atheistic, Mallarmé does not, like Vigny, 'entrust to an all-powerful God the hope that his testament should one day be discovered'. Rather, Mallarmé ensured that it could only be 'his own infinity', namely 'infinite Chance' (NS 117), that could regulate the reception of *Un coup de dés*. As Meillassoux has it, the 'discovery of the procedure can only be accidental' (NS 118). Crucially, this constitutes a striking sublation of Rancière's notion of the irreducibility of the problematic of 'the orphaned letter' (MS 95), that is, the necessarily anarchic logic of the reception of a literary work in the 'aesthetic regime'. As we know, '[n]o writing can designate the rule or the public that testifies for it' (PS 56) in this 'regime'. But in actual fact, on Meillassoux's account, Mallarmé ingeniously incorporated this contingency into the very design of his final work, making it an essential component in his creation of a new Eucharist.

However, as Meillassoux also explains, it is not enough for Mallarmé to have staged such a sacrificial drama. In order to properly sublate Christianity the poet had to become *himself* as infinite and as eternal as God. This identification would occur, of course, according to the properly modern idea according to which the infinite is not the transcendence of the divine but rather 'Chance', this latter being what 'rules effectively [all] the finite and alternative events of our world' (NS 134), from those phenomena that 'seem oriented by an intentional and higher purpose' (NS 30) to those that manifest an 'absence of Meaning' (NS 31). Thus, to be clear, the infinity in question here is what Meillassoux explicitly qualifies as a 'dialectical, rather than mathematical' (NS 31),[2] infinite: in other words, an infinite that 'always-already contains that which is outside of its limit' (NS 31), just as 'the speculative Infinite . . . contains in itself the contradictory totality of alternative possibilities' (NS 183).

How, though, could Mallarmé become identical to this infinity? How could he become eternal like God? To see how, we firstly need to understand precisely what 'Chance' consisted of for Mallarmé. As Meillassoux tells us, 'the infinity of Chance . . . such as Mallarmé conceives of it is in fact characterized by *three* properties':

it is *real* (Chance effectively rules the finite and alternate events of our world), *determined* (its opposing results are always such or such a concrete result) and *eternal* (Chance remains equal to itself, always in act, whether its productions are insignificant or full of meaning). (NS 134 – Meillassoux's emphasis)

In a difficult but rigorous series of demonstrations, Meillassoux now shows that Mallarmé succeeded in conjugating, in a single work, the *reality* and *eternity* of 'Chance'. That is, *Un coup de dés* and its main character 'the Master', with whom Mallarmé identifies, not only have 'the ideal eternity of fictional characters' (NS 137), they are also *real* in so far as their destiny is that of Mallarmé himself – or, more precisely, of Mallarmé in the guise of the 'signatory of *Un coup de dés* who lives forever in the mind of his readers' (NS 144). The drama of the poem's reception is Mallarmé's drama as well; he is a really existing individual who, like 'Jesus, born in Bethlehem under Augustus' (NS 144), also has an eternal existence.

Un coup de dés thus conjugates the *eternity* and the *reality* of 'Chance'. But in order to be *determined* – the third and final property of 'Chance' mentioned above – Meillassoux explains that *Un coup de dés* had to produce a result – a 'total count', or the code itself – that also 'always-already contains that which is outside of its limit' (NS 30 – translation modified): that is, *Un coup de dés* had to produce a code and 'another number close to it, but which does not have a relation to the code' (NS 136). Put differently, Mallarmé's stroke of genius was to include in his code a slight 'indetermination' (NS 135), a slight discrepancy as to the poem's precise number of words. By encrypting both a code and its absence – in other words, by producing a structure that would be isomorphic to the specifically dialectical infinity of 'Chance' – it follows that it is uncertain as to whether Mallarmé actually rolled the dice; that is, as to whether he encrypted his testamentary poem or not. His real act remains infinitely – eternally – a hesitation, just as 'the Master' is 'eternally fixed in pure indecision' (NS 129). But while 'the Master' is a fictional character, the 'indecision' *Un coup de dés* encodes is precisely that of the poet himself as a real individual. We can never determine whether the Mallarmé of flesh and blood actually coded his poem or not: as Meillassoux puts it, 'we would thus have to say that the forever-undecidable uncertainty affecting the Number had refluxed back onto the gesture of the poet, making the latter a being virtually composed of contrary options' (NS 139). Mallarmé thus becomes identical with the infinity of 'Chance', a secular divinity.

But in what does the code's 'indetermination' consist? As Meillassoux shows, there is, in fact, a strict uncertainty as to the count of words in the poem – an uncertainty that falls, ingeniously, on the word *perhaps* [*peut-être*], which, famously, forms part of the phrase that follows the nihilist refrain 'nothing will have taken place but the place': namely, the phrase 'except perhaps a Constellation'. As Meillassoux explains, it is precisely the *perhaps* [*peut-être*] that complicates the count of words that make up the poem: in so far as it could be either one or two words, the *peut-être* 'forbids us any univocal rule in the count of compounded words' (NS 207). Thus, the 'the code is a thing at once fragile and coherent' (NS 216) in a manner precisely analogous to those fleeting moments in Mallarmé's poetry, which Rancière had drawn our attention to, in which the common course of the world is broken for an instant by an ephemeral ideality, such as when a siren emerges momentarily from a thin thread of foam on the sea. For Meillassoux, this fragile gap between sense and non-sense – between the brute identity of a phenomenon and its infinitisation – is also staged in *Un coup de dés* through the figure of the siren. In this case, however, this infinitisation concerns the code itself: 'This leap of the siren, brief and decisive, thus destroys the "rock" of a Meter that had up until then been "fettered" in its arithmetical truth – that is to say, the Meter whose excessive and limited precision "imposed a limit on infinite" (that of 707)' (NS 193). In an unmistakable echo of Rancière's reading of the sonnet 'Hushed to the crushing cloud', Meillassoux then asks: 'As soon as the Siren is glimpsed, it dives back into the ocean: has this infinitization taken place, or only its phantasm?' (NS 186). As the figure that stages the necessary indeterminacy of the code and thus of the poet's successful sublation of the Eucharist, the siren again stands for Mallarmé's poetry as such. Now, however – and against Rancière – we can know that this poetry was successful.

In encountering *Un coup de dés*, then, we are effectively participating in a secular Eucharist involving the real sacrificial drama of a finite, corporeal individual – Mallarmé himself – who has now become eternal, identified as he is with the infinity of 'Chance'. To decipher the poem, to enter into its singular movement, to participate in the sacrificial Passion of a finite man become identical with the infinite – in other words to 'impregnate oneself with the infinity of the Master' (NS 204), this secular successor to Christ – is to absorb the sole sort of Eucharist available to us as moderns. Mallarmé is thus able to recuperate for a secular age the secret of the Catholic Mass – a secret that had ensured its continuity well past the death of God and which a rigorously atheistic civic cult had to appropriate if emancipation from the yoke of religion was to be achieved.

We have now given the explicit set of reasons for why Meillassoux thinks Mallarmé successfully produced a new literary form of the Eucharist. Against Rancière, and indeed against many of Mallarmé's most significant readers, Meillassoux demonstrates that there is now no longer any infinite deferral of the Book, no eternally postponed union of the poet and the people, and no unsurpassable contradiction between the two concepts of writing that, Rancière argues, characterise modern literature as such, namely 'orphaned speech lacking a body that might accompany it and attest to it' (MS 16) – the necessarily anarchic nature of reception – and 'the hieroglyph that bears its idea upon its body' (MS 16) – the perfect coincidence of content and form. Against Sartre, for whom *Un coup de dés* gave expression to the nihilism of the post-1848 bourgeoisie, which postulated that 'everything came down to the same' (NS 132), Meillassoux shows how Mallarmé's testamentary poem is ultimately affirmative. And against Kristeva, who interpreted the religious elements of the poet's work as a regressive cover for the radicality of his 'textual practice', we can now appreciate the rigorously atheistic sublation of Catholicism achieved by Mallarmé in *Un coup de dés*. And finally, against Badiou, for whom the hesitation of 'the Master' had to be 'as eternal as its circumstances' in order to produce the 'absolute symbol of the event' (BE 215), Meillassoux succeeds in showing that Mallarmé did in fact roll the dice – *peut-être*.

For Meillassoux, *Un coup de dés* is singularly capable of transcending all of these interpretations, which themselves are inseparable from a certain understanding of modern literature, in particular of its political destiny. And so, after listing various utopian projects of modernity, from the poetic religions of Lamartine or Hugo, to the revolutionary undertakings of Marx, Meillassoux is able to affirm that

> all this would nevertheless have succeeded in making *one* breakthrough up to our times, one only, and at a precise point – a unique Poem that would traverse the twentieth century like a hidden gem, finally to reveal itself, in the following century, as the strangely successful defence of an epoch we had buried under our disenchantments. (NS 205)

Now that it has been victoriously deciphered, *Un coup de dés* can function as a retroactive justification for the sort of egalitarian and emancipatory thought and practice that has been condemned as 'outmoded' (NS 205) by the soft thought and cynical practice of our apparently post-ideological age. Put differently, the alleged failure of all of modernity's 'Grand Narratives' (NS 205) has been decisively disproved by the successful production, in *Un coup de dés*, of a secular Eucharist, a triumphant literary sublation of the religions of the past. As Meillassoux concludes: 'modernity triumphed and we did not know it' (NS 205). The political significance of Mallarmé's work is thus confirmed for a contemporary audience.

Despite this triumphalism on Meillassoux's part, it is unclear whether the extraordinary claims he makes in his conclusion can stand scrutiny. What is at issue here is not whether or *Un coup de dés* has been successfully deciphered or not, but rather the significance Meillassoux accords the work in so far as his interpretation holds.

Let us return, firstly, to the stated aim of Mallarmé's later work, as Meillassoux himself construes it. For Mallarmé, Meillassoux tells us, 'no society is possible without a strong symbolic link that is capable of founding a civic religion and inspiring the profound adhesion of individuals to the ends of the community' (NS 104). As we know from Rancière, the necessity of such a 'symbolic link' was postulated by Mallarmé as a result of the factitious and finally harmful unity he thought the Republican state and the capitalist market imposed upon people. Meillassoux reminds us that, despite being a Republican, 'Mallarmé consider[ed] as impossible a strict neutrality of public space that would reserve all spiritual *élan* for the intimate sphere' (NS 104). As a consequence, art had to propose a new 'ceremony ... by which the community, delivered from any and all belief in transcendence, could contemplate the immanence of its own divinity' (NS 114). When Meillassoux speaks of *Un coup de dés* as constituting 'the strangely successful defence' (NS 205) of the poet's epoch in which such communitarian projects were commonplace, however peculiar they may seem to our contemporary sensibilities, we should therefore ask whether or not Mallarmé actually succeeded in producing 'a strong symbolic link' for a post-theological community and whether he effectively usurped the role of religion as the necessary spiritual supplement to our abstract unity under the modern state. Whatever its obvious ingenuity, is *Un coup de dés* really the success Meillassoux claims it is?

If we consider this question closely, what we find is that *Un coup de dés*, by 'compensating for the faults of the old religions' (NS 14), in fact simply abstracts from these religions everything except the metaphysics of the Eucharist. The justification for this move is that Mallarmé, as Meillassoux reads him, considered the Eucharist to be the hidden 'treasure' (NS 107) of the Catholic Mass and the reason for the latter's unexpected endurance. Encountering *Un coup de dés* is supposed, then, to be the equivalent of consuming a 'mental host' (NS 221) consistent with the metaphysics of a resolutely modern age. What is then supposed to occur is an 'intimate revolution of the subject' (NS 221) who is now freed from the outdated dogmas of the Church. However, in order to make his testamentary poem into a secular Eucharist, it would appear that Mallarmé was required to fulfil a set of criteria that arguably worked against his art ever becoming a civic religion. To be specific, the fact that it was strictly necessary for Mallarmé to ensure that 'it could [only] be infinite Chance ... that could unveil the truth of the Mallarméan act' – in other words, that it was rigorously necessary for him to run the risk that his poem never be comprehended as such – would seem to work against the fulfilment of his communitarian goals. However ingenious Mallarmé's solution to the problem of producing a literary Eucharists is, its sheer precariousness surely makes *Un coup de dés* an incongruous candidate for the role of successor to religious practices, particularly if we comprehend the latter in their full concrete complexity. Indeed, it could be said that, besides the metaphysics of the Eucharist, Mallarmé simply neglected all of the other concrete components of religious or civic existence, preferring instead to privilege only those that literature was most capable of sublating.

And so, armed with his manifestly exorbitant ambitions, Mallarmé mobilised the immanent resources of literature. However, while these resources were up to the task of responding to certain aspects of what it would take for the poem to be, as Rancière puts it, 'the religion of the future' (PS 56), they manifestly failed to fulfil other criteria necessary for the assumption of this role. For instance, if literature was supposed to have for its task the institution of 'a collective communion' (NS 109) that would help 'build the bonds of the new community' (PS 31), then the community of readers of *Un coup de dés* is a highly precarious, indeed restricted, community – and necessarily so. If Mallarmé succeeded, as Meillassoux says he has, then it is in a demonstrably narrow domain and according to a highly restricted scale of values. To make this even more evident, we could ask – and with reference to another of the nineteenth-century utopians whose projects Meillassoux considers to be continuous with the poet's – the following question: what does it mean for Mallarmé to have succeeded but for Marx to have failed? If *Un coup de dés* is indeed supposed to be a serious component of 'an emancipatory politics' (NS 221), as Meillassoux implicitly claims it is, then it is hard to avoid a conclusion that is the exact opposite of the one he proposes.

It would appear, then, that Rancière's conclusion reasserts itself, albeit in a different form. For what Rancière fundamentally aims to do, we argue, is to render intelligible why modern literature would see itself not only as able, but also as singularly required, to propose a utopian solution to the political ills of modernity. Both the confidence invested in Mallarmé as an agent of emancipation, as well as the criticisms that have been levelled against him when he is seen as failing to fulfil these expectations, follow from the fundamental axioms of the 'aesthetic regime of art'. In restoring the conditions of intelligibility for the exorbitant political ambitions of modern literature, Rancière is not defending them in the contemporary conjuncture. Rather, he seeks to explain why a literary creation like Mallarmé's would mobilise its own resources in order to respond to the key political problematics of modernity, despite the manifest inadequacy of these resources in the face of the latter's enormity. Despite its sheer ingenuity, the secular Eucharist of *Un coup de dés* as read by Meillassoux is thus an ultimate example of the fundamental mismatch between the powers of literature and its utopian political project.

*

As we have seen throughout this work, political appropriations of Mallarmé's writings have very often functioned on the basis of a set of interlinked assumptions made strikingly evident in Meillassoux's recent work. These include the idea that the literary enterprise could have a determinate and indeed privileged role to play in the political struggles of modernity; that it could exert a causal impact upon these struggles; and even that it had the necessary and sufficient resources to definitively resolve them. These assumptions are present not only in Meillassoux's book and in the other works we have explored in the preceding five chapters. They are also present in the most recent work devoted to Mallarmé's political significance: Jean-François Hamel's *Camarade Mallarmé*. As we noted in our introduction, Hamel proposes a 'politics of reading' inspired by past political appropriations of Mallarmé's writings as a task for contemporary hermeneuts, calling upon them to 'augment the power of texts and, with an antagonistic aim, to inscribe within them a form of dissidence' (CM 203). Meillassoux's work, however, has the unexpected effect of making visible the gap between the immanent powers of literature and the tasks it has historically set itself. In a word, it is indeed necessary to 'suspend one's incredulity' (CM 10) to believe that *Un coup de dés* could resolve the problem that it was explicitly created to confront. Even when it is presented in as spectacular a fashion as Meillassoux presents it, *Un coup de dés* is a paradigmatic example of what Laurent Jenny has called the 'excessiveness necessary to the poetic spirit'[3] – an 'excessiveness' that one suspects has characterised the whole history of political appropriations of Mallarmé. Since Jenny considers that the 'time of the revolutionary metaphor is over',[4] in order to determine the contemporary significance of the political appropriations of Mallarmé studied in this book we can conclude by considering the question of the 'excessiveness' of the idea of literature that has consistently been applied to the poet's writings. Do the other interpretations considered in this book also attest to the gap between literature's powers and its political destiny? Have Mallarmé's writings been set a task they were incapable of carrying out? Why, then, has he consistently been considered a 'comrade' of progressive political causes? How, finally, are we to understand the oscillation between considering Mallarmé a hero and a villain?

In our reading of Sartre's career-long engagement with Mallarmé, we delimited two ultimately incompatible estimations of the poet's significance. The first consisted in Sartre's condemnation of Mallarmé as a member of a politically irresponsible generation of writers whose legacy it was imperative to purge from post-war French literature. The second, by contrast, involved Sartre recognising Mallarmé's prescient poetic thinking of an 'ontological drama' (MPN 122) structuring human existence. As we argued, the poet's brilliance as an ontologist did not save him from falling foul of Sartre's exigent Marxist politics, in light of which he remained a counter-revolutionary nihilist. *Mallarmé, or the Poet of Nothingness* thus mobilised two distinct and irreconcilable evaluative frameworks: one political, the other philosophical. Leaving Sartre's philosophical interpretation aside, in terms of his political frame of reference, what might we say regarding the 'excessiveness' – or not – of his judgement of the poet's politics? Did his critique of Mallarmé's and the postromantics' failures participate in an 'excessive' estimation of literature's political capacities?

As Vincent Kaufmann has argued, 'Sartre seems to have been perfectly conscious of the utopian character of his dream of the Book',[5] a 'Book' that was meant to be 'the reflexive presence-to-self of a classless society' and to 'speak to all men',[6] as Sartre demanded in *What is Literature?* For Kaufmann, Sartre's literary ideal did not refer to an actual form of literature, but functioned instead to orient present literary practice and to provide a scale of values with which to judge really existing works. But if it is impossible for any instance of literature to reach this ideal point, what becomes of Sartre's critique of those literary currents, such as late nineteenth-century French postromanticism, that seem to fall well short of this ideal, and perhaps even do so consciously? As we suggested in our first chapter, Sartre's post-war strategy of distinction involved exteriorising onto the 'pure literature' of Mallarmé and his contemporaries those properties possessed by literature that meant it always risked failing to 'speak to all men'. Whatever evidence Sartre could find for charging the postromantics with elitism, the dice were thus loaded in advance: Sartre's critique of his predecessors became more excessive the more he used it as a cover for the inherent risk of failure run by his own preferred form of literature, 'committed literature'. The fact that in *The Poet of Nothingness* and *The Family Idiot* Sartre simply passed over Mallarmé's designs for a literary ceremony with egalitarian aspirations attests to the strategic blindness of his reading. Sartre's Mallarmé was thus caught in the force-field of an idea of literature that enlisted the poet in the service of a political project he could never carry out, and condemned him when he inevitably failed to do so. Sartre's is no doubt one of the most remarkable surveys of nineteenth-century French culture *tout court*. Yet its viciously polemical tone is incomprehensible if we fail to see how it is animated by an 'excessive' conception of literature's political destiny.

In our second chapter, we turned to Julia Kristeva's reading of Mallarmé, which she produced under the auspices of *Tel Quel*, a journal whose fundamental project was to proclaim the transformative political power of literature. Given that Kristeva wrote *Revolution in Poetic Language* in the context of the French university system, meaning that the hidden presuppositions of *Tel Quel*'s literary theory had to be made explicit and rendered internally coherent, her 1974 work offered us a unique opportunity to study and assess the Telquellians' arguments for why literature could have an 'impact' (RLP 620) on the social world as a whole. What we discovered was that Kristeva could only sustain the promise of such a 'revolution in poetic language' if she demonstrated why the 'impact' of Mallarmé's textual practice had been restricted in his time, even if it contained within it the seeds of a future revolutionary literature. To do this, Kristeva identified certain 'fetishes' in Mallarmé's writings – marks at the level of his writings' content that they were products of an unenlightened age. Chief among these 'fetishes' were Mallarmé's references to religion, which *qua* content were meant to cover over the radically disruptive form of his textual practice. If the limits of Mallarmé's writings were to be lifted, Kristeva's argument ran, their regressive content had to be replaced with content that was consistent with the Telquellians' theory of the 'text'. *Revolution in Poetic Language* thus ended with the truly incongruous claim that Mallarmé's writings were a moment in a literary teleology that led to Philippe Sollers' early 'novels', which had supposedly transcended the political limitations of Mallarmé's poetry. Such a patent absurdity reveals the problem at the heart of Kristeva's work on Mallarmé: namely, that there is little point in charging Mallarmé with failing to spark a 'revolution in poetic language' if such a phenomenon is constitutively impossible, or if the only evidence one can provide for its imminent arrival is that novels like *H* or *Lois* are improvements upon works like 'Music and Letters' and *Un coup de dés*. As Badiou claims, it is unsurprising that the political foundations of *Tel Quel*'s literary theory were swiftly dismantled when the context that had supported them had passed away.[7] Like Sartre's Mallarmé, Kristeva's Mallarmé was also caught in the jaws of an impossible dilemma.

With Badiou's *Theory of the Subject*, to which our third chapter was partly devoted, we found a work that at first seemed consistent with Sartre and Kristeva's political appropriations of Mallarmé. That is, Mallarmé emerged from this, Badiou's first philosophical treatise, as both a petty bourgeois conservative and an intellectual radical. Should we therefore not consider Badiou's identification of a 'structural dialectic' in Mallarmé's writings as a species of those readings that submitted his writings to a standard they could never achieve? Was it not implicit in Badiou's interpretative strategy that he believed Mallarmé *should* have produced a poetry of the 'historical', and not simply 'structural', dialectic? In fact, *Theory of the Subject* is a very different work to *The Poet of Nothingness* or *Revolution in Poetic Language*. As we argued, in contrast to these two works Badiou never claims that poetry *does* politics; that it is a species of political action. Identifying Mallarmé's 'structural dialectic' is an intellectual exercise, not a political one. Doing so can at best be a critical ground-clearing exercise for conceiving of a successful political strategy. In a sense, then, Badiou's identification of a 'structural dialectic' in Mallarmé is similar to Sartre's recognition of Mallarmé's 'ontological drama'. Both are extraordinary intellectual and poetic achievements, yet their true significance is distorted if they are seen as substitutes for political action.

In his post-*Being and Event* work, Badiou makes the autonomy of politics from poetry a key pillar of his philosophy. However, we asked why, if this were the case, Badiou frequently mobilised Mallarmé's writings in discussions of the post-'89 political conjuncture. In 'A French Philosopher Responds to a Polish Poet', Badiou presented Mallarmé as a rigorous egalitarian and as a great thinker of the pure form of any and all events, including political ones. This made it seem as if Badiou was in fact judging Mallarmé according to the standards of his own communist politics. The only difference with respect to *Theory of the Subject* – or indeed to Sartre and Kristeva's work – was that this time Mallarmé was presented as Badiou's comrade, not as his enemy. However, we argued that while Mallarmé seemed to incarnate, fortuitously, all of Badiou's most cherished political values, this did not mean that *all* art had to be similarly egalitarian in order to qualify as an artistic truth. For Badiou, art maintains its autonomy irrespective of its explicitly political content, as per his doctrine of *inaesthetics*. If an instance of art were to present a manifest content whose lines of force were elitist or nihilist, this would not render its pretensions to the status of truth illusory. In Mallarmé, Badiou simply finds a set of powerful artistic images of an egalitarian politics, presented by an ingenious artistic ancestor whose prestige adds to the value of Badiou's own position. In the final analysis, however, for Badiou art's politics does not bear upon its essence. Unlike Sartre's or Kristeva's Mallarmé, Badiou's Mallarmé is not subject to the 'excessive' demands of modernity's idea of literature's political destiny.

Jean-Claude Milner's reading of Mallarmé occupies a singular position with respect to the question of the 'excessiveness' of this idea of literature. Milner argues that, in fact, Mallarmé was himself a partisan of just such an 'excessive' vision, albeit in a disguised form. That is, while Mallarmé buried the poetico-political project of his predecessors, his poetry retained their orientation towards an ideal point situated at an infinite distance from the world, yet capable of unilaterally determining the world's value. Poetry's 'cold constellation' was simply another name for an elitist dualism, which summoned the real to attain the ideal point poetry had already reached and then condemned it for failing to do so. As Milner made clear, it was not for nothing that the Russian revolutionaries elected Mallarmé to be their 'comrade'. For Milner, the poet, along with his 'hagiographers' (MT 65), were equally complicit in propounding a vision of the world that rendered the vast majority of human activities meaningless, or subject to an impossibly exigent scale of values. Unlike Badiou, who reads Mallarmé outside of the coordinates of the literary politics that Sartre and Kristeva practised, Milner sees the poet as a paradoxical participant in this politics. Milner's proposed gesture, by contrast, consists in enjoining the rest of us to be done with this literary politics and to turn towards an ethics and politics of the finite, one capable of comprehending and avoiding the traumas of the twentieth century.

In light of our question regarding literature's 'excessive' political destiny, the singularity of Rancière's intervention again comes into view. While he disagrees with Milner that Mallarmé's politics were inscribed within a revolutionary horizon, he agrees with Sartre, Kristeva and Badiou that his poetry still possessed explicitly political aims. As we know, for Rancière Mallarmé sought to produce a 'new Eucharist' that would combat the modern citizen's alienation by the state and the market, all the while producing a strong symbolic bond that was nevertheless not of the order of a community of origins. While Sartre, Kristeva, Badiou and even Milner could all agree with a version of this reading, Rancière's singularity lies in how he positions himself vis-à-vis Mallarmé's politics. That is, Rancière neither proposes to reactivate a literary politics inspired by Mallarmé's example, nor criticises it for its perceived weaknesses or failures. Rancière's work is above all that of a scholar who restores a past literary practice to its proper horizon of significance. At most, his intervention expands the horizon of our contemporary imagination by reconstructing a phenomenon whose singularity has long been obscured. His most essential achievement, however, is to have discerned the reasons why Mallarmé has for so long oscillated between being a comrade and an enemy to progressive political causes. That Mallarmé's egalitarianism and utopianism were structurally indissociable from his elitism is the most important lesson of *The Politics of the Siren*. Yet there is also another key lesson to be learnt from Rancière's Mallarmé: namely, that since both incarnations of Mallarmé make sense only within the horizon of a poetico-political project that is itself struck by an untranscendable contradiction, their very *raison d'être* evaporates once this horizon itself vanishes.

Let us return one final time to the question we posed above. Given how often and systematically Mallarmé has oscillated between being a hero and a villain, a comrade and a class enemy, we can conclude that this oscillation has indeed been determined by the fact that an exorbitant estimation of literature's political significance has been applied to his writings. While at some moments this vision of literature's politics has found in Mallarmé a figure that could give it some credence, it has also made him a focal point for the inevitable moment of critique this vision implies – a moment that comes about when discrete instances of literature fail to live up to the political ideal they have otherwise been exhorted to attain. As we wrote in our introduction, the irony of Hamel's call for a 'politics of reading' inspired by Mallarmé and his interpreters is that Mallarmé has not only been a figure invested with the virtues required of a political militant; he has just as frequently stood for literature's failure to fulfil its political responsibilities or to fully actualise its revolutionary potential. Certainly, Mallarmé has been a veritable 'comrade' for many left-wing French intellectuals of the latter half of the twentieth century. But he has also been the focus of critique – or, in a less polemical context, of the sense of melancholy consequent upon the failure of literature's promises to be kept. If the history of 'comrade Mallarmé' is over, just as the 'time of the revolutionary metaphor' is over, it is not because literature is yet to keep its promise: it is because we now recognise that it never could. The time is ripe for new ways of linking politics and literature to be invented.

NOTES

1. See also Meillassoux's remarks in an essay devoted to the difference between his reading of *Un coup de dés* and that of Badiou: 'Badiou and Mallarmé: The Event and the Perhaps', *Parrhesia*, No. 16 (2013).
2. See also Meillassoux's discussion of the dialectical nature of this infinity in 'Badiou and Mallarmé: The Event and the Perhaps'.
3. *Je suis la révolution*, 213.
4. *Je suis la révolution*, 211.
5. V. Kaufmann, *Poétique des groupes littéraires (Avant-gardes 1920–1970)* (Paris: Presses Universitaires de France, 1997), 148.
6. *What is Literature?*, 122.
7. 'Mallarmé Said It All', 86.

Bibliography

Abastado, C., 'Portrait d'un nihiliste (Sartre, au lecteur de Mallarmé)', *Obliques*, Sartre', Nos. 18–19 (1979), 195–7.
Badiou, A., *Manifesto for Philosophy*, trans. Norman Madarasz (New York: State University of New York Press, 1999).
Badiou, A., *Being and Event*, trans. Oliver Feltham (London: Continuum, 2005).
Badiou, A., *Handbook of Inaesthetics*, trans. Alberto Toscano (Stanford: Stanford University Press, 2005).
Badiou, A., *Metapolitics*, trans. Jason Barker (London: Verso, 2005).
Badiou, A., *Conditions*, trans. Steven Corcoran (London: Continuum, 2008).
Badiou, A., *Theory of the Subject*, trans. Bruno Bosteels (London: Continuum, 2009).
Badiou, A., *D'un désastre obscur. Droit, Etat, Politique* (Paris: L'Aube, 2012).
Badiou, A., 'Is It Exact That All Thought Emits a Throw of Dice?, trans. Robert Boncardo and Christian R. Gelder, *S: Journal of the Circle for Lacanian Ideology*, 'Mallarmé Today', Vol. 9 (2016), 16–30.
Badiou, A., 'Mallarmé Said It All', in Robert Boncardo and Christian R. Gelder, *Mallarmé: Rancière, Milner, Badiou* (Lanham: Rowman & Littlefield, 2017).
Beaulieu, E., 'Une sirène de *polis*', *Spirale: arts, lettres, sciences humaines*, No. 220 (2008), 23–4.
Benda, J., *La France Byzantine, ou le triomphe de la littérature pure. Mallarmé, Gide, Proust, Valéry, Alain, Giraudoux, Suarès, les Surréalistes. Essais d'une psychologie originelle du littérateur* (Paris: Gallimard, 1945).
Bloch, R. H., *One Toss of the Dice: The Incredible Story of How a Poem Made us Modern* (New York: Liverlight Publishing Corporation, 2017).
Bohac, B., *Jouir partout ainsi qu'il sied: Mallarmé et l'esthétique du quotidien* (Paris: Classiques Garnier, 2012).
Boncardo, R. and Gelder, C. R., *Mallarmé: Rancière, Milner, Badiou* (Lanham: Rowman & Littlefield, 2017).
Boschetti, A., *The Intellectual Enterprise: Sartre and* Les Temps Modernes, trans. Richard C. McCleary (Evanston: Northwestern University Press, 1988).

Campion, P., *Mallarmé, poésie et philosophie* (Paris: Presses Universitaires de France, 1994).
Campion, P., 'Mallarmé à la lumière de la raison poétique', *Critique*, Vol. 53, Nos. 601-2 (1997), 467-80.
Catani, D., *The Poet in Society: Art, Consumerism and Politics in Mallarmé* (Oxford: Peter Lang, 2003).
Carey, J., *The Intellectuals and the Masses: Pride and Prejudice among the Literary Intelligentsia, 1880-1939* (London: Faber and Faber, 1992).
Chassé, C., *Les Clés de Mallarmé* (Aubier: Editions Montaigne, 1954).
Compagnon, A., 'La place des Fêtes: Mallarmé et la IIIe République des Lettres', in Bertrand Marchal and Jean-Luc Steinmetz (eds), *Mallarmé ou l'obscurité lumineuse* (Paris: Hermann, 1998).
Davis, O., *Jacques Rancière* (Cambridge: Polity, 2010).
Davies, G., *Mallarmé et le drame solaire: essai d'exégèse raisonnée* (Paris: José Corti, 1959).
Davies, G., *Mallarmé et 'la couche suffisante d'intelligibilité'* (Paris: José Corti, 1988).
Davies, G., *Vers une explication rationnelle du 'Coup de dés' (nouvelle édition)* (Paris: José Corti, 1992).
Deleuze, G., *Nietzsche and Philosophy*, trans. Hugh Tomlinson (New York: Columbia University Press, 1983).
Deleuze, G., *The Fold: Leibniz and the Baroque*, trans. Tom Conley (London and New York: Continuum, 1993).
Denis, B., 'Le dernier des poètes. Sartre lecteur de Mallarmé', *Courrier du Centre international d'études poétiques*, No. 225 (2000), 45-61.
Derrida. J., 'The Double Session', in *Dissemination*, trans. Barbara Johnson (Chicago: University of Chicago Press, 1981).
Dubreuil, L.,'Pensées fantômes', *Labyrinthe*, Vol. 17 (2004), 83-6.
Durand, P., *Mallarmé: Du sens des formes au sens des formalités* (Paris: Seuil, 2008).
During, E., 'L'Acte et l'Idée: Badiou et l'art contemporain', in Isabelle Vodoz and Fabien Tarby (eds), *Autour d'Alain Badiou* (Paris: Germina, 2011).
Faye, J.-P., 'Le camarade Mallarmé', *L'Humanité*, 19 September 1969.
Feltham, O., *Alain Badiou: Live Theory* (London: Continuum, 2008).
ffrench, P., *The Time of Theory: A History of* Tel Quel (Oxford: Clarendon Press, 1995).
Forest, P., *Histoire de* Tel Quel*, 1960-1982* (Paris: Seuil, 1995).
Foucault, M., *The Order of Things: An Archaeology of the Human Sciences* (New York: Vintage Books, 1994).
Gobille, B., 'La guerre de *Change* contre la "dictature structuraliste" de *Tel Quel*. L'avant-garde à l'épreuve de la crise politique de Mai '68', *Raisons politiques*, No. 18 (2005/2), 73-96.
Goldthorpe, R., 'Mallarmé: Sartre's Committed Poet', M. Bowie et al. (eds), *Baudelaire, Mallarmé, Valéry: New Essays in Honour of Lloyd Austin* (Cambridge: Cambridge University Press, 1982).

Goldthorpe, R., *Sartre: Literature and Theory* (Cambridge: Cambridge University Press, 1984).

Greaney, P., '*Mallarmé: La politique de la sirène* by Jacques Rancière', *MLN*, Vol. 113, No. 5, Comparative Literature Issue (1998), 1190–2.

Guillemin, H., *Le Coup du 2 décembre* (Paris: Gallimard, 1951).

Hamel, J.-F., *Camarade Mallarmé: Une politique de la lecture* (Paris: Minuit, 2014).

Hippolyte, J., 'Le *Coup de dés* et le message', in *Figures de la pensée philosophique* (Paris: Presses Universitaires de France, 1971).

James, R., 'Poetic Form and the Crisis of Community', in J. Acquisto (ed.), *Thinking Poetry: Philosophical Approaches to Nineteenth-Century Poetry* (Basingstoke: Palgrave Macmillan, 2013).

Jenny, J., *Je suis la révolution. Histoire d'une métaphore (1830–1975)* (Paris: Editions Belin, 2006).

Kaufmann, V., *La faute à Mallarmé. L'aventure de la théorie littéraire* (Paris: Seuil, 2011).

Kauppi, N., *Tel Quel: la constitution sociale d'une avant-garde* (The Finnish Society of Science and Letters, 1990).

Kauppi, N., *French Intellectual Nobility: Institutional and Symbolic Transformation in the Post-Sartrian Era* (Albany: State University of New York Press, 1996).

Kauppi, N., *Radicalism in French Culture: A Sociology of French Theory in the 1960s* (Farnham: Ashgate, 2010).

König, T., 'Pour une phénoménologie du discours poétique moderne', in C. Burgelin (ed.), *Lectures de Sartre* (Lyon: Presses Universitaires de Lyon, 1986).

Kristeva, J., *Recherches pour une sémanalyse* (Paris: Seuil, 1969).

Kristeva, J., 'Sémanalyse et production de sens, quelques problèmes de sémiotique littéraire à propos d'un texte de Mallarmé: *Un Coup de dés*', in A. J. Greimas (ed.), *Essais de sémiotique poétique* (Paris: Larousse, 1972).

Kristeva, J., *La révolution du langage poétique. L'avant-garde à la fin du XIXème siècle: Lautréamont et Mallarmé* (Paris: Seuil, 1974).

Kristeva, J., *Revolution in Poetic Language*, trans. Margaret Waller (New York: Columbia University Press, 1984).

Lechte, J., *Julia Kristeva* (London: Routledge, 1990).

Lloyd, R., *Mallarmé: The Poet and His Circle* (Ithaca: Cornell University Press, 1999).

Lund, H. P., 'Mallarmé chez Kristeva', *Orbis Litterarum*, Vol. 31 (1976), 229–33.

Lyotard, J.-F., *Discourse, Figure*, trans. Anthony Hudek and Mary Lydon (Minneapolis: University of Minnesota Press, 2011).

Mallarmé, S., *Collected Poems: A Bilingual Edition*, trans. Henry Weinfield (Berkeley: University of California Press, 1996).

Mallarmé, S., *Œuvres complètes, I. Edition présentée, établie et annotée par Bertrand Marchal* (Paris: Gallimard, 1998).

Mallarmé, S., *Œuvres complètes, II. Edition présentée, établie et annotée par Bertrand Marchal* (Paris: Gallimard, 2003).
Mallarmé, S., *Divagations*, trans. Barbara Johnson (Cambridge, MA: The Belknap Press of Harvard University Press, 2007).
Mallarmé, S., *Stéphane Mallarmé: The Poems in Verse*, trans. Peter Manson (Miami: Miami University Press, 2012).
Marchal, M., *Lecture de Mallarmé: Poésies, Igitur, le Coup de dés* (Paris: José Corti, 1985).
Marchal, M., *La Religion de Mallarmé: poésie, mythologie et religion* (Paris: José Corti, 1988).
Marchal, B. (ed.), *Mallarmé (Mémoire de la critique)* (Paris: Presses Universitaires de Paris-Sorbonne, 1998).
Marx-Scouras, D., *The Cultural Politics of* Tel Quel (University Park: Pennsylvania State University Press, 1996).
Mauron, C., *Introduction à la psychanalyse de Mallarmé, suivie de Mallarmé et le Tao et Le Livre* (Neuchâtel: Editions de la Baconnière, 1968).
Meillassoux, Q., *The Number and the Siren: A Decipherment of Mallarmé's Coup de dés* (London: Urbanomic, 2012).
Meillassoux, Q., 'Badiou and Mallarmé: The Event and the Perhaps', *Parrhesia*, No. 16 (2013), 35–47.
Milner, J.-C., *Les noms indistincts* (Paris: Seuil, 1983).
Milner, J.-C., *For the Love of Language*, trans. Ann Banfield (London: Macmillan, 1990).
Milner, J.-C., *Constats* (Paris: Gallimard, 2002).
Milner, J.-C., *L'Œuvre claire: Lacan, la science, la philosophie* (Paris: Seuil, 1995).
Milner, J.-C., *Mallarmé au tombeau* (Paris: Verdier, 1999).
Milner, J.-C., 'Mallarmé Perchance', trans. Liesl Yamaguchi, *Hyperion: On the Future of Aesthetics*, Vol. 9, No. 3, 'On Mallarmé: Part 1' (2016), 87–110.
Milner, J.-C., 'The Tell-Tale Constellations', trans. Christian R. Gelder, *S: Journal for the Lacanian Circle of Ideology Critique*, Vol. 9 (2016), 'Mallarmé Today', 31–8.
Milosz, C., *The Witness of Poetry* (Cambridge, MA: Harvard University Press, 1983).
Minahen, C. D., 'Poetry's Polite Terrorist: Reading Sartre Reading Mallarmé', in M. Temple (ed.), *Meetings with Mallarmé in Contemporary French Culture* (Exeter: University of Exeter Press, 1998).
Mondor, H., *Vie de Mallarmé* (Paris: Gallimard, 1941).
Mondor, H., *Mallarmé plus intime* (Paris: Gallimard, 1944).
Mondor, H., *Eugène Lefébure: Sa vie, ses lettres à Mallarmé* (Paris: Gallimard, 1951).
O'Keefe, B., 'Mallarmé: the politics of the siren', *The Comparatist*, Vol. 37 (2013), 309–16.
Payne, M., *Reading Theory: An Introduction to Lacan, Derrida and Kristeva* (Oxford: Blackwell, 1993).

Pearson, R., *Unfolding Mallarmé: The Development of a Poetic Art* (Oxford: Oxford University Press, 1997).
Pearson, R., *Mallarmé and Circumstance: The Translation of Silence* (Oxford: Oxford University Press, 2004).
Poulet, G., *Etudes sur le temps humain*, 2 (Paris: Plon, 1952).
Rancière', J., *Aux bords du politique* (Paris: La Fabrique-Editions, 1998).
Rancière, J., 'The Politics of Literature', *SubStance*, Vol. 33, No. 1 (2004), 10–24.
Rancière, J., *Et tant pis pour les gens fatigués. Entretiens* (Amsterdam: Editions Amsterdam, 2009).
Rancière, J., *Mallarmé: The Politics of the Siren*, trans. Steven Corcoran (London: Continuum, 2010).
Rancière, J., *Mute Speech*, trans. Gabriel Rockhill (New York: Columbia University Press, 2011).
Rancière, J., *The Politics of Literature*, trans. Julie Rose (Cambridge: Polity Press, 2011).
Rancière, J., *Proletarian Nights: The Worker's Dream in Nineteenth Century France* (London: Verso, 2012).
Roger, T., *L'Archive du Coup de dés* (Paris: Éditions Classiques Garnier, 2010).
Roger, T., 'La faute au mallarmisme', *Acta fabula*, Vol. 13, No. 9, 'L'aventure Poétique' (2012).
Roger, T., '"Camarade Mallarmé": mallarmisme, anachronisme, présentisme', *Acta fabula*, Vol. 15, No. 6, 'Réinvestissement, rumeur & récriture' (2014).
Sartre, J.-P., 'La Nationalisation de la littérature', in *Situations, II* (Paris: Gallimard, 1948).
Sartre, J.-P., *Saint Genet: Actor and Martyr* (New York: Georges Braziller, 1963).
Sartre, J.-P., 'A Long, Bitter, Sweet Madness', trans. Anthony Hartley, *Encounter*, Vol. 22 (1964), 61–63.
Sartre, J.-P., *Baudelaire*, trans. Martin Turnell (New York: New Directions, 1967).
Sartre, J.-P., *Sartre By Himself*, trans. Richard Seaver (New York: Urizen Books, 1978).
Sartre, J.-P., *The Family Idiot: Gustave Flaubert, 1821–1857, Volume One* (Chicago: University of Chicago Press, 1981).
Sartre, J.-P., *Mallarmé, or The Poet of Nothingness*, trans. Ernest Sturm (University Park: Pennsylvania State University Press, 1988).
Sartre, J.-P., *The Family Idiot: Gustave Flaubert, 1821–1857, Volume Three*, trans. Carol Cosman (Chicago: University of Chicago Press, 1989).
Sartre, J.-P., *The Family Idiot: Gustave Flaubert, 1821–1857, Volume Five*, trans. Carol Cosman (Chicago/London: The University of Chicago Press, 1993).
Sartre, J.-P., *Critique of Dialectical Reason, Volume One: Theory of Practical Ensembles* (London: Verso, 2004).

Sartre, J.-P., *Being and Nothingness*, trans. Hazel Barnes (London and New York: Routledge Classics, 2005)
Sartre, J.-P., 'The Purposes of Writing', *Between Existentialism and Marxism*, trans. John Matthews (London: Verso, 2008).
Sartre, J.-P., 'A New Mystic', in *Critical Essays*, trans. Chris Turner (London, New York and Calcutta: Seagull Books, 2010).
Sartre, J.-P., 'Man and Things', in *Critical Essays*, trans. Chris Turner (London, New York and Calcutta: Seagull Books, 2010).
Sartre, J.-P., 'There and Back', in *Critical Essays*, trans. Chris Turner (London, New York and Calcutta: Seagull Books, 2010).
Sartre, J.-P., *What is Literature?*, trans. Bernard Frechtman (London and New York: Routledge, 2010).
Sartre, J.-P., *War Diaries: Notebooks from a Phoney War, 1939–1940*, trans. Quintin Hoare (London and New York: Verso, 2011).
Sartre, J.-P., 'Black Orpheus', in R. Aronson and A. Van Den Hoven (eds), *We Have Only This Life To Live: The Selected Essays of Jean-Paul Sartre, 1939–1975* (New York: New York Review Books, 2013).
Sartre, J.-P., 'Introducing *Les Temps Modernes*', in R. Aronson and A. Van Den Hoven (eds), *We Have Only This Life To Live: The Selected Essays of Jean-Paul Sartre, 1939–1975* (New York: New York Review of Books, 2013).
Sartre, J.-P., 'Merleau-Ponty', in R. Aronson and A. Van Den Hoven (eds), *We Have Only This Life to Live: The Selected Essays of Jean-Paul Sartre, 1939–1975* (New York: New York Review of Books, 2013).
Scherer, J., *Le 'Livre' de Mallarmé. Premières recherches sur les documents inédits* (Paris: Gallimard, 1957).
Scriven, M., *Sartre's Existential Biographies* (London: Macmillan, 1984).
Sollers, P., *Logiques* (Paris: Seuil, 1968).
Sollers, P., '"Camarade" et camarade', *L'Humanité*, 19 September 1969.
Sollers, P., *Sur le matérialisme* (Paris: Seuil, 1974).
Stanguennec, A., *Mallarmé et l'éthique de la poésie* (Paris: Vrin, 1992).
Thériault, P., *Le (Dé)montage de la fiction: La révélation moderne de Mallarmé* (Paris: Honoré Champion, 2010).
Verstraeten, P., 'Sartre et Mallarmé', in *Sartre/Barthes*, *Revue d'esthétique* (1991), 27–38.
Wolfe, C., 'Rethinking Commitment: Ontology, Genre and Sartre's *Mallarmé*', *Diacritics*, Vol. 21, No. 4 (1991), 69–85.

Index

Abastado, Claude, 74n

Badiou, Alain, 1, 9, 15, 16, 119, 122–6, 185, 188, 189, 191, 235, 240, 242
  Being and Event, 2, 5–6, 125, 141, 142–51, 152, 153, 163, 166, 170, 241
  Conditions, 159
  'A French Philosopher Responds to a Polish Poet', 6, 123, 125, 126, 153, 157–60, 162–70, 241
  Handbook of Inaesthetics, 153, 154–5
  'Is It Exact That All Thought Emits a Throw of Dice?', 142–3, 163
  'Mallarmé's Method', 151, 152
  Manifesto for Philosophy, 167
  Theory of the Subject, 2, 5, 125, 126–41, 149, 150, 151, 152, 162, 170, 213, 241
Baudelaire, Charles, 26, 36, 41, 44, 47, 48, 57, 64, 143, 179–82, 178, 183, 184, 198
Blanchot, Maurice, 28, 56, 124, 155, 192, 195–6

Carey, John, 201
Chassé, Charles, *Les Clefs de Mallarmé*, 193
Cohn, Robert Greer, 124

Davies, Gardner, 124, 137, 138, 145, 146, 150, 225n
de Lisle, Leconte, 3, 30, 36, 38, 41, 44, 45, 46
de Vigny, Alfred, 198, 220, 228, 230

Faye, Jean-Pierre, 79
Feltham, Oliver, 147
Flaubert, Gustave, 3, 30, 44, 208

Gelder, Christian, 152
Guillemin, Henri, *Le Coup du 2 décembre*, 30

Hamel, Jean-François, 22, 27, 28, 226n, 227, 243
  Camarade Mallarmé, 9, 10, 13–18, 238
Hegel, Georg, 40, 56, 62, 124, 136, 187, 213, 215, 216
Hugo, Victor, 32, 34, 35, 57, 82, 178, 180, 181, 182, 183, 198, 228, 235

James, Alison, 204
Jenny, Laurent, 238
Je suis la revolution, 9, 11–12

Kaufmann, Vincent, 239
  La faute à Mallarmé, 9, 10–11, 12
Kristeva, Julia, 1, 15, 16, 185, 188, 191, 235, 240–1, 242
  Revolution in Poetic Language, 2, 4–5, 11, 16, 80, 81–119, 240, 241
  Sèméiôtiké, 80, 87

Mallarmé, Stéphane
  'Accusation', 105
  'The Afternoon of a Faun', 52, 57
  'Apparition', 49, 57
  'Arisen from the aspirant rump', 54
  'Art for All', 37–8, 193, 196, 201
  'Autobiography', 54, 64
  'Autumn Lament', 48
  The Book, 113–14, 116–18, 176, 186, 196
  'Bucolic', 48, 115, 186
  'Conflict', 128, 212–13, 222–3
  'Confrontation', 212
  'The Court', 45, 61, 115–16, 200

Mallarmé, Stéphane (cont.)
  'Crisis of Verse', 24–5, 53, 84, 85–6, 144, 185
  'The Demon of Analogy', 182–3, 186
  'Does all Pride smoke of an evening', 54
  'Funeral Toast', 52, 53
  'Gold', 115
  Hérodiade, 49, 57–8, 61, 62, 63, 106–8, 110, 113
  Igitur, 55, 60, 62, 135, 144, 178, 184, 186, 195–6
  'In victory having fled fair suicide', 63
  'An Interrupted Spectacle', 207–8, 212
  'The Jinx', 56, 57
  La Dernière Mode, 184, 187, 202
  'Lace cancels itself out', 57
  Les Dieux antiques, 211
  'Magic', 25, 130–1
  'Music and Letters', 38, 53–4, 59, 60, 116, 129, 200, 240
  'The Mystery in Letters', 90, 169
  'Prose (for des Esseintes)', 90–5, 103, 104, 113
  'Restricted Action', 123, 164, 182
  'Safeguard', 130
  'Scribbled at the Theatre', 200
  'Stilled beneath the oppressive cloud'/'Hushed to the crushing cloud', 131–6, 139, 151, 162, 197–203, 234
  Sonnet en –yx, 54, 136–40, 162
  'Sick of unquiet rest', 49, 199
  'Sigh', 50
  'Toast', 197–203, 209
  Un coup de dés, 50, 61, 96–9, 103, 142–51, 152, 162, 176, 186–7, 219–21, 228–38, 240
  'Villiers de l'Isle-Adam', 57
  'The virginal, enduring, beautiful today', 54, 61, 175–81, 186
  'When the shadow threatened with unalterable law', 60–1
  'The White Waterlily', 52
  'Winter Shudder', 47
Marchal, Bertrand, 6, 8, 9, 15, 186, 200, 210, 211, 212, 214, 229
Mauron, Charles, *Introduction à la psychanalyse de Mallarmé*, 49–51
Meillassoux, Quentin, 1, 3, 15, 16
  The Number and the Siren, 7, 228–38

Milner, Jean-Claude, 1, 15, 16, 152, 242
  Mallarmé au tombeau, 2, 6, 175–90
Milosz, Czeslaw, 153, 154, 201, 209
  The Witness of Poetry, 154–70
Mondor, Henri, 28

Paulhan, Jean, 18, 23, 123

Rancière, Jacques, 1, 3, 15, 16, 227–8, 234, 235, 237–8, 242–3
  Mallarmé: The Politics of the Siren, 2, 6–7, 191, 192–221, 243
  Mute Speech, 192, 202–3, 207, 215, 227
  The Politics of Literature, 192–3, 221–4
  Proletarian Nights, 222–3
Roger, Thierry, 8, 9–10, 12, 13, 15, 64

Saint-Simonism, 192, 203, 211, 215
Sartre, Jean-Paul, 1, 2, 3–4, 6, 8, 15, 17, 18, 81, 106, 112, 116, 122–4, 143, 156, 165, 179, 185, 186, 188, 191, 192, 193, 196, 201, 209, 235, 239–40, 241, 242
  Baudelaire, 26, 28, 41
  Being and Nothingness, 4, 22, 27, 29, 59, 60
  'Black Orpheus', 22, 24
  The Communists and Peace, 30
  Critique of Dialectical Reason, 31
  The Family Idiot, 4, 15, 22, 25, 27, 39, 65, 240
  Mallarmé, or The Poet of Nothingness, 4, 22, 25, 26–8, 29–65, 192, 194, 239–40, 241
  Saint Genet, 22, 30–1
  War Diaries, 27, 28–9
  What is Literature?, 4, 22, 23, 25, 27, 30, 122, 239
Schlegel, Friedrich, 215–16
Sollers, Philippe, 3, 12, 80, 118, 119, 121, 240

Tel Quel, 4, 5, 7, 9, 79, 80, 119, 124, 125, 240

Valéry, Paul, 17, 18, 28
Verlaine, Paul, 36, 37, 41, 47, 48, 50

Wagner, Richard, 192, 203, 211, 214–15, 229

EU representative:
Easy Access System Europe
Mustamäe tee 50, 10621 Tallinn, Estonia
Gpsr.requests@easproject.com